£2.50

D0553389

WITHDRAWN

INTENT UPON READING

To a child who is intent upon reading

all books are children's books.

E. V. LUCAS

Margery Fisher

Intent upon Reading

A CRITICAL APPRAISAL OF MODERN
FICTION FOR CHILDREN

 BROCKHAMPTON PRESS

TO JOHN MASEFIELD

SBN 340 03510 2

First printed 1961
Second impression 1961
Third impression 1962
Second (revised and enlarged) edition 1964
Second impression 1965
Third impression 1967
Fourth impression 1969
Published by Brockhampton Press Ltd, Leicester

Printed and bound in Great Britain
by Hazell Watson & Viney Ltd, Aylesbury

Copyright © 1961, 1964 by Margery Fisher

Typographical designer: Gerald Wilkinson

Contents

Foreword

In the original edition of *Intent upon Reading* I concentrated on the years 1930–1960. It is impossible, of course, to draw a firm line at 1930, and where it suited my purpose I wrote about books published before this date, but there are some classic works which I have dismissed summarily or omitted altogether. I have tried, both in the original edition and in the two new chapters for this edition, to illustrate general points, rather than write a definitive survey; and I have mentioned no books which I have not read.

The material for these new chapters has been accumulated gradually in reviewing and not, as for the original edition, collected all at once for a special purpose. I have been able to focus my attention on a large proportion of the fiction of three years *as it was published*, and my ideas have been able to develop more spontaneously and slowly. No historical change takes place in a moment of time, and no trend in literature, however clear-cut it may seem, can truly be said to have begun in any one calendar month. I am confident in saying that children's fiction is steadily improving in quality and that as a form of literature it is receiving more attention than ever before. For anything more specific than this, I have tried not to be too dogmatic about tendencies that I have noticed during the past three years. These tendencies are usually floated on the tide of good, but not necessarily outstanding, fiction: the prizewinners, the future classics, seldom owe anything to fashion and are often unclassifiable. The average story-book, which is published, reviewed and then falls back to make room for the productions of the next month, is well worth studying in detail, and I hope that in providing full reading lists I may draw attention to some books which have suffered from the tremendous tide-race of publication in our time.

There have been only two brief periods in my life when I was not reading some books for children—the first eighteen months, before I began to look at books, and my four university years, when time had to be kept for other kinds of reading. The first of my six children began to be aware of books twenty-four years ago. Between them and at different times they have shown an astonishing variety of tastes. I have pursued books which I have felt they might like and have read every book that they have read. For ten years I was sole reviewer of children's books for a national monthly magazine. In May 1962 I started my own magazine of reviews of children's books, *Growing Point*. I have been able to see and read all those books which the publishers themselves feel are worthy of note, and I am grateful to all those publishing houses which regularly supply me with books for review.

My enjoyment of children's books has changed in character, but not diminished, now that I must read as an adult. Reading, to a child, is an occupation engaging his immediate attention and confirming his own experience in a memorable way: detachment is out of the question. I approach a child's bookshelf now, with a sharpened critical sense and with a parent's selectiveness. So my opinions are of two kinds. Certain stories which were formative in my childhood (among them, *The Water-Babies*, Masefield's *A Book of Discoveries*, and *The Story of a Red-Deer*) can never again be merely books to read; they are so full of associations that, re-reading them, I can fancy myself a child again and can see them as a child would. I cannot read the stories of today like this, however much I enjoy them, but when I talk to children I can see in them the same experience. To keep in touch with the likes and dislikes of the young is essential for any critic of their literature.

There are classified reading lists at the end of each chapter. Dates in brackets refer to original publication. Those books marked with an asterisk are mentioned in the text, and most of the books so marked, together with all the rest, are recommended. In most cases I have not mentioned ages for which books might be suitable. This is a tricky business and the choice (surprising though it may often be) is best left to the child concerned.

The drawings have been chosen because they illustrate points that I have made in the text. They are reproduced here by permission of the publishers in whose books they appear.

I acknowledge gratefully the help of the Superintendent and staff of the British Museum Reading Room, the Librarian of the American Information Service in London, the Book Information Bureau of the National Book League and Miss Eileen Colwell of the Hendon Children's Library; and especially my thanks are due to Miss B. M. Makepeace and the staff of the Northampton County Library for the help they give me whenever I need it. I am indebted also to John Spence, A.L.A., for checking the index for the original edition and for compiling the new index for the present edition. Finally, my thanks are due to Antony Kamm, who as an editor has shown unfailing good humour and perspicacity and, as a friend, has been bracing or encouraging at just the right moments.

MARGERY FISHER

Ashton, 1964

Chapter 1 | *The Way Back*

Is it good? Will it sell? What is it about? Will little Johnny like it or is it more suitable for Jane? There is less and less time to ask all these necessary questions as the output of children's books grows with every year that passes. Thirty years ago it was possible for a literary critic to look at those books written specially for children, and those which children could read, and see them as a whole. Today it is hard to keep abreast of new publications, let alone keep a sense of proportion about them. There is little time to look back at the classics, to recommend them to children who, following the habit of their elders, take the easy way out and ask for the latest story by So-and-so. This time and space have to be found. Some thread must be held out to the young reader as he wanders in the maze of volumes of today and yesterday. Some advice must be offered to him, if only because his reading is so much more thorough, so much more definite in its impact, than the reading of an adult.

Whether their books have been many or few, children have always read intensely. Seventy-two years ago an American critic wrote:

> . . . somewhere about the house, curled up, may be, in a nursery window, or hidden in a freezing attic, a child is poring over The Three Musketeers, lost to any consciousness of his surroundings, incapable of analyzing his emotions, breathless with mingled fear and exultation over his heroes' varying fortunes, and drinking in a host of vivid impressions that are absolutely ineffaceable from his mind. We cannot read in that fashion any longer, but we only wish we could.
> Agnes Repplier. *What Children Read*, in BOOKS AND MEN (Houghton Mifflin, Boston, 1888) pp. 64–5.

We must help the child to choose his books so that the ineffaceable
impressions will be worth while; and this means that we must regard
children's books, primarily, not as toys or merchandise, but as a
form of literature.

In the last fifty years and more, many critics have reviewed the
history of children's books and have discussed the psychology of
children's reading. Literary principles (formulas and intentions,
style and technique) have nearly always been incidental. And
although some of the best evaluation of children's literature comes
to us in this way, as it does in Harvey Darton's balanced comments
in his definitive work, CHILDREN'S BOOKS IN ENGLAND,
this is not really enough. We need constantly to revise and restate
the standards of this supremely important branch of literature;
constantly, because of the overwhelming number of books published each year.

The best full literary discussions of children's books are already
out of date. Geoffrey Trease's surefooted and vigorous TALES OUT
OF SCHOOL was published in 1949, and E. S. Turner's BOYS WILL
BE BOYS, with its shrewd comments on school stories and periodicals,
in 1948. Dorothy Neal White's ABOUT BOOKS FOR CHILDREN
came out in 1946 in England (and is rather particularly concerned
with American books, many of them not available here); her
delightful BOOKS BEFORE FIVE is dated 1954. Roger Lancelyn
Green's TELLERS OF TALES only takes us up to 1953, and his many
stimulating articles are scattered in periodicals, some of them not
easy to find. Frank Eyre's TWENTIETH CENTURY CHILDREN'S
BOOKS stops at the previous year, and in its limited space this
excellent pamphlet can only briefly survey the crowded shelves of the
'thirties and 'forties. In 1960 the Bodley Head launched a series of
monographs on children's writers, and those which have so far
appeared have filled a very real gap. Shrewd in literary comment and
interesting in their biographical and bibliographical detail, these
little volumes are essential for anyone who is studying a particular
author, or, indeed, for any student of literature for children.

Reviews and book lists, certainly, make it their business to keep
up to date. Book lists are not expected to deviate into literary
criticism, but the very fact that they are selective gives them this
status. Kathleen Lines's FOUR TO FOURTEEN, a magnificently
catholic classified list, which now takes us up to 1956, has un-

doubtedly done much to help parents find the best books for children, and both the Library Association and the National Book League publish very useful lists from time to time in pamphlet form. Two periodicals, the *School Librarian* and the *Junior Bookshelf*, keep abreast of children's books in reviews which are long enough for useful general points to be made, and this is the case also with the special supplements issued by *The Times Literary Supplement* two or three times a year. These supplements, and the far too sporadic reviews in daily and weekly newspapers, deserve a better fate than to be used for lighting fires; for although reviewers are lamentably restricted in space, they can (and the best of them do) fit in the happiest and most stimulating ideas about the books they are discussing.

I join the ranks of this growing regiment of critics and reviewers with a lively sense of my debt to them. Without their work I should not have known where to begin.

These preliminary remarks may seem to herald a solemn book. I hope it will not be so. In the long run, the real motive for criticism should be the exchanging of favourites, the recommendation 'Try this, it's good.' Rash as it would be to suppose that this is the motive of all literary criticism, in fact I believe it almost always is in the case of writing about children's books. For a good book for children is not, and never has been, the sole property of children. C. S. Lewis has remarked that he is 'almost inclined to set it up as a canon that a children's story which is enjoyed only by children is a bad children's book.' There is a moral for critics here, as well as a prescription for good writing.

Enjoyed. That is the word to note in Lewis's remark. When we write about children's books we are in a special position. We bring an experience of reading to bear on books which are not intended primarily for us, in which we share by invitation. We should not make public pronouncements about such books if we do not like them or if we do not like the kind of book which they are perhaps failing to be. If we have forgotten the delight of sailing sticks down a gutter, we cannot really get far with chronicles of a four-year-old's day. If we think of horses simply as large and alarming, we should leave pony books alone. Enjoyment must come first. And then, we must try to remember what it is like to read like a child, with that pure, headlong, unguarded enthusiasm Agnes Repplier described.

And, remembering this, we must look for the virtues that a child looks for in his books—energy, sincerity, imagination. All this must be reconciled with the duty of a literary critic to state standards and measure books against them. The average child does not think, when he is reading a story, how good the style is or how well drawn the characters; but we know he will get more lasting pleasure from reading Walter de la Mare or Arthur Ransome than more sensational, superficial writers. We have to recommend from an adult standpoint: at the same time, we have to read with what knowledge we have of the tastes of childhood.

Obviously, any criticism of children's books is going to be prejudiced, not only by personal taste but also by the passage of time. I could not write in the same spirit about THE WATER-BABIES and AT THE BACK OF THE NORTH WIND. Kingsley's story was one of the formative books of my childhood. I must have read it thirty times between the ages of six and ten. When I read it now I am aware of elements which made no impression on me then—like the satire of contemporary ideas and events or the pattern of religious thought. But I can remember, too, my simple enjoyment of the descriptions of place and people, of those glorious lists of polysyllables. I can still read the book as a child would read it. Because I did not read any of George Macdonald's books when I was young, I have to try to find out at second-hand how he affects a child, and my children can only give me a partial answer. So, like all critical books, this will be a mixture of guesswork, analysis, partiality and fact, spiced, I hope, with continuous enjoyment.

I shall be dealing entirely with children's fiction. Factual books, which become more numerous and more competent every day, demand a book on their own. I shall leave out, too, any particular consideration of volumes of verse for children. In writing about children's stories one is, very often, writing about poetry; imagination takes its own shape, especially in children's books. Probably it is arbitrary to make a distinction between fact and fiction, but it makes more sense, at any rate, than a distinction between prose and poetry when we are discussing, for instance, a fantasy or a fairy-tale.

A curious form of snobbery is growing up today, the idea that the child who reads non-fiction is somehow more meritorious, more worthy of respect than the child who reads fiction. The librarian who really feels this is so is, I suppose, thinking only of the *best* non-fiction and the *worst* fiction. I can only hope so. All the same, it is a dangerous view, let it mean what it may. Sometimes a child wants to read a book with a factual slant, a textbook on electricity or trains or carpentry or cooking, because he wants to collect facts for a particular purpose. Another time, he wants to read a story, to discover not facts first of all but ideas, suggestions, pictures, imitations and versions of the facts he knows. He is not *better* at one time than at another; he is different. The child who looks at a photograph of a chair is learning something; the same child, looking at Edward Lear's picture of the chair and table walking together, is also learning something. The child who looks at a map of the Amazon basin, and the child who reads Ronald Syme's RIVER OF NO RETURN— why should one be thought of as more virtuous than the other? The wise librarian and teacher is making this distinction one of convenience only, but there still seems to be some need to affirm the value of imaginative fiction, and that I shall try to do.

Why is the child held fast in his window-seat, rapt into another world? Which books will hold him like that? Which books will merely occupy his time? In his early years a child is willing to accept any world the writer creates, not with conscious, conscientious belief in its truth, but by participation. The critic, as I have said, must try to achieve something of this whole-heartedness, while not losing his literary sense. But what about the writer?

A reviewer, perhaps suffering from a weekend surfeit of junior novels, wrote sadly:

> Writers should every now and then be rigidly kept from writing for a year. If at the end of that time they have a nervous breakdown from frustration, they should be allowed to write. If, on the other hand, they are quite fit and happy, they should be put on to office work, knitting, gardening, or some other pleasant occupation, permanently and full-time. This would be fairer to children.
> 'Something of Value'. *The Times Literary Supplement*, Children's Books Section, 4 December 1959, p. ix.

Let us assume, however much we may agree with this complaint, that the writer wants to write, and is not merely using a piece of experience because he believes it is saleable in story form. Why does he choose to write for children, and what is he setting out to do?

First, obviously, he is setting out to create a world to suit a child, whether that child is two or ten or fifteen—a world scaled down in an appropriate way from the adult world. He is using a set of facts and ideas in a certain way. Graham Greene, when he wrote THE LITTLE STEAM ROLLER, was using the concept of smugglers at an airport which, if treated in another way, could have gone into one of his adult Entertainments. Alison Uttley, when she wrote A TRAVEL-LER IN TIME, was using facts which would have been unaltered in themselves if they had been used in an adult historical novel, instead of in a story centred on a schoolgirl and the perceptions of a school-girl. Invented creatures and invented landscapes—Tolkien's Ents and Hobbits, the Snark, Palmer Brown's land beyond the pawpaw trees—work their way up from adult dreams and preoccupations and memories.

All these things are ready to be adapted to the world of a child, and they can be adapted simply by an intellectual effort; but anyone who enters the child's world, whose dreams and wishes in some measure become merged into a child's dreams and wishes, will produce a better book than the writer who writes, as it were, from the top of his head. One will write a story about a rabbit who runs away and gets into mischief: the other will write PETER RABBIT.

The author must be involved. He must somehow enter into the world of his book or it will never come to life. He must either go back to childhood, consciously or unconsciously, or he must share the childhood of young people round him. When he creates his imaginary world he must start with his own knowledge and work outwards. If he is involved like this it is almost axiomatic that he will not be writing to order but because he wants to, because (as C. S. Lewis puts it) a children's story is the best art-form for something he wants to say, 'just as a composer might write a Dead March not because there was a public funeral in view but because certain musical ideas that had occurred to him went best into that form.'*

The author's return to the world of a child is governed by adult compulsion, sometimes simple, sometimes alarmingly complex. Sometimes it is a compulsion just to tell stories. When Patricia Lynch was a child she was privileged to listen to Mrs Hennessy, one of the last of the travelling story-tellers. Her response was immediate and

* Three Ways of Writing for Children. I. The Proper Meeting between Man and Child: C. S. Lewis. (In *Fifty-Two*, A Journal of books and authors from Geoffrey Bles. Autumn 1959, no. 4, p. 5.)

complete. Her love of stories grew along with her love of telling them. The old woman's technique, her lilting vernacular, her easy relations with her listeners, her compelling formulas and repetitions, all sank into the child's mind and returned to her when she began to write herself. There is hard work behind Patricia Lynch's stories but there is also an innate, joyous love of story-telling. To take a different kind of case, when Mary Treadgold wrote that splendid pony story, WE COULDN'T LEAVE DINAH, her adult skill was fused with emotions revived from childhood. She wrote, she tells us, 'in a passion of recollection', after she had heard the news of the invasion of the Channel Islands. She wrote, too, remembering how, when she was fourteen, she had longed to be different, 'extrovert, with clear-cut and developed values, plenty of courage, and good at games—I having been the kind of child who had and was none of these things.'* This reconsideration of childhood was, presumably, the least conscious element in her writing, but it is what makes the story so good.

Sometimes the return to childhood is not really a return. Kenneth Grahame, for example, had in some ways never left the pastures and paths of childhood, and although this added to the perplexities of his adult life, it meant that THE WIND IN THE WILLOWS, behind its sociological comment, its satire, its allegory, its private jokes and portraits, is one of the freshest and most appealing books that ever engaged the attention of a child.

The 'escape' into humour of Lewis Carroll and Edward Lear, whatever it revealed of their temperamental needs, does not undo the fact that they strike straight at the hearts of adults as well as of children; it explains it. Biographical criticism can, of course, lead a long way from the texts in question; can even, sometimes, spoil a childhood favourite if we read it with a morbid preoccupation with its deepest origins. Harvey Darton has said the last word on this in his wise remarks about ALICE IN WONDERLAND:

> There is no need here to articulate, as it were a skeleton, the alleged dual personality of Dodgson. It can be done, with a reasonable amount of insight, by anyone who is able to guess at the mind of a bachelor specialist in a precise subject, living in a period of accepted inhibitions, who suddenly, for a few glorious

* In CHOSEN FOR CHILDREN (Library Association, 1957), p. 28.

moments, sees quite clearly and lovingly all that mixture of credulity, acumen and innocence which we call a child, and becomes ageless himself.

F. J. Harvey Darton. CHILDREN'S BOOKS IN ENGLAND (Cambridge University Press, 1958 edition) p. 267.

There is no need to be alarmed or affronted by the idea that some of the best children's books provided escape or compensation for their authors. It is interesting to know why an author has tracked back to his childhood, but it is more important to examine how he does it and what use he makes of his journey.

The impulse that makes him write for children is, almost literally, a journey, for it will be more often associated with places than with people. For children, people take their place along with kettles and kittens, in a wide landscape that has its own order, and memory holds the key to this special order. Imagination and memory together pick out objects, people, atmosphere and impulses, on a principle that no grown-up can consciously work by. John Masefield has said that he wrote THE MIDNIGHT FOLK 'from memories of childhood, and from scenes and images that had been in my mind for a long time, and imaginings about places that had been important to me as a child, and are important to me still.' Before these memories were sorted and chosen for the story, they had their own order, their own relevance to a child's life. Very often the memory of a place is the motive force for a story in which it seems to take second place; but as you read and reread the story, the setting seems to spread and swallow the whole. It is so with THE MIDNIGHT FOLK, and with A TRAVELLER IN TIME, where the house, Thackers, based on a house Alison Uttley knew and loved as a child, dominates the story. Philippa Pearce, when she was lying awake in a hospital bed night after hot night, longing for coolness and water, began deliberately to imagine herself, step by step, back at the river of her childhood. So MINNOW ON THE SAY began, and, behind the lively characters, the ingenious plot and the rounded picture of the activities of two small boys, the Say flows on, through the imagination, never forced into the foreground, but always present. Her second book, TOM'S MIDNIGHT GARDEN, grew round a house she had known as a child, and I remember her remark that a friend had commented on the size of the house in the story, saying it must have been a mansion. It was, in fact, a house of ordinary size, but the writer, completely one with her story, had drawn it with a child's memory.

For Edward Ardizzone, too, the backgrounds of his stories, in words and pictures, are the backgrounds of his own life:

> Tim's house by the sea is a house we stayed in as very young married people at Walmer, near Deal. The docks and the ships and the sailor men—I knew them all as a very small boy in Ipswich before the war when I and my cousin Arthur played truant and spent our days mucking about among the ships and barges. We were always allowed on board, to poke our noses into the engine room and mess about all day long.
>
> Edward Ardizzone, speaking at the National Book League, 18 February 1960, on Book Illustration (in *Books*, no. 329, May–June 1960, pp. 94–5).

These backgrounds are visualized with the enjoyment of recaptured youth and the enjoyment of communication as well, for the stories of Tim and Lucy and Ginger were written for his own children, as the Babar books were written for the young de Brunhoff, as Alice grew out of a story told to three small girls, as Rat and Mole and Toad and Badger were the characters in bedtime tales for Alastair Grahame, as the stories of Teddy Robinson were told to a little girl about her own bear. Innumerable stories, particularly for small children, have as their beginning an easy, pleasurable alliance of adult and child. If narrator and listener are in sympathy, and if the narrator is not trying to demonstrate any imagined superiority, the book that comes from this kind of partnership will have some good about it even if it is not skilfully written, for it will have the qualities of sincerity and truth.

Of course there will be some adult comment even in stories which began at bedtime. The adult writer cannot shed all his prejudices and become, literally, a child again. His training and skill will have some value, and above all in giving a purpose to his story. It is the fashion nowadays to decry the story with a moral, but no story can be written without one, though it may not take the sermon form familiar to the child of the last century. The nursery virtues are to be found in Alison Uttley's tales of Tim Rabbit as they were found in the stories of Mrs Molesworth. The adventure story of today proclaims courage and honesty and self-reliance in a different tone of voice but no less unmistakably than it did a century ago. Among other things, the writer for children is an interpreter of life, especially of contemporary life, and in this sense the child expects that writer to inform him, to make categorical statements to him which he is not old enough to make for himself.

We may conclude, then, that a child's story must, ideally, be written from the heart and from at least some memory of and contact with childhood. It must appeal directly to the imagination of the reader, must create a unique world into which the child will go willingly and actively. It must, necessarily, contain some proportion of adult comment, but this must be delivered as from one intelligent individual to another, not in a spirit of condescension. And it must be written, within the demands of the particular story, as well as possible.

Reading List

(Books mentioned in the text are marked * throughout the lists)

1.*General works on children's books and children's reading*
*Bodley Head Monographs. Bell, Anthea. E. NESBIT. Clark, Leonard. WALTER DE LA MARE. Crouch, Marcus. BEATRIX POTTER. Green, Roger Lancelyn. J. M. BARRIE, LEWIS CARROLL. Meek, Margaret. GEOFFREY TREASE. Shelley, Hugh. ARTHUR RANSOME. Sutcliff, Rosemary. RUDYARD KIPLING. *Bodley Head* 1960.
*Crouch, Marcus, *ed.* CHOSEN FOR CHILDREN. *Library Association* 1957.
*Darton, F. J. Harvey. CHILDREN'S BOOKS IN ENGLAND: five centuries of social life. *C.U.P.* (1932) 1958.
*Eyre, Frank. TWENTIETH CENTURY CHILDREN'S BOOKS. *Longmans* 1952.
*Green, Roger Lancelyn. TELLERS OF TALES. *Ward* (1946) 1953.
Junior Bookshelf (Tower Wood, Windermere, Westmorland: annual subscription 17s. 6d.).
*Library Association (Chaucer House, Malet Place, London, W.C.1). Printed book-lists are issued from this association from time to time.
*Lines, Kathleen. FOUR TO FOURTEEN. *C.U.P.* for N.B.L. (1950) 1956.
*Lynch, Patricia. A STORY TELLER'S CHILDHOOD. *Dent* 1947.
*Meigs, Cornelia, and others. A CRITICAL HISTORY OF CHILDREN'S LITERATURE. *Macmillan of New York* 1954.

*National Book League (7 Albemarle Street, Piccadilly, London, W.1).
    Annual lists of children's books from 1957, occasional special lists, and
    articles in their monthly magazine, *Books*.
*Repplier, Agnes. *What Children Read*, in BOOKS AND MEN. *Houghton
    Mifflin*, Boston 1888.
**School Librarian* (Journal of School Library Association, 29 Gordon Square,
    London, W.C.1). Some articles of general interest.
*Trease, Geoffrey. TALES OUT OF SCHOOL. *Heinemann* 1949.
*Turner, E. S. BOYS WILL BE BOYS. *Michael Joseph* 1948.
*White, Dorothy Neal. ABOUT BOOKS FOR CHILDREN. *O.U.P.* 1949.
*White, Dorothy Neal. BOOKS BEFORE FIVE. *O.U.P.* 1954 (first published by
    N.Z. Council for Educational Research).

2.*Story-books mentioned in the text*
*Grahame, Kenneth. THE WIND IN THE WILLOWS (see Chap.4).
*Greene, Grahame. THE LITTLE STEAM-ROLLER (see Chap.2).
*Kingsley, Charles. THE WATER-BABIES (see Chap.6).
*Macdonald, George. AT THE BACK OF THE NORTH WIND (see Chap.5).
*Masefield, John. THE MIDNIGHT FOLK (see Chap.6).
*Pearce, A. Philippa. MINNOW ON THE SAY (see Chap.14).
*Pearce, A. Philippa. TOM'S MIDNIGHT GARDEN (see Chap.7).
*Syme, Ronald. RIVER OF NO RETURN (see Chap.12).
*Treadgold, Mary. WE COULDN'T LEAVE DINAH (see Chap.10).
*Uttley, Alison. A TRAVELLER IN TIME (see Chap.7).

Chapter 2 | *Pictures in the Nursery Fire*

The style of a child's story matters no less at the picture-book stage than it does later. Children first become acquainted with books by looking *and* listening; at this stage it is looking first, for most of them, but what goes in one ear does *not* come out of the other. It stays embedded in the memory. A child's taste in words, no less than in the visual arts, gets its start here, for better or for worse.

For these first years, though, the pictures must carry the story as much as the words do. Sometimes they will be predominant, the words merely acting as links. In William Nicholson's CLEVER BILL, for example, each picture is accompanied by three or four words at most; they are no more than captions. It is the pictures that tell you, with dash and colour, how the little soldier, left behind in the packing, runs across country to rejoin his mistress at the dockside. This is how a painter tells a story, and the artist/author Françoise is working in something of the same way. If a mother reads Françoise's neat little anecdotes about Jeanne-Marie to a three-year-old, she will find the stories perfectly shaped to suit him, but if the child is left alone with one of these books he will be able to follow what happens by the pictures. The scenes by the Seine, at a country fair and in the meadow are illustrated in simple blocks of colour. Booths, sheep, passers-by, trees and the little girl herself stand out against a background merely suggested. Gay and firm, the pictures lead the child into a whole world of miniature incidents and dramas to which the words supply an accompaniment.

Verbal description must be cut drastically in books for small children, for words tire them more quickly than pictures do. The wise writer for this age (Beatrix Potter is one shining example) reserves adjectives, as it were, for the illustrations, where innumerable small points, some of them sophisticated, can be stressed.

Phyllis Krasilovsky, in THE COW WHO FELL IN THE CANAL, tells in a series of simple statements how Hendrika floated down to a small town and was taken home by lorry. It is a starting-point, this text. The full story is told in Peter Spier's pictures, and the atmosphere of a Dutch town is established in a way which would have been impossible in words. There is, besides, the artist's comment, his attitude to this lively and improbable story. This comes out as clearly in his pictures as the author's does in the cheerful style of her prose. A commonplace tale can be touched to new life by this personal idiosyncrasy—and, for small children's stories, most often in pictures. I remember for instance the folk tale of the Turnip, as it is illustrated by Lewitt-Him in the volume of verse-tales, LOCO-MOTIVE, with its enormous, jovial humour expressed in washes of succulent colour, and the feeling of mystery which shines through Ray Bradbury's SWITCH ON THE NIGHT. This fable uses the most commonplace incidents of a child's life, and Madeline Gekiere's pictures enliven it with their deliberately simplified colour, including the device of the coloured page, and their use of abstract design.

Personal feelings communicate themselves so readily in pictures like these. To go back to a very different kind of illustration, take Kate Greenaway's books for children. The verses are laboured and sometimes absurd, but in her pictures she has recorded all the enjoyment, the gaiety and the busyness of small children. She communicates at once the sympathy of a grown-up watching children, and the child enchanted by her play. A good illustrator can always annotate the world of childhood for parents as well as for children. Adrienne Adams's drawings for Rumer Godden's IMPUNITY JANE express beautifully a child's absorption in small things. Jean de Brunhoff and his nephew have shown another mood in their pictures of Babar's three children, sliding down the banisters, dressing up in Indian costume, racketing about like any human children. Sympathy and imagination together have made miniature worlds which need pictures. It is through pictures most of all that small children will see their own inclinations and actions as if in a mirror; words would have killed these moods stone-dead.

What small children are looking for, of course, is a description of the world as they see it. The heroes of their picture-books may be trains or elephants or they may be children like themselves. The action may be familiar or fantastic. It is usually, in fact, a combina-

tion of the two. The appeal of Diana Ross's stories about the little
red engine lies in the welding together of everyday and far away.
The child follows with delight, in words and pictures, when the engine
goes out into the world, adventuring as boldly as the child does in his
fancy, challenging larger and more powerful engines, venturing to
London, to India, even to the Moon, but always coming back to
Taddlecombe, to his friends, little dog Hurry and the gamekeeper's
cat. Very little of the background of the stories, the shifting of scene,
can really be expressed in words; they are there to deal, simply, with
the story; nor can the endearing personality of the engine be shown
except in pictures, and this Lewitt-Him and Leslie Wood have done
with superb success.

Diana Ross's chief contribution to these stories is the device of
repetition which she has made peculiarly her own. Her stories, like
so many others for this stage of childhood, are incantations, lulling a
child to sleep and filling his mind with images and ideas which recur
for his delight. Best of all Diana Ross's stories in collaboration
with Leslie Wood is WHOO WHOO THE WIND BLEW, a cumulative tale in which we follow the fate of various garments as the
wind snatches them away one by one from their disgruntled owners.
The procession of odd individuals grows longer and longer. Rich
old grandmother, corporation dustman, famous singer and the rest,
they all follow the growing skein of errant clothes in picture after
picture, and the fun gets faster and better as the words build up to a
ridiculous climax.

Repetition, the multiplication of objects—this can produce
pleasing patterns to the eye as well as pleasing groups of words.
Wanda Gág's nursery tale, MILLIONS OF CATS, is a good example
of this. As the old man selects cat after cat, accumulating a con-
course of animals, the repeated phrase 'hundreds of cats, thousands
of cats, millions and billions and trillions of cats' is pointed by the
author's amusing designs.

Wanda Gág's work has always the quality of folk tale. It is at once
fantastic and homely. Part of the charm of this tale lies in the oddity
of the country through which the old man journeys, and part of it
lies in the conclusion, when the battle is over and the lamplight shines
on the happy old couple with their own cat, the most beautiful cat
in the world because he is their own. The reassurance of domestic
security, so vital for small children, comes across better in the

Drawing by Peter Spier for Phyllis Krasilovsky's THE COW WHO FELL IN
THE CANAL (World's Work)
Below: Drawing by Reiner Zimnik for his DRUMMERS OF DREAMS (Faber). A
design which depends on repetition

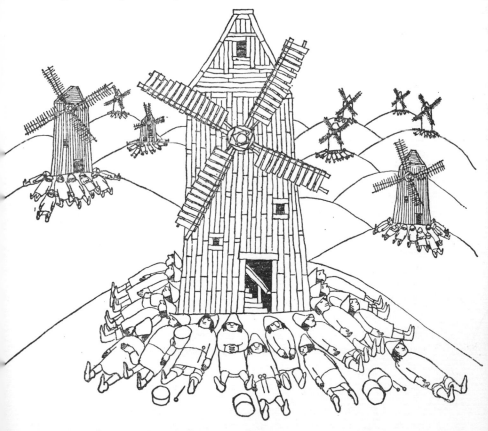

pictures than in the words; any expression of this lamplit mood would be heavy and sentimental in words.

Children need not always see themselves in their own world. They need not always look at scenes where children are children. Against the safe background of nursery tea, the infants of Kate Greenaway dress up and copy the manners and modes of their elders. In the picture-books which Caldecott made for the nursery, the world is a robust adult world of hunting parsons and coy maidens, where children tag along and have a wonderful time; but in SING A SONG FOR SIXPENCE the world is handed over to the young. Here is a boy king, his crown set down on the table, earnestly counting his money beneath pictures of nursery heroes, while his sister rules demurely in a delightful nursery filled with toys. It is all a glorious game of make-believe.

Nothing pleases children more, of course, than to be made free of the adult world through picture-books. In Jean de Brunhoff's stories, Babar the elephant is, clearly, a small boy, privileged by a double magic to lead a human and an adult life. The text offers merely a plain statement of what the elephants do, but in the pictures the whole delightful invasion of the adult world is made clear. Celeste dipping her croissant into her coffee, as the pair breakfast in bed; Babar being fitted for a suit (and, like any child, riding up and down in the store lift); Celeste in her nurse's costume, tending the wounded elephants under instruction from the useful old lady; Babar and Celeste, wrecked on a desert island, setting up camp:

> Ils ont dressé leur tente, puis, assis sur de grosses pierres, ils mangent avec appétit une excellente soupe au riz cuite à point et bien sucrée. 'On n'est pas si mal sur cette île,' dit Babar.
> Jean de Brunhoff. LE VOYAGE DE BABAR (Jardin des Modes, 1932) p. 9.

The elephants imitating a small boy and girl imitating a bourgeois couple—it is an irresistible sequence. It is the same with Ardizzone's glorious picture-books about Tim and his friends. Here is the world he knew as a child, illuminated by his sympathy as a parent. Here all the dearest wishes of childhood come true. Charlotte learns to make pastry, Lucy has a real party frock, and Tim is the prototype of all small boys, squaring up in the post-office to send a telegram, spying on the mutineers, shouldering his worldly goods in a handkerchief, always resourceful, always cheerful, always with a tip-tilted look of concentration and curiosity. Now and then in Ardizzone's books we hear the authentic voice of authority: 'Well dash my wig. Boys, boys and a dog in the cab of my engine. Can't have them here. Impossible. Against Company regulations. Go away at once.' So the engine-driver, in NICHOLAS AND THE FAST-MOVING DIESEL. But the two boys do drive the train, and, like the succession of mayors and sea-captains in the *Tim* books, the railway officials give way to youth and pin medals on their chests.

Now this is not only a joke. The child is pleased to see another child doing grown-up things, and the effect is one of comedy rather than of humour. This comedy will lie, for the child, mainly in the pictures, so that a simple, short text is all that is necessary. For this reason I think Kathleen Hale's books about Orlando the marmalade cat fall just short of the top rank, though from the decorative point of view they are superb. She puts too much into words. She spoils her good jokes (built on the incongruous meeting of two worlds) by forcing them into words. The free, spontaneous, gorgeous detail of her lithographs does not need elaboration in the text, but it sometimes gets it. Not always. One of her best stories, ORLANDO'S INVISIBLE PYJAMAS, turns round the unfortunate baldness of the marmalade cat's hindquarters as a result of an accident with some paraffin. Grace knits him a replica of his own coat, so that he can face the world without embarrassment. And he does, until he meets a dog and tries to put his fur up. In the text, this is stated simply. It is elaborated in the pictures—first, of a dog rocking with derisive laughter at Orlando's smooth back, then of the same dog turning tail when he sees that the cat's fur has grown and that he is really in earnest. This is fine technique, for the joke is essentially a pictorial one. Elsewhere, Kathleen Hale adds unnecessarily to the pictures. In ORLANDO KEEPS A DOG, the wonderful double-spread (pp. 24–5) of Grace and her poodle hurtling across a snowbound landscape is redrawn in words:

They raced over ploughed fields that looked like white corduroy; past trees wearing mittens and jerseys of ivy; they followed the tracks of the rabbit round a snow-covered haystack, that reminded Bill of an iced cake. They were startled by what they thought was a strange beast with antlers, swishing his tail and stamping, but it

was only Orlando's friend Vulcan, the horse, who was scratching
his head against a fallen branch.
Kathleen Hale. ORLANDO KEEPS A DOG (Country Life, 1931)
p. 24.

The comic items here, especially the trees with jerseys, misfire in
words but are triumphantly amusing in line and colour, and there
is, besides, the beauty of design, of the detailed foreground and the
lovely distant view of a little town encircled by the river. The point
does not need driving home in words as well as pictures. Children
are more likely to appreciate the full horror of Mr Cattermole's
supper, for instance ('a horrid mess of raw onions, peppermint-
creams and fish') when they see it, in colour, and surrounded by
other surrealist evidences of the recluse's housekeeping.

The earlier books about Orlando are much simpler. The artist
enjoys herself making designs and lets the pictures carry most of the
story. We know far more about Grace in those early stories, by
seeing her take a carpet-sweeper into a pigsty or dip Tinkle carefully
into a river pool, than we do later, when there are more verbal
comments on her maternal devotion, her efficiency and her gentle-
ness. There are, in fact, too many words in these later books, and
these words express too much, so that we have a text suitable for
an eight-year-old linked with pictures which are just right for
children of three and four. Not that older children do not get a lot of
pleasure out of Orlando; but the perfect Orlando age, I think, is
four.

At the same time, picture-books must have a text, and this text
must sound right. They will be read aloud, and therefore they will
depend above all on good, easy, musical sentence-rhythms. The
simplest sentence can have a good shape. One of the best books I
know for small children is Alastair Reid's I WILL TELL YOU OF A
TOWN, a poet's impression of a fishing town from early morning till
sunset, presented in prose embellished by verse and by delicate line-
drawings, all three mediums knit into a beautiful whole. There is
nothing complicated in the language of a passage like this:

> The day is ticking away, and the old clock, which has watched
> over the town for centuries, is counting the children on their
> shouting way to school. Six little fishing children from the corner
> cottage, five from the red house by the fire station, four from the

farm, three from the white lighthouse, twins from the gardener's hut, and one alone, little Billy from the bakery, waving to his mother with a red woollen cap.

Alastair Reid. I WILL TELL YOU OF A TOWN (Hutchinson, 1959) p. 15.

Or of this falling close:

Swish, swish. The waves are hushing on the beach. Sleep, sleep. The dogs are dreaming of bones. The boats in the harbour stir slowly round and bump softly together as the tide turns. The seagulls fold their careful wings, and the chickens cluck softly in the still farmyard. Only the light in the lighthouse is still awake, blinking a welcome or a warning to any ships at sea, across the rocks and the chasing tides.

Ibid., p. 36.

This is the prose of a writer who hears the rhythms of human speech. Nobody telling a story, if he has any talent at all, keeps his voice at the same level, his words at the same length or his sentences in the same shape; and the writers whose work will live are those who have the story-telling gift, the true narrative rhythm. One of the most attractive tales to read to small children is E. M. Hatt's THE CAT WITH A GUINEA TO SPEND, a cumulative tale. An old lady decides to give a party for her twelve great-grandchildren (the roll-call of their names rings through the story). She sends her cat, Nod-by-the-fire, to do the shopping, with certain conditions and warnings; each of these is taken up and developed, and they are neatly woven into the quiet end after the party. The book is a delight for its originality and sparkle, for Leslie Wood's striking pictures, and for the crisp, rich style. Here is the story-teller enjoying words:

As Noddy passed by the rattling, creaking mill, out popped a dusty mill mouse and made him a mocking grimace. 'Poor Noddy!' she taunted him, 'aren't you a foolish cat to be off to town on a fine Spring day, when you might be chasing field mice among the meadow-sweet and mill mice among the meal-sacks!' And Noddy shook his head most remarkably quickly to and fro, which meant 'Of course I'm not!'

E. M. Hatt. THE CAT WITH A GUINEA TO SPEND (Faber, 1947). n.p.

Simplicity does not mean short, blunt sentences, and it does not mean short, blunt words. The opening of PETER RABBIT is simple; not basic. In her books, if Beatrix Potter wanted to use a long or an unfamiliar word, she did. Enid Blyton and others think that children are taxed too much if they are confronted by so much as a poly-syllable, but generations of them, as young as three, have enjoyed without too much intellectual effort the end of Tom Kitten's adven-ture—'My friends will arrive in a minute and you are not fit to be seen; I am affronted,' said Mrs Tabitha Twitchit'; or Jemima Puddleduck's search for a 'convenient dry nesting-place' or Sally Henny-Penny's 'remarkable assortment of bargains.' It is learning without tears, if you like. It is also an enormous pleasure, the sharp shock of a new, exciting word; a pleasure for the listening child, and a pleasure for the adventurous reader getting at it phonetically and making a guess at its meaning.

There are authors who have deliberately catered for this particular taste. Leslie Brooke, for instance, in those ingenious rhymed tales, JOHNNY CROW'S GARDEN and JOHNNY CROW'S PARTY, and Ludwig Bemelmans in his comical verses about Madeline, which depend for their point on the apt placing of unusual words. But this must be as it comes. Every author must be free to write as he pleases, not tied down by fear that a child might not be able to understand what he writes, nor by any snobbish feeling that he has to show off. He only needs to remember that children are bold and experimental, that they like a mixture (in words and in pictures) of the rational and the irrational, the simple and the crowded, the known and the unknown.

In all these books, pictures and words are interdependent and of equal importance. But it is not long before the child who has been used to books begins to listen more than to look. Now he needs stories, still illustrated, but with the text putting in a stronger claim to his interest. This is the time (perhaps when a child is four) for the nursery chronicle, the picture in words of the child's life; an exten-sion of picture-books, because it is still a simple survey of the life he knows. When he reads, or listens to, the stories about Minikin or Milly-Molly-Mandy, he is reliving his own life, enjoying the expected.

A simple survey, this is what children enjoy, but not an over-simplified one. It may sound easy to write a tale about a perfectly

"Once upon a time there were two huge great fairies."

I tell you a story? Once upon a time there were two huge great fairies——"

"Mary-Mary!" said Miriam. "Go away at once. You shouldn't have been listening."

"—and their names both began with an M——" went on Mary-Mary.

"Oh, do go away!" said Miriam and Meg.

"—they were called Margarine and Marmalade——" said Mary-Mary.

"Shall we push her out?" said Martyn.

"Take me away!" said Mary-Mary in Moppet's voice. "I don't believe in fairies—I only believe in mice."

Mary-Mary crawled out from under the table, saying to Moppet, "Very well, I'll take you away and tell you a mouse story." And she went into the kitchen where Mother was busy cooking the dinner.

Mary-Mary sat under the draining-board and told

A page from MARY-MARY (Harrap) by Joan G. Robinson (illustrated by the author) ordinary day in the life of a perfectly ordinary child: anyone who has tried it knows it is extremely, painfully difficult. It is one thing to recall to yourself the pleasures of playing pirates or looking for hidden treasure, quite another to reconstruct, honestly, and without being arch or patronizing, the special joy, to a four-year-old, of feeding a stray kitten or walking in the rain. Few writers have done this without taking a deep breath and adopting an attitude, and this of course at once separates them from the child reader. One of the sterling exceptions is Jane Gross, who in an unassuming volume of tales, HARRIET AND SMITH, succeeded in presenting the daily adventures of a small girl and her cat with almost photographic fidelity and with no trace of affectation. Harriet talks to Smith as if he were another child; Smith behaves as he pleases, now like a cat, now like an odd but pleasant companion. The relationship between the two gives a new twist to stories which are very ordinary as far as their subject is concerned.

It takes courage to play the theme of early childhood absolutely straight, and it takes ingenuity to vary the pattern of tiny domestic adventures. Joan G. Robinson, in her tales of Mary-Mary, gets attention at once because of her heroine, one of the most amusing naughty girls I know in fiction. Diana Ross, in WILLIAM AND THE LORRY and NURSERY TALES, uses repetition and verbal pattern brilliantly. Doris Rust, in numerous stories for small children, constantly changes the emphasis in what are quite ordinary incidents. So, in ALL SORTS OF DAYS, the story of a rainy day is centred on the umbrellas in the stand, their personalities and their fate; it is through their talk that you see what is going on in the home. A foggy day is described through the comments of a ship's tug on the river, a train, a green car and so on. A sunny day has frogs for its chief characters, and a windy day the wind himself. All the stories reflect the ordinary everyday life that a child knows and loves to have repeated.

But it must be repeated honestly and with sympathy. It is no use talking down to children, in books, and it is no better to treat them with ostentatious respect. They must be addressed *as children*—as beings with their own values, walking beside us, not in front or behind. I cannot imagine a child of seven, or even of five, being satisfied with the tone of H. B. Creswell in MARYTARY, as he tells how a clever dog discovered two lost children:

Off he ran into the wood, and at first he did not find any smell worth telling about. Then he came to a quite nice smell, and he followed it, and it was a pretty white cat, but it ran up a tree. And next he met a lovely smell, all furry like Mummy's stole, but more; and he followed the smell along the ground and it was a beautiful bunny rabbit with black ears, but it ran into a hole in the bank. Next of all he smelt a most delicious scrumptious smell, nicer than anything; and what do you think it was? It was the fish bones that Johnny had thrown down, frizzling in the fire, far, far away. So the old dog followed where the smell came from till he reached the river. Then he put up his nose, sniffed, said 'Bow wow,' jumped in and swam over to the island. Wasn't it clever of him?
H. B. Creswell. MARYTARY (Oxford University Press [1928] 1950) pp. 12–13.

But I can imagine a child of that age responding to this:

The door of Mr Parfitt's cottage was opened by a young girl in a red frock. Tony was relieved. Everything about Mr Parfitt's cottage had looked and smelt so very odd, that he would not have been greatly surprised if the door had been opened by the cat, with a white apron round its tabby waist.
Olive Dehn. THE PIKE DREAM (Hamish Hamilton, Reindeer Books, 1958) p. 29.

The date of publication of these two books is important. Olive Dehn's is thirty years later than H. B. Creswell's, and in those thirty years our ideas about seven-year-olds have changed a good deal. All the same, there is still much sorting to do among contemporary stories before we can find books for this age where the author really shares the recollected pleasures and pains of childhood. We must throw aside puppies and kittens in favour of cats with dash and character. We must put aside trivial catalogues of nursery events and look for family chronicles with humour and imaginative energy. Above all, we must criticize out of existence books that adopt a monosyllabic style and an infantile manner. It is no use thinking of a young listener as infantile. It is true that he is still clinging to his own world, still seeing pictures in the nursery fire; the books he enjoys and needs keep him close to his own world, where lie affection and security. But, to him, that familiar world is always new and exciting, and the writer can keep it so.

Drawing by Edward Ardizzone for his TIM AND CHARLOTTE (O.U.P.)

Reading List

(*Unless otherwise stated, the books in this section are illustrated by their authors*)

*Ardizzone, Edward. LITTLE TIM AND THE BRAVE SEA CAPTAIN (1936),
   redrawn and with additional text 1955, LUCY BROWN AND MR GRIMES
   1937, TIM AND LUCY GO TO SEA (1938), redrawn and with additional text
   1958, TIM AND CHARLOTTE 1951, TIM TO THE RESCUE 1949, TIM IN
   DANGER 1953, TIM ALL ALONE 1956. *O.U.P.* (See also p. 382.)

*Ardizzone, Edward. NICHOLAS AND THE FAST MOVING DIESEL (1948) 1959,
   JOHNNY THE CLOCKMAKER. 1960 *O.U.P.*

Ardizzone, Edward. PAUL, THE HERO OF THE FIRE. *Penguin* 1948.

Bannerman, Helen. LITTLE BLACK SAMBO. *Chatto* (1899) continuously in
   print. Best of all repetitive tales for the very young.

*Bemelmans, Ludwig. MADELINE (1939 U.S.A.) 1954, MADELINE'S RESCUE
   (1953 U.S.A.) 1954. MADELINE AND THE BAD HAT (1957 U.S.A.) 1958. *Deutsch.*
   (See also p. 382.)

Berg, Leila. LITTLE PETE STORIES. *Penguin* (Puffin Story Books) (1952) 1959.
   Illustrated by Henrietta Garland. Subtle humour, sure understanding of
   a four-year-old's pleasure in puddles, drains, his shadow, etc.

Bettina. PAOLO AND PANETTO. *O.U.P.* 1960. Exquisite tale of rich boy, poor
   girl and faun playing in a dream world: superb illustrations by the author.

*Bradbury, Ray. SWITCH ON THE NIGHT (1955 U.S.A.). Hart-Davis 1955.
   Illustrated by Madeline Gekiere.

*Brisley, Joyce Lankester. MILLY-MOLLY-MANDY STORIES. *Harrap* 1928, and
   many other titles.

*Brooke, Leslie. JOHNNY CROW'S GARDEN 1903, JOHNNY CROW'S PARTY 1907, JOHNNY CROW'S NEW GARDEN 1935. *Warne.*

*Brunhoff, Jean de. THE STORY OF BABAR THE LITTLE ELEPHANT (1931 France) 1934, BABAR'S TRAVELS (1932 France) 1935, BABAR THE KING (1933 France) 1936, BABAR'S FRIEND ZEPHIR (1936 France) 1937, BABAR AT HOME (1938 France) 1938. BABAR AND FATHER CHRISTMAS (first published in France 1941) 1940. *Methuen.*

*Brunhoff, Laurent de. BABAR AND THAT RASCAL ARTHUR (1947 France) 1948, PICNIC AT BABAR'S (1947 France) 1950, BABAR'S VISIT TO BIRD ISLAND (1951 France) 1952. *Methuen.* (See also p. 382.)

Burton, Virginia Lee. THE LITTLE HOUSE (1942 U.S.A.). *Faber* 1947. How the city grew round a country house: lovely pictorial procession of the seasons.

*Caldecott, Randolph. PICTURES AND SONGS. *Warne,* from 1878.

Chönz, Selina. A BELL FOR URSLI (1946 Zürich) 1950, FLORINA AND THE WILD BIRD (1952 Zürich) 1952. *O.U.P.* Translated by Anne and Ian Serraillier. Illustrated by Alois Carigiet. Verse tales from Switzerland with rich illustrations.

*Creswell, H. B. MARYTARY. *O.U.P.* (1928) 1950.

*Dehn, Olive. THE PIKE DREAM. *Hamish Hamilton* (Reindeer Books) 1958. Illustrated by Sonia Markham.

Drummond, V. H. MRS EASTER'S PARASOL 1944, MISS ANNA TRULY 1945 THE CHARMING TAXI-CAB 1947, MR FINCH'S PET SHOP 1953, MRS EASTER AND THE STORKS 1957. *Faber.* Gay, humorous fantasies, as pointed in words as in the author's pictures.

Flack, Marjorie. THE STORY ABOUT PING (1933 U.S.A.). *Bodley Head* (1935) 1956. Enchanting story of a duckling on the Yangtse: superb coloured pictures by Kurt Wiese.

*Françoise. JEANNE-MARIE COUNTS HER SHEEP 1955. JEANNE-MARIE IN GAY PARIS 1957, SPRINGTIME FOR JEANNE-MARIE 1958, JEANNE-MARIE AT THE FAIR 1959. *Brockhampton.*

*Gàg, Wanda. MILLIONS OF CATS. *Faber* 1929.

*Godden, Rumer. IMPUNITY JANE. *Macmillan* 1955. Illustrated by Adrienne Adams.

*Greenaway, Kate. UNDER THE WINDOW (1879) 1956, MARIGOLD GARDEN (1885) 1959. *Warne.*

Greene, Graham. THE LITTLE TRAIN 1946, THE LITTLE FIRE-ENGINE 1950, THE LITTLE HORSE-BUS 1952, THE LITTLE STEAM-ROLLER 1953. *Parrish.* Illustrated by Dorothy Craigie. Crooks and spirited vehicles in lively tales.

*Gross, Jane. HARRIET AND SMITH. *Hulton* 1958. Illustrated by Paddie Spratley.

*Hale, Kathleen. ORLANDO THE MARMALADE CAT: A CAMPING HOLIDAY 1938, ORLANDO THE MARMALADE CAT BUYS A FARM 1942, ORLANDO THE MARMALADE CAT: A TRIP ABROAD 1949, ORLANDO THE MARMALADE CAT: A SEASIDE HOLIDAY 1952, ORLANDO THE MARMALADE CAT: HIS SILVER WEDDING 1944, ORLANDO BECOMES A DOCTOR 1944, ORLANDO KEEPS A DOG 1949. *Country Life.*

Hale, Kathleen. ORLANDO THE JUDGE 1950, ORLANDO'S ZOO 1954, ORLANDO'S MAGIC CARPET 1958, THE FRISKY HOUSEWIFE 1959. *Murray* (Harlequin Books).

Hale, Kathleen. ORLANDO'S HOME LIFE 1942, ORLANDO'S EVENING OUT 1941, ORLANDO'S INVISIBLE PYJAMAS 1947. *Penguin.*

*Hatt, E. M. THE CAT WITH A GUINEA TO SPEND. *Faber* 1947.

*Hillyard, Mary D. MINIKIN'S VISIT 1953, MINIKIN'S NEW HOME 1954, MINIKIN AND HER FRIENDS 1955, TIMOTHY, MINIKIN AND ALL 1956, A TREAT FOR MINIKIN 1958. *Dent.* Illustrated by A. H. Watson.

Jones, Harold. THE VISIT TO THE FARM 1941, THE ENCHANTED NIGHT 1947. *Faber.* Charming, rather mannered tales of small girls.

Kaye, Geraldine. THE BOY WHO WANTED TO GO FISHING. *Methuen* 1960. Simple tales of two small children in Malaya, sliding from everyday to glimpses of the supernatural. Exquisite drawings by Peggy Fortnum.

Kellway, Mary. HAPPY DAYS. *Hutchinson* 1959. Illustrated by Sheila Rose. Red-letter days of a five-year-old who lives by the sea.

*Krasilovsky, Phyllis. THE COW WHO FELL IN THE CANAL (1957 U.S.A.). *World's Work* 1958. Illustrated by Peter Spier.

*Lewitt-Him. LOCOMOTIVE. *Minerva Publishing Co.* 1939. Adapted from the Polish by Bernard Gutteridge and W. J. Pearce.

Lewitt-Him. THE FOOTBALL'S REVOLT (1939). *Sylvan Press, Nicholson and Watson* 1944. Humour, fantasy, odd bright pictures.

Lewitt-Him. FIVE SILLY CATS. *Minerva Publishing Co.* 1944. Cumulative tale for the very young.

McCloskey, Robert. MAKE WAY FOR DUCKLINGS. *Viking*, New York 1941. Family of ducks reared in Boston city: enchanting and amusing pictures.

*Nicholson, Sir William. CLEVER BILL (1926). *Faber* 1958.

*Potter, Beatrix. THE TALE OF PETER RABBIT. *Privately printed* 1900. *Warne* 1902, continuously in print; as are the many other titles.

*Reid, Alastair. I WILL TELL YOU OF A TOWN. *Hutchinson* 1959. Illustrated by W. Lorraine.

*Robinson, Joan G. MARY-MARY 1957, MORE MARY-MARY 1958, MADAME
MARY-MARY 1960. *Harrap.*

*Ross, Diana. THE LITTLE RED ENGINE GETS A NAME. *Faber* 1942. Illustrated
by Lewitt-Him.

*Ross, Diana. THE STORY OF THE LITTLE RED ENGINE 1945, THE LITTLE
RED ENGINE GOES TO MARKET 1946, THE LITTLE RED ENGINE GOES TO
TOWN 1952, THE LITTLE RED ENGINE GOES TRAVELLING 1955, THE
LITTLE RED ENGINE AND THE ROCKET 1956, THE LITTLE RED ENGINE
GOES HOME 1958. *Faber.* Illustrated by Leslie Wood.

Ross, Diana. NURSERY TALES 1944, WILLIAM AND THE LORRY 1956. *Faber.*
Illustrated by Irene Hawkins.

*Ross, Diana. WHOO WHOO THE WIND BLEW. *Faber* 1946. Illustrated by
Leslie Wood.

*Rust, Doris. A WEEK OF STORIES 1953, A STORY A DAY 1954, ALL SORTS OF
DAYS 1955. *Faber.* Illustrated by Shirley Hughes.

Sisson, Rosemary Anne. MR NOBODY. *Macmillan* 1956. Illustrated by Rosamond
Stokes. Cumulative and repetitive tales with a slight flavour of fantasy.

*Zimnik, Reiner. JONAH THE FISHERMAN (1954 Germany) 1957, translated by
Richard and Clara Winston. THE PROUD WHITE CIRCUS HORSE (1956
Swizerland) 1958, DRUMMERS OF DREAMS (1958 Germany) 1960, translated
by E. M. Hatt. *Faber.* Stories with a moral, decorated with the author's
sharp, fascinating drawings.

(See also p 382.)

Chapter 3 | *There and Back by Tricycle*

So far the young reader has had it all his own way. He has been the hero of his own bedside story, time and again, and he is still the hero even when the story takes an improving turn. Nursery morals make themselves felt gently through many picture-book characters, from Kate Greenaway's well-behaved exemplars to that industrious and domesticated pair, Babar and Celeste; and, more flatteringly, through the mischievous and ingenious monkey, Zozo, in Harry Rey's stories, as he calls up the fire-station, falls into a pudding mixture and knocks himself out with ether at the hospital. The charm of Zozo is not that he is a naughty boy, but that he is a naughty monkey. Sin and retribution are felt indirectly and the lesson is put a stage further away from the child, who is free to enjoy the fun. Toys, in particular, are useful scapegoats as well as attractive subjects for a story.

The classic example, Carlo Collodi's PINOCCHIO, with its irresistible jumble of virtuous improving fairies and mischievous boys, is still on the fringe of the overtly moral period; it first appeared in England in 1892; but the story has never lost its appeal for children, though they are now less accustomed to straight moralizing, because the author writes with such joviality and lets his sympathy for Pinocchio come out so clearly through the moral. This nursery classic makes a curious contrast with a counterpart of the present day, MONKEY BEHAVE by Margaret Behrens, a lively tale with a toy monkey standing all through between a boy and his mischief. Here the moral is introduced in a very different fashion. Behind the book is all the weight of Freudian psychology; the child must be persuaded, studied, cajoled. A vade-mecum for modern parents, this is also a most amusing story, and few children will realize, when they first read it, that, like Pinocchio, it is an oblique study of a boy growing up and learning to live with his fellows.

Stories about toys give children a wonderful chance to be naughty by proxy. They also give them a delightful miniature picture of a domestic world. The little girl who first listened to the tales of Teddy Robinson, and the countless little girls who have followed her, see their own world dramatized. Teddy Robinson does everything that young Deborah does (and the author's delightful drawings make you believe this). As she imitates her elders, camping, cooking, shopping, visiting, so her toy, with the bumbling humour of all teddy bears, imitates her. Whether read aloud to a three-year-old or read word by laborious word by a forward five, stories like these provide safety and excitement at the same time.

Helen Clare gives children a different kind of pleasure in her stories of the five dolls, for young Elizabeth Small is able to shrink and take part in the minute contrivances of her own dolls' house. When she enters that tiny portal she ceases to be a child. She becomes instead a visitor, behaving with decorum and politeness. She may no longer move her dolls about to suit her whim, but must accept them as they are, conceited Vanessa, kindly Jane, Jacqueline with her few words of English, and all. When the front of the dolls' house is taken off, it shows a tiny version of the adult world, and the dolls serve as models, as it were, for the child whose life is broadening before her. It is for the advantage of this view of life, I am sure, that Rumer Godden has chosen dolls as the central characters of many of her fables for children. Candy Floss, the mascot of a coconut-shy; Impunity Jane, a Victorian pocket doll with the spirit of a buccaneer; gentle Holly in the Aylesbury toyshop—they have personality as well as appearance. Above all, there is THE DOLLS' HOUSE. This is a miniature novel, a tale full of situations that come frighteningly near those of adult life. Totty, the farthing doll, in her contest with the sinister Marchpane, is as interesting to an adult reader as to a child, and for different reasons. A child watches the drama entranced, dotes on little Apple, holds his breath to see what Marchpane will think of next, despairs for feather-headed Mrs Plantagenet. The adult catches echoes of domestic discord everywhere, admires the surreptitious satire of the story, and admires, too, the impression of stiff shrewdness which the author gives to her dolls. Like the family in Edward Bawden's lithograph, THE DOLLS AT HOME, they behave exactly *like* dolls pretending to be people.

So that, while it might seem that stories about toys were bound to keep a child within the nursery walls, in fact they can very easily take him outside them. Sometimes the adult note is struck only irregularly. A. A. Milne, in his stories of Pooh, uses some of his characters for satire. Owl and Kanga and, most of all, Eeyore, belong properly with all those animals, from Æsop's dog down to George Orwell's pig, who have given a devastating imitation of human temperaments. Lightly handled (they are toys, after all), Milne's little creatures can sometimes send a shiver down your spine. At the same time, Pooh and Piglet are facets of the child, and Pooh's house brings the same domestic pleasure to a child reader as a dolls' house does. So far, so good. The snag is that Milne, though he writes easily and with charm, does not seem to me entirely at home in the child's world.

Pooh belongs to the period of nannies and nurseries, when a parent was a parent, and, however friendly father and son may be, they are in two different worlds. This is emphasized by the bedtime-story framework ('Coming to see me have my bath?' 'I might,' I said. 'I didn't hurt him when I shot him, did I?' 'Not a bit.' and so on). The narrator is always there, occupying something of the position, physical and mental, of the Tramp in Čapek's *Insect Play*, and his asides and interpolations have an air of facetiousness which is uncongenial to some children of today. The interpolations, the free use of capital letters for comic emphasis ('Would you read a Sustaining Book, such as would help and comfort a Wedged Bear in Great Tightness?'), the lapses into sentimentality, are blemishes, to my mind, on a set of tales which, for their inventive energy, their verbal wit and their sheer exuberance have earned a permanent place on children's bookshelves.

WINNIE-THE-POOH and THE HOUSE AT POOH CORNER have picked up much of the soft atmosphere of children's writings in the 'twenties. There is at least one toy story of the period which has conspicuously avoided this, a book which should never have been allowed to go out of print. POOR CECCO, by Margery Williams Bianco, which came out in 1925, is something on its own, full of character, full of incident, delivered straight from child to child, as it were, with no middleman. Cecco, the wooden dog, with his conscientious, rather laborious care for the other inmates of the toy-cupboard; lonely, home-loving Jensina; Tubby and Bulka, the two sentimental, rather witless plush dogs; the wax dolls, Gladys and

Virginia, with their snobbish idiom; and the rascally cat, Murrum; they are all as real and exciting as their adventures. The story, told in a vivid style, is perfectly adjusted to a child's world. Listen to this comment on the marriage of Tubby and Bulka:

> Scarcely was the ceremony over, and every one had crowded round to kiss the bride, than the Lion came forward, with Anna sidling along behind. They too wanted to get married, seeing how simple it all was. Harlequin was willing, but Poor Cecco put his foot down.
>
> 'Nonsense!' he declared. 'One wedding at a time! It's Tubby's turn to-day, and besides, there are no more gifts ready. Anna has spent all the summer shilly-shallying on account of that stupid green meadow of hers, and now she must just content herself with being engaged for the present!'
>
> So they were engaged, formally; Anna, after some coyness, consented to wear a grass ring round her left ankle, and she took off her bell and hung it about the Lion's neck.
>
> Margery Williams Bianco. POOR CECCO (Chatto & Windus, 1925) p. 173.

and what child could resist the picture of Jensina's house on the ash-heap:

> She was an industrious little person, one could see at once, and had not wasted her time, for when she led them presently round the side of the ash-heap there stood a cosy little house which she had built herself, out of an old soap-box, and of which she had every reason to be proud. She had spread a bit of carpet on the floor and made a sofa to sleep on, and pillows stuffed with thistle-down, and she had hung the walls with scraps of wall-paper and fine pictures of tomatoes and peach-orchards, saved from old fruit cans. She had even a little kitchen, with plates and egg-cups and a real coffee pot, and all these things she had gathered one by one on the dump-heaps and brought home. Only the coffee pot, being too large, had to stand outside, but it looked very well there, and gave an air of hospitality to the place.
>
> Ibid., p. 66.

In this story we have left the nursery for a more spacious and varied world. The small child can go on a conducted tour of many lands hand-in-hand with a travelling doll. This is no new story-telling device. It is more than a century since MEMOIRS OF A LONDON DOLL appeared (though it is still, perhaps, the best of its kind ever written). The jointed wooden doll, Maria Poppet, who leaves the establishment of Sprat the toy-maker in High Holborn, sees London in many aspects before she settles down at Ashbourn Hall; sees the inside of a pastrycook's, watches a child toiling in a milliner's, goes to the opera, sits to a celebrated portrait-painter, sees the Lord Mayor's show and a pantomime at Drury Lane—all through the eyes of a doll, which is to say, through the eyes of a child sharpened by adult experience. The pantomime is described as a child would see it, with the final significant detail:

> ... now and then through one side of the curtain we caught a glimpse of something so bright that went by, like tall flags on painted poles, and tops of spears, and parts of mantles of people's dresses; and once, underneath the bottom of the dark green curtain, we saw run along a little pair of bright silver feet.

> 'Mrs Fairstar'. THE MEMOIRS OF A LONDON DOLL (Harrap 1923. First published 1855) p. 148.

but the Lord Mayor's show is seen as if by a doll:

> ... I also saw the principal dolls of this wonderful show—I mean the Lord Mayor in his coach, with the wooden Sword-bearer and the gingerbread Mace-bearer—at least, they looked like wood and gingerbread; and, indeed, so did the Lord Mayor himself ... He gave a sigh as he passed us, and laid his hand upon his fine stomach, and then he gave a smile.

> Ibid. pp. 130-31.

The doll's point of view, egocentric and unique, gives piquancy to small adventures. There is Rachel Field's inimitable wooden doll, Hitty, through whose eyes we see a panorama of American social history. Hitty is afraid many times in the course of her travels, but even when she is washed overboard from a whaler and is in danger of being swallowed by a hungry fish, her dignity is unruffled. Conscious arrogance and unconscious humour combine to give a special flavour to this story, as to Dorothy Ann Lovell's tale of Emma the royal doll, who travels through the lanes of England in search of her high-born relatives, and, in all her curious adventures, preserves a dainty wooden dignity.

Some of these doll stories, with their emphasis on character, will appeal more to girls than to boys, but out of the toy-cupboard, too, come innumerable animated engines and aeroplanes, tractors and cars, from Hardy Gramatky's Little Toot to the Rev. W. Awdry's absurd and endearing engines (not forgetting the Fat Controller, one of the best portraits of a bureaucrat in fiction). No child who enjoys bustle and change can do better than to start solo reading on Elizabeth Chapman's series about Marmaduke the lorry and his adventures with Joe, his cheery driver, Archibald the engine, and all the men, women, animals and vehicles he hobnobs with on his trips in the hills round Manchester. Simple and direct, these stories give great pleasure for their gay common-sense, and because Marmaduke trundles through a world not so very different from the world of everyday. And a child's world. Marmaduke is as unpredictable as any small boy. We are not expected to read too much into these airy fables; like the drawings that accompany them, they are spun out of simple things.

The style of these stories was selected to suit children from four to about seven. Ursula Moray Williams had no particular age in mind when she wrote THE ADVENTURES OF THE LITTLE WOODEN HORSE—or so I suppose, for the book is wise, mature, richly written, and has the ageless appeal of fairy-tale. It has the fairy-tale point too, for the little horse, with his scratched paint and his indomitable courage in adversity, is the younger son of a Grimms' tale, even to

Drawing by Eccles Williams for Elizabeth Chapman's MARMADUKE THE LORRY (Brockhampton)

the way he ends up in a palace. This is a story that will last a child
for many years. When he is five he can listen to it as an adventure
story, and at ten he can reread it and hear the voice of poetry speaking, a little melancholy, a little distant. And he may notice, now, that
the wooden horses' involvement with the world has been by no means
simple. He has not always found people agreeable, and he has
certainly not found them easy to understand.

There is so much to attend to in a story like this that you cannot
assign it to any particular age, but you *can* say that it will help
younger children when they are taking that last step from the
nursery into the outside world. And that is what they must now do,
in their reading. The nursery chronicle is no longer capacious enough
to contain all they want to discover. They must get on their tricycles
and venture out to see what the world is like.

To find suitable books for children of six to nine is not at all easy,
and it is probably less easy now than it used to be. Forty years ago
the customers for children's books belonged mainly to reading
families; they were children who read early, who read easily, and
who could move on pretty quickly from their primers to THE WIND
IN THE WILLOWS or TOM SAWYER. Nowadays, among the countless thousands of children demanding books for first solo reading,
there are many who are reading late—at six or seven instead of
four or five. These children need stories that go further than the
mere chronicling of junior pursuits, to tempt them on. They want a
story. Brockhampton Press was the first publishing house to produce
specially for the young reader, the slow reader or the reluctant
reader, what may be called 'domestic episodes'; and other publishing houses (among them Hamish Hamilton, with Antelope and
Reindeer books, Burke with Wren books, Bodley Head with Acorn
books) have followed their example. Each of these domestic episodes
has a short, clear-cut, single story, with a point rather than a sequence
of domestic events. Each, at its best, shows an intelligent combination
of the ordinary and the unordinary, a little twist of the familiar,
and this is often underlined by the illustrations.

The daily round of sand-castles, dolls' tea-parties and dressing-up
has been changed, and not only the scene but the whole outlook of
the actors. For these domestic episodes reflect homes where nurseries and nannies have given place to a free and easy atmosphere.
The change in our social life, the mix-up of classes, the new know-

Drawing by Prudence Seward
for Bruce Carter's TRICYCLE
TIM (Hamish Hamilton). The
ordinary is made unordinary,
and the stairs of a manor
house become a
runway

ledge children are acquiring, almost without knowing it, of the work
and play of all sorts of people—these are reflected in the stories now
being offered to five-year-olds and their slightly older brothers and
sisters. Just as the social background of reading children has enormously expanded, so has the range of subjects that are used in children's stories. An illustration would be the work of Mary Cockett, who
writes for children of six and over. JAN THE MARKET BOY and
SEVEN DAYS WITH JAN might seem, at first glance, to resemble very
closely a type of family chronicle. But Jan lives in a working

family. His father has a stall on the market, and Jan's play is tied
up with work all the time. When he races caterpillars, it is down the
side of an empty crate he is supposed to be shifting; when he discovers the back streets of the little town, it is while he is on his way
to deliver goods to his father's customers. Again, in ROLLING ON,
Mary Cockett tells of a town boy who goes to stay with his grandfather in the country. But this is no ordinary visit. Grandfather
lives in a caravan attached to a steam-roller, and his work takes him
all over the place. Dan not only has to learn country ways, he has to
meet children from the village and learn to get on with them in the
village school; he has to discover all the protocol and the interest
of a new environment. It is not only because of the unusual social
scene that this story is different; it is also because it is the story of a
child exercising his own wits on his own life, finding out how to get
on with people, how to learn. It is right in the line of modern theory,
this story, with its new freedom in a child's life.

Leila Berg's clever tale, THE HIDDEN ROAD, also moves firmly
out of the middle-class nursery world, and (which is more important)
gives children their own function among people of varied ages and
opinions; for Jeremy and Nicola learn to accommodate themselves
to the families in the council flats they have so much resented, and
from the oldest inhabitants of this London backwater, whose house
was once the Big House of the neighbourhood, they get something
to think about:

> 'And the squirrels have gone,' wailed Nico, 'and the ducks. They've
> been frightened away . . . driven away. *Why* do all the best things
> go?'
> 'Oh, but they don't, my dear.' The old lady seemed surprised.
> 'I loved the fox. He was beautiful and bright. But I knew he
> killed the chickens . . . The famous old gentleman who had tea
> down there a hundred years ago was very clever and really very
> kind, but he was a very rude man who upset a lot of people, I
> daresay. . . . You mustn't think that everything that goes is nice,
> and everything new is horrid.'
> 'Most things,' said Jeremy suddenly, 'are a bit nice and a bit
> horrid.'
> The old lady nodded vigorously. 'So you've found that out,
> have you?' she said.

'Oh, I've known that for ages,' said Jeremy, as if it wasn't important.
Leila Berg. THE HIDDEN ROAD (Hamish Hamilton, Antelope Books, 1958) pp. 99–100.

The moral purpose of the nineteenth century is oddly echoed in stories like these. The tone is different, but the moral, less directly offered, is essentially the same—that children must learn to live honestly and usefully in the world as they find it. Rosemary Garland, in particular, never lacks a social point. In THE SECRET CURTAINS, an English child and her French neighbour opposite make friends with the freemasonry of children, though they cannot speak each other's language. In DONKEY BOY, an unmanageable street-Arab finds a niche in the country. In THE COUNTRY BUS, a group of children help an elderly man down on his luck.

These theories of daily life, carefully adapted to the young, add spice and point to the stories; they certainly do not restrict them in any way. The Victorian child took it for granted that his stories would have an improving note and I think our children will end up by doing the same. Certainly the morals in their stories will be more lightly stated and stated with more humour, for when children live cheek by jowl with their parents, authority has to wear a different, less noticeable guise. A story like Pauline Clarke's THE ROBIN HOODERS strikes the typical note of today. Robert, Serena and Tom, who live in a village, decide to do good deeds; but not because they want to be good. Serena has been rereading stories of Robin Hood and they think robbing the rich to help the poor would make a good game. They are not under instructions from tracts or parents, and they have to find the path to generosity through mistakes and minor successes, until the major triumph when they discover (by accident) a treasure which helps their dear Miss Laurel to regain her manor house. In a word, they are children learning to behave suitably and with energy in a very mixed world.

The kind of book I have been discussing often has some indication of age on its dust-cover. These indications are a convenience so long as parents and librarians do not take them literally. Obviously, it is a pity to give a child a book that is too childish; a good deal less harm is done if you give one that is too old (so long as it is not absurdly out of range). Children develop in jumps and, in their reading, they need always to be a jump ahead of themselves, with books that are just too old, just too deep, so that they can be always moving on. Anyone choosing for a child must appraise, select, be guided first by the publisher's note of age, but afterwards, and much more, by a knowledge of the individual child.

Most of these books are designed for first solo reading, and their style is carefully organized to that end. It is dangerous to aim at 'simple, clear language', as the advertisement of one series states, if this is to imply any control or any restriction on the use of long words; but the danger will be avoided so long as we are concerned with authors of the calibre of Norman Dale, Meriol Trevor, Leila Berg, Olive Dehn and Barbara Euphan Todd (to mention only a few). They have taken their own line and have given children books which are within their capacity, but which, because of individual style, will not hold them back. Children who read early will soon gobble up these domestic episodes and will look for tougher, richer reading. But the slow and reluctant reader will find plenty to think about, for the subjects of these stories are expandable. A feud between families in adjoining holiday caravans, the building of a council estate on a beloved playground, a move from town to country or from country to town—these are events which affect children and their parents and neighbours in different ways, and in the best domestic stories the child is well aware of many strands of meaning. The citizen of tomorrow is today being better served with his first stage in story-books than he was five years ago.

Reading List

1.*Stories of dolls and toys*
Ainsworth, Ruth. RUFTY TUFTY THE GOLLIWOG 1952, RUFTY TUFTY AT THE
     SEASIDE 1954, RUFTY TUFTY GOES CAMPING 1956, RUFTY TUFTY RUNS
     AWAY 1957, RUFTY TUFTY FLIES HIGH 1959, RUFTY TUFTY'S ISLAND
     1960. *Heinemann.* Illustrated by Dorothy Craigie. Agreeable, comical tales
     in which a golliwog has the kind of small domestic adventures a child
     would enjoy. (See also p. 367.)
*Awdry, Rev. W. RAILWAY SERIES. *Ward* 1945 onwards. Illustrated by John
     Kenney.

Bailey, Carolyn Sherwin. MISS HICKORY. *Viking*, New York 1946. Illustrated by Ruth Gannett. Spirited tale of a twig-doll with a nut head fending for herself in winter in the New Hampshire country: full of delightful detail.

*Behrens, Margaret. MONKEY BEHAVE. *Hart-Davis* 1958.

Berg, Leila. THE STORY OF THE LITTLE CAR. *Epworth Press* 1955. Illustrated by Sillince. Everyday adventures of an attractive little vehicle.

*Bianco, Margery Williams. POOR CECCO (1925 U.S.A.). *Chatto & Windus* 1925. Illustrated by Arthur Rackham.

Brisley, Joyce Lankester. ADVENTURES OF PURL AND PLAIN. *Harrap* 1941. Delightful domestic adventures of two wooden dolls. Illustrated by the author.

Carson, Hilda. PLAIN MARY JANE 1957, MARY JANE AND THE VISITORS 1959. *Harrap*. Illustrated by Astrid Walford. Adventures of a doll's house family.

*Chapman, Elizabeth. MARMADUKE THE LORRY 1953, MARMADUKE AND JOE 1954, RIDING WITH MARMADUKE 1955, ADVENTURES WITH MARMA-DUKE 1956, MERRY MARMADUKE 1957, MARMADUKE AND HIS FRIENDS 1958, MARMADUKE AND THE ELEPHANT 1959, MARMADUKE AND THE LAMBS 1960. *Brockhampton*. Illustrated by Eccles Williams. (See also p. 368.)

*Clare, Helen. FIVE DOLLS IN A HOUSE 1953, FIVE DOLLS AND THE MONKEY 1956, FIVE DOLLS IN THE SNOW 1957, FIVE DOLLS AND THEIR FRIENDS 1959. *Bodley Head*. Illustrated by Cecil Leslie. (See also p. 377.)

*Collodi, Carlo (pseud). PINOCCHIO. *Dent* (Children's Illustrated Classics) 1951 (in original English translation of M. A. Murray, first published by Fisher Unwin in 1892). Illustrated by Charles Folkard.

*'Mrs Fairstar' (Richard Hengist Horne). MEMOIRS OF A LONDON DOLL (1855). *Harrap* 1923.

*Field, Rachel. HITTY (1929 U.S.A.). *Routledge* 1950. Illustrated by Dorothy P. Lathrop.

Fletcher, David. MISS PRIMROSE. *Hutchinson* 1955. Illustrated by Rosalie Fry. Travels of a conceited doll and her reformation; unusually good characterization.

*Godden, Rumer. IMPUNITY JANE 1955, THE FAIRY DOLL 1956, THE DOLLS HOUSE 1947, THE STORY OF HOLLY AND IVY 1958, CANDY FLOSS 1960. *Macmillan*. Illustrated by Adrienne Adams.

*Gramatky, Hardy. LITTLE TOOT (1939 U.S.A.). *World's Work* 1958. Illustrated by the author.

Judah, Aaron. TALES OF TEDDY BEAR. *Faber* 1958. Illustrated by Sheila Hawkins. A bear and his friends leading more or less human lives: most individual humour.

*Lovell, Dorothy Ann. THE STRANGE ADVENTURES OF EMMA. *Faber* 1941.
Illustrated by Irene Hawkins.

McFadyen, Ella. PEGMEN TALES. *Angus & Robertson* 1959. Selected from
PEGMEN TALES 1946, and PEGMEN GO WALKABOUT 1947. Illustrated
by Edwina Bell. Australian children and home-made toys that come to life.

*Milne, A. A. WINNIE-THE-POOH 1926, THE HOUSE AT POOH CORNER 1928.
Methuen. Illustrated by Ernest Shepard.

*Rey, H. A. ZOZO. *Folding Books* 1942. Illustrated by the author.

*Rey, H. A. ZOZO RIDES A BIKE 1954, ZOZO TAKES A JOB 1954, ZOZO GETS
A MEDAL 1958. *Chatto & Windus.* Illustrated by the author. (See also p. 384.)

*Robinson, Joan G. TEDDY ROBINSON 1953, MORE ABOUT TEDDY ROBINSON
1954, TEDDY ROBINSON'S BOOK 1955, DEAR TEDDY ROBINSON 1956,
TEDDY ROBINSON HIMSELF 1957, ANOTHER TEDDY ROBINSON 1960.
Harrap. Illustrated by the author.

Symonds, John. LOTTIE. *Bodley Head* 1957. Illustrated by Edward Ardizzone.
Eighteenth-century setting, adventures of a doll and a dog. Wholly enchanting.

Tozer, Katharine. THE WANDERINGS OF MUMFIE 1935, HERE COMES MUMFIE
1936, MUMFIE THE ADMIRAL 1937, MUMFIE'S MAGIC BOX 1938, MUMFIE'S
UNCLE SAMUEL 1939, MUMFIE MARCHES ON 1942. *Murray.*
Illustrated by the author. Adventures of a toy elephant in his own magic land
and in ours: comical fantasy with poetic undercurrent.

Williams, Ursula Moray. HOBBIE. *Brockhampton* 1958. Illustrated by the author.
Spirited toy collects a gang of hobby horses and escapes to the seaside.

*Williams, Ursula Moray. THE ADVENTURES OF THE LITTLE WOODEN
HORSE. *Harrap* 1938. Illustrated by the author.

2.'*Domestic episodes*' (See also p. 339.)

*Berg, Leila. THE HIDDEN ROAD. *Hamish Hamilton* (Antelope Books) 1958.
Illustrated by B. Chapman.

Berg, Leila. ANDY'S PIT PONY. *Brockhampton* 1958. Illustrated by Biro. Fact
and feeling beautifully blended.

Carter, Bruce. TRICYCLE TIM 1957, BALLOONING BOY 1960. *Hamish Hamilton*
(Antelope Books). Illustrated by Prudence Seward. Crisp tales in which small
boys find wonderful outlets for their energy and initiative.

*Clarke, Pauline. THE ROBIN HOODERS. *Faber* 1960. Illustrated by Cecil Leslie

*Cockett, Mary. JAN THE MARKET BOY 1957, SEVEN DAYS WITH JAN 1960.
Brockhampton. Illustrated by Peggy Beetles.

*Cockett, Mary. ROLLING ON. *Methuen* 1960. Illustrated by Shirley Hughes.
(See also p. 340.)

Dale, Norman. JOHNNIE-BY-THE-RIVER. *Hamish Hamilton* (Antelope Books) 1957. Illustrated by Zélide Teague. Adventures of tough river-boy in fair weather and flood.

*Garland, Rosemary. A SWARM IN JUNE 1957, illustrated by Valerie Taylor. THE COUNTRY 'BUS 1958, THE LITTLE FOREST 1959, illustrated by Cecil Leslie. *Hamish Hamilton* (Antelope Books).

*Garland, Rosemary. DONKEY BOY. *Hamish Hamilton* (Reindeer Books) 1958. Illustrated by Constance Marshall.

*Garland, Rosemary. THE SECRET CURTAINS. *Harrap* 1959. Illustrated by Sheila Rose.

Hough, Charlotte. THE TRACKERS. *Hamish Hamilton* (Reindeer Books) 1960. Illustrated by the author. Adventures, exciting and sometimes absurd, of two boys and a small girl on an island in a lake.

Kennett, John. THE CRUISE OF THE COOT. *Brockhampton* 1959. Illustrated by Joan Milroy. Boating story with mildly satirical note: well written.

Kyle, Elisabeth. THE MONEY-CAT. *Hamish Hamilton* (Reindeer Books) 1958. Illustrated by Cecil Leslie. Unusual treasure-hunt in a cottage.

MacGibbon, Jean. PETER'S PRIVATE ARMY. *Hamish Hamilton* (Antelope Books) 1960. Illustrated by Janet Duchesne. A boy's adventures with toy soldiers—exceptionally real characters and conversation.

Mayne, William. THE FISHING PARTY. *Hamish Hamilton* (Antelope Books) 1960. Illustrated by Christopher Brooker. Village school on special day. Clear-cut, wonderful tale of children enjoying themselves in their own way.

Williams, Ursula Moray. THE MOONBALL. *Hamish Hamilton* (Reindeer Books) 1958. Illustrated by the author. Children find magic creature from outer space.

from THE CRUISE OF THE COOT (see above)

Chapter 4 | ## Mrs Bunny and the Rabbits

One of the pictures my children liked most when they were small was Jean de Brunhoff's impression of the monkey town in BABAR'S FRIEND ZEPHIR. Zephir the monkey is home for the holidays. Here is the station in the background, father busy with the luggage and the children skipping with excitement like any human brothers and sisters. There are the tree-houses, with monkeys leading suburban lives—reading the paper, watering flowers in a window-box, stirring soup. A fantasy, and at the same time a picture based on accurate observation. If children go to the monkey-house at the Zoo they do not expect to see a chimpanzee stirring soup, but they can often see female chimpanzees being motherly. It is quite as natural to put monkeys into houses, in a story, as it is to tell a domestic tale to children through the agency of a dolls' house, and animal stories for the younger children have, more often than not, an element of fantasy in them.

From time to time, and particularly in the late nineteen-thirties, there has been criticism of this way of interpreting nature, but this seems to have had as little effect on stories about rabbits or monkeys or horses as the several attempts to bring reason into fairy-tales. It hardly seems likely, in fact, that a child will classify beetles and butterflies inaccurately in his teens as a direct result of having been given, in childhood, pictures of butterflies dancing in evening dress or beetles wearing mackintoshes. Certainly it seems a good thing to protest (and I am sure it should be done more often) against the travesty of animals that you find in some cheaper picture books. There can be no excuse for putting funny hats on hippopotamuses or making monkeys talk in bursts of facetious slang; and it is equally necessary to take a stand against the prettifying of animals, particularly the smaller animals. There are only too many writers who think they can do as well as Beatrix Potter did by dressing up a rabbit and calling her Mrs Bunny. So long as a rabbit behaves like a rabbit, I see no reason why she should not have human attributes as well as a human name; but the very word 'bunny' has picked up a sentimental connotation since the days of Benjamin Bunny and his uncompromising papa. Inaccuracy, vulgarity, sentimentality—these are the three dragons that haunt the path of the writer of animal stories. Children can very easily be deluded by the stories they are given in their first years, and silly books about animals are among the most corrupting influences they can meet.

Good fantasy is another matter. This will attach itself more easily to some animals than to others. Cats and dogs have by centuries of domestication drifted on to the fringes of human behaviour. In family tales, indeed, they are apt to be treated as supernumerary characters, though this has to be done with some tact if it is not to be sentimental; and it is only one step to turn them into pirates, nurses or explorers in space. As for mice, they are, as Beatrix Potter has taught us, perfectly fitted for the dolls' house and the doll-size tale, in their daintiness and dressability. The many writers who use a mouse family to make a domestic tale for a small child have necessarily concentrated on this aspect, and have left out the messy, marauding side. In Eve Titus's books about Anatole there is even a wry admission of this. This strong-minded mouse becomes a cheese-taster in a factory, to emphasize to men the usefulness of his race, and the notes he pins on the various samples are in fact most useful to the manufacturers. The joke is well within a child's range, but the joke they prefer is the more simple one of mice keeping house, like so many little dolls. In stories like THE FLY-BY-NIGHTS by Averil Newell or Rosalind Vallance's tales of Tittymouse and Tattymouse, animals are so deeply immersed in human doings that illustration must come to the rescue to redress the balance. Very little exaggeration—a pair of spectacles here and a gesture of the paw there—and your mice are tiny human beings and still perfectly mouselike.

So long as a writer does not falsify natural fact, except by the initial changing of mice into humans, children may be left to enjoy innumerable ways of treating them in fiction. They will even understand something of Rumer Godden's purpose in THE MOUSEWIFE, a tender tale built round an anecdote in Dorothy Wordworth's Journal, about a friendship between a mouse and a caged dove.

The author has made of this a parable about the oppressed, but it still remains a delicate and readable story about a mouse and a dove, matched with delicate naturalistic drawings by William Pène du Bois.

Humanization can only be successful if something is preserved of the original animal. Beatrix Potter's tales depend on the fact that the animals behave like themselves masquerading as humans. They are humans only in order to appeal more directly to the children who read about them. The animal is always the starting-point; she works outwards from there. She never brings her animals into relation with each other unless this would naturally happen (as, for instance, in Jemima Puddleduck's meeting with the fox, or the same fox's contest with Tommy Brock). Alison Uttley's method is somewhat different. The friendly alliance of Little Grey Rabbit, Squirrel and Hare is not based on natural fact, nor is the character of Grey Rabbit particularly rabbitish (though Hare's irresponsibility is a legitimate extension of the behaviour of hares in spring). Yet in the Grey Rabbit stories, and in the tales of Snug and Serena, the field mice, and of Little Red Fox, the small animals of the countryside are most sympathetically humanized. Successfully, because this has been done very moderately, and because the background of the stories, in words and in pictures, is so lifelike. It is idealized, of course. Here are wild flowers in full bloom, rich autumn hedgerows, good weather. If it does snow, the mice go out with mufflers and lanterns; they do not starve. But the picture of the country is as true as we need it to be in this kind of story and it depends on a knowledge as sound as that of Beatrix Potter or Kenneth Grahame.

In Alison Uttley, too, there is the particular charm of folk lore and legend. Her animal stories are really fairy-tales. The swan, in LITTLE RED FOX AND THE MAGIC MOON, is a fairy-tale princess; the country superstitions about hedgehogs are used with gentle humour in the tales of Fuzzypeg and his milkman father. The characters of Wise Owl (in the Grey Rabbit books) and Toad (in the stories of Snug and Serena) preserve something of immemorial folk mystery. The same element is present, in a more robust form, in the rustic tales of Sam Pig and Tim Rabbit which are always popular with children. And in none of these stories is there any trace of sentimentality or flippancy. Listen to the beginning of another woodland tale, THE UPSIDE-DOWN MEDICINE by Racey Helps:

Do you like eating nuts? You do? And so do squirrels, but even squirrels can eat too many. Tippety Nippet was a squirrel and he was VERY fond of nuts; but once he ate far too many, as you shall see.

Just as Tippety Nippet was a nice sort of squirrel, so his tree-house was a nice, cosy sort of house. No doubt it would seem a little queer to you, for it had only one room. Tippety told people it had four rooms, for he called the blue-carpet part the bedroom (as it truly was, for there stood the little green bedstead), while he called the flowered-carpet part the dining-sitting-room-kitchen. Racey Helps. THE UPSIDE-DOWN MEDICINE (Collins, 1946) p. 1.

This is a clever and amusing story, like the rest of the series about Barnaby Littlemouse and his friends; the pictures are attractive to look at, though a little too near grotesqueness for my liking; but they are marred, text and pictures, by an uneasy jocosity, and I am sure part of this is due to the fact that the author has chosen his animals arbitrarily. The stories do not rise out of the nature of rabbits, squirrels or tortoises; they are accounts of what happened to these animals because the author intended that they should.

It is, of course, unfair to compare any writer with Beatrix Potter, but for most of us she is a standard, not only for animal fantasies for the very young but also for straight animal stories. MRS TITTLE-MOUSE, after all, can be read as an ecological study of a mouse burrow, and a very accurate one it is too. The other things in the book—the glancing humour, the shrewd character-drawing, the loving but matter-of-fact precision of the domestic background—each element gains from the others. It has been said that generations of middle-class children owe their mature taste in landscape to the Peter Rabbit books, and it has been said, besides, that generations of middle-class housewives have an ambivalent attitude to mice because of them. It is always worth repeating that generations of children have, unconsciously, learned to observe carefully and accurately the world of animals through this most conscientious of observers. Beatrix Potter is the final answer to the determinedly practical reader. In late middle age she became a notable breeder of Herdwick sheep. Her specialist knowledge at county sales did not stop her from writing, in THE FAIRY CARAVAN, a piece of charming conversation among ewes on a hillside, and of expressing pictorially the woolly, anxiously maternal side of her flock. Her books teach children how to live with animals and how to know them.

This is, of course, what any good animal story will do. Beatrix Potter's indirect method of teaching is more in line with modern practice than the frankly instructive technique of some of her contemporaries. Edmund Selous's JACK'S INSECTS, an extreme example of the educational story, would seem unutterably prim and improving to children today, although the conversations between Jack and the creatures he meets have a dry humour that gave me a lot of pleasure when I was six or so. Sermonizing is not altogether a matter of date. Rutherford Montgomery and René Guillot, writing in the present day, are almost as explicit in their plea for the proper treatment of animals as Anna Sewell was when she wrote BLACK BEAUTY more than eighty years ago. Other writers widely separated in date—Kipling and Meindert De Jong, for example—bury their moral purpose more deeply.

If you have a moral, you are humanizing animals in a sense, and this is inevitable in stories for older children, just as it was in fantasies for the young. In spite of an increasing specialist vocabulary, the biologist still has to use some human terms when he describes animal behaviour. The writer who presents the life history of an animal to children, when he has described environment factually, must use his own experience and idiom to describe the imagined emotions of that animal. The most accurate and detailed account of the birth and early days of a young animal—like Niko Tinbergen's THE TALE OF JOHN STICKLE—cannot do without the ideas of home, maternal care, education. The author's illustrations, too, take us much further than the purely scientific standpoint. Each drawing is precise as to fact, but each has a strong element of design and expresses the author's aesthetic pleasure in the natural world.

Every author will make such compromise as suits him. A classic animal story, the Hon. J. W. Fortescue's* STORY OF A RED-DEER, draws the Hind as a kind of Lady of the Manor (even the belligerent Vixen addresses her with respect) and the rest of these Exmoor animals have their proper accents, from the Cockney of the half-domestic rabbits to the rich Devonshire of the old buck rabbit and the muddle-headed woodcock. The hierarchy of a nineteenth-century country parish is reproduced quite naturally and with

*Afterwards Sir John Fortescue.

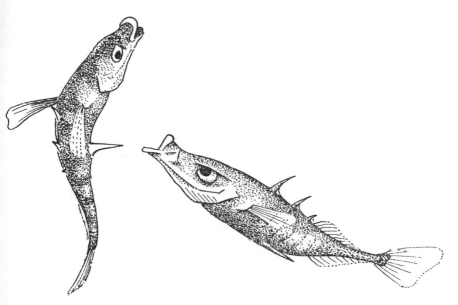

Drawing by Niko Tinbergen for his THE TALE OF JOHN STICKLE (Methuen)

delightful comedy, in the conversation and relationships of the animals, and at the same time the home and adventures of an Exmoor stag are described with absolute fidelity. The beautiful ending of the story shows how the author has fused his point of view with his intuitive rendering of the feelings of the deer:

> And the wild baying ceased; and he heard nothing but the chorus of the waters in his ears. Once he struggled to raise his head, and the great brown antlers came looming up for a moment through the eddies; but as he passed down to the deep, still pool beyond the fall, the water called to him so kindly that he could not but obey . . .
>
> So the waters closed over the stern, sharp antlers, and he bowed his head and was at peace.
>
> Then men came and pulled the great still body out of the water; and they took his head and hung it up in memory of so great a run and so gallant a Stag. But their triumph was only over the empty shell of him, for his spirit had gone to the still brown pool . . . So there he remains; for he had fought his fight and run

his course; and he asks for nothing better than to hear the river
sing to him all the day long.

Hon. J. W. Fortescue. THE STORY OF A RED-DEER (Macmillan,
1919 ed.) pp. 210–12.

Sixty years later, H. Mortimer Batten drew an equally striking
picture of a red deer's life, in THE SINGING FOREST. This time the
scene is the Highlands of Scotland, the hero Corrie, a stag hand-
reared by the laird's children and afterwards released. This is a
more objective story than the older one. The deer has a personality,
in a limited sense, but there is no attempt to equate him with a social
type. He is observed by people, who present their picture of him, and
indeed of a whole complex of natural life, as accurately as possible.
And as sympathetically, for the author has in common with Sir
John Fortescue the fact that he has known and loved the country he
describes and has watched the animals there.

These are more than animal stories. They are poems, if you like,
of country life, not as an extension of civilization, but as a world in
itself, owning man merely as an inhabitant. To an imaginative child,
such books are an unforgettable experience. Again, to read Henry
Williamson's life stories of Tarka the otter, Salar the salmon and
the rest is to be made more intensely aware of the natural world.
When Williamson writes about animals he thinks of them, not as
humans, but as individuals. He follows Tarka through the seasons,
through dangers and delights, with an intuitive sympathy not in the
least impaired by his extreme accuracy in matters of fact. He puts
thoughts into the minds of his characters (and we must call them
'characters') but they are probable thoughts only. The mantle of
Williamson has fallen on David Stephen, whose style, less poetic,
has the same fine selective quality. A passage like this is an illustration in itself:

In the Mossrigg wheatfield, cushats and magpies staggered
and side-stepped as they fed on the fast-freezing ground. The
ragged trousers of the parchment-faced rooks whipped about in
the wind, as they delved with much wing-flicking and tail-fanning.
Pica was one of sixteen bellicose magpies dibbling in the hardening
earth crust, and time and again he was almost toppled forward
on to his beak when the wind tipped him under the tail. The
pigeons danced in unwilling circles as cupped wings caught the

wind. Across the pasture, beyond the fence, sheep plodded in
twos and threes to the shelter of the Strip, while the wind combed
the wool on their spines into a variety of ephemeral partings.
David Stephen. STRING LUG THE FOX (Lutterworth, 1950)
pp. 82–3.

It is an illustration of a special kind, of course; it seeks, through
words, to create an intense atmosphere of cold, but not a precise
picture of a place. This the reader cannot get from words; whatever
picture floats into his mind will be fragmentary, vivid in one or two
particulars that strike him, changing, probably, if he rereads such
passages. The drawings for STRING LUG THE FOX, by Nina Scott
Langley, naturalistic and detailed, do not carry the imagination
forward as the words do; they add an actuality to certain scenes in
the book. It would perhaps be true to say that the illustrator can
do more to fix fact in the reader's mind than the writer can; pictures
like these are functional, like the more decorative drawings
of Maurice Wilson for another book by Stephen, THE RED
STRANGER. But they are not solely functional. These two artists,
and more strikingly, Charles Tunnicliffe in his drawings for TARKA
THE OTTER, show their enjoyment and understanding of natural
life as much as the authors do.

Stephen's stories are full of this enjoyment, this appreciation of
the teeming life of the Lowland grouse-moors, the keepers and
farmers and landowners who are concerned with the busy, secret
ways of fox and owl and stoat. His command of detail is tremendous
and his power to vary it and change the focus from man to wild
creature and back again. At the end of a book like STRING LUG
THE FOX we know a good deal more of the minutiæ of wild life than
we knew before, but we are not conscious of having been taught.
We know more, too, about the way a fox thinks—but not more
than we legitimately should. Here is an account of the fox detecting
a gin on one of his regular routes:

. . . he did not jump on to the boulder. He wanted first of all to
investigate the matter of its changed appearance. Wading out to
it, shoulder deep, he sniffed critically. Through the odour of the
moss, and in spite of the scent-destroying wash of water, he
recognized the smell. . . . Steel! String Lug pondered, but did not
paw. He gripped the outer fuzz of the moss covering and jerked,

sliding back on his haunches till he almost fell in the water. The gin lay exposed, slick on his stepping-stone, with jaws spread to catch his feet.

At that moment String Lug knew fear—real fear. It is doubtful if he realized at once that the gin had been set specially for himself, or that Pate was the man responsible. What he did appreciate was that he might well have walked right into it had he not stopped to consider the boulder's altered appearance. But when he found another gin carefully planted beside his favourite rowan tree on the ridge, he knew that it was meant for him. And that was the beginning of trap wisdom for String Lug.

Op. cit., pp. 80–81.

This is not to offer children a spoof insight into the minds of animals, but to present probabilities worked out by observation; and, above all, to present cause and effect so they tie up into a stirring story.

For the good animal story is not only about an animal. It is about a whole environment, the heritage of all young readers. The life stories of animals, of this classic kind, belong with BEVIS and B.B.'s matchless BRENDON CHASE and Masefield's fine chronicle for boys, A BOOK OF DISCOVERIES, for they represent the wish that lives in us all, young and old, beyond the pastoral convention or nationalist sentiment, to identify ourselves with the land around us.

There is the other side of the picture, too. If animals achieve characters when they are placed in the centre of their habitat, they get a reflected character when they are involved in a human story.

Chiang Yee's YEBBIN gives a picture of social life in a small town in Southern China, with its rituals of behaviour and its rigid class distinctions. Yebbin the monkey is a 'character'. He enjoys human company, he readily learns tricks, and because of his natural inquisitiveness he comes to be a deciding factor in the troubled love affair of the herb dealer's son and the daughter of the scholar next door. At the same time the animal is observed and described as an animal (more successfully in line and water-colour than in the rather diffuse and undistinguished text). BLACK BEAUTY is a piece of social history. From the reminiscences of Beauty and Ginger and Merrylegs there emerges a picture of England a century ago, in village and city. The documentation is important in linking the two themes, human relations and kindness to animals, in rather the same

way as the social and poetic themes are linked in AT THE BACK OF
THE NORTH WIND. Meindert De Jong's touching story, THE
WHEEL ON THE SCHOOL, combines the yearly cycle of a stork with
a vignette of a Dutch village; and a later story, ALONG CAME A
DOG, sets a dog and a crippled hen against the background of an
American smallholding. Every move the hen makes, in the yard,
the chicken-house or the riverside where she hides, is meticulously
described against an equally meticulous background. The tiny farm-
house drama is played out almost visibly for the reader, and behind
it there is De Jong's invariable moral—'He prayeth well, who loveth
well, Both man and bird and beast.' There is no fuss about this
moral. In SHADRACH, a touching story of a small boy and his pet
rabbit, there is not a word that does not contribute directly to the
story. But the folk-lore simplicity of this, and the other stories,
takes them straight to the heart, and Maurice Sendak's drawings
likewise show the warmth of homely affection in its proper setting.

Stories about domestic animals necessarily follow a double
pattern. The life of an animal is cut into the life of a man, and the
success of each story will depend on the author's honesty and good
sense when he is describing the emotions of animals. Horse stories—
perennially popular with children—offer a wide choice of techniques.
There is the purely factual piece, like BEN by Primrose Cumming, a
panorama of the life of a cart-horse in London and the country,
illustrated with photographs. There is the horse-breaking story,
where men and animals share the centre of the stage. In Don Patton's
BROWN JUG, for instance, with its vivid picture of Canadian horse-
breakers and trappers, the bond between the horse and his half-
breed rider is fairly and movingly described, with attention to both
characters. There are tales where a man's adventures run side by
side with those of a horse; Will James's cowboy tale, SMOKY,
is a classic example, and H. M. Peel's FURY, SON OF THE WILDS,
a splendid picture of Australian horsemanship, is a worthy successor.
All these stories hint at the supposed feelings of the horse, and dwell
on the affection that is recognized between man and beast. HORSE
IN THE CLOUDS is bolder in its approach. This story about an
Argentine ranch and the colt Pampa was written by Helen Griffiths
when she was sixteen. Her very evident love of horses and her young
spontaneous love of writing have carried her through a story which
might have led many older writers to disaster. She has really suc-

Drawing by Maurice Wilson for David Stephen's THE RED STRANGER
(Lutterworth)
Below: Drawing by Astrid Walford for Rosalind Vallance's TITTYMOUSE
AND TATTYMOUSE (Harrap)

ceeded in following the thoughts in an animal's mind—for Pampa is far more important and more interesting than the English boy who finds him or the Spanish boy who breaks him in. Perhaps we can draw a moral from this free-moving story, the moral that though there are many things to avoid when you write an animal story, you probably have the best chance of avoiding them if you write from the heart more than from strict biological theory.

Mary Elwyn Patchett's Australian stories are written in this free, friendly spirit. The writer is looking back on a childhood spent with animals. The horses in TAM THE UNTAMED, the dingoes and kangaroo dogs in WILD BROTHER, are just as well described as the sheep station and the people who live and work there, and their feelings are just as believable. So it is, too, with Rutherford Montgomery's stories of Northern Canada, like CARCAJOU and MISTER JIM. Jim, the grizzly, has, from living with men, developed characters of humour and sociability which are, obviously, latent in wild grizzlies. In CARCAJOU, the character of the wolverine is observed, as it were, from further off, drawn almost like the villain in a melodrama and yet with accurate detail. These tales look back to the enchanting stories of Ernest Thompson Seton, but the climate has changed in the last thirty or forty years. Seton's bear cubs and beavers were described as if they were small boys and girls playing. Montgomery's stories are, first and foremost, stories about the wilds, and the humanization is only secondary to the factual picture.

Nowadays a serious animal story will less often use direct speech than did the stories of thirty years ago; but the Kipling type of stylized dialogue used by animals has been used brilliantly by René Guillot in his series of tales about African animals. Guillot knows Senegal and the Sudan well, and the hunter-naturalist Marlow, who plays some part in all the stories, may be taken to be a self-portrait of the author in his relation of interested patron to jungle animals. Guillot writes as accurately as a naturalist but as vividly as a poet. He deliberately enters into the minds of his characters. In OWORO, for instance, he relates the chimpanzee's pattern of thought to that of aboriginal tribes, and the story is haunted by the quest of the monkey for the secret spring, Koguli, famed in monkey tradition:

Oworo, as a child with the tribe, knew nothing of this at first but soon he began to guess the meaning of their annual migration

through the heart of Africa in obedience to a law as old as the
world. But it is not the rains that lead the chimpanzee—they go
quite at random, rather as black men do who hear the rumours
of gold and, trusting to luck, quit their villages and go wandering
in search of the wonderful river that flows with nuggets of gold.
René Guillot. OWORO. Translated by Gwen Marsh. (Oxford
University Press, 1954) Foreword, p. vi.

Animals talk in Guillot's books, they feel, they reflect. The cheetah
in KPO THE LEOPARD thinks about her adoption of the leopard cub;
Sama the young elephant thinks about the dangers he may meet in
the jungle. They give human expression to their instinctive behaviour.
Guillot is a poet, in that he believes in an affinity between man and
animals, an affinity better shown in action than in philosophy;
symbolized by the friendship of Sirga the lioness and the African
boy Ulé. These stories are unique. Some children will find them
difficult to read; the style, though verbally simple, is very com-
pressed. A few may be impatient with the way plot and reverie are
woven together. For the discriminating child, and the child who
likes to send his imagination far and wide, they offer at once a firm
statement about man's duty towards animals and a series of imaginative exercises which would be hard to beat in any sphere of
children's writing.

Guillot has followed Kipling in giving his animals free expression
for their thoughts, but Kipling keeps his animals nearer to the human
world. They have personality as well as speech, in human terms.
Bagheera, aristocrat of the jungle, with his pride and his cere-
monious way of talking; Baloo the bear, clumsy and affectionate;
Kaa the snake, a coiled Svengali; the surly, greedy, deceitful tiger,
Shere Khan; these are as near to human character as they are to
animal behaviour. Occasionally they carry a weight of satire; the
Bandar-log do, for instance, those fickle, conceited monkey-people.
It is no new thing to use animals for satire; probably they made their
first appearance in literature in satirical fables, like those of Æsop,
and the use of animals to point morals about human behaviour first
brought them, through simplified forms of medieval bestiaries, to
the attention of children in this country. Probably children take little
note of the satirical twist in stories like Hugh Lofting's about Dr
Dolittle; but, though these were begun, it is said, as a relief from the

atmosphere of the first world war, they are, in one sense, commentaries on human beings. This makes the characters less naturalistic, of course. If you compare, say, Jemima Puddleduck with Dab-Dab, you can see at once which is the real duck, which is a fussy housewife disguised as a duck. Lofting's animals are human types in animal shape, and the humour of the books depends on the incongruity of animals behaving like humans. This satire is far less observable in Lofting's simplified drawings. Here, the animals are drawn *as* animals, though in a slightly grotesque manner, and when they perform any action which is more proper to humans, it is done stiffly, as if they are holding positions they have been taught.

So that we have here neither pure satire nor a picture of the animal world. We are tracking back to the fantasies for small children, and the books are so gay and light-hearted that it is quite possible for children to enjoy them without noticing any of the sharpness at all. When the Doctor gives Nightshade the vixen various strong-smelling essences to put on her cubs' pads, to protect them from hounds, children are amused in just the same way as they are amused by Prince Bumpo's proposal to use gum of different flavours on the postage-stamps of Jolliginki. In fact, one is a good joke; the other is an expression of strong feeling. But the feeling does not upset the easy-going pace of the story.

I am not so sure about the consistency of E. B. White's STUART LITTLE, that odd (and, to me, rather frightening) fantasy about an American wife who unexpectedly produces a mouse as her second son. Doctor Dolittle's animals are touching when they go in for human activities because they do these things as an animal would. But the enumeration of all Stuart's special arrangements, for washing, for climbing up to the basin by way of the bath-chain, for sitting at table, and so on, all emphasize the fact that he is trying, agonizedly, to act as a human being. His shrewd remarks about humans seem to me to have the same nastiness as the pert remarks of a precocious child at a tea-party. This American story is neither satire nor fantasy, but a surrealist mixture, and there is nothing of the charm of animal life to take the taste of the satire away, for Stuart's life is led entirely in a New York apartment.

The atmosphere of THE WIND IN THE WILLOWS, though this book is a far more searching satire, is wholesome and fresh, redolent of the country (even if it is idealized country), and it is the continuous picture of the river, and of the animals that live on and round and near it, that carries through the many threads of the story, conscious and unconscious, tragic and comic, revealing and secret. This is not a child's story pure and simple. Neither is GULLIVER'S TRAVELS. Neither is STUART LITTLE. Neither is ANIMAL FARM. Yet there is so much that children will find for themselves in these books that they will be read many times before they are completely understood. Grahame's story, in fact, when it was first published, baffled the attempt of various critics to pigeon-hole it. Peter Green, in his biography of Grahame, quotes Richard Middleton's review in *Vanity Fair* as one of the very few which kept a clear head:

> The book for me is notable for its intimate sympathy with Nature and for its delicate expression of emotions which I, probably in common with most people, had previously believed to be my exclusive property. When all is said the boastful, unstable Toad, the hospitable Water Rat, the shy, wise, childlike Badger, and the Mole with his pleasant habit of brave boyish impulse, are neither animals nor men, but are types of that deeper humanity which sways us all . . . And if I may venture to describe as an allegory a work which critics, who ought to have known better, have dismissed as a fairy-story, it is certain that *The Wind in the Willows* is a wise book.
> Peter Green. KENNETH GRAHAME (Murray, 1959) p. 259.

THE WIND IN THE WILLOWS is a wise book; it is a complicated book; yet it has given more pleasure to children than almost any other. Firm and strong it certainly is in its implications, but it is a long way from the derisive and shattering propaganda of Erich Kästner's THE ANIMALS' CONFERENCE or George Orwell's ANIMAL FARM, in which animals stand for so much of human error that they have almost ceased to be animals at all. Grahame's story will not push philosophy or satire at a child. It will rouse in him, at different times, pity and anger, enjoyment and laughter; it will satisfy the desire for these things as it satisfied Grahame when he wrote it; and it will leave the animal world where it was, untouched by human sentiment or speculation. The animals return to the river and the wood unchanged; but the reader, young or old, can never again feel blank or indifferent towards them.

Reading List

1.*Horse Stories* (See also p. 345.)

Ball, Richard. BRONCHO. *Country Life* 1930. Illustrated by G. D. Armour.
Life-story of a horse, especially in cavalry regiment in First World War.

Downie, John. GALLOPING HOOFS. *Nelson* 1936. Illustrated by the author.
First-person story told by horse-breaker on cattle station in N.W. Australia.

*Griffiths, Helen. HORSE IN THE CLOUDS. *Hutchinson* 1957. Illustrated by
Edward Osmond. (See also p. 345.)

*James, Will R. SMOKY. *Scribner's*, New York (1926) 1929. *Penguin* (Puffin
Story Books) 1941. Illustrated by the author.

Mitchell, Elyne. THE SILVER BRUMBY. *Hutchinson* 1958. Illustrated by Ralph
Thompson. Life-story of a wild horse in Australia; straightforward and vivid.

*Patton, Don. BROWN JUG. *Routledge* 1936.

*Peel, Hazel M. FURY, SON OF THE WILDS. *Harrap* 1959. Illustrated by Joan
Kiddell-Monroe.

*Sewell, Anna. BLACK BEAUTY (1877). *Dent* (Children's Illustrated Classics)
1948. Illustrated by Lucy Kemp-Welch. *Ward, Lock* 1954. Illustrated by
Lionel Edwards.

Wayne, Mel. WILD HORSE KINGDOM. *Collins* 1960. Illustrated by Christine
Price. First-person story of a young man establishing breeding-ranch in
Wales: vigorous and exciting.

2.*Fantasies about cats*

Coatsworth, Elizabeth. THE CAT WHO WENT TO HEAVEN (1930 U.S.A.). *Dent*
1949. Illustrated by Lynd Ward. Fairy-tale of the Buddha, beautifully written
and illustrated.

Coblentz, Catherine. THE BLUE CAT OF CASTLE TOWN (1949 U.S.A.). *Longmans*
1949. Illustrated by Janice Holland. Gentle moral tale with nineteenth-century
American background.

Grigs, Mary. THE YELLOW CAT. *O.U.P.* 1936. Illustrated by John and Isobel
Morton-Sale. Travels in foreign countries.

Simson, C. Fraser. CANAL CATS. *Blackie* (Frederick Books) 1955. Illustrated
by Maurice Wilson. Robust domestic tales of feline house-keeping in
Regent's Park.

Todd, Ruthven. SPACE CAT (1952 U.S.A.) 1955, SPACE CAT VISITS VENUS
(1955 U.S.A.) 1956. *Chatto & Windus*. Illustrated by Paul Galdone. Witty
stories with topical adventures.

3. *Fantasies about Mice*

Austin, Margot. PETER CHURCHMOUSE (1941 U.S.A.) (1943) 1958, GABRIEL
CHURCHKITTEN (1942 U.S.A.) 1958, GABRIEL CHURCHKITTEN AND THE
MOTHS (1948 U.S.A.) 1959, TRUMPET CHURCHDOG (1948 U.S.A.) 1959.
World's Work. Illustrated by the author. Comical tales of village church
and its unofficial visitors.

Bell, Vicars. ORLANDO AND ROSALIND. *Faber* 1960. Illustrated by Dorothea
Patterson. Sophisticated tales of literary-minded mice at home.

*Godden, Rumer. THE MOUSEWIFE. *Macmillan* 1951. Illustrated by William
Pène du Bois.

*Helps, Racey. THE UPSIDE-DOWN MEDICINE. *Collins* 1946, and many other
titles in the Barnaby Little Mouse series. Illustrated by the author.

*Newell, Averil. THE FLY-BY-NIGHTS. *Black* 1947. Illustrated by Kathleen
Hilken.

Sharp, Margery. THE RESCUERS. *Collins* 1959. Illustrated by Judith Brook.
Adventure story appropriate to mice but with adult humour and characterization. (See also p. 375.)

*Titus, Eve. ANATOLE (1956 U.S.A.) 1957, ANATOLE AND THE CAT (1957
U.S.A.) 1958. *Bodley Head*. Illustrated by Paul Galdone. (See also p. 385.)

*Uttley, Alison. SNUG AND SERENA PICK COWSLIPS. *Heinemann* 1950, and
many other titles in the Little Brown Mouse series. Illustrated by Katharine
Wigglesworth.

*Vallance, Rosalind. TITTYMOUSE AND TATTYMOUSE 1946, TITTY AND
TATTY BY THE RIVER 1949, TITTY AND TATTY'S HOUSE-WARMING 1958.
Harrap. Illustrated by Astrid Walford.

4.*The British country scene and its animals*

*'B.B.'. BRENDON CHASE. *Hollis & Carter* 1944. Illustrated by the author.

*Batten, H. Mortimer. THE SINGING FOREST. *Blackwood* 1955. *Penguin* (Puffin
Story Books) 1958. Illustrated by Maurice Wilson.

Budden, John. CHARLIE THE FOX. *Country Life* 1932. Illustrated by G. D.
Armour. Open-air story of the hunting field and the woods.

Ferry, R. H. WHERE THE RIVER RAN. *Hodder & Stoughton* 1960. Illustrated by
Margaret Ransome-Block. Elegantly written story of an otter in the West
Country, her relations with men and beasts; notable illustrations.

*Fortescue, Hon. J. W. (afterwards Sir John Fortescue). THE STORY OF A
RED-DEER. *Macmillan* (1897) 1958.

*Jefferies, Richard. BEVIS, THE STORY OF A BOY (1882). *Cape* 1932. Illustrated
by Ernest Shepard.

Masefield, John. A BOOK OF DISCOVERIES. *Wells Gardner* 1910. Illustrated by Gordon Browne.

*Stephen, David. STRING LUG THE FOX, illustrated by Nina Scott Langley, 1950. THE RED STRANGER, illustrated by Maurice Wilson, 1958. *Lutterworth.*

*Uttley, Alison. THE SQUIRREL, THE HARE AND THE LITTLE GREY RABBIT. *Heinemann* 1929, and numerous other titles in the Little Grey Rabbit series. Illustrated by Margaret Tempest.

*Uttley, Alison. LITTLE RED FOX AND THE WICKED UNCLE 1954, LITTLE RED FOX AND CINDERELLA 1956, LITTLE RED FOX AND THE MAGIC MOON 1958. *Heinemann.* Illustrated by Katharine Wigglesworth.

Uttley, Alison. THE ADVENTURES OF NO ORDINARY RABBIT, illustrated by Alec Buckels. *Faber* 1937, and numerous other titles in the Tim Rabbit series. (See also Chap. 6).

*Uttley, Alison. TALES OF THE FOUR PIGS, illustrated by Alec Buckels. *Faber* 1939, and other titles in the Sam Pig series. (see also Chap. 6).

*Williamson, Henry. TARKA THE OTTER. *Putnam* 1927. *Penguin* (Puffin Story Books) 1937. Illustrated by C. F. Tunnicliffe.

Williamson, Henry. THE HENRY WILLIAMSON ANIMAL SAGA. *Macdonald* 1960. Comprising TARKA THE OTTER, SALAR THE SALMON, THE EPIC OF BROCK THE BADGER, CHAKCHEK THE PEREGRINE.

5.*Miscellaneous* (See also p. 374.)

Barker, K. F. BELLMAN: THE STORY OF A BEAGLE. *Black* 1933. Illustrated by the author. Training and experience on the Westmorland fells: sporting atmosphere.

Baudouy, Michel. OLD ONE-TOE (1957 France). *Methuen* 1960. Translated by Marie Ponsot. Illustrated by Ralph Thompson. Family of children and their relationship with a fox: beautifully written, with understanding of man and beast.

*Brunhoff, Jean de. BABAR'S FRIEND ZEPHIR. (see Chap. 2).

Fallada, Hans. THAT RASCAL FRIDOLIN (1955 Germany). *Heinemann* 1959. Illustrated by Imre Hofbauer. Humorous, natural tale of badger's maraudings.

Finger, Charles. A DOG AT HIS HEEL. *Harrap* 1937. Australian sheepdog and his work; a touching and interesting tale.

*Guillot, René. SAMA (1950 France) 1952, SIRGA (1951 France) 1953, OWORO (1951 France) 1954, KPO THE LEOPARD (1955 France) 1955. *O.U.P.* Translated by Gwen Marsh. Illustrated by Joan Kiddell-Monroe.

*Jong, Meindert De. THE WHEEL ON THE SCHOOL (1954 U.S.A.) 1956, SHADRACH (1953 U.S.A.) 1957, ALONG CAME A DOG (1958 U.S.A.) 1959. *Lutterworth.* Illustrated by Maurice Sendak.

Karazin, N. CRANES FLYING SOUTH (1936). *Longmans* (Heritage of Literature Series) 1952. Translated by M. P. Krovsky. Migration from Russia to Egypt and back: accurate details, personalized birds, jaunty humour.

*Kipling, Rudyard. THE JUNGLE BOOK (1894) 1950, THE SECOND JUNGLE BOOK (1895) 1950. *Macmillan.* Illustrated by Stuart Tresilian.

*Montgomery, Rutherford. CARCAJOU. *H. C. Arrowsmith* 1937. *Penguin* (Puffin Story Books) (1943) 1948.

*Montgomery, Rutherford. MISTER JIM. *Faber* 1952.

*Patchett, M. E. TAM THE UNTAMED. *Lutterworth* 1954. Illustrated by Joan Kiddell-Monroe.

*Patchett, M. E. WILD BROTHER. *Collins* 1954. Illustrated by John Rose.

*Potter, Beatrix. THE FAIRY CARAVAN. Privately printed 1929, *David McKay* Phil., 1929. *Warne* 1946. (See also Chap. 2).

*Selous, Edmund. JACK'S INSECTS. *Methuen* (1910) 1920. Illustrated by J. A. Shepherd.

*Tinbergen, Niko. THE TALE OF JOHN STICKLE. *Methuen* 1954. Illustrated by the author.

Wilson, Erle. COORINNA. *Deutsch* 1953. Life story of Tasmanian (marsupial) wolf, distinguished in style, and fascinating in setting.

*Yee, Chiang .YEBBIN: A GUEST FROM THE WILD. *Methuen* 1947. Illustrated by the author.

6. Animal Satire

*Grahame, Kenneth. THE WIND IN THE WILLOWS. *Methuen* (1905) 1931. Illustrated by Ernest Shepard.

*Kästner, Erich. THE ANIMALS' CONFERENCE (1949 Switzerland). *Collins* 1955. Translated by Zita de Schauensee. Illustrated by Walter Trier.

*Lofting, Hugh. THE STORY OF DOCTOR DOLITTLE 1922, THE VOYAGES OF DOCTOR DOLITTLE 1923, DOCTOR DOLITTLE'S POST-OFFICE 1924, DOCTOR DOLITTLE'S CIRCUS 1925, DOCTOR DOLITTLE'S ZOO 1926, DOCTOR DOLITTLE'S CARAVAN 1927, DOCTOR DOLITTLE'S GARDEN 1928, DOCTOR DOLITTLE IN THE MOON 1929, GUB GUB'S BOOK 1932, DOCTOR DOLITTLE'S RETURN 1933, DOCTOR DOLITTLE AND THE SECRET LAKE 1949, DOCTOR DOLITTLE AND THE GREEN CANARY 1951, DOCTOR DOLITTLE'S PUDDLEBY ADVENTURES 1953 (posthumously published stories collected and edited by his wife). *Cape.* Illustrated by the author.

*Orwell, George. ANIMAL FARM. *Secker & Warburg* 1954.

*White, E. B. STUART LITTLE (1945 U.S.A.). *Hamish Hamilton* 1946. Illustrated by Garth Williams.

Chapter 5 | *The Land of Faerie*

Satire is a late experience in a child's reading life. Until he is in his teens he is likely to see, in Toad and Rat and Badger and Mole, animals who divertingly behave like human beings; he will not see them as types of humanity. But when he meets cats and bears and snakes personified in fairy-tale, he will respond to their inward meaning imaginatively and at once.

The attitude of primitive man to animals was not far from that of the child who meets them in fairy-tale. He assumed human characteristics for them. He liked them, feared them, exploited and placated them, and no doubt from earliest times he clarified his own view of them by putting them into stories. When he told a story in which an animal did something *for* him or *to* him, he was getting to terms with the natural world. In the same way, he could people the natural world with imaginary beings, spirits of wood and tree and mountain, beings which were sometimes friendly (like brownies and other household spirits) or sometimes malicious and even hostile (like trolls and ogres and gnomes). If this is not the only explanation for the fairy race as we now know it, it is at least a satisfactory one.

The magical origins of fairy-tale are far away from us now. From earliest times, oral tradition has been enriched by the writing down of tales or by the telling of them by specialists, bards and itinerant poets, who added their own twists and conceits. Local and national events and characteristics, allegory and moral, domestic anecdote and detail—all these have been shaping the fairy-tale for centuries and sophisticating it. Yet no fairy-tale is worth anything without the two primitive emotions in which lie the beginnings of magic—fear and wonder. Storm and cold, fire and the loneliness of mountains, the fear of the elements is implicit in traditional fairy-tales from the Maori to the Spanish, from Russia to Africa. It is at the very root of

George Macdonald's stories, in the magnificent rushing end of THE
PRINCESS AND THE GOBLINS and in Diamond's adventures with
the North Wind:

> For a few moments, Diamond seemed to be borne up through the
> depths of an ocean of dazzling flame; the next, the winds were
> writhing around him like a storm of serpents. For they were in the
> midst of the clouds and mists, and they of course took the shapes
> of the wind, eddying and wreathing and whirling and shooting
> and dashing about like grey and black water, so that it was as if
> the wind itself had taken shape, and he saw the grey and black
> wind tossing and raving most madly all about him.
>
> George Macdonald. AT THE BACK OF THE NORTH WIND (Dent,
> Children's Illustrated Classics, 1956) p. 60.

It gives imaginative unity to J. R. R. Tolkein's impressive contemporary epic of magic:

> Suddenly a song began: a cold murmur, rising and falling. The
> voice seemed far away and immeasurably dreary, sometimes high
> in the air and thin, sometimes like a low moan from the ground.
> Out of the formless stream of sad but horrible sounds, strings of
> words would now and again shape themselves: grim, hard, cold
> words, heartless and miserable. The night was railing against the
> morning of which it was bereaved, and the cold was cursing the
> warmth for which it hungered.
>
> J. R. R. Tolkein. THE FELLOWSHIP OF THE RING (Allen &
> Unwin, 1954) p. 152.

Another modern writer, Angela Ainley Jeans, has built two fine
stories, LISTEN TO THE WIND and THE KINGDOM OF THE WINDS,
on a personification of the elements which has more than a touch of
primitive grandeur.

The good illustrator of fairy-tale will try to convey this general
feeling rather than struggle in vain to put down in line the intangible
happenings of fairy lands. What happens in traditional fairy-tale
does not take on a concrete semblance in a child's mind. As he reads,
he is beset by haunting visions just out of reach. He knows what is
happening, he feels the mystery and magic of it, but he does not
want to see it. All the same, it can be *suggested* in illustrations. They
can show us a scene that will put us in the right frame of mind for a

Drawing by Peggy Fortnum for Patricia Lynch's JINNY THE CHANGELING (Dent). The mood of one kind of fairy-tale. Below: Drawing by Joan Kiddell-Monroe for James Reeves's ENGLISH FABLES AND FAIRY STORIES (O.U.P.)

fairy story, a scene which evokes fear and wonder in us. Joan Kiddell-Monroe, in particular, has a style well suited to do this.

Fear in one story may be wonder in another: the two are never far apart. Both rise from an apprehension of the supernatural which still nourishes fairy-tale in our own day. The tiny visions of Diana Ross's Miss Pussy; the valley with its mist-enlarged, galloping horse, which the little changeling sees in Patricia Lynch's JINNY THE CHANGELING; the glimpses Eleanor Farjeon gives us, in THE SILVER CURLEW, of moonlit mystery; the haunting landscapes of Walter de la Mare's story of THE THREE ROYAL MONKEYS; these are all much nearer to primitive fairy-tales than their style might suggest.

The Land of Faerie is a place to fear and to marvel at; to see in dreams or to imagine in snatches. It is also a place that enshrines human wishes. For a fairy story is more than a description of nature. There is something happening; and it is usually something fortunate, in the long run, to compensate for the world as it really is. Fairy-tales are made out of a natural desire to change life in imagination if it cannot be changed in fact. George Macdonald's North Wind is grand and terrifying; she can also be gentle, and can even up the inequalities of life for little Diamond. Beside the terrors of snake-filled marshes and icy wastes and burning deserts, there are pictures of ideal worlds, paradises for those who are willing to search for them. They may be worlds described in very human terms, like the civilized world in a Chinese fairy's magic box, with its wide city streets and shops and 'dragons of many colours, all horned and fire-breathing'; or they may be suggestions, like the land of Nowhere in an Australian aboriginal legend, 'oceans of nothingness and soft billowing clouds, topped with pink and gold', or they may be worlds rounded out with symbolism, like Hans Andersen's description of the Garden of Eden:

> The lion and the tiger darted like lithe cats through the green thicket that smelt like the blossom of the olive, and the lion and the tiger were tame; the wild wood-pigeon shining like the fairest of pearls fluttered the lion's mane with its wings, and the antelope, that elsewhere is so timid, stood still and nodded its head, as if it too would like to join in the play.
> Hans Andersen. FORTY-TWO STORIES. Translated by
> M. R. James (Faber, 1953 ed.) pp. 134–5.

By the time fairy stories come to us they have been considerably sophisticated. The youngest son does not want compensation for his lowly place in the tribal hierarchy, he wants to win half a kingdom and marry a princess. The basic wish, though, is still, as it always was, a wish for luck. Something from outside—a little black man, a snake saved from a forest-fire, a god from a mountain-top, whatever it is—something with magical powers is going to make up to us for our lack of good fortune. Children or adults, we all need this feeling of compensation, whether we believe in it or not. When we go to see *Peter Pan* on the stage, and clap to revive Tinker Bell, we are not clapping because we believe in fairies so much as because we all have somewhere in us the desire that fairies should exist.

The young man, then, swineherd or woodcutter or farm-hand, wants to marry a princess. There are no fairy stories that I know of where a young prince wants to become a swineherd—not permanently, that is, though now and then for a joke, perhaps, or as relaxation from his lofty station. Traditional fairy-tales are the property of children and simple folk. They begin in the kitchen, and more often than not they have been told there. They are simply told and concerned with simple things. Their stage properties are chairs and chests, the spinning-wheel and the axe, spiders' webs and bejewelled toads and attentive, friendly robins. No fairy-tale will be right for children, or right for anybody for that matter, unless the magic is simple and unless it is accepted completely within the terms of the story. Self-consciousness kills a fairy-tale more quickly than a pedestrian style or a lack of imagination.

The idea of disbelief should never enter in at all. By a paradox, the magical element should be completely matter-of-fact. A domestic fable, by James Reeves, *The Old Woman and the Four Noises*, tells how an old countrywoman learned to live at peace with the inhabitants of the creaking board, the squeaking door and the rattling window-frame:

'Don't be afraid,' said the voice. 'I am an elf. You cannot see me, but I live in your front door and I bring you luck. Every time the door is opened or closed, I squeak just to remind you I am here.'

'Well, what an odd thing,' said the old woman. 'I never knew before that there was such a thing as a door-elf that squeaked, but now I come to think about it, I see no reason why there shouldn't be. Won't you come in and make yourself at home?' James Reeves. PIGEONS AND PRINCESSES (Heinemann, 1956) p. 29.

This story was written only a few years ago, but it has the attitude of true fairy-tale. Traditional fairy-tales are very direct; there is no fumbling or apologizing; you are in the magic world straight away:

> Long, long ago, in the days when wishing was still some use, a King's son was put under a spell by a wicked old witch. As soon as he was quite in her power, she shut him up in a great iron chest. Then, by means of her magic, she set Prince, chest, and all, down in the middle of a lonely and enchanted forest.
> *The Great Iron Chest,* in GRIMMS' FAIRY TALES, freely translated by Amabel Williams-Ellis (Blackie, 1959) p. 163.

Not all writers of modern times have been able to strike this casual note, and, obviously, it is most easily done in the retelling of old tales. Ruth Manning-Sanders is particularly happy in her opening paragraphs in PETER AND THE PISKIES, a collection of old Cornish legends and folk-tales. Here is the beginning of *Skillywidden*:

> A man was cutting furze. And where the furze was growing higher than his head, he cut a way into the middle of it, so that he would have more room to swing his hook. And what should he see in the middle of that furze brake, lying on a bed of wild thyme, but a little fellow no bigger than a mouse. He was dressed in a smart green coat and sky-blue breeches, and he had little square-toed shoes on his feet with diamond buckles. He had pulled his bit of a three-cornered hat down over his eyes to shade him from the sun, and he was fast, fast asleep.
> Ruth Manning-Sanders. PETER AND THE PISKIES (Oxford University Press, 1958) p. 7.

To the Cornish, fairies are natural enough. Irish writers, from Frances Browne to Patricia Lynch, have the same complete ease of manner. It is fatal to try to avoid the traditional formulas, the 'Once upon a time' which never wears out.

This is not because it is a formula that pleases children. Fairy-tales are not the sole property of children, and it is only perhaps in the last

two centuries that they have come to be regarded in this way. They
are a form of poetry, and belong to everyone in whom imagination
is active and free. To children most of all, therefore, because they
have not yet learned that the imagination has any limits. When
adults claim fairy-tales for themselves, there are often odd results.
Charles Perrault, at the end of the seventeenth century, offered
traditional tales to the French court as a luxury entertainment,
with primitive fear well hidden under the cloak of reason, with
sardonic rhymed morals tacked on at the end. To sum up Red
Riding Hood like this:

> This story teaches that the very young,
> And little girls more surely than the rest—
> Sweet, dainty things, clothed in their Sunday best—
> Should never trust a stranger's artful tongue.
>   Small wonder if these guileless young beginners
>   Provide the wolf with some of his best dinners.
> THE FAIRY TALES OF CHARLES PERRAULT, translated by
> Geoffrey Brereton (Penguin, 1957) p. 25.

is to change the terror of the woods for the perils of the city. Cinderella, Beauty and the Beast, Puss in Boots, Bluebeard, these were
all country tales turned by Perrault into period pieces. The two
brothers who attack Bluebeard at the critical moment might come
straight from Dumas; 'one a dragoon and the other a musketeer'
and each benefiting from their sister to the extent of a captain's
commission. Cinderella, finding husbands for her ugly sisters, is a
very different person from the anonymous waif of the Grimms'
version or the romantic lady in Eleanor Farjeon's nineteen-twentyish
piece, THE GLASS SLIPPER. In our own day, James Thurber has
offered an adult view of fairyland. The shadow of the *New Yorker*
hangs over his witty pieces, like MANY MOONS, THE THIRTEEN
CLOCKS and THE WHITE DEER, with their farrago of satire, legend,
fancy and verbal flapdoodle. But it is still fairyland that we enter
through these stories. Prince Thag, journeying in search of the
enchanted deer, meets this kind of adventure:

> Four redbirds in a tangle bush sang 'verti verti verti go' as Thag
> closed his mouth and held his breath and shut his eyes and
> galloped on through the stingish ringy smoke and the trickish sicky

smell, and after a long moment he rode out of the growth of
gnarled and toppling trees, and beheld before his eyes the shining
Valley of Euphoria.

The air sparkled with the high fine sparkle of crystal which
made the three men who approached Thag seem larger than they
really were. The three men stood beside Thag's horse and bowed
and smiled and bowed. Thag saw that each man held in his hand
a mask exactly like his face, but the first mask was stern, the
second mask was sad and the third mask was solemn. The first
man giggled, the second man chuckled, and the third man
chortled. The first man bowed and spoke. 'We wear our masks on
yesterdays and on tomorrows.'

The second said, 'And since those sad days never come—'

The third man said, 'We know no sorrows.'

James Thurber. THE WHITE DEER (Hamish Hamilton, 1946)
pp. 53–4.

Parody and magic adventure go side by side in passages like this.

Part at least of the humour in these tales will only be discovered
by a child from the tone of voice of an adult reading them aloud,
and that same child will miss some of the point of another modern
writer of fairy-tales, Diana Ross. Volumes like THE BRIDAL GOWN,
CHILD OF AIR and THE WILD CHERRY present tales of traditional
sort with various implications. Occasionally these overweight the
story, as in the very philosophical story called *Necessity the Mother
of Opinion* (in CHILD OF AIR). In *The Pest Child* (from THE BRIDAL
GOWN) and *The Young Man with Music in His Fingers* (from THE
WILD CHERRY) and in many others, narrative and meaning are
beautifully welded together. Her best work is to be found in the cycle
of stories about Miss Pussy and Jackanapes. In these, like Perrault,
she has brought stylish artistry to bear on very simple plots. She has
given her peacable, determined little cat a domestic background—on
the face of it a very definite background, a village, faintly Regency in
character, where Jackanapes, the roistering monkey, unwelcome in
polite society, sets himself by his tricks to disturb Miss Pussy's com-
posure. So far, we are in almost a Beatrix Potter world. But the
horizon is shifting and unclear. Transformation is the keynote of the
tales—the change from grave to gay, from ordinary to magical.
Miss Pussy lives on the very edge of fairyland. *The Enormous*

Apple Pie tells how she invited her nephews and nieces to a party and how Jackanapes and Snatch, his boon companion, ate the contents of the pie and filled the case with frogs. No child could resist the careful detail of the making of the pie, or the sudden magical sequel to the trick:

> For now that the frogs are all out of the pie they gather them-selves in order around the largest among them, and he, with a great air, draws a fiddle from under his arm, and each of the others produces a musical instrument, till here is a complete orchestra of flutes and strings, and bowing to Miss Pussy who is dumb with amazement they strike up a pleasant tune. Motioning to Miss Pussy that she shall follow them they lead the way back into the pie.
> What! Follow a band of frogs into an apple pie! Why, the thing is impossible! But as Miss Pussy and her nieces and nephews crowd round to peer into the pie the opening seems to widen, and quite easily they find themselves walking in a mossy glade, so delightful and charming they think they have found the way to paradise.
> Diana Ross. THE ENORMOUS APPLE PIE (Lutterworth, 1951) pp. 17–18.

The Phœnix begins in lively style, with the kittens finding treasures in Miss Pussy's garden, including a locket which she had lost and which Jackanapes covets. Suddenly the tone changes and we are in a different world:

> So with a solemnity which would do justice to Solomon in judg-ment he takes out his pocket-knife and prises open the locket.
> Oh! But the wonder of it!
> A bright shining light which yet does not dazzle fills the whole room; a rosy light which quivers and seems to live, and in the heart of the light which centres in the locket a Phœnix lies, golden and beautiful, and as it raises its jewelled head the light ripples as if the Phœnix stirred in a pool, and there is a smell of such sweet-ness as if every scented flower in a forest of spices were being stirred by a warm wind.
> Ibid., pp. 91–2.

This magic world can be over the horizon, up in the sky, under ice, or in the kitchen. Diana Ross makes magic out of ordinary things— a swing, a photograph album, a pie-dish, an old shirt. Sometimes it is pure magic—as when Miss Pussy, riding high on the swing, looks for a moment into fairyland. Sometimes, as in *Mid-summer Eve*, when Jackanapes is punished by Miss Pussy's fairy friends, the effect is richly comic just because of the ordinary domestic details:

> He staggers to the kitchen to make himself some strong coffee, but when he gets the tin from the shelf, what is this? It is full of gravel and cinders. He swears savagely and reaches for the tea caddy, frowning and trying to figure out what he did with the coffee. But when he opens the tea caddy there is nothing in it at all except thousands of little spiders which run out all over the place when he drops the caddy in disgust. And yet he can swear he filled it only yesterday with a pound of tea.
> Ibid., pp. 58–9.

But then, of course, fairy-tales have always been practical as well as poetic: the magic has always started from simple beginnings. From the folk-tales of Grimm, which are so easily acclimatized in England, to J. B. Haldane's scientific fantasy, MY FRIEND MR LEAKEY, or Naomi Mitchison's GRAEME AND THE DRAGON, we have seen the combination of ageless and contemporary. Your writer of true fairy-tale has always in the background a magical land which no man ever sees and all men long for; in the foreground are the comfortable pots and pans, or whatever ordinary circumstance is to be illuminated by the sun of that magical land. And your writer of true fairy-tale will display no uneasiness when moving from one world to another. To read Patricia Lynch's stories, in fact, is to be in two worlds at once. In THE GREY GOOSE OF KIL-NEVIN or THE TURF-CUTTER'S DONKEY, animals speak, leprechauns move about freely at country fairs, small objects become enchanted and then, in a flash, are ordinary objects again. Inside the humble cottage everything is peaceful and secure, but, once outside, the enchantment is everywhere, sometimes dangerously alluring, sometimes treated with humorous disrespect. Celtic twilight doesn't come into this, but plenty of Celtic easiness with the fairy folk, such as one gets also in the simply-told stories of Frances Browne in GRANNIE'S WONDERFUL CHAIR, still fresh and lively after a

century, or in more modern stories like Helen Simpson's volume of
Irish tales, MUMBUDGET, which veers between humour and the
magic of the supernatural. From an exquisite tale of a small boy
learning the music of nature, with a fairy pipe, we go on to a delicate
comedy of a brownie who leaves his prim London home to give a hand
in an Irish household. His help is so effective that nobody can find
anything 'for how could they know that the eggs had been put tidily
into a bowl on the dresser, and the rice in a tin labelled RICE.'
There is a story about an elemental who comes to work on a farm, a
story terrifying in its intensity and pathos, and there is a rollicking
bit of fun about a banshee whom William tries to re-educate:

> 'That's not the way my mother taught me,' said she. 'She took
> pride in my voice, as well she might, though I say it, for when I
> was younger I could best a March wind at its height. My mother
> taught me to render misfortune only. Who ever heard of a person
> would howl for joy?'
> Helen Simpson. MUMBUDGET (Heinemann, 1928) p. 160.

Poetry, mysterious happenings, jokes and absurdity, they are all
there, mixed with artless art by a writer who is perfectly at home in
the land of the fairies.

In all these stories the domestic background serves as a starting-
point. It is the same background—the hut, the cottage, the kitchen—
from which men go off to find strange adventures, in GRIMMS'
FAIRY TALES. Mrs Molesworth, writing half a century after English
children had first wandered into that dangerous land, took fairy-
tales back into a mid-Victorian middle-class nursery. Her descriptions are gentle and general, her enchantments always turn out for
the best, and the most delightful of her fairies are nothing but
cotton-reels transformed. *The Reel Fairies* is a fancy designed for
the young. A little girl (the author in childhood) falls asleep by the
fire and dreams (or is it a dream?) that she has been made Queen of
the cotton-reels she has been playing with. She is enthroned in her
mother's work-box, which is drawn as a carriage by her subjects.
How many writers, at this point, would have loaded the story with
gauze and glitter. Mrs Molesworth makes no mistake. She sees the
work-box as a child would:

> . . . she settled herself in the place the fairies had kept for her, the
> nice little division lined with satin, in which her mamma's thimble

Drawing by Peggy Fortnum for Diana Ross's THE ENORMOUS APPLE PIE (Lutterworth)   Below: Drawing by Pauline Baynes for C. S. Lewis's THE LION, THE WITCH AND THE WARDROBE (Bles)

and emery cushion always lay. It was pretty comfortable, only rather hard. . . .

Mrs Molesworth. FAIRY STORIES (Harvill Press, 1957) p. 77.

And at the end there is a gentle hint from the mother. It was not so pleasant, was it, to be a Queen? Better to be a good child safe in the nursery.

Yes, safe. Behind all Mrs Molesworth's stories lies the idea of security, the security of a happy and comfortable home. In *Ask The Robins*, when Linde is preparing for her dangerous night journey to the robins' wood, her sister first gives her a cup of 'good hot soup' and makes her put on all her wraps. In THE CARVED LIONS, one of her best stories, the lions make no magic, and nobody expects them to; but they bring to the homesick girl, even if only in a dream, the illusion that she has seen her parents, that she is still part of a family.

Perhaps these are not fairy-tales in the strict sense of the word. The enchantment is slight, and we never have to consider how much of it is supposed to happen and how much is merely *felt* by the characters. Similarly, Mrs Ewing uses fairy lore as a beautiful background for stories which are full of family discipline and affection, coloured with a strong feeling for the rural past. Foreground and background are connected with fact. In *Amelia and the Dwarfs*, for example, we watch Amelia change from a spoilt, destructive young miss to a thoughtful little girl. Whether she really becomes the dwarfs' slave or whether it was merely a feverish dream concerns neither author nor reader. What matters is the atmosphere of danger, the feeling of lurking mischief in the little creatures, which any child will believe could have changed Amelia's behaviour.

This domestic note makes the magic very easy to accept, but although stories like this are a long way from the traditional fairy-tale, there is the faint echo of elemental music in them. The world C. S. Lewis has created, in our own day, in his cycle of fairy adventure stories about Narnia, looks at the outset as homely as the world of these Victorian tales. In the first book of his series, THE LION, THE WITCH AND THE WARDROBE, we find four children playing hide-and-seek. Lucy, hiding at the back of a wardrobe, suddenly finds herself in a winter landscape, walking towards—a lamp-post. The transition to the magic world is superbly managed in the text, and in Pauline Baynes's drawings which subtly interpret it. The first person Lucy meets is Mr Tumnus, a faun. He is carrying an umbrella and several parcels, and he gives her a good tea in his suburban tree-root dwelling. But it is not Lucy who finds out the secret of this strange land. When she gets back to her own world, her next brother, Edmund, jeers at her story, and when he in his turn wanders into Narnia he still pretends she is making it all up. He is duly punished when he becomes the protégé of the White Witch, usurper Queen of Narnia. Like Kay with the Snow Queen, he hugs his fault to him until his conscience is awakened and he joins the others to overthrow the witch and become one of the rulers of Narnia.

Events in the kingdom may seem at times rather surprising, but they have not the complete inconsequence of events in traditional fairy-tales. Everything is the result of character, whether mortal or supernatural, and this makes it perfectly possible to believe in the beasts in PRINCE CASPIAN who have lost their freedom and power of speech but who recover them when the four children help to overthrow the prince's wicked uncle; to believe in the changing of their cousin Eustace Stobbs, in THE VOYAGE OF THE DAWN TREADER, from a priggish, vegetarian schoolboy to an eager and enterprising traveller in strange lands; to believe in the extraordinary underground kingdom in THE SILVER CHAIR, where a lost prince, heir to old Caspian, is held underground in slavery to a green lady until certain conditions are fulfilled.

These conditions show the same mingling of magic and mysticism which you find in medieval poems like *Sir Gawain and the Green Knight*, and it is no accident that this story so much resembles the poem, with its magical details. C. S. Lewis is a leading exponent of medieval allegory, and if scholarship sits lightly in these stories, his allegorical purpose gives them meaning that children will not even try to grasp at a first reading.

In these tales he shows a fairy-tale picture of the redemption of man and his right to immortality. The virtues of courage, loyalty and generosity, the faults of greed, conceit and treachery, are familiar in fairy-tale. But Aslan the mysterious Lion, king over all temporal rulers of Narnia, son of the Emperor over the sea, Aslan who comes and goes without warning, who dies to save his subjects, who fills children and beasts alike with awe and love—Aslan is an emblem of Christ.

At the end of THE LAST BATTLE, Aslan explains to the children that they will not, as in the previous books, return to their own world:

'There *was* a real railway accident,' said Aslan softly. 'Your father and mother and all of you are—as you used to call it in the Shadowlands—dead. The term is over: the holidays have begun. The dream is ended: this is the morning.'

And as He spoke He no longer looked to them like a lion; but the things that began to happen after that were so great and beautiful that I cannot write them. And for us this is the end of all the stories, and we can most truly say that they all lived happily ever after. But for them it was only the beginning of the real story. All their life in this world and all their adventures in Narnia had only been the cover and the title-page; now at last they were beginning Chapter One of the Great Story which no one on earth has read: which goes on for ever: in which every chapter is better than the one before.

C. S. Lewis. THE LAST BATTLE (Bodley Head, 1956) pp. 183-4.

I respect C. S. Lewis for coming so unaffectedly to the climax which is obviously, for him, the only possible one; but from a literary point of view the transition from adventure (which has its own ideas and importance) to Christian apologetics seems too abrupt. The history of Narnia, as he presents it, is full of implicit allegory which is enough to carry worlds of meaning to any thoughtful child. The passage I have just quoted comes after a long description of the breaking up of Narnia after the last battle with the Calormenes, the forces of unbelief; it is a description of dis-creation which has the simple intensity of a poem by Blake, and is one of the finest pieces of writing in this kind of story. Like the mythological passages in George Macdonald's stories, it goes behind religious doctrine and speaks to the awe-struck ancestor who survives in all of us. The descriptions in these books tell us more than the sermonizing. They have a literary value as well, for they hold all the stories together.

C. S. Lewis makes us believe in Narnia, rich, fertile, and hospitable; in Archenland, mountainous and mysterious; in Calormen, with its walled cities, its pomegranates and perils, the Eastern feeling which comes out also in the illustrations. Not by the maps which he provides to establish the frontiers, the principal cities and rivers for the seeing eye, but in the words, the evocative names and the finely realized landscapes with which he fills the eye of the imagination, so that you go with the four children to the Stone Table, see the boy Shasta crossing the desert, see the animals dividing at the great Door. In moments of joy, of fear and of poetic vision, this is a very real country.

So is the world J. R. R. Tolkein has described in THE HOBBIT and in the trilogy, THE LORD OF THE RINGS, a world drawing inspiration from Malory and Spenser and from Beowulf most of all.

I can remember Professor Tolkein reading Beowulf aloud at Oxford, pacing up and down the lecture-room with his gown flying, giving us an inkling of what bardic poetry ought to sound like; and his fairy-tales, if you can call them that, have the same bardic quality. They read aloud extremely well. The language is alive, thrusting, moving, plunging, piercing; even at its quietest it has the tension of near-movement.

It all began with THE HOBBIT. This is a straight fairy-tale, published in 1937, about a hero who is persuaded by a wizard to try to destroy the dragon Smaug, who lies guarding his treasure inside a hill and sallies out to terrorize the nearby villages. But this is not an ordinary fairy story. First, the hero is neither a fairy nor a human. He is a Hobbit: exactly described for us, with his stature (large Hobbits can ride small ponies), his tastes (they claim to have discovered tobacco) and his domestic life. Our particular Hobbit, Bilbo Baggins, is a sort of Hornblower with fur, a peace-loving creature elevated to be hero. 'Dear me!' he exclaims, 'what a fool I was and am! . . .I have absolutely no use for dragon-guarded treasures, and the whole lot could stay here for ever, if only I could wake up and find this beastly tunnel was my own front-door at home!' Qualities which he takes for granted help him to win in the end—his courage (which is partly lack of imagination), his sense of humour and his tenacity.

On his journey Bilbo meets by an underground river an extraordinary, malicious, slimy animal called Gollum. This is in fact not his name but an onomatopœic rendering of the swallowing noise he makes. His name we learn later, in more sinister circumstances, for, nearly twenty years after the publication of THE HOBBIT, THE FELLOWSHIP OF THE RING appeared, beginning an epic tale unique in plot and in style.

THE LORD OF THE RINGS is a quest story, like THE HOBBIT. It

has the same freshness and precision, but it is a more serious affair altogether. In the previous tale, Bilbo had won by a trick from Gollum a little rough ring which that creature called his Precious. This proved to be the One Ring which unites all other Rings, at once a symbol of power and an actual object which the whole of Tolkein's magic world is seeking. Whoever holds this ring can rule all people and all places, but he will almost certainly lose his soul.

We enter this vast, incredible world on the eve of crisis. Sauron, brooding shadow of evil, wants the ring. Gandalf, that same wizard who sent Bilbo after the dragon, knows the ring must be destroyed, thrown into the Cracks of Doom in the Fire-Mountain, which is under the eye of Sauron. The ring has for many years lain hidden in Bilbo's house, but in his old age he gives it to a young relation, Frodo, and it is Frodo, in the end, who takes on the task of seeing the Ring destroyed. His companions on the journey, assembled by degrees, are two young Hobbit friends, Merry and Pippin, Samwise (Frodo's faithful servant), Gimli the dwarf and Legolas the Elf, and two men of a high heroic race, Aragorn, a prince wandering in disguise, and Boromir, a flawed, tragic knight of the Arthurian sort. THE FELLOWSHIP OF THE RING describes how the band collected and starts them on their adventures. THE TWO TOWERS follows the enterprise into side-issues, while the armies of good and evil gather for the final battle, and this is fought out in THE RETURN OF THE KING.

These books are not in the strictest sense children's books, as THE HOBBIT is. I do not mean children cannot read them. Every child should read them, somewhere between the ages of eleven and sixteen, and everyone with a feeling for poetry, of any age, should read them too. They are immensely exciting and compelling stories, but beyond the adventure there is the poetry of vast ideas, of appearances wonderfully visualized, of a country given form and contour, colour and weather, of people (elves and Ringwraiths, magicians and hobbits, tree-wights and knights) each one perfectly realized. I have never met anyone who was lukewarm about Tolkein's books. Either you will think he has made a considerable fuss about nothing, or you will accept the world he has invented and find it complete and satisfying. It is not a fairy-tale world so much as the world of Arthurian legend, where enchantment is at once human and supernatural. It is an extraordinarily varied world; you move from a

86 INTENT UPON READING

rough village inn to the stately hall of the Elves, from the dark, deadly caves of Moria to the earthy, infinitely reassuring home of Tom Bombadil the elemental. And as the scene changes, so does the style.

Action calls out some of Tolkein's best writing. The struggle between Gandalf and the Balrog, deep in Moria, is epic and demands archaic style:

> Long I fell, and he fell with me. His fire was about me. I was burned. Then we plunged into the deep water and all was dark. Cold it was as the tide of death: almost it froze my heart . . . Yet it has a bottom, beyond light and knowledge . . . Thither I came at last, to the uttermost foundations of stone. He was with me still. His fire was quenched, but now he was a thing of slime, stronger than a strangling snake.
>
> We fought far under the living earth, where time is not counted. Ever he clutched me, and ever I hewed him, till at last he fled into dark tunnels.
>
> J. R. R. Tolkein. THE TWO TOWERS (Allen & Unwin, 1954) p. 105.

And, in contrast, there is Merry's slangy account of the fantastic attack by the Ents, the tree-herds, on Isengard:

> When Treebeard had got a few arrows in him, he began to warm up, to get positively 'hasty', as he would say. He let out a great *hoom-hom*, and a dozen more Ents came striding up. An angry Ent is terrifying. Their fingers, and their toes, just freeze on to rock; and they tear it up like bread-crust. It was like watching the work of great tree-roots in a hundred years, all packed into a few moments.
>
> They pushed, pulled, tore, shook, and hammered; and *clang-bang, crash-crack*, in five minutes they had these huge gates just lying in ruin; and some were already beginning to eat into the walls, like rabbits in a sand-pit.
>
> Ibid., p. 172

Now plain, now bardic, now rough and clanging, the magnificent prose drives you forward through this astonishing story. It is like traditional fairy-tale in one way. It has no moral teaching. There are ideas in plenty in the three books, especially the idea behind the

Ring, that power corrupts; but this is presented as a danger, not as
a moral. Time after time we realize that the Ring is changing Frodo,
that it is trying to bend him to its purposes. Frodo faces this as a
danger, in the same spirit as he faces Shelob or Sauron. Of course we
can read morals into the books, and we are all bound to read them
with thoughts of tyranny and dictatorship in our minds. But,
though they reflect the climate of our time, they have the universal,
dateless quality of imagination.

Tolkein's is an intensely active, bardic work. It grew out of
family story-telling over many years and it is communicated very
directly to the reader. With Walter de la Mare we have a country
described by a poet, where appearances matter as much as events,
sometimes more. Here we have come back to the land of traditional
fairy-tale, but we are seeing it through a magnifying glass. Take
Dick and the Beanstalk for example. What a beanstalk it is—not *a*
beanstalk but *the* beanstalk. When Dick came upon it, that rimy
afternoon in Gloucestershire, he was bound to recognize it. How
sharply visualized every detail is in this brilliant tale. Here are the
giant uncles in the strange land at the top of the beanstalk:

> Dick crept forward, and, leaning out a little between the bases of
> the balusters of the gallery, peeped down. They were intent on a
> game that looked like common dominoes, though the pieces or
> men they played with were almost as big as tombstones. In no story-
> book he had ever read had Dick chanced on the like of these
> giants. They sat like human mountains at their game, and the
> noise of the dominoes was like Pharaoh's chariots. And when
> one of them, laying down a domino on the table, mumbled,
> *Double!*, it was like the coughing of a lion.
> Walter de la Mare. COLLECTED STORIES FOR CHILDREN
> (Faber, 1957) pp. 38–9.

The barn where Grackle, the young giant, lies hidden, the giants'
kitchen where Dick is nearly caught, the ogre's widow, the hills
Dick sees in the distance, the very hair and hide of his pony—everything is precisely and superbly described.

This is a cheerful story, because Dick is a cheerful lad who does
not worry about a little danger. In most of de la Mare's work there
is an undercurrent of sadness, mystery and fear. He knows what is
involved in a glance into the fairy world, however brief. His appar-

itions have nothing to do with the gauzy and inept creatures our children see on birthday-cards. It seems hardly right to call de la Mare's beings *fairies*, even using the word in its oldest sense. Perhaps the being in *Miss Jemima* is the nearest to a fairy:

> '. . . on the other side of the flat gravestone a face appeared. I mean it didn't rise up. It simply came into the air. A very small face, more oval than round, its gold-coloured hair over its wild greenish eyes falling on either side of its head in a curous zigzag way . . .'

At least it is an extraordinarily evocative and mysterious picture. An early illustrator of this story, Irene Hawkins, did try to represent the fairy, and so put her picture some way away from the mood of the story. Robin Jacques, in a drawing for the same scene, makes you see the fairy through the raptly reflective face of the young Jemima.

Then there are the strangers in *The Three Sleeping Boys of Warwickshire* who appeared like this in the water-meadows:

> . . . of middle height, with garments like spider-web, their straight hair of the colour of straw falling gently on either side their narrow cheeks, so that it looked at first glimpse as if they were greybeards. And as they trod on their narrow feet, the frozen grasses scarcely stirring beneath them, they turned their faces from side to side, looking at the children. And then a fairness that knows no change showed in their features, and their eyes were of a faint flame like that of sea-water on nights of thunder when the tide gently lays its incoming ripples on some wide flat sandy strand of the sea.
> Ibid pp. 110–111.

Or the more traditional but still unique dwarf in *A Penny a Day*:

> He was of the height of a child of five; he had pointed ears, narrow shoulders, and a hump on his back. And he wore a coat made of a patchwork of moleskins. He stood there—as stock-still as the stones themselves—his bright colourless eyes under his moleskin cap fixed on her, as if Griselda was as outlandish an object to him as he was to Griselda.
> Ibid., pp. 55–6.

Drawing by Irene Hawkins for Walter de la Mare's *Miss Jemima* in THE
MAGIC JACKET (Faber)

How could his beings fail to be unique, when he sees everything as freshly as a child would? One of his stories, *Maria-Fly*, illustrates not only the nature of a child but also of the poetic impulse. Maria, alone in a room, suddenly sees a fly. It seems to her as though she had never seen one before. She tries to communicate her vision, to the cook, to her father, to the gardener. Each one answers after his kind, each utterly fails to understand her. She goes on trying to explain:

> 'I—have—just—seen—a—fly. It had wings like as you see oil on water, and a red face with straight silver eyes, and it wasn't buzzing or nothing, but it was scraping with its front legs over its wings, then rubbing them like corkscrews. Then it took its head off and on, and then it began again—but I don't mean all that. I mean I sawn the fly—saw it, I mean.'
> Ibid., p. 354.

It is all there—the vision, the effort to communicate, the picture that comes to us. Maria, too, was a poet.

Even in this short, artless story, there is a feeling of precariousness, of one world dissolving into another. The fairy world of de la Mare is precise in detail but hazy in outline, a country unmapped and largely uninhabited. Even in a story like *The Three Sleeping Boys*, the harsh world of hunger and cold and soot, which is a version of historical fact, merges without effort into a silvery dreamland where the boys are at peace. In that incomparable piece of myth-making, THE THREE ROYAL MONKEYS, the characters are the animals of the African plain and jungle, their names fancifully modified, and the country is, on the face of it, equally recognizable. But this, too, is a magic land, the land where the traveller must seek the fabulous stone called Kiph, the land of de la Mare's poems. Here all is strange and remote. An ancient hare makes magic; Nod, youngest of the monkey princes, is at once child, pongo and fairy; there is poetic hyperbole in the descriptions of fearful mountain passes and the beautiful gardens of Tishnar. Homely, prosaic details are fused with otherworldly beauty, as in the superb passage which tells of the monkey brothers arrived at Tishnar's meadows:

> For there, in the midst between the fountains, was a long low table spread with flowers and strange fruits and nuts, and lit with clear, pear-shaped flames floating in the air like that of the Wonder-

Drawing by Robin Jacques for Walter de la Mare's *Miss Jemima* in
COLLECTED STORIES FOR CHILDREN (Faber)

stone, but of the colours of ivory and emerald and amethyst; with nineteen platters of silver and nineteen goblets of gold. And presently they heard in the distance the grasshopper voices of the Hill-Mulgars, as they came stubbling along with Thimble's litter in their midst, carrying their heavy faggots and bottles and bundles, their pink eyes blinking, their knees trembling, not knowing whether to be joyful or afraid.

Walter de la Mare. THE THREE ROYAL MONKEYS (Faber, 1946) p. 226. First published in 1910 as THE THREE MULLA-MULGARS.

You believe in all these mysterious places because of the associations of the words that are used to describe them; the shorthand of poetry is easier to read (above all, easier for children to read) than the more painstaking longhand of more prosaic travellers.

Best of all de la Mare's stories is *The Lord Fish*, perhaps the most perfect example of imaginative prose, in fairy-tale idiom, of the present century. Here is the English countryside, tree, river, cottage, great house and all, but with the light of enchantment hanging over it. Here lives John, who tries to help his needy, hard-working mother, but who is led astray time and again by his passion for fishing. One day he leaps a stone wall, finds a mer-maiden in a stone tower, undergoes a transmogrification, and at last returns home with a princess for wife and a box of jewels. These are the bare bones of the story. How is it at once actual and magical, simple and full of overtones? Not with what happens, certainly, but with word after word a spell is woven round ordinary events. The house is different from any other, and yet the same:

> ... John suddenly found himself staring up at the walls of a high dark house with but two narrow windows in the stone surface that steeped up into the sky above. And the very sight of the house set his heart beating faster. He was afraid. Beyond this wall to the right showed the stony roofs of lesser buildings, and moss-clotted fruit trees gone to leaf. Busying to and fro above the roof were scores of rooks and jackdaws, their jangled cries sounding out even above the roaring of the water, for now close beneath him the stream narrowed to gush in beneath a low-rounded arch in the wall, and so into the silence and darkness beyond it.

Walter de la Mare. COLLECTED STORIES FOR CHILDREN (Faber, 1957) p. 239.

The changing of John when he rubs himself with the green ointment
is almost clinically described, yet there is magic in it too:

> ... a dreadful darkness and giddiness swept over him. He felt his
> body narrowing and shortening and shrinking and dwindling.
> His bones were drawing themselves together inside his skin;
> his arms and legs ceased at last to wave and scuffle, his eyes seemed
> to be settling inside his head. The next moment, with one con-
> vulsive twist of his whole body, he had fallen plump into the water.
> Ibid., p. 248.

There is the Lord Fish who catches John, with grey glassy eyes and a
cod-like chin and a hand that was 'little else but skin and bone';
there is the little maid with grey-green plaits and an ageless face who
saves him; there is the larder where he hangs, with its glass jars of
dried roots and lily-bulbs and various herbs for flavouring fish,
and the great leaden casket stamped with an A for Almanara. All
these things are precise and clear, but round them is an atmosphere
of mystery, of other-worldliness. True, the village has a name; but
the house has not, and the steward is only the Lord Fish; in short,
behind the meticulous detail, the setting remains truly anonymous
as it is anonymous in the tales of Grimm and Perrault.

It is noticeable that Robin Jacques's pictures for de la Mare's
COLLECTED STORIES FOR CHILDREN give us no landscapes, only
odd, attractive people who are not quite of this world. The landscape
of this, as of other magic worlds, is to be visualized by each reader
in his own way. For as he reads he will see in his mind's eye patterns
and colours, scenes from real life, fragments from pictures half-
remembered. Each of us makes a particular picture for each fairy-
tale scene, so that illustrations do not represent the story to us. They
decorate it, and help to send our imaginations off on a voyage which
has no goal and no limit in time or space. De la Mare's stories
reconcile the poet's skill and insight with the instinctive marvelling
of a primitive mind. This is the true land of fairy-tale.

Reading List

Traditional fairy-tale and modern variants, with emphasis on the setting of fairy-tale
*Andersen, Hans. FORTY-TWO STORIES. *Faber* (1930) 1953. Translated by M.
   R. James. Illustrated by Robin Jacques. HANS ANDERSEN'S FAIRY TALES:
   A SELECTION. *O.U.P.* (World's Classics) 1959. Translated by L. W. Kings-
   land, with original illustrations. FAIRY TALES. World Edition, *Ward* 1951
   et seq. Translated by R. P. Keigwin. Illustrated by Vihelm Pedersen.
Bonnet, Leslie. CHINESE FAIRY TALES. *Muller* 1958. Illustrated by H. Toothill.
*Browne, Frances. GRANNIE'S WONDERFUL CHAIR (1857). *Blackie* 1955.
   Illustrated by Barbara Freeman.
*de la Mare, Walter. *The Lord Fish*, in ANIMAL STORIES. *Faber* 1939. Wood
   engravings from Topsell. And in COLLECTED STORIES FOR CHILDREN,
   illustrated by Irene Hawkins. *Faber* 1947. Illustrated by Robin Jacques.
   Faber 1957.
*de la Mare, Walter. THE THREE ROYAL MONKEYS (1910 AS THE THREE
   MULLA-MULGARS). *Faber* 1946. Illustrated by Mildred E. Eldridge.
*de la Mare, Walter. THE MAGIC JACKET. Illustrated by Irene Hawkins.
   Faber 1943.
Downing, Charles (retold by). RUSSIAN TALES AND LEGENDS. *O.U.P.* 1956
   Illustrated by Joan Kiddell-Monroe.
Durack, Mary and Elizabeth. THE WAY OF THE WHIRLWIND. *Angus &
   Robertson* 1957. Australian folk-tales, brilliantly illustrated by the authors.
Duvoisin, Roger. FAIRY TALES FROM SWITZERLAND. *Muller* (1943) 1958.
   Illustrated by the author.
*Ewing, Juliana Horatia. THE BROWNIES AND OTHER STORIES (1870, 1885).
   Dent (Children's Illustrated Classics) 1954. Illustrated by Ernest Shepard.
*Farjeon, Eleanor. THE SILVER CURLEW 1953, THE GLASS SLIPPER 1955.
   O.U.P. Illustrated by Ernest Shepard.
Garner, Alan. THE WEIRDSTONE OF BRISINGAMEN. *Collins* 1960. Set in
   Alderley Edge, Cheshire, with a multiplicity of magical creatures, good and
   evil, and a centuries' old spell resolved by two children.
*Grimm, Jacob and W. K. FAIRY TALES. *Blackie* 1959. Edited by Amabel
   Williams-Ellis. Illustrated by Pauline Baynes.
Guillot, René. THE ELEPHANTS OF SARGABAL (1956 France). *O.U.P.* 1956.
   Translated by Gwen Marsh. Illustrated by Felix Hoffmann. Indian legend of
   boy leader of jungle outcasts rescuing princess: exotic and thrilling.

*Haldane, J. B. S. MY FRIEND MR LEAKEY. *Cresset Press* 1937. Illustrated by Leonard Rosoman.

Herda, H., *ed.* FAIRY TALES FROM MANY LANDS. *Thames & Hudson* 1956. Illustrated by Gerhard Grossmann, Hilde Koeppen and Ursula Wendorff-Weidt.

Jacobs, Joseph. CELTIC FAIRY TALES. *Muller* 1958. Selected by Lucia Turnbull. Illustrated by John D. Batten.

*Jeans, Angela Ainley. LISTEN TO THE WIND 1955, illustrated by Disley Jones. THE KINGDOM OF THE WINDS 1957, illustrated by V. H. Drummond. *Parrish.*

*Lewis, C. S. THE LION, THE WITCH AND THE WARDROBE 1950. *Penguin* (Puffin Story Books) 1960. PRINCE CASPIAN 1951, THE VOYAGE OF THE DAWN-TREADER 1952, THE SILVER CHAIR 1953, THE HORSE AND HIS BOY 1954. *Bles.* THE MAGICIAN'S NEPHEW 1955, THE LAST BATTLE 1956. *Bodley Head.* Illustrated by Pauline Baynes.

Lines, Kathleen, *compiler.* A RING OF TALES. *O.U.P.* 1958. Illustrated by Harold Jones.

*Lynch, Patricia. THE TURF-CUTTER'S DONKEY 1934, illustrated by Jack B. Yeats. THE GREY GOOSE OF KILNEVIN 1939, illustrated by John Keating. JINNY THE CHANGELING 1959, illustrated by Peggy Fortnum. *Dent.*

MacAlpine, Margaret. THE HAND IN THE BAG. *Faber* 1959. Illustrated by Richard Kennedy. Haunting tale of the Highlands, a delicate mixture of magic and domestic detail.

Macdonald, George. AT THE BACK OF THE NORTH WIND (1871) 1956, THE PRINCESS AND THE GOBLIN (1872) 1949, THE PRINCESS AND CURDIE (1883) 1949. *Dent* (Children's Illustrated Classics). Illustrated by Charles Folkard.

*Manning-Sanders, Ruth. PETER AND THE PISKIES. *O.U.P.* 1958. Illustrated by Raymond Briggs.

Manning-Sanders, Ruth, *ed.* RED INDIAN FOLK AND FAIRY TALES. *O.U.P.* 1960. Illustrated by C. Walter Hodges.

*Mitchison, Naomi. GRAEME AND THE DRAGON. *Faber* 1954. Illustrated by Pauline Baynes.

*Molesworth, Mrs. M. L. *The Reel Fairies*, in TELL ME A STORY. *Macmillan* 1875. And in FAIRY STORIES. *Harvill* 1957. Edited by Roger Lancelyn Green. *Ask the Robin*, in FAIRIES AFIELD. *Macmillan* 1911.

*Molesworth, Mrs. M. L. THE CARVED LIONS (1895). *Faith Press* 1960.

*Perrault, Charles. FAIRY TALES. *Penguin* 1957. New translation by Geoffrey Brereton.

Picard, Barbara Leonie. THE MERMAID AND THE SIMPLETON 1949, illustrated by Philip Gough. THE FAUN AND THE WOODCUTTER'S DAUGHTER 1951, illustrated by Charles Stewart. *O.U.P.* Exquisite fairy-tales in traditional manner.

Picard, Barbara Leonie (retold by). FRENCH LEGENDS, TALES AND FAIRY STORIES. *O.U.P.* 1955. Illustrated by Joan Kiddell-Monroe.

*Reeves, James (retold by). ENGLISH FABLES AND FAIRY STORIES. *O.U.P.* 1954.

*Reeves, James. PIGEONS AND PRINCESSES. *Heinemann* 1956. Illustrated by Edward Ardizzone.

*Reeves, James, *ed.* A GOLDEN LAND: STORIES, POEMS, SONGS NEW AND OLD. *Constable* 1958. Illustrated by various artists.

*Ross, Diana. THE WILD CHERRY 1943, THE BRIDAL GOWN 1952. *Faber.* CHILD OF AIR. *Lutterworth* 1957. Illustrated by Gri.

*Ross, Diana. THE ENORMOUS APPLE PIE 1951, THE BRAN TUB 1954. *Lutterworth.* Illustrated by Peggy Fortnum. These are all about Miss Pussy, and there are two stories about her in THE WILD CHERRY. The story that began it all can be found in THE GOLDEN HEN. *Faber* 1942. Illustrated by Gri. (See also p. 379.)

*Simpson, Helen. MUMBUDGET. *Heinemann* 1928.

*Thurber, James. MANY MOONS 1944, THE WHITE DEER 1946, THE THIRTEEN CLOCKS 1951. *Hamish Hamilton.* Illustrated by the author. (See also p. 381.)

*Tolkein, J. R. R. THE LORD OF THE RINGS, comprising THE FELLOWSHIP OF THE RING 1954, THE TWO TOWERS 1954, THE RETURN OF THE KING 1955. *Allen & Unwin.*

*Tolkein, J. R. R. THE HOBBIT. *Allen & Unwin* 1937. Illustrated by the author.

Vacher, Gwyneth. THE SHOEMAKER'S DAUGHTER. *Blackie* 1957. Illustrated by Peggy Fortnum. Journey of an orphan through the Forest of Nowhere.

Wells, Ann E. TALES FROM ARNHEM LAND. *Angus & Robertson* 1959. Illustrated by Margaret Paice. Folk-lore of Northern Australia linked with the adventures of a child in the present day.

Williams-Ellis, Amabel (retold by). FAIRY TALES FROM THE BRITISH ISLES. *Blackie* 1960. Illustrated by Pauline Baynes.

Zajdler, Zoë. POLISH FAIRY TALES. *Muller* 1959. Illustrated by Hazel Cook.

Chapter 6 | The Conversation of Witches

The Land of Faerie owes its existence to primitive fears of the natural world, but there is the human element to be considered as well. More often than not, tales of giants and elves illustrate not so much the dangers of wind and weather as of man living in a community. They offer the earliest descriptions of the human situation, couched in fanciful terms and presented impersonally.

This impersonal attitude soon became untenable. Rationalists from the sixteenth century at least had cast scorn on the race of giants and dragons, but it was left for the English critics of the nineteenth century to take the final step against the fairy world. They insisted that writers of fairy-tales should make them purposive, should give them a moral. Dismayed by the anonymous and illogical tone of Grimms' tales, which had appeared in England in 1823, they asserted that tales such as these should be brought into line with social morality.

It is easy to see why moralists thought Grimms' tales bad for children. They would naturally disapprove of stories like *The Three Dancing Princesses*, for instance, where a casual act of kindness brings what seems a disproportionate return to the hero, or like *Rumpelstiltskin*, where the miller is rewarded for his foolish boasting by becoming father-in-law to a king, or like *The Master-Thief*, which puts a premium on cunning. It never satisfied them that such tales made firm, categorical, uninhibited statements about human nature and human wishes. They felt fairy-tales should point the way to virtue. But of course no child who reads the story of Cinderella is going to think that she gets the prince because she is *better* than her sisters, only that she is nicer and more fortunate; and this is useful knowledge for anyone, child or adult. The Grimm brothers themselves certainly set great store by the victory of goodness over evil in the tales they collected. 'Notice too,' they said,

> 'that in this fairy-tale world the powers of darkness—such as
> robbers, witches and man-eating giants, are always foiled. Even
> the Devil has a grandmother, while in the case of danger from
> robbers or monsters, a friendly wife or daughter is likely to be at
> hand, who is sure to know some way of averting Fate. In short, the
> tales all end well and indeed usually with a suggestion of ever-
> lasting happiness. . . .'
> Amabel Williams-Ellis. GRIMMS' FAIRY TALES (Blackie, 1959)
> p. 331.

But this was not to claim a moral purpose for the tales, but only to
point out that we are all, at bottom, optimists.

Of course it is not the business of fairy-tales to teach children to be
good, nor, for that matter, to suggest that they should be naughty.
Andrew Lang said, in the mid-Victorian period, he had 'never yet
heard of a child who killed a very tall man merely because Jack
killed the giants.' But the moral had come to stay. Kingsley, in THE
WATER-BABIES, enforced it by a compelling narrative style and by
his passionate interest in everything he wrote about. George Macdonald enforced it by the grandeur of his conceptions. No child is
ever likely to forget a warning against godless living put across like
this:

> One day at noon, when life was at its highest, the whole city fell
> with a roaring crash. The cries of men and the shrieks of women
> went up with its dust, and then there was a great silence.
>
> Where the mighty rock once towered, crowded with homes and
> crowned with a palace, now rushes and raves a stone-obstructed
> rapid of the river. All around spreads a wilderness of wild deer,
> and the very name of Gwyntystorm has ceased from the lips of
> men.
> George Macdonald. THE PRINCESS AND CURDIE (Dent,
> Children's Illustrated Classics, 1949) p. 238.

Mrs Molesworth and Mrs Ewing charmed children gently into the
nursery virtues with their domestic sprites. Ruskin, in THE KING
OF THE GOLDEN RIVER, preached his sermon in the urbane tones
of a man about town. All these tones of voice may be heard in our
own times. Čapek speaks with the voice of Kingsley; C. S. Lewis

sounds the mythic note of George Macdonald; Diana Ross has inherited the charming moral tone of the Victorian ladies and Thurber the worldly advising of Ruskin.

Still, it will be said, modern fairy-tales have freed themselves from the need to sermonize. All the same, they have never recovered the irresponsible, inconsequent shape of the past. Certainly the demand for the pure fairy-tale still exists. The past fifteen years have seen a noticeable increase in the reprinting of volumes of traditional tales, headed by the Oxford Myths and Legends series and Muller's splendid series of national fairy-tales. British regional tales, new versions of the Arabian Nights, unfamiliar stories from Australasia, from the Eskimos and Red Indians, from Africa, as well as new versions of the Arthurian legends and the Greek myths, keep fairy-tale alive. But we are not fancy-free and presumably never can be again. If we imitate the traditional tale in the present-day, we add something of comment, of purpose. We are always trying to say something definite about people and their lives.

But our fairy-tales do not derive so much from the moral versions of the last century as from Hans Andersen, the 'father of modern fairy-tale'. Drawing from the same traditional material as older story-tellers, he turned the anonymity of folk lore to personal use. His method is certainly in tune with modern practice. He did not preach, but in his tales he expressed his own disappointments and regrets and his observations of the way of the world. In some stories, like *The Snow Queen*, it is possible to find lessons, but I doubt whether anyone who reads the story is concerned with learning them; rather, he perceives the gentle glow that comes from the character of Gerda, he recognizes the tough acceptance of life in the whole plot of Kay's enchantment and his rescue from the ice-palace, he enjoys the marvellous sequence of scenes, from the sunny beginning under the rose-trees to the terrors of the robber girl and the Lapp woman. In other stories, like *The Tinder Box*, children will see a rogue living successfully on his wits; but what child thinks the witch has been unjustly treated? Yet how much can be learned from the tales, and in how many different ways. You can observe the workings of snobbery and affectation in an Emperor or a shirt-collar, a snail or a barndoor fowl. You can see stupidity getting its deserts in a gloomy underground land of enchantment or in a provision-dealer's shop.

Hans Andersen can make a pin or a match or a lead soldier into a personality, and that is of course one of the secrets of his permanent place on children's shelves. There are plenty of writers since Andersen who have animated tin soldiers—Little Noddy, surely, has had plenty of dealings with them. But to draw tears and smiles, quite spontaneous and genuine, on account of a lead soldier with one leg and a paper doll—that takes genius. Not cleverness or wit or ingenuity but the power to compel truth out of yourself that has grown slowly out of childhood impressions. This is how writers of fairy-tale work—this is how Eleanor Farjeon worked, and Patricia Lynch, and Walter de la Mare, and Hans Andersen, the ancestor of them all. This is what he said himself, about the cottage in Odense where he lived as a child:

> That one little room which was almost filled with the cobbler's bench, bed and the turn-up bedstead on which I slept, was the whole of my childhood's home; but its walls were hung with pictures; on the chest of drawers stood pretty cups, glasses and knick-knacks, and above the workbench by the window was a shelf with books and broadsheets. In the little kitchen, above the store-cupboard, was a rack filled with plates. To me the little room appeared large and rich; the very door, whose panels were painted with landscapes, meant as much to me then as a whole picture gallery now. In the kitchen was a ladder leading on to the roof and there in the gutter between our house and our neighbour's was a box of earth in which grew chives and parsley, and that was all my mother's garden.
>
> THE MERMAID MAN: the autobiography of Hans Christian Andersen. A new abridged translation by Maurice Michael. (Arthur Barker, 1955) pp. 7-8.

It is because there is not a shadow of guile or faking here that Hans Andersen belongs to children and can give them more than anyone else—can give them, above all, a humour that rises out of household objects as often as out of people.

'Painters beget pictures,' Picasso has said, 'as princes beget children—not with princesses, but with country-girls. One never paints the Parthenon, or a Louis XV chair. One makes pictures out of a hovel, a tobacco-pack, or an old stool.' It is apt to be so, too, with fairy-tales. Fire-irons, tin soldiers and porridge-bowls are hallowed by tradition and belong to the cottage world from which fairy-tales sprang. Edith Nesbit's princess 'in a simple little morning frock of white chiffon and diamonds' whose suitors are summoned by telephone is under a slight disadvantage. We are not used to this kind of drawing-room character in the magic world, nor to this kind of stage property. But there is plenty of room for humour in fairy-tale, and in our time this may well be topical. There can be magic in modern gadgets.

Richard Hughes, in a present-day story called THE SPIDER'S PALACE, describes how a little boy discovers that his torch-glass, when reversed, will turn people into toys and give toys the power to act like people. This is high fantasy, but it is presented with absolute logic and conviction:

> And he put it to his eye and looked at his father and mother, and so it was: they were immediately wooden Mr. and Mrs. Noah out of the Ark. To make sure, he took a pin, and keeping the glass firmly in his eye he tried to stick it in his mother. But it wouldn't go in, for she was now quite hard: it only scratched a little paint off. Then he took the glass away, and they were his mother and father again. But just to make sure he stuck the pin in again. This time it went right in, and his mother sat up with the most awful yell.
> Richard Hughes. THE SPIDER'S PALACE. (Chatto & Windus, 1931) p. 134.

Lorna Wood is just as ingenious in RESCUE BY BROOMSTICK. A vital history-book has been stolen and hidden in a waste-disposer. Dowsabel, the witch, gets it back by using a reversing spell, but it is then discovered that, in its pages, Henry VIII signs the Magna Carta and Boadicea invents the cinematograph. The joke has been taken to its logical conclusion, Anyone who was fortunate enough, as I was, to read the proper, unabridged stories about the Kingdom of Oz, will remember what humour and excitement and mystery Frank Baum drew out of machines and chemical experiments, and J. B. S. Haldane's MY FRIEND MR. LEAKEY follows the same prescription, with its surreptitious scientific learning.

Mr Leakey is a dragon, and this is important, for humour in a fairy-tale (one of the most obvious ways in which adults can convey their views) comes best from the more robust supernatural beings.

Fairies themselves are too ethereal for laughter. You cannot define them in human terms and so there can be nothing to laugh about. Brownies and leprechauns, giants and witches, nearer to the human race, can be imagined to act as humans do, and so can be laughed at. Barbara Sleigh's CARBONEL, a modern family story with incidental magic, is one of the best examples of this kind of humour. There is, of course, an extra twist to the humour in fairy-tales. It comes, at its best, from a delicate use of incongruity, a balance between the fairy world and our own, and is particularly well-suited to children, who are willing to believe themselves committed to both worlds.

CARBONEL is the story of Rosemary, a London schoolgirl whose mother sews for a precarious living, and who one day, when she goes to a street market to buy a broom, runs into a witch who is just retiring to keep a sweet-shop. The witch's cat, Carbonel, sold to Rosemary for her three Queen Victoria farthings, has to serve the girl unless she can unwind the spell, and for this she has to find the witch's hat and cauldron and spell-book. The story runs an exciting course as Rosemary and her new friend John, son of her mother's richest client, follow up clues, helped by the resourceful and temperamental cat, who provides most of the humour in the story. He is very much on the spot, in both magic and real world. When Rosemary suggests mending the worn broom with string, he puts her right:

> 'Good gracious, no! You can't mend magic with string! . . . You will be suggesting glue and tin-tacks next. A few weeks ago the cauldron sprang a leak, and SHE insisted on filling up the hole with one of those pot-mender things you get at an iron-monger's, at sixpence a card. And what was the result? . . . Her spells worked out lumpy . . .'

Barbara Sleigh. CARBONEL (Parrish, 1955) p. 34.

But Carbonel can also evoke a more poetic world:

> 'I took to the broomstick business like a duck to water. Oh, those were the days, when you raced together through the tumbling sky, with the Milky Way crackling below, and the wind in your fur strong enough to tear the whiskers off you! Or leaping and plunging through the midnight sky with a host of others, and the earth twirling beneath you no bigger than a bobbin!'

Ibid., p. 27.

The witch herself makes a wonderful reappearance in THE KINGDOM OF CARBONEL, as the kidnapper of the royal kittens, and her sly, dry, faintly sinister attitude to life is exactly what you would expect of a witch. And who could resist the absurd eccentricities of Lorna Wood's hag Dowsabel? Who could help laughing with her, as well as at her, when, riding on her broomstick with Jane one night, she kicks out at a weathercock and sends it spinning:

> 'Never could stand that bird,' she said with satisfaction. 'Too smug by half. Now he won't be sure which is east and which is west and I think I've knocked the S off South.'
> Lorna Wood. RESCUE BY BROOMSTICK (Dent, 1956) p. 29.

Mary Norton's BED KNOB AND BROOMSTICK starts, in contrast. on a very ordinary note. Miss Price lives in the Bedfordshire village where Carey, Charles and Paul go to stay with an aunt:

> She wore grey coats and skirts and had a long thin neck with a scarf round it (made of Liberty silk with a Paisley pattern). Her nose was sharply pointed and she had very clean, pink hands. She rode on a high bicycle with a basket in front, and she visited the sick and taught the piano.
> Mary Norton. BED KNOB AND BROOMSTICK (Dent, 1957) p. 8.

When Paul first sees her lurching past his bedroom window on her broomstick, he thinks what an inefficient witch she is; in fact, being too ladylike to ride astride, she is often in difficulties, and it is because the children help her home after a fall that she confides to them her plans for study. She even does an advanced spell for them, and with the help of Paul's bed-knob they journey to distant places and distant periods, escaping from cannibals, from the police, and finally from Restoration London after the Great Fire. It is on this last journey that they meet, and bring back to their own times, the lugubrious necromancer Emelius Jones, whose neglected appearance rouses Miss Price's maternal instincts. If there is plenty of humour in these two eccentric characters, there is far more in Mary Norton's comments on the technique of witchcraft. No child could resist the description of Miss Price's workroom, or her explanation to Carey who wonders why she can't make money:

> '. . . you can't get the ingredients. What people don't realize . . . is that there are very few spells that can be done without para-

phernalia. You must, if you understand, have something to turn
into something and something to turn it *with*.'
Ibid., p. 57.

or the picture of Emelius's work with his old master, who made him
do all the dirty work of collecting cats from graveyards and bats
from belfries, or Miss Price's earnest exhortation:

'I never scrape the scales from an adder . . . It takes force from any
spell except those in which hemlock is combined with fennel. The
only time I ever scrape the scales from an adder is in spells against
St. Vitus's dance, then for some reason, it gives better results . . .'
Ibid., pp. 152–3.

Mary Norton makes her comic points so well because of her close
attention to detail. In her three stories about the Borrowers, everything depends on incongruity—on creatures of another race behaving like humans—but this time humour is merged into tenderness
and poetry. The Borrowers are tiny people who live in the interstices
of human dwellings. Humans, to them, exist to supply them with
small objects, like safety-pins, matchboxes or chessmen, which they
can use for their own purposes—even to supply them with their
scraps of names. To us, as we read, the Borrowers are not miniature
humans; they are *reminders* of what humans are like.

The first of three books about these little people sounds a note of
pathos. We are told that the race is dwindling, that Pod, Homily and
Arrietty, who live under the kitchen floor of an old house in Bedfordshire, have long ago said goodbye to the Harpsichord family and the
Overmantels, and it is a long time since they saw their relations the
well-to-do Clocks. For the moment, however, the family is safe, so
long as they are not 'seen'.

One day Pod *is* seen, by a boy staying in the house, and though the
boy becomes their ally, he is the cause of their having to leave their
home in a hurry. In THE BORROWERS AFIELD we follow their fortunes as they camp in an old boot, as they search for the badger-sett
where Uncle Hendreary is said to live, and as they meet Spiller, a gipsy
Borrower who sees no need for relatives or any of the gentilities that
Homily clings to. In THE BORROWERS AFLOAT we find the little
family under a roof again, but an inhospitable one. With the help of the
gamekeeper's son they have found Uncle Hendreary behind the
skirting in a cottage; but his wife, Aunt Lupy, is unpleasant to her

Drawing by V. H. Drummond for Barbara Sleigh's CARBONEL (Parrish)

poor relations, food is short, and they are housed in a draughty
garret. Urged on by young Arrietty, with her longing for the open,
mother and father venture into the wilds again, and under Spiller's
guidance they voyage downstream in a knife-box, hoping to find a
model village they have heard of, which they believe is the perfect
home. Mary Norton has said that they will find the village and settle
down, in a fourth book. How passionately she makes her readers
hope that they will. This is not only because her Borrowers remind
us of all the dispossessed, the small and valiant and under-privileged
people of this world and of all worlds. The books must be read with
this in mind, but, as with Tolkein, it is an idea, not a moral. These
are fairy stories, and they make their impression as much by their
style as by their story.

Mary Norton is a most skilful story-teller. First, she is absolutely
consistent. She is herself short-sighted, and she has a sure, sharp
vision of small things. She can see *exactly* how half a pair of
embroidery scissors would be used by the Borrowers, or a knob of
sealing-wax or a button; and her illustrator, Diana Stanley, has
exquisitely transposed this vision of littleness into drawings.
Secondly, this magical world (only a few inches away from our own
world of chairs and teacups) is reached by a roundabout route.
These are stories within stories. At first we listen to old Mrs May
telling young Kate about her brother and *his* tales about the Borrowers. Old Tom Goodenough, in the gamekeeper's cottage, Mrs
Driver the cook, the gardener Crampfurl who abetted her in getting
rid of the 'mice dressed up', all add their mite of detail and authenticity to the story.

But if there were still any doubt of the existence of the Borrowers,
it would be dispelled by their personalities. Arrietty, bright as a
button, chronicler and enthusiast; Homily keeping her integrity
as a housewife through danger and misfortune (when she arrives,
dishevelled and dirty, at Aunt Lupy's gracious home, she refuses to
be patronized: 'Poor dear Lupy', she was saying, glancing wearily
about, 'What a lot of furniture. Whoever helps you with the dust-
ing?'); and Pod, brave as a lion, common in speech, full of sensible
philosophy—('There's a lot of worse food, when you care to think
of it, than a piping-hot, savoury stew made of corn-fed field-mouse.').
They are as real as many characters we or our children will meet in
real life, and just as real is the setting of the stories—the dirty world

Drawing by Diana Stanley for Mary Norton's THE BORROWERS AFLOAT
(Dent)

under the floorboards, the damp hedge with its safe corners, Spiller's kettle, the pile of sticks in the water where they hide from Wall-Eye the Gypsy, and the spread of Midland landscape, whole and real and touched with poetry.

If fairy-tales are universal, they are also regional. Hans Andersen or Perrault or Patricia Lynch can be placed at once in their place of origin, and many English writers can be as easily labelled. They draw their characters from British folk lore—the sproggins and drowners of Cornwall, the lob or hobgoblin of English villages—and they draw their scenes from an unchanging countryside. Mrs Ewing's tales take us back to an older England of familiar spirits, an England already threatened by the forces of industry and progress when she wrote, an England derived from Shakespeare and Drayton and even earlier writers. Kipling, too, gave us a piercing vision of a fairy past that had nothing to do with Denmark or Germany. PUCK OF POOK'S HILL and REWARDS AND FAIRIES are full of the romance of other lands and other times, but most children remember them best for the Sussex country scenes, incidental to the plot but essential to the character of the stories, for Old Hobden and Puck with his capricious ways and unruly tongue, for the bridleways older than the Romans and the magically, eternally old and new leaves of oak, ash and thorn.

Alison Uttley's stories communicate to children a picture of old England filtered through a magic haze. Stories like *The Leadminer*, with its tender lapping up of the lonely, wizened, leather-clad dwarf into the farmhouse warmth; or *Young Lambs for Sale*, with its picture of centuries-old Cotswold; or *John Barleycorn*, with its simple, unearthly evocation of the corn-spirit; or *The Merry-go-round*, where a bronze Roman whistle sets the painted horses galloping through the night; or that strange, mysterious tale of the old farm-hand who brings good luck to the place, *Orion Hardy*; each sets its own exact atmosphere. This delicate combination of history and fairy-tale can be seen at its best in *Upon Paul's Steeple*, where a chance-dropped apple-pip grows into a fine tree:

> The little boys came running as soon as school was over, from all the streets of London, up the hill of Ludgate, down the street of Fleet, carrying baskets and sticks, bags and crooks, to try to hook the lowest branches. The watchman prevented them from

Drawing by Philip Hepworth for Alison Uttley's *The Merry-go-round* in
JOHN BARLEYCORN (Faber)

throwing stones lest the precious windows of Saint Paul's should be broken.

From many a little wooden house in London came the smell of apples roast, apples baked, apples in pies, and apples in dumplings, and every spice shop was sold out of cloves. They were the sweetest, nicest apples anyone had ever tasted, and even King Charles had apple-pasties.

Alison Uttley. MAGIC IN MY POCKET (Penguin, 1957) p. 145.

This is not the only one of Alison Uttley's stories that is poised on a nursery rhyme, and this way of capturing elusive associations is used also by Eleanor Farjeon, whose numerous and varied tales are full of the vivacity and alertness of a child. One very shapely tale, *Elsie Piddock Skips in her Sleep*, grows naturally out of an old skipping-rhyme, and Sussex games provide a framework for two collections of stories, MARTIN PIPPIN IN THE APPLE ORCHARD and MARTIN PIPPIN IN THE DAISY FIELD. Martin is a resourceful countryman living in a rustic setting. At a deeper level he is a wandering enchanter, who knows the minds of men, and centuries of magic are hinted at through him. He is also a medieval jongleur, weaving an airy and delicate pattern of romantic love after the pattern of William Morris and Sydney's *Arcadia*.

THE SILVER CURLEW, a version of the English tale *Tom Tit Tot*, combines the magical and the rustic likewise. Beside sweet, stupid Doll and the petulant young king of Norfolk there is the mysterious Charlee Loon communing with birds on the beach, and the ancient, fearful Witching Wood where the Black Imp holds his court and where he binds Charlee and young Poll with spiders' webs as firm as steel.

And so to the most English writer of them all—John Masefield, whose two magic adventure stories, THE MIDNIGHT FOLK and THE BOX OF DELIGHTS should be on every child's bookshelf. These two books are built upon the past. First, upon the Herefordshire country where the poet lived as a child and which is the background of so much of his writing. They well up, especially THE MIDNIGHT FOLK, from memories of childhood, from imagination playing upon the places that were then his world. The old house, Seekings, where Kay is rapped over the knuckles by his governess; the warrens where the friendly cat Nibbins and Bitem the Fox frustrate the keeper's knavish tricks; the millpool where Kay plays with the otter;

the stable where he finds the ancient pistols of Benjamin the highwayman; the night sky where he swoops with Bat and hears the village people chatting below him; all the sounds and smells of summer days and summer nights are packed into the story, the whole feeling of a country world where time has stood still and the centuries have telescoped, where witches and cats and humans can quite easily lead parallel lives.

THE MIDNIGHT FOLK is the story of a quest for the great treasure from the cathedral of Santa Barbara, which had been entrusted to Kay's grandfather, Captain Harker, in time of revolution. Two parties are looking for the treasure, lost so many years ago—the witches, urged on by Abner Brown, whose grandfather was a mutineer on Captain Harker's ship, and the guards, Kay's old toys, who have marched off from Seekings to follow up a clue. Kay is drawn into the adventure by Nibbins, whose blood still stirs at the sound of incantations, but who wants to put things right in the old house.

The narrative is impeccable; but this may not be obvious to a child at first reading, for it is also complex. The story inches itself forward as first one party and then the other gets a little more information about what happened to the treasure and where it might be. Thus there is, inset in the adventure, a tiny sea-story of mutiny in a hot, far-off country, which is fascinating in itself. Information comes from various sources. Now Kay flies at night to a house in the north where he sees 'a wicked old woman in a very gay dressing-gown . . . reading a sprightly story'—Miss Susan Pricker, daughter of another mutineer. Now the witches get a little warmer when they call up and interrogate apparitions—a glittering child, a youth crowned with ivy-leaves, and others less helpful. Now the disreputable Rat brings a snippet of information to Kay in return for bacon-rind. Now Blackmalkin, the sneaking cat, overhears something useful to her mistress the witch.

Everywhere you feel the writer along with you, taking you into the English country or into the red muddy stretches of South American country, enjoying every picture as he draws it.

It is a real Christmas stocking of a book, packed with parcels of all shapes and colours—with adventure, by day and night, with witches and foxes, requiring wit and courage, speed and stealth; with humour in the characters of Rat the cellarman, or the riotous

Miss Susan Pricker, or the splendid witch Mrs Pouncer. And at the bottom of the stocking is the orange—the poetry shining everywhere, lighting a paragraph with an unexpected word (but just the one word that will do), making mermaids and weathercocks absolutely real, making hollow trees and lumps of sugar and brooms mysterious, as though never seen before.

THE MIDNIGHT FOLK is essentially a summer book, but THE BOX OF DELIGHTS is set in a winter landscape, in the neighbourhood of Seekings, shrouded in snow, and in the Chester Hills, sinister under a grey sky. The story started with a question in the author's mind. Exactly what would happen to the Christmas services in a cathedral town if all the clergymen disappeared? Abner Brown suggested himself as a character in this drama, and the author, with his zest for details, consulted authorities, including a Bishop, before he gave Abner his head. Like so many of Masefield's stories, THE BOX OF DELIGHTS has a vein of happy boyish humour; but there are many more threads in its rich weave. Kay is older now, and Abner Brown is more determined and more ruthless. The treasure itself is more valuable—none other than a magic box which can carry its possessor back into the past, and so to the discovery of the elixir of life. This is no ordinary adventure, though there is excitement enough to satisfy any child. There are gangsters, but there is a more primitive danger as well; magic solves problems better than kidnapping does, though Abner and his spouse (once Sylvia Daisy Pouncer, Kay's governess) try both. When Kay and Cole Hawlings, the wandering alchemist, are imprisoned underground and in danger of drowning, they escape by sympathetic magic. Kay has to draw— a man sculling a boat, with a bunch of keys, a pair of horses:

In fact, the drawings did stand out from the paper rather strangely. The light was concentrated on them; as he looked at them the horses seemed to be coming towards him out of the light, and, no, it was not seeming, they were moving; he saw the hoof casts flying and heard the rhythmical beat of hoofs. The horses were coming out of the picture, galloping fast, and becoming brighter and brighter. Then he saw that the light was partly fire from their eyes and manes, partly sparks from their hoofs.

John Masefield. THE BOX OF DELIGHTS (Heinemann, 1935) p. 378.

So even this adventure is not quite ordinary, not quite straight-forward. Masefield's sense of the past, of its colour and mystery above all, so superbly shown in his poetry and novels, works itself into this child's tale. Kay, carrying the magic box, hides behind a stockade and watches Celts fighting marauding wolves. He sees a Roman legion on the march. He comes to the walls of Troy just after the siege is over:

> After the party had gone past with the wailing captives and cursing guards, Kay went into the Skaian Gate and looked about him at the desolation. The doors of all the houses were open; the things which had not been worth carrying away lay smashed or torn in the ways. There was nobody left in the city except a stray cat or two, mewing in misery. The pigeons which had once nested in the temples were flying about in the smoke. As Kay went up towards the temples a gust of wind caught the fire; it burst out with a savage crackle and fierce flame.
> Ibid., pp. 281–2.

The past, everywhere, is as real as the present. It hangs about the mysterious stranger who comes to warn Cole, with the brooch shaped like a cross for a sign. It breathes in the study at Seekings, where Cole makes immemorial magic for the children. It is an evocation as subtle as it is strong. This return to the past is a special form of fantasy, allied to fairy-tale, owing much to it, but with different aims and feelings. In Masefield's two books it is part of a more complicated whole; but there are writers who have written fantasies simply to recall the past, in a special way distinct from historical novels, and some of these I must mention in detail in a separate chapter.

Reading List

The modern fairy-tale; humour and character
'B.B.'. THE LITTLE GREY MEN 1942, DOWN THE BRIGHT STREAM 1948. *Eyre & Spottiswoode*. Illustrated by the author. The last gnomes left in England, their adventures by stream and mill, and their departure for Ireland. Rich, evocative picture of a vanishing rural England, with light-hearted humanizing of animals and country spirits.

'B.B.'. THE FOREST OF BOLAND LIGHT RAILWAY. *Eyre & Spottiswoode* 1955. Illustrated by the author. Gnomes running a railway in defiance of enemy leprechauns: inventive and ingenious, full of wit and absurdity.

*Baum, Frank. THE WIZARD OF OZ. From 1900. Unfortunately only the first Oz story is now available in England, in an abridged version and with poor illustrations.

*Capek, Karel. FAIRY TALES (1932 Prague). *Allen & Unwin* 1933. Illustrated by Joseph Čapek.

Dixon, Marjorie and Kennedy, Richard. THE GREEN-COATED BOY. *Faber* 1957. Illustrated by Richard Kennedy. Two children wandering in search of a black goat, in Ireland, and going over the frontier of the real world.

Duggan, Maurice. FALTER TOM AND THE WATER BOY. *Faber* 1958. Illustrated by Kenneth Rownell. Fable of the world under the water.

*Farjeon, Eleanor. MARTIN PIPPIN IN THE APPLE-ORCHARD (1921) 1952, illustrated by Richard Kennedy. MARTIN PIPPIN IN THE DAISY-FIELD (1937) 1954, illustrated by Isobel and John Morton-Sale. *O.U.P.*

Guinness, Bryan and Pym, Roland. CATRIONA AND THE GRASSHOPPER. *Heinemann* 1958. Illustrated by Roland Pym. Vivacious tale of chases and parties in an entertaining land of fantasy.

Hughes, Jean. DITTA'S TREE. *Penguin* (Puffin Story Books) 1952. Illustrated by Mary Willett. An Indian tree-spirit and his unpredictable mischief and help to the villagers nearby.

*Hughes, Richard. THE SPIDER'S PALACE. *Chatto & Windus* 1931. Illustrated by George Charlton.

Kendall, Carol. THE MINNIPINS (1959 U.S.A.). *Dent* 1960. Illustrated by Erik Blegvad. Miniature race in land between mountains, fighting the Mushroom People. Allegory of individualism: clever details of local customs and characteristics.

*Kingsley, Charles. THE WATER-BABIES (1863). *O.U.P.* 1948. Illustrated by A. E. Jackson.

*Kipling, Rudyard. PUCK OF POOK'S HILL (1906), REWARDS AND FAIRIES (1910). *Macmillan*, continuously in print. Latest editions illustrated by Stuart Tresilian.

Lagerlöf, Selma. THE WONDERFUL ADVENTURES OF NILS (1906–7 Sweden). *Dent* (Children's Illustrated Classics) 1950, 1953. Translated by Velma Swanston Howard. Illustrated by Hans Baumbauer. English edition published in two parts, the second entitled THE FURTHER ADVENTURES OF NILS, and in a form slightly abridged from American edition. Superb, long, varied tale of a Swedish farmer's son who is changed into an elf as punishment for cruelty to animals, and flies with wild geese on migration. Adventures with people and animals, plenty of humour, a warm human interest.

Lofting, Hugh. THE TWILIGHT OF MAGIC. *Cape* (1931) 1958. Illustrated by the author. Droll, sober and mysterious by turns, a tale of medieval witch-craft and what the witch was really like.

*Masefield, John. THE MIDNIGHT FOLK (1927) 1957, THE BOX OF DELIGHTS (1935) 1957. *Heinemann.* Illustrated by Rowland Hilder.

Masefield, Judith. THE MARVELLOUS MERLAD. *Collins* 1952. Illustrated by Shirley Hughes. Extravaganza set in Ireland about a merboy.

*Nesbit, E. *Melisande* (1901), in MODERN FAIRY STORIES, edited by Roger Lancelyn Green. *Dent* 1955. Illustrated by Ernest Shepard.

*Norton, Mary. BED KNOB AND BROOMSTICK. *Dent* 1957. Illustrated by Eric Blegvad. A composite of THE MAGIC BEDKNOB 1945 and BONFIRES AND BROOMSTICKS 1947.

*Norton, Mary. THE BORROWERS 1952, THE BORROWERS AFIELD 1955, THE BORROWERS AFLOAT 1959. *Dent.* Illustrated by Diana Stanley. (See also p. 378.)

*Ruskin, John, *The King of the Golden River* (1830), in MODERN FAIRY STORIES, edited by Roger Lancelyn Green. *Dent* 1955. Illustrated by Ernest Shepard.

*Sleigh, Barbara. CARBONEL 1955, illustrated by V. H. Drummond. THE KINGDOM OF CARBONEL 1959, illustrated by Michael Leonard. *Parrish.*

Sleigh, Linwood. THE BOY IN THE IVY. *Faber* 1955. Illustrated by Kate Adamson. Witchcraft full of humour but with mysterious undertones.

Sleigh, Linwood. THE TAILOR'S FRIENDS. *Faber* 1956. Illustrated by Robert Spearman. Ordinary people leaving our world in a party of mysterious personages bound for a lost Celtic land.

*Uttley, Alison. CUCKOO CHERRY-TREE 1943, THE SPICE-WOMAN'S BASKET 1944, illustrated by Irene Hawkins. THE WEATHER-COCK 1945, illustrated by Nancy Innes. JOHN BARLEYCORN 1948, illustrated by Philip Hepworth. THE COBBLER'S SHOP 1950, illustrated by Irene Hawkins. *Faber.*

Uttley, Alison. MAGIC IN MY POCKET. *Penguin* (Puffin Story Books) 1957, illustrated by Judith Brook. A collection from the above and the volumes of animal stories. (See Chap. 4).

*Wood, Lorna. THE PEOPLE IN THE GARDEN 1954, RESCUE BY BROOMSTICK 1956, THE HAG CALLS FOR HELP 1957, HOLIDAY ON HOT BRICKS 1958, SEVEN-LEAGUE BALLET SHOES 1959, HAGS ON HOLIDAY 1960. *Dent.* Illustrated by Joan Kiddell-Monroe.

Chapter 7 | *Travellers in Time*

Every piece of fiction is written twice over—first by the author and then by the reader. The author is making a journey into a new world and he leaves signposts which will help the reader to find the way there in his turn. In a time fantasy the journey is a double one. The child who reads goes first on a straight road, introduced to a character or characters like himself and belonging to his own time. These characters take over the function of guide and the reader follows them back into the past, forgetting his own world and taking the world of the traveller with him. He becomes the traveller—or, if he does not, the journey has been in vain. For this impressive and exciting kind of fantasy exercises the imagination in a way that no other does.

You have, then, a story within a story, and one depends absolutely on the other. This kind of book is very different from the straight historical tale. HOUSE OF ARDEN by E. Nesbit, Alison Uttley's A TRAVELLER IN TIME, Edward Eager's THE TIME GARDEN— these give you far more than just a story of Elizabeth's reign. They give you, in various moods, the *feelings* of boys and girls moving in history but still remembering their own times. The reactions of the children to what they see and hear, the way they are changed by their experience—it is for these things that we make the journey. What we learn on the way is incidental. We may come back knowing some of the facts of the Babington plot, or with a picture in our mind of an Elizabethan feast, or with a more lively impression of Queen Elizabeth herself. But the child who reads these books will have learned something beyond fact. He, too, will be a little changed by his imaginative experience.

In every one of these time fantasies there is one question we can justifiably ask. Has the author made us believe in his manipulation of time? Has his illusion been successful? There are various ways in which writers have helped the reader through the double journey, and one is by a magic talisman. Masefield's THE BOX OF DELIGHTS has such a talisman. Isolated and illuminated by a poet's hand, it is so real to a child that he can believe in everything that the box causes to happen. Magic clings round it as it clings round Frances Browne's story-telling chair or round Desdemona's handkerchief. These objects are focal points. They collect and concentrate the magic of a story. So, in THE GAUNTLET, Ronald Welch uses a mailed glove as the way back to twelfth-century Wales. In THE FIFTH OF NOVEMBER, L. A. G. Strong's boy hero snatches up a piece of crumbling stone and plaster from the torture-chamber of the Tower of London, and sleeps with it under his pillow; only then, in his dreams, does he live through the story of Guy Fawkes. Hilda Lewis, in THE SHIP THAT FLEW, pricks the imagination with a little model ship, which young Peter found in an antique-shop, a Viking ship which grows to fit its intended crew and which can take them anywhere in space and time. The ship is not only a conveyance; its history and fate are important to the story. The children discover it had been the property of the Norse god Frey, and at Asgard they bargain with him for it, before they re-trace its adventures in ancient Egypt and play some part in the rescue of Pharaoh's son from his enemies.

E. Nesbit, whose magic has always a sensible, even prosaic beginning, understood this device very well. In THE STORY OF THE AMULET the magic object has two functions. It is the means by which the children reach the past, but it is also the object of their journeyings. At the beginning of the story they only possess half of it, rummaged from out of a tray in a junk-shop. To get their heart's desire, they must find the whole amulet at some stage before it was broken. If they can do this, they will somehow be able to bear the whole object back to their own time, even though they know that one half was completely crushed in the past. This is straining credulity to the utmost, but so persuasively does E. Nesbit establish the magical nature of the amulet, so skilfully does she mix fantastic events with historical background, that we believe everything, even that the amulet does end up, years after the children are dead and gone, in a case at the British Museum.

We believe it, in the end, because E. Nesbit believes it, and because in the realm of fact she is so sure and safe. With relatively few details at her disposal about Egypt or Babylon or Atlantis, she strikes a drum-note of awe, distance and magnificence. She gives the reader a feeling of the past.

THE STORY OF THE AMULET, for all its scholarly background and vivid detail, is no text-book. There is plenty of incidental humour, especially coming from the Psammead (the central figure of FIVE CHILDREN AND IT, now making a brief appearance). His grudging assistance, his grumblings and exactions, his fear of damp and love of praise, provide an acceptable contrast to the more thoughtful parts of the book. E. Nesbit shares with her readers the doubts and terrors of a journey to the distant past. She never talks down to them; she believes they are capable of appreciating mature distinctions of right and wrong, good and evil. On the other hand, unlike some writers of fantasy, she never plunges her young characters into adventures beyond their scope. Although the scenes in THE STORY OF THE AMULET are impressively accurate, there is nothing in any of them which could not have come from the imaginations of intelligent and well-read children thoroughly acquainted with the galleries of the British Museum. And from time to time, as they face angry rulers or clever priests, a word or a phrase will remind us that they are children, distinct and individual, meeting each situation as a child would meet it.

Obviously it is the amulet, the magical object, which holds together the various episodes of this exciting story. In some time fantasies it is a place, a building or a hill or a piece of country, which has accumulated magic through the centuries. Here the author is on safe ground. Most of us have at some time or another had a flash of understanding of the past when our knowledge of history has been awoken by a particular place, a local repository of great events.

Two striking stories, THE CHILDREN OF GREEN KNOWE and THE CHIMNEYS OF GREEN KNOWE, by Lucy M. Boston, are built round an old home, partly Norman, where a small boy stays with his great-grandmother Oldknow. Green Knowe (based on a real house, and lovingly described) sits four-square in the story, with its large, partly wild garden, and its topiary work, including the terrifying Green Noah which involved Tolly in the most exciting of his adventures. The story is warmed by the feeling of past generations—old walls, old toys, old tales of bygone Oldknows. At first Tolly wonders about these ancestors, then he studies their portraits, then, slowly, begins to see them—children of the seventeenth century, with their old names (Linnet, Toby, Alexander), their odd way of talking, of coming and going, of snatching Tolly up in their long-past exploits. It is not historical fact, but atmosphere, that the author is after, the feeling of a past century linked to the present by the spontaneous laughter of children and the superstitious terror of the great moving bush whose fall portends the end of the magic.

For it is magic, a curious, oblique, almost conversational magic, built round little things—a pet squirrel, a patteran in the garden, a chaffinch that flies in at Tolly's bedroom window. In the first book, THE CHILDREN OF GREEN KNOWE, it is a very simple magic, a matter of companionship across time. THE CHIMNEYS OF GREEN KNOWE has a more strictly planned story. This time Tolly makes a friend from the end of the eighteenth century, blind Susan, daughter of a seafaring Captain Oldknow, who brought back from the West Indies a little black boy to be her servant and companion. Tolly learns their story, chiefly from his great-grandmother, snatch by fascinating snatch, as she sits mending the old patchwork quilt in which pieces of the Captain's corduroy and his wife's muslin, of black Jacob's monkey-suit and the striped apron of the sneaking servant Caxton, are all stitched.

So they sit at night, not old woman and child, but two friends playing a game of pretending, and by day Tolly ranges the house, tapping the walls to find the jewels which were lost when the new wing was burnt down, and 'listening' to the house which is 'full of secrets'. He adds to his grandmother's tales. Once or twice he becomes an actor in old dramas, but his treasure-hunt, once he has collected enough clues from the past, is brought to a successful conclusion in the present when, exploring among the roof-timbers, he finds the chimney of the blocked-up room that had belonged to the evil servant, and drags out the jewels that mean new life for the old house.

In these beautifully written stories, imagination spans time. They are not fairy-tales. There is nothing supernatural in them; this is the magic of personality and of atmosphere. The author's intention in this has been understood entirely by her son, who is her illustrator. To illustrate *directly* what happens would be to break the spell of the fantasy. Peter Boston's pictures are backgrounds,

establishing the place where strange things happen. For THE
CHILDREN OF GREEN KNOWE he has devised illustrations in a
unique combination of green on black which seem almost to emanate
from the story, and the black and white drawings for THE CHIMNEYS
OF GREEN KNOWE have a strange, appealing delicacy. So, in text
and pictures, Green Knowe comes to life with its odd corners, its
stone walls imposing yet 'gentle and curving to touch, almost warm,
to be patted like living creatures'; full of past generations, enshrining
layers of experience.

Drawing by Peter Boston for L. M. Boston's THE CHIMNEYS OF GREEN
KNOWE (Faber)

Alison Uttley's exquisite story, A TRAVELLER IN TIME, re-creates
the past by the same method. Thackers, the house where young
Penelope stumbles upon the past, is based on a farm-house where
the author spent her early years, and where she heard her father talk
of the Babingtons and their championing of Mary Queen of Scots
as though they were neighbours in the present. The tunnels which
Anthony Babington had planned and started were tradition only
when Alison Uttley heard of them, but very strong tradition, passed
on to her by people who believed it. Her imagination, as she tells us
in her foreword, seized on these tales:

Many of the incidents in this story are based on my dreams, for in
sleep I went through secret hidden doorways in the house wall and
found myself in another century. Four times I stepped through
the door and wandered in rooms which had no existence . . . and
I talked with people who lived alongside but out of time, moving
through a life parallel to my own existence.
Alison Uttley. A TRAVELLER IN TIME (Faber, 1939) p. 12.

Just so Penelope, a visitor from London to her aunt and uncle at
the farm, strays through a door and finds herself talking to an aunt
kneading dough in a wooden trough in an Elizabethan kitchen;
finds that this is the favourite country house of the Babingtons and
that Anthony is hopelessly committed to the cause of the tragic
queen. Through her aunt, housekeeper to the family, she meets and
talks to the Babingtons. At first her visits to the past are brief and she
is not anxious about her return; but as she is swept up into the plot,
she grows more aware of danger—to herself as well as to the Babingtons. Her whole heart is engaged, and she tries to communicate
to them her knowledge of what must be Mary's fate. Her distress
when nobody will listen to her gives poignancy to the simple incidents of the story. When she sees Mary sewing with her ladies in
Wingfield Manor, she recognizes her loneliness and remembers her
danger. 'Oh, take care! They read your letters.' she calls outside the
window, and turns away from the past, miserable because she cannot warn the queen, afraid lest she should be too deeply involved in
her fate. All the same, she cannot wish for the end of her visions, and
as she grows older and realizes that the power cannot last, she regrets
the clear sight of younger days:

There was a clatter of hooves from the court-yard and Master
Anthony rode out with two horses. Francis sprang to his mare's
back and away they went, down the drive and along the winding
valley. I waited there, shivering with cold, but the hoofbeats were
only the clamour of the brook's waters, and nobody returned.

The peacefulness of Thackers which had held the seasons for
five hundred years flowed through me, giving me strength and
courage as it had done to those others, uniting me and them. I
knew I had seen them for the last time on this earth, but some day
I shall return to be with that brave company of shadows.
Ibid., pp. 330–1.

More than the story of the romantic Babingtons, or the atmosphere
of the old house, or the mysterious movements in time, the character
of Penelope dominates the book, and it is her wondering and her
fear that are the real reason for it.

Personal experience, transmuted by imagination and fine writing—
these are found also in Philippa Pearce's TOM'S MIDNIGHT GARDEN.
In this story, time loses its limits for two people. First, for Tom, a
schoolboy sent to stay with a rather unenterprising aunt and uncle
while his brother has measles. The Kitsons live in a flat in a large
converted house, and Tom, disturbed by rich food and lack of exercise, lies awake at night listening to the unregulated and eccentric
chimes of the grandfather clock in the hall. He is soon to prove the
truth of the clock's motto—Time No Longer; for though he in-
tends to keep his promise not to stir out of bed between bedtime
and breakfast time, he is given an hour outside time.

One night the clock strikes thirteen. Tom goes down to investigate, opens the back-door and finds himself not in the concrete
yard with dustbins and clothes-lines but in an apparently limitless
garden. In this garden it would seem that Tom is a ghost; or so he
appears to Hatty, the small girl he meets there and who accepts him
as a playmate in her Victorian world. He believes that he can share
everything that happens to Hatty before he has to return to the
present. This is not to be. Although time stands still in Tom's world
while he is in the past, it does not stand still for Hatty. She is growing
up even as Tom plays with her, and the magic, the wonder of the
garden, the transcending of time must come to an end with the ending of her childhood. This familiar ending to time fantasies is beautifully handled, with great sympathy for the boy who suddenly sees
his companion as a young woman. And there is a bold twist to the
ending which sends the whole book back on itself, sends the reader
rethinking the whole. For Tom, on the very day he is due to go home,
meets the owner of the house, old Mrs Bartholomew, who lives in
seclusion upstairs. He climbs to her flat, opens the door—and finds
that she is Hatty. So, did he go back in the past, or did she create
the past with her dreams as she lay in bed, an old woman?

The subtlety of this circumstance is something children may pay
more attention to if they reread the book in their late teens. As a
child's story it is magnificent. It is at once philosophical, swift and
gay. The conversations of Hatty and Tom are natural, the incidents

Drawing by Susan Einzig for Philippa Pearce's TOM'S MIDNIGHT GARDEN
(O.U.P.)

probable and presented with beautiful clarity. The style is impeccable
—loose-jointed and flexible, colloquial when the occasion demands,
at other times rhythmical and poetic. The fantasy will be real to
children because it is real to the author; she has carried out C. S.
Lewis's advice that 'the matter of our story should be part of
the habitual furniture of our minds.' This means that although in
some ways the book is too old for an eight-year-old, in other ways
it is exactly right. The immediate mysterious sympathy between Tom
and old Mrs Bartholomew can be paralleled in another magnificent
story, BARBOCHE by Henri Bosco, which tells how young Pascalet
(who appeared earlier in THE BOY AND THE RIVER and THE FOX
IN THE ISLAND) goes on a journey with his old aunt Martine to

revisit the village where she lived as a child. Her vision of the past
merges into the present, as two pieces of film scenery can melt
together. Where she sees fine formal gardens and prosperous cottages, Pascalet sees ruin, weeds and decay; but such is the bond between the two, and the atmosphere of magic into which they journey,
that he can almost see the village of the past as well as of the present.

The mysterious half-magic of this story rises partly from the
Provençal landscape, partly from the superstitious, dreamy characters of young Pascalet and his aunt. TOM'S MIDNIGHT GARDEN, likewise, is a book about people and their feelings. It is also, very much,
a book about Time. The author is preoccupied with Time and its
problems. Is it circular? Is it continuous? If Hatty carves Tom's
private mark on a tree (which in present Time stands in the middle of
a new housing estate), will the mark be visible to Tom in the present?
And, if so, was it made *now* or *then*? Tom, always conscious of being
in two worlds, never finds the answer to this, but he does make one
firm attempt to conquer the limits of Time. He visits the garden on
one occasion in winter, and finds Hatty skating. As he has no skates,
he makes a plan; he begs her to wrap up her skates and hide them in
her secret hiding-place (which, in the present, is in Tom's bedroom).
Tom then returns to the present, finds the skates, takes them back
into the past, and is soon skating blissfully on the Fens, the skates
mysteriously duplicated. This bold stroke succeeds by its simplicity.
The author, wisely, attempts no explanation. As Edward Eager makes
one of his characters say, in THE TIME GARDEN, when a red handkerchief exists simultaneously in two periods, 'it's all part of the Mystery
of Time.' Authors who try an elaborate analysis, or who lay down
rules for a journey into Time, hold up the action of the story and
only succeed in bewildering the reader.

Past may be linked with present in ordinary, non-magical terms.
One of the neatest links I know of this kind is in a short story by
Margaret J. Baker in TIP AND RUN. Two children, helped by a
Tudor stone-mason who descends from a stained-glass window, go
back to the Victorian period, where they find that two small cousins
are ill. They need blankets; the children get to the village and choose
some, but the shopkeeper refuses to accept their modern money.
There is only one thing to do; they run off with the blankets, and pay
when they return to the present, by post. The nineteenth-century
bill, with the twentieth-century notes, is taken to the manager:

'I recollect it well,' he said to himself. 'I was just a lad and fresh to the job with shoes that pinched. It's proper money, the little lass said, and they've got to have them. We'll pay, it's a promise. She's honest enough for credit, I thought, but the manager, he were a tartar. "No credit," he said, and she and the boy took the blankets and ran. We traced them in the carrier's cart to Sunflower Hampton. A terrible snowy night it were, and I could have sworn I saw their footprints in the snow leading straight for the church door. But when we looked inside, they weren't to be seen. I've puzzled about it from that day to this.'

Slowly he dipped his pen in the ink-well, and beside the item in the ledger he wrote the words *Account Settled in Full*.

Margaret J. Baker. TIP AND RUN. (Brockhampton, 1958) pp. 34-5.

It is a masterly ending, fantasy comfortably equated with reality. This little story is meant to entertain, but it has a crisp certainty in the handling of Time.

There is one problem in time fantasies which cannot be written off by the word *mystery*. If you embroil your characters in the past, are they to be passive spectators or are they, in effect, to alter the course of history? Of course any author who tried to alter accepted fact drastically would court disaster. Professor Branestawm says the last word on this, when he and his friend Colonel Dedshott go back in time and participate in the Squiglatanian revolution:

'This is all wrong, you know . . . it was the king's troops who won really. We've done something nasty to history, I'm afraid. I had no idea we should alter the battle like that.'

Norman Hunter. THE INCREDIBLE ADVENTURES OF PROFESSOR BRANESTAWM (Penguin 1950) p. 17.

Alison Uttley, as we have seen, lets Penelope remember what the fate of Mary Queen of Scots was, but the girl has no power to communicate this to her friends in the past. In E. Nesbit's fine story, HOUSE OF ARDEN, Elfrida finds herself dancing round a maypole in Tudor times, watched by Henry VIII and his new Queen Anne Boleyn. She can only say, 'Mind your darling head', and nobody heeds her. The touch of sadness here fits better in the story than the more exciting way of letting children from the present make mischief in the past. Richard Arden, for example, chats about the Gunpowder Plot before it is discovered and is promptly put in the Tower; so is Eliza, in THE TIME GARDEN, when she informs her royal namesake that she will soon be having Essex beheaded.

It is safer, and perhaps wiser, to confine yourself to domestic pictures in the past or to obscure or imagined events. The fourteenth-century siege which Ronald Welch so vividly reconstructs in THE GAUNTLET takes place in an unknown castle on the Welsh marches. Patricia Lynch, in ORLA OF BURREN, uses legendary material, about Granuaile, piratical and romantic queen of Galway in Elizabethan times, and in FIONA LEAPS THE BONFIRE she tells of Queen Maeve and Cuchullain. Other writers offer, as it were, lessons in social history, avoiding great events but giving their characters the power to enter the lives of ordinary people. E. Nesbit's HOUSE OF ARDEN and HARDING'S LUCK are really adventure stories, stories about a quest for treasure through the past. Edred and Elfrida and their cousin Richard, through the magic made by the snappish white Mouldiwarp, badge of their house, and by Dickie's magic seeds and coral, visit many periods, but they are nearly always involved in the private affairs of private families. In any case, history is not the main purpose in these excellent stories. They are studies of character, of brother and sister relationship, of the reaction of children to danger and perplexity and responsibility beyond their years, to their duty as landowners.

THE GOLDEN SHORE by Elinor Lyon, on the other hand, has a serious historical purpose. The two young people concerned have ancient Greece much in mind. Penelope's father is a schoolmaster who is coaching her cousin John for a scholarship. An essay subject, 'Describe in your own words the life of an ancient Greek peasant', starts the ball rolling. Grumbling about this, John urges Penelope out of doors. They jump a stream, fall in on the far side, and find themselves in an unknown world, where a group of Hellenes, threatened by barbarian invasion, have entrenched themselves behind the stream (in the children's world the Lifferli, to the Greeks Lethe). The waters of Lethe have had their effect on John and Penelope. They are only dimly aware of being out of their own time, but they throw themselves eagerly into the new skills and occupations they are offered. The adventures in the story are familiar enough—battles and chases which can be found hundreds of times over in stories—but they are lifted from ordinariness by the author's historical sense, her splendid picture of the Greeks clinging to their old customs and traditions. Because of her imaginative sympathy, her story is likely to teach children, indirectly, far more about Ancient Greece than a more factual story might, and I would put this book, well-written and compelling as it is, on a level with E. Nesbit's excursions into the pre-Christian world.

The use of the river Lethe makes this story something more than a piece of factual history. Though far from the poetry of Alison Uttley or Philippa Pearce, it has a strong element of fantasy in it. Other books which have an even stronger element of the didactic have sacrificed something of poetry, I think. Noel Streatfeild's tour de force, THE FEARLESS TREASURE, pursues ideas of inheritance and social obligation through various periods of British history. It is informative and brilliantly pictorial; but although the six children concerned are guided into the past through imagination, the boy or girl who reads the book—and it is best for the over-twelves, I think—will find their interest caught rather than their emotions. The same is true of Meriol Trevor's SUN SLOWER, SUN FASTER, in which the author sets out to survey the Catholic faith—first to illuminate its tenacity through persecution, neglect and corruption, and then to trace faith itself back to a primitive sun-worship which clinches the title of her book. Four people go back to various scenes in history—Bristol when Brunel's ship, the *Great Western*, sails in; Bath, visited by James II; the Norman Abbey in Bristol; a Saxon village, and so on. We watch these people affected in different ways by the religious aspect of what they see, and the doctrinal aim of the story really puts any feeling of poetry or magic out of the question.

There is no reason, of course, why this device of a journey in time should not be used in various ways. There is a good deal of humour to be got out of a character from the past visiting the present—like Norman Matilda in THE SHIP THAT FLEW, whose piece of Bayeux tapestry enlivens a present-day village fête, or Victorian Louisa (in Elizabeth Denys's light-hearted adventure, SEVEN DAYS' WONDER) who so much enjoys car-rides and television. This is all good fun and is not meant either to create a magical atmosphere or preach a moral. A visit to the future is a different matter.

Inevitably the writer, when he projects himself forward in imagi-

nation, takes with him his own idea of the present. Usually he will
be suggesting the consequences, good or bad, of a logical change
from our own pattern, that pattern being always discernible. When
the children in THE STORY OF THE AMULET have a glimpse of the
not-very-distant future, they see a London fresh and clean and full
of flowers, where people are gentle and generous-hearted. All Edith
Nesbit's Fabian principles and desires are behind the picture, which
is made more telling when the woman they are talking to looks out
of the window for a moment into the past and recoils with dismay
from its ugliness.

Light, air, flowers, honesty and grace—ideals natural enough to
writers of our time—these are the points, too, round which Meriol
Trevor builds an ambitious story, THE OTHER SIDE OF THE MOON.
This is not exclusively a children's book, though, on the face of it,
it is one more venture to the Moon, with a boy in his teens as chief
character. But there is no restriction of either terror or teaching,
and in its imaginative sweep it occasionally approaches the three
extra-terrestrial novels of C. S. Lewis (OUT OF THE SILENT PLANET,
PERELANDRA, THAT HIDEOUS STRENGTH). Meriol Trevor
describes two races on the Moon. The inhabitants of Cordeluc, with
their twin kings, romantic as well as democratic, their language
going back to Creation, their conviction that they are in touch with
the First Giver of Life, represent the ideal man, a man who has
taken from the past simplicity, myth-making and knight-errantry,
and has turned his back on the worst elements of mechanization.
These men of Cordeluc live on 'the other side of the Moon', in a
small area of warmth and fertility, whereas the Half People live on
the edge of the dead side, in underground cities ruled by dictators
and always at war. The description of the people shows how they
derive from our own times:

> . . . they all seemed to wear uniform, or if not, their ordinary
> clothes looked like uniforms, for they were mass-produced in
> standard sizes in a factory which Brett showed them. Men and
> women alike wore loose trousers and a sort of blouse jacket, with
> a belt. Everyone wore a tag on his shoulder with his name and
> number, and the same on his or her cap . . . Everybody looked
> grim or gloomy or cross or worried; they all stared at the visitors
> but none of them said anything, though they chattered to each

other in an ugly language full of hisses and guttural croaks. Meriol Trevor. THE OTHER SIDE OF THE MOON (Collins, 1956) p. 120.

A few Half People win the right to return to Cordeluc, and a few of the noble folk are either stolen or tempted over to Coldeaston, where they are brainwashed and kept as citizen-slaves. This is the fate that threatens the men of the *Moondart*, when they are lured into the city after a sojourn with the twin kings. The odd combination of social satire and magic in the book (the quest of the Moonstone is fairy-tale with a religious note) is only made possible, as so often in fantasy, by the careful drawing of the characters, each influenced one way or the other by the people on the Moon. Gil has the clear, unprejudiced courage of a schoolboy; Tracy Kingville, the American playboy, has his own jocular bravery; the bigoted scientist, Oliver, recoils from too much knowledge; the pilot belongs by nature to the Half People; while Anselm, the navigator, who alone can touch the Moonstone, is the good man, the scapegoat. Together, these men stand for humanity. The moral is not pressed too much, the thrilling story is not hampered by it, but it is there all the same.

No journey in time is completely lacking in magic, even if it teaches a lesson; but time fantasy is freer and goes nearer to the heart of the matter. It makes the reader feel in tune with the past or the future; it gives him the feeling of moving naturally in strange worlds, the heir to many places and many times.

Reading List

*Baker, Margaret J. TIP AND RUN. *Brockhampton* 1958. Illustrated by Terence Freeman.

*Bosco, Henri. THE BOY AND THE RIVER (1955 France) 1956, THE FOX IN THE ISLAND (1956 France) 1958, BARBOCHE (1957 France) 1959. *O.U.P.* Translated by Gerard Hopkins. Illustrated by Lynton Lamb.

*Boston, L. M. THE CHILDREN OF GREEN KNOWE 1954, THE CHIMNEYS OF GREEN KNOWE 1958. *Faber.* Illustrated by Peter Boston. (See also p. 374.)

Capon, Paul. FLIGHT OF TIME. *Heinemann* 1960. Illustrated by Marina Hoffer Four teenagers discover a time-machine and journey to 2600 A.D. and 1960 B.C.

Chauncy, Nan. TANGARA. *O.U.P.* 1960. Illustrated by Brian Wildsmith. Beautifully written, touching story of a girl in Tasmania going back in time and making friends with the last blackfellows.

Dawson, Carley. MR WICKER'S WINDOW. *Faber* 1955. Illustrated by Lynd Ward. Quest for jewelled tree belonging to Chinese princess, starting in present-day Washington and moving back to the eighteenth-century port of Georgetown.

*Denys, Elizabeth. SEVEN DAYS' WONDER. *Collins* 1959. Illustrated by Margery Gill.

Dickinson, William Croft. BORROBIL 1944, illustrated by John Morton-Sale. THE EILDON TREE 1947, illustrated by James S. Richardson. *Cape.* Two children are admitted to a fairy past.

Dickinson, William Croft. THE FLAG FROM THE ISLES. *Cape* 1951. Illustrated by Eric Tansley. The same children meet James IV of Scotland and play their part at Flodden Field.

*Eager, Edward. THE TIME GARDEN. *Macmillan* 1958. Illustrated by N. M. Bodecker.

Fitzroy, Olivia. THE HUNTED HEAD. *Cape* 1956. Illustrated by Raymond Sheppard. Boy returns to eighteenth century and re-enacts adventure of his ancestors with Bonny Prince Charlie.

*Hunter, Norman. THE INCREDIBLE ADVENTURES OF PROFESSOR BRANE-STAWM (1933). *Penguin* (Puffin Story Books) (1946) 1950. Illustrated by Heath Robinson. (see also Chap. 9).

*Lewis, C. S. OUT OF THE SILENT PLANET 1938, PERELANDRA 1943, THAT HIDEOUS STRENGTH 1945. *Bodley Head.*

*Lewis, Hilda. THE SHIP THAT FLEW. *O.U.P.* 1939. Illustrated by Nora Lavrin.

*Lynch, Patricia. ORLA OF BURREN 1954, illustrated by Joan Kiddell-Monroe. FIONA LEAPS THE BONFIRE 1957, illustrated by Peggy Fortnum. *Dent.*

Lynch, Patricia. THE BOOKSHOP ON THE QUAY. *Dent* 1956. Illustrated by Peggy Fortnum. Boy who loves reading wanders at night in Dublin, meets and talks with Swift.

*Lyon, Elinor. THE GOLDEN SHORE. *Hodder & Stoughton* 1957. Illustrated by the author.

Lyon, Elinor. DAUGHTERS OF ARADALE. *Hodder & Stoughton* 1957. Illustrated by the author. Three children reconstruct a Stuart incident in their family history.

Maddock, Reginald. THE TIME MAZE. *Nelson* 1960. Illustrated by Robert Hodgson. Two boys diverted in a magic cave to prehistoric times and then to the future.

*Nesbit, E. THE STORY OF THE AMULET (1906) 1957, FIVE CHILDREN AND IT
(1902) 1957, illustrated by H. R. Millar. THE HOUSE OF ARDEN (1908)
1949, HARDING'S LUCK (1903) 1949, illustrated by Desmond Walduck.
Benn.

Pardoe, M. ARGLE'S MIST 1956, ARGLE'S CAUSEWAY 1958, ARGLE'S ORACLE
1959. *Routledge.* Illustrated by Audrey Fawley. Three children and a school-
master mysteriously visit Britain in the time of Cymbeline, Hampshire in the
twelfth century, and Greece at the time of Alcibiades and Socrates.

*Pearce, A. Philippa. TOM'S MIDNIGHT GARDEN. *O.U.P.* 1958. Illustrated by
Susan Einzig.

Sauer, Julia. FOG MAGIC. *Viking*, New York 1943. Illustrated by Lynd Ward.
Girl in Novia Scotia joins life of village of long ago, now lost; a beautiful
and impressive story.

Severn, David. THE FUTURE TOOK US. *Bodley Head* 1958. Illustrated by Jillian
Richards. Two schoolboys go forward to Kent and London in 3,000 A.D.

Severn, David. DREAM GOLD. *Bodley Head* 1949. Illustrated by A. K. Lee. Two
schoolboys in Cornwall follow in dream an ancient adventure of pirates and
treasure.

Severn, David. DRUM-BEATS! *Bodley Head* 1953. Illustrated by Richard
Kennedy. Children in co-educational boarding school see into Africa and the
fate of an expedition lost years before.

*Streatfeild, Noel. THE FEARLESS TREASURE. *Michael Joseph* 1953. Illustrated
by Dorothy Braby.

*Strong, L. A. G. THE FIFTH OF NOVEMBER. *Dent* (King's Treasuries of Literature Series) (1937) 1940. Illustrated by Jack Matthew.

*Trevor, Meriol. SUN SLOWER, SUN FASTER 1955, illustrated by Edward
Ardizzone. THE OTHER SIDE OF THE MOON 1956, illustrated by Martin
Thomas. *Collins.*

*Uttley, Alison. A TRAVELLER IN TIME. *Faber* 1939. Illustrated by Phyllis
Bray.

Wallace, Kathleen. THE PRIZE ESSAY. *Heinemann* 1953. Illustrated by Richard
Kennedy. Mature story for girls of fourteen and over. Two schoolgirls
begin to see and talk to the Brontës, while studying their lives and work.
Very moving and done with masterly tact.

*Welch, Ronald. THE GAUNTLET. *O.U.P.* 1951. Illustrated by Terence Freeman.

Chapter 8 | *Magic Carpets*

The setting of fairy-tale is customarily (though not invariably) an enchanted country which we must seek in what Jung called the collective unconscious. We may more properly call those stories *fantasy*, which bring the magic and the irrational into our own world. Fantasy takes known objects and scenes and reshapes them in its own terms. This, at least, is one way of classifying the numerous tales which are not fairy-tales, although they may have traditional elements. Some will be only arbitrarily sorted. Where, for example, can we put THE PHOENIX AND THE CARPET, or THE LITTLE MATCH GIRL, or, for that matter, ALICE IN WONDERLAND ?

The very simple dramatizing of a child's experience, through an animal or a toy that comes to life, though it is technically fantastic, can be very near to fact, just because the child takes it literally. A four-year-old has only to tie a bonnet on a kitten and force it into a doll's pram to make it, instantly, a baby. To this child there is nothing out of the way in Mrs Tiggy-Winkle wearing an apron and wielding a flat-iron. Nor is the everyday world really changed. Plates and spoons, cats and foxes, may change their rôle and their clothes in stories, but to a child they are not essentially different. Merely, the story has gratified his wish for a world where nothing is impossible; it is still the world he knows. Fantasy for young children is best if it is a matter of one simple incident which, for a time, enlarges and irradiates the everyday world.

In two volumes of enchanting stories from Norway, LITTLE OLD MRS PEPPERPOT and MRS PEPPERPOT AGAIN, by Alf Prøysen, we meet an ordinary housewife with one unusual habit. From time to time, unexpectedly, she shrinks to the size of a pepperpot, and while she is small she can understand the speech of animals. The accidents that rise from this are all founded on the facts of everyday.

The magic shines over a grocer's shop with a drawer of macaroni, a small girl's doll, a brass bedstead, a magic fulfilling the unspoken wish of many a child to be able to enter the world in a different guise. There is shrewd psychology in these tales. Mrs Pepperpot (a very real character, in words and in pictures), is quick to exploit her power, even if she cannot have it to order. For a long time she has suspected mice of raiding her larder, but one day she learns otherwise, when she goes small and they describe to her a 'monster' who can only be her husband; with quick opportunism, she appoints a mouse as her 'penny watchman' and stops her husband's marauding. Then there is her neighbour, who has earned the nickname Mrs Calamity because of her love of omens. Mrs Calamity has a habit of stealing plants and one day she sets to work on Mrs Pepperpot's best geranium; but Mrs Pepperpot, going small, makes the most of her chance. Following the thief, she enlists the help of a wagtail, a black cat and a magpie, and with one stroke puts an end to her neighbour's superstition and her thieving ways. Everything that happens is just one remove from the familiar world of a bustling woman. These simple tales have some of the same attractive ingredients as Mary Norton's more complex stories about the Borrowers.

Drawing-magic is another device of this simple kind. Look at, for instance, that delightful little tale, THE MAGIC BUTTON by Kathleen Guthrie. One day, as Kitty draws a mouse and a caterpillar, she rubs the top button of her blouse, thinking at the same time how wonderful it would be if they could talk to her. At once, of course, they do, and the three of them go for a glorious spin round the town on thistledown parachutes. Kitty is taken out of her world and yet she never leaves it. The direct style and the comical drawings fit perfectly together; this is a beautiful exercise in creative imagination.

The magic in a pencil is not always so simple and light-hearted. Most stories that use this device take it at its face value, but drawing is, after all, one of the forms of sympathetic magic, and fear lurks behind it. This is one of the compelling fears, like the thought of infinity, which comes to strong imaginations. It would be possible for a timid child to read, say, the drawing incident in THE BOX OF DELIGHTS (see pp. 373–9) and remain unmoved, but an imaginative child would very likely feel a pang of terror as Kay's pictures come to life. This is not a harmful thing, I am sure, but a necessary stretching of that child's poetic feeling. A fascinating story by

Catherine Storr, MARIANNE DREAMS, illustrates this point.

This is the story of a girl, kept in bed by illness, who finds a pencil with magical properties. There begins a dream-relationship with Mark, who is also ill. The two children have not met, though the same tutor visits them both, but through Marianne's drawings they share a weird adventure, besieged in a bleak house on a moor by huge, one-eyed stones which, each day, move nearer and nearer. Marianne's ordinary world is confused and shifted as the adventure gets more and more alarming, until the children escape in the healing beams of a lighthouse which she had sketched on the horizon.

The story is sometimes frightening, but the terror is held in check because the children are learning to control it through the pencil. Using their wits, they think out, step by logical step, what they can draw that will be most useful, and they deduce by observation, gradually, that safety lies in light. In one way this story can be read as a fantastic adventure, but it is also a study of children coming to terms with some of the harsher aspects of life. It is a little allegory, wonderfully turned.

This is certainly a book for the child older than the little girl who can light-heartedly imagine herself flying on a piece of thistledown and talking with a mouse and a caterpillar. All the same, everything develops from Marianne's simple, child-shaped drawings. Reality is always there—that is the secret—from the simplest stories about agreeably odd happenings to those dream-stories which, as it were, create a country through imagination, almost map the country of the imagination itself. Palmer Brown has written two exquisite stories, BEYOND THE PAWPAW TREES and THE SILVER NUTMEG which are fantasies within fantasy, for the country where Anna Lavinia lives and her house shielded by a high wall are both real and unreal. Here are the domestic events of an ordinary world, with mother making preserves (pawpaw preserves) and little girl enjoying her pets. But the air is different; this is a country unknown to travel-agencies. Anna Lavinia's mother likes to believe what she sees, but the child's father, who has been absent for a long time, is, in his wife's words, 'always chasing rainbows', and his daughter inclines to his point of view:

Though she had not seen him for more than two years, Anna Lavinia remembered clearly his bright red beard and the pocket microscope which he always carried to examine the motes in sunbeams. He often promised to let Anna Lavinia look at them too, but somehow he never got around to it.

Palmer Brown. BEYOND THE PAWPAW TREES (Methuen, 1956) pp. 8–9.

So, in this book, she sets out on a visit to her aunt Sophia Maria prepared for all that may happen, dealing equally well with the matter-of-fact fat lady in the train and with the mirage on which a town is perched, and where she finds her aunt and her father. She has found something else, too, on her journey, a silver key which her father has been searching for; together they take it back to the desert oasis and find 'fourteen small iron pots all full of gold'. It is real gold, as Anna Lavinia's father assures her, and at last she knew 'why her father was always chasing rainbows, and she felt sure that her mother would feel better about it when she knew too.' This is having the best of both worlds.

Drawing by Palmer Brown for his THE SILVER NUTMEG (Methuen)

In THE SILVER NUTMEG, Anna Lavinia, still exploring, goes through a dew-pond into an upside-down world where gravity does not exist, and where a permanent band of recoverers pull down things that float out of their proper sphere. Anna Lavinia and the boy who is her companion in this world enjoy playing together, and they enjoy too the discovery that the sad lady, his aunt, was once betrothed to Anna Lavinia's wandering uncle (an engaging char-

136 INTENT UPON READING

acter who peddles spices and who is united to his love in the end).
The odd, entrancing illustrations, feathery and delicate, encrusted
with detail, underline this fascinating amalgam of fantastical and
familiar. The tale is made of the very spirit of childhood, curious,
aware and reaching out to the unknown.

Under water, too, or reflected, is the world Theresa Whistler has
imagined in THE RIVER BOY. This is the story of Nathaniel, who
lives in an old house remote in deep country, a boy whose imagination keeps him company, who wants something and at last finds it
in his dreams—his reflection, the river boy. For Nathaniel's valley
has no river, but in his dreams and reveries he and the river boy play
in a wonderful stream, and journey down it towards the sea. The
journey itself is symbolic of growing up. When Nat reaches the sea
and sees the last of the river boy, he realizes as well as we do that
the adventure is over. The fantasy swings at will between the simple,
concrete wishes of a boy and the half-formed wishes of his mind
thrusting towards his older self. Beside the delights of finding birds'
nests, seeing a mill at work or scything corn, there are intimations of
deeper desires. At the mill, Nat feels the presence of an unseen people.
He is drawn strongly towards the farm seen across the valley:

It was then that he realised with a strange, sharp surprise, that the
tower cast no shadow at all. All round it beneath him the twelve
roofs lay in the bright sunlight of evening, which was drawing
from his own feet already so long and dark a shadow, stretching
out far beyond the shadow of the stack. Yet the whole farm, and the
ancient tower, and the flowering trees, lay in a circle of untroubled
radiance. Gazing at them long and silently, Nathaniel felt as
though something he had always minded had been put right, as
though he had found something he did not know he had lost.
Theresa Whistler. THE RIVER BOY (Hart-Davis, 1955) p. 115.

It is because he struggles to reach the farm by his own efforts that
the dream momentarily swings into a nightmare, to a long vision of
the river boy lying motionless in the snow, tended by an old woman
—Nature herself. Then Nat finds the sea and enters upon the next,
rational stage of everyday life, refreshed, taught, enlivened by the
imaginary journey.

The meaning of the story will rise in the mind of an intelligent
child long after he has enjoyed the concrete images, the beautiful

pictures that children naturally create in a dream. A white horse in moonlight, a village with its church, 'like a string of goslings behind a grey goose', a snail 'waving delighted horns in the air', an old mill at work—the floor trembling, the three cats whisking about 'in the mealy gloom', the miller himself with every crease of his clothes giving off flour 'as a puffball spurts brown dust when you stamp on it'. I can't praise too highly this unusual, shining book, with its exquisite drawings, its rich, graceful style and its overtones of meaning. This is indeed the transformation of one world into another, for while there is nothing here outside a boy's experience, there is nothing quite ordinary in this river world. The ordinary and familiar have become magical, new and vibrating with colour and light.

The balance between real and unreal, between fact and imagination, is the key to good fantasy. You can accept the improbable (that is, you can believe in it with your imagination) just so far as you can believe in the realistic beginnings from which the fantasy springs. Belief is taxed to its utmost when the fantasy is closest to the real. The works of Rosemary Anne Sisson, to take an example, are at first glance realistic: they are best called romantic. In THE IMPRACTICAL CHIMNEY-SWEEP we have a rustic scene idealized but still only one remove from the world we know. The story tells how John William, who climbs chimneys for his father, loses his job because he prefers to watch the sunrise from the top of Lord Summerset's chimney-stack. John William's sense of values provides the point of the story. Setting out with a horse and cart, he sweeps his way from house to house in country unknown to him, picking up as wages various objects which seem useless but which come in handy in the end:

Then Miss Ellen kissed John William and gave him the sea-shell, and he said goodbye to her and to Commander Peters and to Jane, and he went away inland, with his brush over one shoulder and his bundle of flints over the other, and his leather halter pulled up tight with the silver buckle. And long after the little white house was out of sight, and the sea was only a blue and silver gleam behind him, he put Miss Ellen's shell to his ear, and there he could hear the waves breaking on the shore and the wide sea singing, singing in the wind.

Rosemary Anne Sisson. THE IMPRACTICAL CHIMNEY-SWEEP (Macmillan, 1956) p. 136.

Drawing by Theresa Whistler for her THE RIVER BOY (Hart-Davis)

And John, whom his father scorns for his unworldliness, ends up with a beautiful gypsy bride and a blessing from the Romany queen:

> 'You shall climb chimneys all your life . . . and you shall never grow too stout for it. At the end of every chimney you shall see the silver stars, and the soot shall never blind you to them.'
> Ibid., pp. 158–9.

The events of this odd story are offered as fact, as something that happened. At the other extreme are two remarkable books by William Mayne which push real-life adventure just to the edge of fantasy, but never beyond, through the imaginations of the central characters. THE BLUE BOAT, which shows this method at its simplest, is the story of two small boys spending a spring holiday in a prim seaside villa with a prim landlady. Escaping from her fussing, they play by a mere where they borrow a boat—a magic boat, it seems to them, for they come upon it just after they have wished for it. By the mere, too, they meet a giant, a goblin and an alchemist, and the fact that they later discover these to be friends lying up between circus seasons makes no difference to their enjoyment. It is all, to use Hugh's splendid word, 'disordinary', and they separate fact and fantasy, partially and happily, as children naturally would:

> Christopher sat in the back of the car and heard no more of any-one's conversation. He was sorting out all the muddling facts that had appeared to him, starting with the goblin and ending with the friendliness of the giant. It was easy, he thought, for Hugh to think they were slightly magic; but whatever Hugh thought or imagined there was no magic, no sudden land of goblins and giants and princes beyond the Mere. Yet they had been there, without any sort of fancying at all, and seen the goblin and the giant, and been called princes . . .
> The explanation came to him gradually: it had to, because it troubled his mind all the time to find himself in a place he did not believe in. If the goblin pretended to be a goblin, and the giant pretended to be a giant, and really they were friends . . . But they are goblin-sized and giant-sized . . . Yet they are only pretending, and playing a game, and we are playing it too . . . If I play it instead of trying to make it into sense, will that be better?
> It was better, he found at once. He looked at Mrs Wrigley in the front of the car, and found she was a witch, quite certainly . . .

Pretending certainly, that is . . . And Dad was a king . . . That
could very likely be so, because he was a kingish man used to
ordering people and sending them to do things.
William Mayne. THE BLUE BOAT (Oxford University Press, 1957)
pp. 122–3.

In A GRASS ROPE there is a deeper feeling of mystery. Set in the
Yorkshire dales, this is a treasure hunt, like so many of William
Mayne's books, but with the difference that one of the characters,
young Mary, believes so firmly in magic that her interpretation of
events dominates the story rather than her parents' common-sense
or Adam Forrest's grammar-school reasoning. The treasure, they
know, belonged to Sir Owland (an ancestor of Nan and Mary) who
lost a pack of hounds and a hunting unicorn and, with them, all his
wealth, which was said to be 'fastened' to them. The older children
follow up clues, in story-book fashion: but Mary plaits the traditional
grass-rope to catch the unicorn, and goes off in the night down an
old mine-shaft, which she firmly believes is the gate to fairyland.
Down in the darkness she finds a creature she takes for the unicorn
(it is a fox-cub fallen into the shaft); groping in the grass she finds
some wire, twists it into a collar and lead, and fastens one end to
the fox, the other to a 'white peeled stick'. When she is found and
pulled out by her anxious family, the wire is found to be the silver
collars joined together of the long-dead hounds, the 'white stick' a
piece of an animal's skull with a central horn. So strong is William
Mayne's power of fantasy that most children will refuse, as Mary
does, to listen to the father's rational explanation of this. As Mary
says, when she sees the collars being polished, 'One for each of us,
and one for each animal . . . And all because I believe in fairies.'

It is certainly not inappropriate to use the word 'magic' of a story
where the author makes you aware of the irrational all the time, the
poetic below the events of ordinary life, and does this while keeping
his characters absolutely real, not eccentric or peculiar, but people
with character and drive and personal idiom.

Mayne's particular contribution to the fantastic adventure is the
way he makes the vision of certain of his characters override actual
events. In these two books, which have simple, almost hackneyed
plots, the tone is set by Mary's belief in fairyland and by the interpretation Hugh and Christopher put on the people they meet. All

else—narrative, clear-cut dialogue, implied description—follow along behind, brilliant but subsidiary. The same compulsive imagination runs through an odd, intriguing story, THE DOUBLING ROD, by Ada Harrison. This is the story of the Hinnabels, who by chance find a forked stick which has the power to duplicate any object or event. The Hinnabels gradually come to understand, and sometimes to fear, the power of the rod. They use it to get back an Etruscan bronze figure which is stolen while Mr Hinnabel is keeping it for a museum, but the rod only works because the Hinnabels believe in it. The magic is not really from outside; it depends on character, and is believable because of this. There are plenty of adventure stories like this one which have been given a new life and vigour by a small, easy touch of magic—for instance Meta Mayne Reid's stories, in which a group of Irish children are instructed by Tiffany, the cat, in magical lore. The magic does not advance the plot noticeably in any of these stories, but it adds tension and glamour to stories that are otherwise familiar enough.

Meta Mayne Reid blends magic and reality without any self-consciousness, and so does Janet McNeill in her amusing stories of Specs McCann, school stories which, without the touch of fantasy, would still be notable for their wit, their complete lack of cliché in word or event, their precisely delineated characters. But Specs, an Irish boy at boarding-school, has 'queer things' happen to him. He is taught the crawl by a mermaid, he hatches a dragon from an egg found in a cave, he changes a master into a white rabbit; the droll joke runs through two volumes and is always fresh and entertaining. Sometimes the fantasy is extreme (as with the dragon); sometimes it is subtle, as in *Specs and the Cuckoo Clock*, a small masterpiece. Tusky, a rival schoolboy, has planted a moth-ball in Specs's clock, and has made Specs look a fool, for he was sure the bird had laid it; but Specs has the last word:

Tusky came in at the end of the period to borrow a dictionary. He looked rather excited and pleased, but we didn't make any remark and just handed the book over. It was half a minute to five and he hung about looking up his word. Then the doors on the clock opened and the cuckoo came out. 'Cuck–' she said, and stopped. For a moment she hung there with her little wings stretched wide, and her bright little eyes looked at Tusky. She

knew who'd made a fool of her. Then she went into her house and
shut the doors with a tiny vicious bang.

Tusky didn't say a word. He just stood there, looking at the
clock and his face got redder and redder. Then he turned and went
out. Specs went over to the clock. It was still ticking busily. He
bent down close to the little doors. 'Thank you, ma'am,' he said.
Janet McNeill. MY FRIEND SPECS MCCANN (Faber, 1955)
pp.95–6.

How easily the author bounces from one mood to another, how
lightly she carries off the joke, not a matter for laughter so much as
for smiles, for beyond it there is a mystery, something more than the
mere fact of a small boy exercising, sometimes outrageously and
inappropriately, an unusual gift. And the more seriously you take
the magic, the more you are kept in bounds by the shrewd psychology, the accurate picture of small boys at school.

With the intrusion of fantastic creatures into an everyday world,
the factual foundation is most important. The swing between fact
and fancy produces an agreeable humour. We believe in the odd
things that happen to Specs McCann because he is such a real boy.
How does Barbara Euphan Todd make us believe in *her* fantastic
characters? For she makes a band of scarecrows settle down with
such success in everyday life that you constantly forget they are
fantastic. Some credit, certainly, is due to her illustrators, who have presented her scarecrow characters in different but always in interesting ways. To John Harwood, who illustrated WORZEL GUMMIDGE
AND SAUCY NANCY, it is the woodenness of the creatures that is
most striking; he makes you see the humour of sticks and clothes
suddenly animated. Jill Crockford is very much aware of the magic
of the transformation, and in her drawings there is an off-beat poetry
that suits the stories perfectly.

Then, the scarecrows come to life by association with the human
characters, so very real themselves—the children, Tom and Susan
and towny Robin, the farmer's wife, who looks after them at Scatterbrook, the egregious Mrs Bloomsbury-Barton. But there is more to
it than this. That adventures happen at all depends on the premise
that Worzel Gummidge is alive, that he can walk and talk, and that
the same power is extended to his wife, Earthy Mangold, lugubrious
Hannah Harrow, and the rest of the crew. But *what* happens de-

Drawing by John Harwood for Barbara Euphan Todd's WORZEL GUMMIDGE
AND SAUCY NANCY (Hollis & Carter). Below: Drawing by Jill Crockford for
WORZEL GUMMIDGE AND THE RAILWAY SCARECROWS (Evans)

pends on character, and most of all on the intentions of Gummidge
himself, with his Will Rogers brand of philosophy that matches so
well his bottle-straw feet and his hedgehog hairbrush. Whatever
humans do, whatever he does to them, to Gummidge 'humans is
daft'. When Earthy Mangold, as a new scarecrow, says she would
rather try to learn being a human first, Gummidge storms at her:

> 'Go and be human then . . . Go and live complicate. Spend your
> mornin's bringin' mud into the house, and your arternoons takin' it
> out again, and puttin' rags into water, and hangin' 'em out to dry.'
> 'Is that what humans does?' asked Earthy.
> 'Ooh, Aye! I've caught 'em at it. It's enough to make anyone sulk.'
> Barbara Euphan Todd. EARTHY MANGOLD AND WORZEL
> GUMMIDGE (Hollis & Carter, 1954) p. 41.

and he is just as rude when John asks him the time:

> 'Humans is daft, the way they goes on about time. I allus defies
> it. The human as started choppin' days and nights into hours, and
> hours into minutes did a great deal o' harm. Time goes wriggling
> on just like a worm, and it don't make no differ if you chops it up
> or not. All humans is daft.' Ibid., p. 52.

Most of the adventures in these books arise simply from Gummidge's mistaken self-confidence. He is prepared at a moment's
notice to take on the semblance of an elephant-trainer, an amateur
naturalist (what he calls a badger-badgerer) or almost any variant of
village worthy, and the authentic, crabby, racy tone echoes through
all his impersonations; perhaps at its most typical when he opens
the Scatterbrook bazaar, after borrowing the clothes belonging to
Lady Piddingfold, the guest of honour:

> Mr Perkins interrupted quickly by saying, 'I will now ask our
> kind friend, Lady Piddingfold, to say that the bazaar is open.'
> He bowed towards Worzel Gummidge, who seemed to have got his
> fingers knotted together in the strings of the sponge-bag.
> 'All right,' he said in his loudest, crossest voice. 'If you say
> the thing's open, it *is* open. I didn't come here to start arguments.
> It's never been shut that I know of.' Then he coughed violently,
> and walked away.
> Barbara Euphan Todd. MORE ABOUT WORZEL GUMMIDGE
> (Hollis & Carter, 1938) p. 65.

This is rollicking humour, but now and then we are pulled up short by moments of poetry, when the children see the country purely, as it should be seen. Robin's night ride on Dapple Grey, the merry-go-round horse (in WORZEL GUMMIDGE AT THE CIRCUS), with the animals and scarecrows crowding round him, is one such moment, and so is the description of John and Susan waking at dawn in the railway cutting where they have spent the night with Gummidge and his friends (in WORZEL GUMMIDGE AGAIN). These stories are popular partly because they give children an outlet for their wish to be rude, dirty and untrammelled; Gummidge carries on, for them, a perpetual mutiny against the world of grown-ups. At the same time he satisfies their latent desire for mystery and magic.

Talking animals are more difficult to draw successfully than fantastic semi-humans, at least when they are to be involved in human affairs, and I would give high praise to Margaret J. Baker for her handling of Homer the tortoise. This pedantic personage first appeared in a story called, suitably, NONSENSE! SAID THE TORTOISE, in which he was bought by three sisters from a local pet-shop. His name is important. In this first book Homer is very useful to Lettice's younger sister Mouse in a spelling-test at school, acting as a crib in her desk. In HOMER SEES THE QUEEN he gets into the British Museum Reading Room and establishes friendly relations with a professor. In HOMER GOES TO STRATFORD he is quite equal to conversations about The Bard, as he calls him, and eventually insinuates himself into an open-air performance of *A Midsummer Night's Dream*. Homer is a splendid character and the adventures which result from his unusual accomplishments are almost all well chosen and reasonable; but there is one point where Margaret J. Baker has gone too far. Fantasy must be consistent. It must have its own limits, and the extra-human events must not clash too seriously with the events of the real world. In NONSENSE! SAID THE TORTOISE Homer has one adventure which illustrates the perfection of fantasy, and one which is, I think, in the wrong key.

First, the good example. Homer is confiscated at school by Miss Weston, a mistress whom most of the girls find prim and alarming. The girls, anxious about their pet, creep out at night and peer in at Miss Weston's window:

They stood on tip-toe peering through a slit in the curtains. Miss

Weston was sitting in a rocking-chair before the gas stove with a mug of cocoa in her hand and a chessboard arranged on the table by her side . . . Sitting on the opposite side of the table, studying the chessmen and shifting one very cautiously with his clubbed foot, was Homer, looking very pleased with himself.

'Checkmate, I think,' he said, 'and thank you for a most enjoyable evening.'

'Not at all,' said Miss Weston, 'your skill was really too much for me. You play a really remarkable game. Now if you have everything for the night, I think I will retire. It's past one o'clock and those children will require all my energies tomorrow.'

Margaret J. Baker. NONSENSE! SAID THE TORTOISE (Brockhampton, 1949) pp. 61–2.

Miss Weston's sang-froid is beautifully conveyed, and there is not a word wasted in this delightful scene. Later in the book, however, Homer's gift is used in a way I find indefensible. In the garden of Sir George Clewisham's mansion the tortoise overhears two men plotting to steal his jewels. He tells the children and they warn Sir George, but too late; Homer has to settle the crooks himself, by shouting at them as they get over the wall, so that they drop the jewels. Now this is too serious an affair to be settled by fantasy; the whole balance of the incident is upset.

A similar point comes up in THE MAGIC WALKING-STICK, a pleasant adventure story by John Buchan, in which an Eton schoolboy finds a stick which will carry him anywhere he wants to go. Bill gets involved in the affairs of young prince Anatole of Gracia and his wicked uncle Kuno, and uses the stick to rescue Anatole and to maroon Kuno, first on St Kilda, then in the Highlands, and finally (a nice Buchan touch) in a suburb of Moscow. Nobody is going to question the logic of all this, for the adventure is an unreal Ruritanian affair. But earlier on the magic has been used in a more questionable way. Bill's aviator uncle is lost in the Sahara on a record-breaking flight. Bill finds him, gives him food and sends a rescue-party from the nearest French frontier-post. Now this puts the fantasy into direct contact with real life, where the danger is too serious, too stringent to be solved by fantastic means. Again, the balance of a story has been spoiled.

This is a mistake that E. Nesbit never made. She tells us exactly how far the magic is supposed to go and coaxes us to believe in it by her cunning detail and by the moderate amount of oddity that we are asked to believe. In that classic wish-story, FIVE CHILDREN AND IT, there are two limits to the magic power which the Psammead exercises, often grudgingly, on behalf of the children. First, it is over by sundown. Secondly, only the children can perceive its effects. These conditions keep the story within bounds and lead to some amusing situations. When Robert wishes to be in a besieged castle, the servants are quite unaware of the change in circumstances, and serve a normal lunch to the children, who hungrily go through a pantomime of eating. There is another twist to the siege incident, for Cyril, pouring water through a hole over the portcullis, in lieu of the customary boiling oil, unfortunately chooses the first moment of sunset, with the result that Martha, back from her day out, receives an undeserved wetting.

Situations like this have a purpose. Reconsideration is the keynote of the book. In the gayest way, E. Nesbit explodes the very idea of the magic wish. Delightful as each day seems at its outset, before the magic has ended some disaster or disconcerting mistake is bound to make the children think again, so that they gradually learn to be careful and to avoid casual wishes. To be rich beyond the dreams of avarice is, after all, not much use when the local shopkeepers do not recognize your currency.

Nobody can fail to believe in E. Nesbit's fantasies, for they are so firmly rooted in character and in circumstance. Everything that happens joins on somewhere to the ordinary world. In THE PHOENIX AND THE CARPET, when Anthea and the rest have used their magic carpet, under the Phœnix's instructions, for several quite exacting journeys, it begins to wear rather thin. E. Nesbit means this literally. A clergyman, transported to a desert island to marry the cook and the burglar, appears only as half a man and half a shadow, because he is standing on a worn part of the carpet, and there comes a moment when two of the children actually fall through a large hole—fortunately on to a handy roof-top. Similarly, THE MAGIC CITY is a series of dream-fantasies based firmly on the conditions of Philip's life. He has built the city out of anything that comes to hand. The citizens whom he finds terrorized by the Giant Sloth turn out to be his Halma men; the city is saved by Cæsar, who marches his forces out of *De Bello Gallico* to attack the barbarians who have already escaped from its pages; the animals are ark-animals, under Mr Noah's rule. As for the city itself, Mr Perrin, the carpenter, says:

> 'All the cities and things you ever built is in this country. I don't know how it's managed, no more'n what you do. But so it is. And as you made 'em, you've the right to come to them—if you can get there. And you have got there. It isn't every one has the luck, I'm told. Well, then, you made the cities, but you made 'em out of what other folks had made, things like bricks and chessmen and books and candlesticks and dominoes and brass basins and every sort of kind of thing. An' all the people who helped to make all them things you used to build with, they're all here too. D'you see? *Making's* the thing. If it was no more than the lad that turned the handle of the grindstone to sharp the knife that carved a bit of a cabinet or what not, or a child that picked a teazle to finish a bit of the cloth that's glued on to the bottom of a chessman—they're all here. They're what's called the population of your cities.'
>
> E. Nesbit. THE MAGIC CITY (Benn, 1910) pp. 105–6.

Beyond the magic happenings, too, there is the feeling of human relations—Philip's growing friendship with Lucy, his advances towards the step-brother he so strongly resented; there is a feeling of growing up, of stretching, of youthful experience. Gay and rollicking though the book is, there is enough wisdom in it to fill out hundreds of wishy-washy family stories of today.

The same sturdy realism anchors to the earth the tugging, sky-bound stories about Mary Poppins by P. L. Travers. Mary Poppins occupies in the Banks family the place filled in Miss Nesbit's books by the Mouldiwarp, the Psammead and the Phœnix. Like them, she is crusty, unpredictable and fond of speaking her mind. Magic is something she is obliged to perform and which she feels will do her charges no good. But she cannot help being magic, for she is an elemental. Sun and stars defer to her at a sky-fête; she is an old friend of the Greek gods; she appears out of the sky on a kite-string; she orders the elements and promotes the unlikely everywhere. That is one side of her. The other side is the Nannie, with her expressive sniff, her despotic commands, her love of the last word.

These lively stories take you into a madder, more completely fantastic world than the world of E. Nesbit, though with the same homely domestic foundation. There is *Bad Wednesday,* a terrifying piece, when Jane is whisked into the world of a Royal Doulton bowl; there is *Mrs Lark's Andrew,* a splendid piece of nonsense about a respectable dog and a mongrel; there is *The Marble Boy,* an incident in the park which combines sharp social comedy with a deep apprehension of the antique; there is the vivid *Hallowe'en,* where comic characters and natural objects all obey Mary Poppins as, with her Dutch doll hair and her immovable, bourgeois hat, she foots it through the night. She is always respectable. When, in *Peppermint Horses,* she whirls the children up into the sky, she is still very much the Nannie:

> 'I'll race you to the oak tree, Jane!' cried Michael, as she trotted up.
> 'Quietly, please! No horseplay, Michael! Put your hats straight and follow me!'
> Mary Poppins, on her parrot umbrella, rode past them at a canter. Neatly and primly, as though she were in a rocking chair, she sat on the black silk folds. In her hand she held two leading strings attached to the Twins' pink sticks.
> P. L. Travers. MARY POPPINS OPENS THE DOOR (Peter Davies, 1944) pp. 124–5.

These stories depend mainly on the character of this strange personage, and because her character is so important, Mary Shepard's illustrations are of the first importance too, for they present Mary Poppins to us visually in a way that establishes her for ever. It is because of Mary Poppins, because she is as she is, that these books are at once gay and serious, superbly entertaining, but always probing into depths of mystery and poetry.

This deeper meaning is essential in fantasy. For the characters involved, there is no need for very deep thought. They can enjoy the pleasure of realizing their dearest wishes, only occasionally speculating about their origin. Sometimes (as in E. Nesbit's stories) they can be changed a little, can learn a little from their adventures, as they miraculously travel the world, change their shape, or exploit the power of a button, a lamp-post or a pencil. But the reader who vicariously enjoys these delights should expect something more. The fantasy should exercise his imagination. For the characters in the story there is little time for Why and How. Questions are blown away as they rush from one adventure to another. But the reader can and should ask How and Why. He should be left with a sense of expansion, as if he himself had been flying on a magic carpet and breathing an air more rarefied than his accustomed oxygen, a world which he wants to know more about. Then, and only then, has the fantasy fulfilled its purpose.

Drawing by Mary Shepard for
P. L. Travers's MARY POPPINS OPENS
THE DOOR (Collins)

Reading List

Fantasy starting in everyday life

*Baker, Margaret J. NONSENSE! SAID THE TORTOISE 1949, HOMER SEES THE
    QUEEN 1956, HOMER GOES TO STRATFORD 1958. *Brockhampton.*
    Illustrated by Terence Freeman. (See also p. 376.)

Bourne, Holly. PERIWINKLE. *Heinemann* 1959. Illustrated by the author. Two
    children take home a mermaid from a fish-shop, with amusing consequences.

*Brown, Palmer. BEYOND THE PAW-PAW TREES (1954 U.S.A.) 1956, THE
    SILVER NUTMEG (1956 U.S.A.) 1957. *Methuen.* Illustrated by the author.

*Buchan, John. THE MAGIC WALKING-STICK. *Bodley Head* 1932.

Forester, C. S. POO-POO AND THE DRAGONS. *Michael Joseph* 1942. Illustrated
    by Robert Lawson. Ordinary family copes with two large, affectionate dragons.

*Guthrie, Kathleen. THE MAGIC BUTTON. *Brockhampton* 1959. Illustrated by the author. (See also p. 368.)

*Harrison, Ada. THE DOUBLING ROD. *Bodley Head* 1957. Illustrated by Robert Austin.

Hopp, Zinken. THE MAGIC CHALK (1948 Norway). *Ward* 1960. Illustrated by Gian Berto Vannio. Inspired nonsense, for all ages from about six. Travels of Jon and his companion Sofus (whom he has drawn).

Howard, Jean. THE THIRTEENTH IS MAGIC (1950 U.S.A.). *World's Work* 1958. Illustrated by Adrienne Adams. Boy and girl in New York flat have adventures with an enchanted pencil.

Lang, E. H. THE CURIOUS ADVENTURES OF TABBY. *Faber* 1956. Illustrated by Shirley Hughes. Small girl has all her most extraordinary wishes granted.

*McNeill, Janet. MY FRIEND SPECS MCCANN 1955, SPECS FORTISSIMO 1958. *Faber.* Illustrated by Rowland Friers.

*Mayne, William. THE BLUE BOAT 1957, illustrated by Geraldine Spence. A GRASS ROPE 1957, illustrated by Lynton Lamb. *O.U.P.*

*Nesbit, E. FIVE CHILDREN AND IT (see Chap. 7).

Nesbit, E. THE PHOENIX AND THE CARPET (1904) 1956, THE MAGIC CITY 1910 *Benn.* Illustrated by H. R. Millar.

*Norton, Mary. THE BORROWERS, etc. (see Chap. 6).

*Prøysen, Alf. LITTLE OLD MRS PEPPERPOT (1957 Sweden) 1959, MRS PEPPERPOT AGAIN (1958 Sweden) 1960. *Hutchinson.* Translated by Marianne Helweg. Illustrated by Björn Berg. (See also p. 378.)

*Reid, Meta Mayne. CARRIGMORE CASTLE 1954, TIFFANY AND THE SWALLOW RHYME 1956, THE CUCKOO AT COOLNEAN 1956, STRANGERS AT CARRIGMORE 1958. *Faber.* Illustrated by Richard Kennedy. (See also p. 337.)

Ropner, Pamela. THE GOLDEN IMPALA. *Hart-Davis* 1957. Illustrated by Ralph Thompson. African adventure, with a legendary animal helping a girl.

Severn, David. FOXY-BOY. *Bodley Head* 1959. Illustrated by Lynton Lamb. Child on lonely visit to country aunts makes friends with a boy of the wilds.

*Sisson, Rosemary Anne. THE IMPRACTICAL CHIMNEY-SWEEP. *Macmillan* 1956. Illustrated by Fritz Wagner.

*Storr, Catherine. MARIANNE DREAMS. *Faber* 1958. Illustrated by Marjorie-Anne Watts.

*Todd, Barbara Euphan. WORZEL GUMMIDGE (1936). *Hollis & Carter* (1943) 1946. *Penguin* (Puffin Story Books) (1941) 1946. Illustrated by Elizabeth Alldridge.

Todd, Barbara Euphan. WORZEL GUMMIDGE AGAIN (1937). *Penguin* (Puffin Story Books) 1949. Illustrated by Will Nickless.

Todd, Barbara Euphan. MORE ABOUT WORZEL GUMMIDGE (1938) 1951, WORZEL GUMMIDGE AND SAUCY NANCY 1947, illustrated by John Harwood. WORZEL GUMMIDGE TAKES A HOLIDAY 1949, illustrated by Will Nickless. EARTHY MANGOLD AND WORZEL GUMMIDGE 1949, illustrated by Jill Crockford. *Hollis & Carter.*

Todd, Barbara Euphan. WORZEL GUMMIDGE AND THE RAILWAY SCARECROWS 1955, WORZEL GUMMIDGE AT THE CIRCUS 1956, WORZEL GUMMIDGE AND THE TREASURE SHIP 1958, *Evans.* Illustrated by Jill Crockford.

*Travers, P. L. MARY POPPINS 1934, MARY POPPINS COMES BACK 1935, MARY POPPINS OPENS THE DOOR 1944, MARY POPPINS IN THE PARK 1952. *Collins* (formerly *Peter Davies*). Illustrated by Mary Shepard.

Ward, Patricia. THE SILVER PENCIL. *Collins* 1959. Illustrated by Nicole Hornby. Pencil writes messages which lead Anne to adventure.

*Whistler, Theresa. THE RIVER BOY. *Hart-Davis* 1955. Illustrated by the author.

White, T. H. MISTRESS MASHAM'S REPOSE. *Cape* 1947. Adult novel, for any imaginative child of twelve or over. Girl living at Stowe discovers descendants of Lilliputians on island in lake. Brilliant fantasy anchored by precise detail.

Drawing by Björn Berg for Alf Prøysen's MRS PEPPERPOT AGAIN (Hutchinson)

Chapter 9 | *Climates of Humour*

The preamble to the Penguin edition of THE MAGIC PUDDING, a humorous tale by Norman Lindsay, ends with the recommendation: 'For ages from eight to eighty, allowing for brief blind periods now and again in between.' It is these blind periods (brief, perhaps, but numerous) which make it difficult to write specifically humorous books for children. I doubt whether many small children really recognize humour as such at all. To do so, they need the experience to sort out the incongruous from the congruous, the likely from the unlikely; and, for them, the distinction hardly exists. They will almost always accept ALICE IN WONDERLAND, for instance, as serious fantasy. Alice's rapid changes in size, the behaviour of the sheep in the wool shop or the flutterings of the White Queen, seem to them exciting and odd rather than laughable.

Perhaps an appreciation of humour begins, most usually, at seven or eight, with practical jokes and the more innocent types of coarseness. This is the period when THE MAGIC PUDDING, or Coppard's PINK FURNITURE, or William Pène du Bois's gay fancies, or Professor Branestawm's nightmarish adventures come into their own; the period when children will read and enjoy comic verse of all shades of wit from Eliot's PRACTICAL CATS to Ian Serraillier's ballads or the ingenious rhymes of Eleanor Farjeon—not necessarily finding their full measure, but enjoying the smiles they provoke.

Children of later school age do not so often look for funny books. Humour *in* stories suits them better. Humour in school stories (though by this time Billy Bunter is a bit of a bore); humour in a sophisticated family idiom, as in Elizabeth Enright's stories about the Melendys, or in William Mayne's choir-school tales; humour in fairy-tale, when the ordinary world is turned upside-down. All kinds of humour by the way, but not humour for its own sake.

This is hardly a 'blind period'. It is a period of change, when the young spontaneous laugh is less frequent than it was before. The capacity for enjoying humour and nonsense will return, and later, too, will come the real blind spots, which are the result of character rather than of age. For adults can, and very often do, laugh at the humour in children's stories (and not only in a retrospective way), but it may be doubted whether children are ever well served by truly adult humour—that is, by humour deliberately keyed to adults.

I do not mean that children will not laugh at humorous books written for adults. They will, of course. They delight in the geometrical absurdities of Leacock about the landlady's bed and her catering, or in the difficulties Bertie Wooster has with the social niceties. They enjoy the Edwardian slapstick of THREE MEN IN A BOAT. But these are forms of humour which belong to a Peter Pan world, where the regular and the orthodox are turned upside-down and destructiveness has a special licence. Adults and children happily meet here and find something they both need, and this may be the reason why so many fathers (perhaps fewer mothers) can still pick up Richmal Crompton's *William* books and find pleasure in them.

For children, though, humour *must* be simple and spontaneous. A manufactured, elaborate joke will not do. I do not mean by this that jokes for children have to be short. On the contrary, a child can wear a joke a long time without getting bored (as parents know only too well), so long as it is a lively and natural one. THE MAGIC PUDDING, which I have already mentioned, is a case in point. This is a splendid, racy, jovial Australian story which is, in fact, one simple expanded joke. Bunyip Bluegum, travelling for pleasure, joins up with Bill Barnacle the sailor and Sam Sawnoff, the penguin, who have already as their companion Albert, a magic, self-perpetuating pudding. Albert is coveted by a Possum and a Wombat, whose plots and stratagems lead them finally into court in the backblocks town of Tooraloo—after which the three friends build a house in a tree, with a paddock for Albert, and settle down to a life of peace and gastronomic bliss. The one point—the to-ing and fro-ing of the Puddin' —is magnificently varied, in a story that moves quick and sharp as the crack of a stockwhip, never overdoing a detail, never missing a chance for one more absurd variation on the theme. It is the simplicity that does the trick.

Take, for instance, our first glimpse of the Puddin':

Bunyip Bluegum was too much of a gentleman to invite himself to lunch, but he said carelessly, 'Am I right in supposing that there are onions in this pudding?'

Before Bill could reply, a thick, angry voice came out of the pudding, saying—

'Onions, bunions, cows and crabs,
Whiskers, wheels and hansom cabs,
Beef and bottles, beer and bones,
Give him a feed and end his groans.'

'Albert, Albert,' said Bill to the Puddin', 'where's your manners?'

'Where's yours?' said the Puddin' rudely, 'guzzling away there, and never so much as offering this stranger a slice.'

'There you are,' said Bill. 'There's nothing this Puddin' enjoys more than offering slices of himself to strangers.'

Norman Lindsay. THE MAGIC PUDDING (Penguin, 1957) p. 15.

One word too many, and the joke might become tedious; but it never does.

Drawing by Norman Lindsay for his THE MAGIC PUDDING (Angus & Robertson)

This wonderful little story has in it both the types of humour that particularly appeal to children—the humour of situation (horse-play and accident) and verbal wit. The various stratagems of pudding-thieves and pudding-owners, illustrated in rollicking style

are introduced by absurd touches. When the friends come upon
the thieves disguised by curious headgear, the Possum stumps
them by remarking 'No removing people's hats. Removing hats is
larceny, and you'll get six months for it.' Bunyip Bluegum's solution
is to stand to attention and strike up God Save the King, whereupon
the crooks are revealed. In the other vein, there are conversations
in the height of lunatic vigour, like the one between Bill Barnacle
and Henderson Hedgehog the deaf Horticulturist:

> 'Have you seen a SINGED POSSUM?' roared Bill.
> 'To be sure,' said Henderson, 'but the turnips are backward.'
> 'Turnips be stewed,' yelled Bill in such a tremendous voice that
> he blew his own hat off. 'HAVE YOU SEEN A SINGED POSSUM?'
> 'Good season for wattle blossom,' said Henderson. 'Well, yes,
> but a very poor season for carrots.'
> 'A man might as well talk to a carrot as try an' get some sense out
> of this runt of a feller,' said Bill, disgusted. 'Come and see if we
> can't find someone that it won't bust a man's vocal chords gettin'
> information out of.'
> Ibid., pp. 49–50.

Or, in a different idiom, the Kookaburra's rude come-back to the
staring sailor, 'all I can say is that if yer don't take yer dial outer the
road I'll bloomin' well take an' bounce a gibber off yer crust'.

There are echoes of ALICE IN WONDERLAND all through this
book, but its raw, violent, bustlingly energetic humour is unique.
In the same vein, and coming from an equally rollicking and energetic writer, are Eric Linklater's two adventure stories for children,
THE PIRATES IN THE DEEP GREEN SEA and THE WIND ON THE
MOON. Linklater is a superb writer and his greatest virtue is that he
never writes down to children. Certainly his subjects are chosen to
suit them. THE PIRATES IN THE DEEP GREEN SEA is a phantasma-
goria of cutlasses, treasure-chests and talking octopuses which has
clearly grown out of bedtime stories, and in THE WIND ON THE
MOON the hilarious incidents arise from the one comic circumstance
of two sisters unexpectedly turning into kangaroos. But if the subjects
of his adult novels, like POET'S PUB or THE MERRY MUSE, are more
sophisticated, the technique is the same in all Linklater's books—
the bubbling up of nonsense, the rollicking slapstick, and the verbal

wit to tempt the discriminating child—like the description of Davy Jones's Locker, where:

> Above the throne two mermaids had arranged some branches of coral in the handsomest style, and now, below the coral, they were hanging a long broad ribbon of pale blue on which, in darker letters, was written:

FLOREAT ETONA

> And in smaller letters below the motto—for the benefit of sailors who had forgotten their Latin—was the English translation: *Let Eton flourish.*

Eric Linklater. THE PIRATES IN THE DEEP GREEN SEA (Macmillan, 1949) p. 235.

Adult writers who write one or two children's books for special occasions are rarely as generous with their skill as Linklater has been. The answer is, I imagine, that he has kept the natural love of a good joke in which adults and children can meet as equals (though they rarely do).

The success of these comedies for children comes partly from their closeness to real life. A child can readily imagine himself under the sea with Hugh and Tim without, as it were, taking a step out of his own backyard, and yet there is a fantastic twist that provokes laughter. William Pène du Bois, similarly, strikes humour out of the familiar, but turns it with a swift movement into the unlikely and the surprising, in THE GREAT GEPPY, the story of a horse-detective, and his magnificent travelogue THE 21 BALLOONS, which tells of the adventures of Professor William Waterman Sherman on the island of Krakatoa. Much of the humour in this book derives from absurd scientific inventions, like the labour-saving house of the M's (which, after nearly twenty years has come a good deal nearer to reality) or the super-ingenious aerial merry-go-round which the Professor so much enjoys.

The mechanical erudition of small boys is flattered by this book, and no less by Norman Hunter's THE INCREDIBLE ADVENTURES OF PROFESSOR BRANESTAWM, which is illustrated, appropriately, by Heath Robinson. The humour here is based entirely on physical things, on absurd machines or phenomenal absence of mind (always a popular subject). There is the nightmarish story, *The Wild*

Waste Paper, with its echo of M. R. James; there is the wry logic of *The Too-Many Professors*, when the Professor comments on his invention to bring pictured things to life:

> 'It is rather a pity,' said the Professor, spraying a picture of a box of chocolates to life, 'that it costs more to make the liquid for doing this than it would cost to buy the things.'
> Norman Hunter. THE INCREDIBLE ADVENTURES OF PROFESSOR BRANESTAWM (Penguin, 1946) p. 123.

and there is the almost brutal slapstick of *Pancake Day at Great Pagwell:*

> The Professor struggled out of his pancake just in time for another one to drop over him. Two pancakes were on the clock, four were draped over the light. The Mayor was eating his way through a complete set of pancakes of varying sizes that had fallen in front of him. The four firemen put their helmets on and brandished their axes, but only succeeded in smashing two cups, one saucer and the sugar basin. Mrs. Flittersnoop put her head gingerly out from under the table and was immediately gummed to the carpet by a three-foot pancake two inches thick that had just shot out. Ibid., pp. 189–90.

Each story enshrines one piece of absurdity, expanded but never overdone, provoking laughter, and, as well, reaching down to the creative energy of schoolboys. Jay Williams and Raymond Abrashkin take the idea of absurd scientific invention as far as possible in two light-hearted stories, DANNY DUNN AND THE ANTI-GRAVITY PAINT and THE HOMEWORK MACHINE. Simple and entertaining though they are, these stories are not merely farce. The children who so much enjoy feeding their school problems to a computer, in the second story, are very well drawn, and this makes their difficulties credible and amusing. Besides, there is an implied comment on the dangerous side of automation that gives the book ballast. Their chief purpose, all the same, is to promote fun and laughter over ordinary things going wrong.

This is the kind of humour which is often found mixed with other elements in the pages of the Jennings stories. I am doubtful whether, in fact, books are ever written with the *sole* intention of making children laugh; but in so far as they are, they do this, almost always, through the element of fantasy. There is, in other words, another world lurking behind the laughter, a world where what seems funny here may in fact be perfectly serious and logical there. Leila Berg's stories about Chunky, besides showing brilliantly the bustling activity of comical small boys, has a touch of this other-worldliness. So has A. E. Coppard's PINK FURNITURE, to an even more marked degree. The story of Toby Tottel's quest is in the finest tradition of meaningful nonsense:

> Then he went on, and on and on he went until he came to the house of the Baldheaded Woman who was renowned for her surpassing wisdom. But she was absent now; only her son was left at home, and his name was Stinker. It was a good name for him. He was a lanky man, with long black gloves and a very high beaver hat, and he always walked backwards and never saw anybody coming. Whenever it rained his boots became dusty, and in times of drought he carried an open umbrella and got wet as a herring.
> A. E. Coppard. PINK FURNITURE (Cape, 1930) p. 28.

The books I have discussed so far have been perfectly understandable in terms of our own world, and have made relatively little demand on the imagination. But nonsense of this kind, of the Edward Lear kind, is mysterious. It is poetry first, humour afterwards. It can carry a child out of himself or it can let him down with a bump, if he resists it with a matter-of-fact attitude.

Nonsense can, of course, be simple and easy. For children of five or so there are Donald Bisset's enchanting bits of idiocy, ANYTIME STORIES and SOMETIME STORIES, with stories where pencils talk and even a silence can have an existence. Sheer absurdity is only valid when the writer is completely committed to it, as Rowland Emett so obviously is in his railway fantasies, ANTHONY AND ANTIMACASSAR and NELLIE COME HOME. This is absurdity verbal and visible. A child can take in his stride a sentence like this: 'The last thing Anthony saw as they left the Branch Line was the Woodchopper chopping the steam into infinitesimal pieces in a fit of amazement and despair.' It is to be enjoyed slowly, like the accompanying drawing, with its shapely but fantastic detail.

There is no age limit for nonsense, and it is possible for anyone to enjoy the Norwegian tale, THE SINGING TOWN by Thorbjørn

Egner, about the town of Kardemomma, and a band of comic-opera thieves who learn to be good citizens.

I am always a little surprised when foreign humour translates and transplants well, but this vividly coloured tale, with its interspersed songs, its world of eccentric tram-cars and odd people, has been warmly welcomed by English children. Tove Jansson and her Finnish books about the Moomins have, perhaps, a smaller and more select band of admirers. Here we have something very subtle, nonsense stories full of melancholy wisdom and terror, neither wholly fantasy nor wholly humour. It is impossible not to compare these stories with the work of Edward Lear and Lewis Carroll. Who would not see cousinly resemblances between the Hattifatteners and the Dong with a Luminous Nose, or between the Moomin parents and Mr and Mrs Discobolos, or between Snufkin and some of Lewis Carroll's touching small animals? The resemblance in each case is not one of feature or idiom; it lies in the mature atmosphere of the stories, the sunny sky of comedy in which there is always drifting a distant cloud of sadness and unease.

The Moomins are presented by their creator in drawings which also have this strange, melancholy feeling. They look, these endearing little animals, like hippopotamuses at the head end (but lively, twinkling hippopotamuses) and they are neatly porcine in body. The Moomins who concern us live in a lonely valley with various peculiar friends—the Snork Maiden, flapping her long eyelashes, who comes of Moomin stock; lively, restless Snufkin, son of an old family friend; the Hemulen, moody and stamp-collecting, who comes to stay and never leaves. Whether these creatures are pure inventions or whether they are based on folk lore figures I do not know. In any case, they are extremely real to me, for their personalities have been cleverly established by what they say and what they do. And in the world they live in there is plenty doing. In COMET IN MOOMINLAND there is danger not only from outer space but also from flood and drought. In MOOMINSUMMER MADNESS the peaceful valley is disturbed by a volcanic eruption which brings an earthquake and a tidal wave. In FINN FAMILY MOOMINTROLL the finding of a Hobgoblin's magic hat precipitates events in which natural and supernatural are both represented. Indeed, the supernatural, or the feeling of it, is never far from this wide, tundra landscape. MOOMINLAND MIDWINTER, perhaps the oddest and most enchanting of all the books, is, simply, a poem to winter, and the poetry is never swamped by the absurd things that happen to Moomintroll when he wakes half-way through hibernation.

Certainly there is humour in these stories, but I doubt whether reviewers or publishers are right in classifying them as 'humorous'. There is, to be sure, the continuous, muted, delightful humour of odd creatures doing ordinary everyday things. Sniff and Moomintroll looking through the Observatory telescope in the Lonely Mountains, respectfully listening to the scientists as they explain the comet; Moominmamma making a cake to welcome her son back from a dangerous adventure; the Snork Maiden adjusting her hair before thanking Moomintroll for rescuing her from the poisonous bush Angostura; Moominpappa, like any mildly arrogant family man, reading extracts from his memoirs to a politely inattentive family.

There is the humour of idiosyncrasy, in the character of the Hemulen aunt, who, in EXPLOITS OF MOOMINPAPPA, is such a nuisance to the roving young men, and who suggests as suitable entertainment for them 'a little sock-darning contest' or 'a nice history quiz', or, in the same book, there is the Carrollian note of parody in Moominpappa's conversation with a chance-met ghost:

The room had suddenly grown cold with an icy draught, and the ghost sneezed.

I don't know how you'd have felt, but for my part I immediately lost much of my respect. So I crawled out from under the bed and said: 'Cold night, sir!'

'Yes,' replied the ghost in an annoyed tone. 'A bleak night of fate resounding with the horrible wails of the phantoms of the gorge!'

'What can I do for you?' I asked politely.

'On a night of fate like this,' the ghost continued stubbornly, 'the forgotten bones are rattling on the silent beach!'

'Whose bones?' I asked (still very politely).

'The *forgotten* bones,' said the ghost. 'Pale horror grins over the damned island! Mortal, beware!' The ghost uncurled, gave me a terrible look and floated back towards the half-open door. The back of his head met the door-jamb with a resounding bang.

'Oop!' said the ghost.

I didn't hide my delight.

With a last hiss the ghost glided downstairs and out into the moonlight. Down on the ground he turned and bade me farewell with three horrible laughs.

Tove Jansson. THE EXPLOITS OF MOOMINPAPPA (Benn, 1952) pp. 112–14.

But all this is humour that belongs to no particular age, and to some ages it will not really seem to be humour. Tove Jansson has done as Lewis Carroll and Lear did. She has corkscrewed her way down into a world of childhood where the unlikely is readily accepted, where incongruity seems entirely natural and at the same time can be comic. But she has kept her adult wits about her, so that we are always aware of shape and logic and order in an unusual world. As with ALICE IN WONDERLAND, these Moomin books are folk lore and fantasy to young children, humour to older boys and girls, and poetry to all. For what binds the elements of nonsense, absurdity, satire and wit together is an underlying note of seriousness, of speculation, an implication of the uncertainty of human wishes and human knowledge. Most compelling of all Tove Jansson's creatures, to me, are the Hattifatteners, those wraith-like people who, like the lemmings, are governed by migratory compulsions. Moominpappa describes them thus:

In that moment I caught sight of a whole flotilla of small ships putting out to sea. Light as butterflies they went gliding away over their own reflections. All were manned by a silent crew: little grey-white beings huddling close together and staring out towards the horizon.

'Hattifatteners,' Hodgkins said.

'Hattifatteners!' I whispered excitedly. 'Putting out on their endless voyages . . .'

'Mind you don't touch them if there's a thunderstorm about,' said Hodgkins. 'Makes them electric. Sting like nettles.'

Ibid., pp. 62–3.

Put beside this extract any of the poems of Edward Lear, with their haunting refrain of vanishing, loss, plaintive longing (*The Courtship of the Yonghy-Bonghy-Bò*, or *Calico Pie*, or most of all, *The Dong with a Luminous Nose*) and you can see the same deep humour of the heart, the humour of poetry which knows no geographical limits nor age limits either.

Lewis Carroll, explaining his portmanteau word 'frumious' in *Jabberwocky*, ended like this:

If your thoughts incline ever so little towards 'fuming', you will say 'fuming-furious'; if they turn, by even a hair's-breadth, towards 'furious', you will say 'furious-fuming'; but if you have that rarest of gifts, a perfectly balanced mind, you will say 'frumious'. Lewis Carroll. THE HUNTING OF THE SNARK (Zodiac Books, 1948) Preface, vii.

A perfectly balanced mind. Yes, it is this above all that is needed in a true nonsense book, a book that is going to remain the treasure and activating possession of child and adult alike. A mind balanced between the spontaneous, irrational, exploratory laughter of a child, and the poetically irrational, energetic, appraising laughter of a well-stored older mind. Let us see how far Lewis Carroll has satisfied both these sections of the thinking, laughing public.

Tragedy may be the obverse side of humour, and it may therefore be natural to find in the realm of nonsense a melancholy belonging properly to it. But melancholy, sometimes tilting into apprehension, is also to be expected in Lewis Carroll's works, as in Lear's, because of their temperaments. To both of them, nonsense provided an escape, a world of fantasy in which they could forget that they were not entirely at ease in their own world. In ALICE IN WONDERLAND and THROUGH THE LOOKING-GLASS Carroll celebrates the wonder of childhood as he saw it, from his own needs. Alice he described* as 'loving and gentle, loving as a dog and gentle as a fawn; courteous—courteous to *all*, high or low, grand or grotesque, king or caterpillar; trustful, curious—wildly curious with the eager enjoyment of life that comes only in the happy hours of childhood.' But if he was trying in these two books to satisfy a child's curiosity and spontaneous love of life, he put into them, too, his own doubts, his fears and nightmares, and something of the barbarity of childhood as it survived in himself. Alice as he saw her gives us one facet of childhood, but there are others. There is the near-cruelty of the Pig and Pepper chapter in ALICE; there is the devastating truth of remarks like those of the Gnat in the sequel:

*From an article in *The Theatre*, April 1887, quoted in Puffin edition of THROUGH THE LOOKING-GLASS, 1948, p. 13.

'Crawling at your feet,' said the Gnat (Alice drew her feet back in some alarm), 'you may observe a Bread-and-Butterfly. Its wings are thin slices of Bread-and-butter, its body is a crust, and its head is a lump of sugar.'

'And what does *it* live on?'

'Weak tea with cream in it.'

A new difficulty came into Alice's head. 'Supposing it couldn't find any?' she suggested.

'Then it would die, of course.'

'But that must happen very often,' Alice remarked thoughtfully.

'It always happens,' said the Gnat.

Lewis Carroll. THROUGH THE LOOKING-GLASS (Penguin, 1948) pp. 69–70.

Obviously, these are books which have a special meaning for different ages. Alice's character, which young people take for granted, can seem, when they are older, rather tiresome and priggish; and perhaps she is never (except for Carroll himself) more to anyone than a centre round which the delightful and peculiar creatures can revolve. My own memory of the two books from my childhood is one of very mixed pleasure. I enjoyed the puns and nonsense verses, but I can remember more vividly the pathetic scenes, and particularly the upsetting effect Bill the lizard had on me, when he was hurled from the rabbit's roof by a giant Alice and when he sat helpless and mortified in the jury box, trying to write with his finger on his slate because Alice had confiscated his squeaking pencil. It was the helplessness of childhood I noticed then, not the sombre, crazy philosophy of the White Queen and the Mad Hatter, or the energetic proliferation of jokes and puns.

Anyone can make jokes, but nobody can write another ALICE IN WONDERLAND. I feel this all the more after reading the gallant attempt of Yates Wilson to do just that, in MORE ALICE. It is clearer to me than ever that Lewis Carroll was not trying to be funny and that he could only be funny because he was not trying. Yates Wilson is held up by his publishers as a writer who can echo 'the master of pure nonsense—Lewis Carroll.' But Lewis Carroll was no master of pure nonsense. His books are not *pure* nonsense, nor were they intended to be so. Yates Wilson, on the other hand, has produced a crazy procession of creatures with no substance behind them,

Drawing by Yates Wilson for his MORE ALICE (Boardman)

though his drawings are deliberately reminiscent of Tenniel. The
concord of thought and laughter in ALICE is regrettably absent.
For instance, when Ethelred is arming for battle, his courtiers
answer his call for his accoutrements of battle with loud cries
about his 'ACCOUTRITHINGUMMIES.'

This rather hoary joke is the kind which adults think children
enjoy, though I doubt if they often do. In any case, Carroll could
never have made it, for long words always have their rights in his
books; they are written on the assumption that the reader will either
recognize long words or at least respect them if they are unknown.
Many of the jokes in this latter-day ALICE are good, but they are
none of them natives of Carroll's world. You can see this clearly if

you compare the description of Ethelred arming for battle with Carroll's similar scene. Here is Wilson:

> Alice crept into a corner to watch proceedings.
>
> 'I can't wear *that* shirt in battle,' Ethelred was roaring. 'I wouldn't be seen dead in it—hand me that flour-bag instead—that's it—now my spats.'
>
> 'HIS SPATS!' everyone chorused. 'Not *those*,' as a well-meaning young lobster was rushing towards the King with a string of fish. 'SPATS! not SPRATS!'
>
> 'Help me on with my hot water bottle!' yelled Ethelred.
>
> 'I wonder why he wants *that*?' Alice thought.
>
> 'In case the field needs airing,' said Ethelred as though he had heard her. 'Now my fire-irons!' he roared, '*and* my bellows, idiot—now my morning paper in case we find some fish and chips—that's it! Now my armour. Not *that* way—here, give it to me—*ouch*! this armour hasn't been warmed—now my visor—not *that* way, fool, I haven't got eyes in the *back* of my head—oh *you*! That's more like it . . .'
>
> Suddenly there was a silence and a stillness, broken only by Ethelred's surprised cry, 'I'm *ready*!'
>
> 'He's ready!' yelled everyone.
>
> There was a mad dash for the door and in a moment the room was empty and the noise of the stampede faded on the afternoon air.
>
> Yates Wilson. MORE ALICE (Boardman, 1959) pp. 60–2.

This is pantomime humour. All the directions are here for the clowning and the by-play; nothing is left to the imagination. If the modern idiom, and the occasional vulgar adverbs and verbs, did not put this very far from Carroll, the technique of the humour would do so, for Carroll's account is infinitely reserved, depending on hints and suggestions:

> 'Of course you agree to have a battle?' Tweedledum said in a calmer tone.
>
> 'I suppose so,' the other sulkily replied, as he crawled out of the umbrella: 'only *she* must help us to dress up, you know.'
>
> So the two brothers went off hand-in-hand into the wood, and returned in a minute with their arms full of things—such as bol-

sters, blankets, hearth-rugs, table-cloths, dish-covers and coal-scuttles. 'I hope you're a good hand at pinning and tying strings?' Tweedledum remarked. 'Every one of these things has got to go on, somehow or other.'

Alice said afterwards she had never seen such a fuss made about anything in all her life—the way those two bustled about—and the quantity of things they put on—and the trouble they gave her in tying strings and fastening buttons—'Really, they'll be more like bundles of old clothes than anything else, by the time they're ready!' she said to herself, as she arranged a bolster round the neck of Tweedledee, 'to keep his head from being cut off', as he said.

'You know,' he added very gravely, 'it's one of the most serious things that can possibly happen to one in a battle—to get one's head cut off.'

Op. cit., pp. 89-90.

Wilson's numerous exclamation marks are of no more consequence than his loud verbs—'he roared', 'he yelled', and all the rest; they are signs of weakness, and their absence in the lunatic paragraphs of Carroll is a matter for thankfulness; for, above all, Carroll was a dignified writer. He never pestered his readers.

I would put THE MAGIC PUDDING on a level with ALICE in its lively inventiveness; and for the poetry of oddity, A. E. Coppard makes as strong an impact on me. But ultimately anyone who tries to imitate Carroll has to reckon with his style, and this is inimitable. His is the tongue of the university man, scholarly, urbane, a little diffident, absolutely uncondescending but conscious of superiority, repressed but generous. It belongs to the Establishment, to a particular way of life which is now part of history.

In some ways it is a bad thing that these two books have the air of the Establishment round them. Not that we would want to do without the gravity and stylishness of ALICE simply because people nowadays do not live as the author had lived; but because the fact of their special flavour has given rise to an absurd amount of snobbery about the books. They are spoken of with reverence; two words quoted from them, by a dignitary of the church or state, bring roars of sycophantic laughter; they may not be criticized. All this is absurd. No book is as good as this. And the result of this persistent adulation is that children nowadays either read ALICE in the potted form in which she appears in comic papers, or they read her with the adjurations of their parents ringing in their ears and feel let down when they have finished (if, indeed, they ever do finish). In many middle-class circles it is as important to know ALICE as it is to use the word napkin and not the word serviette; but this intellectual snobbery cuts the ground from under Carroll's feet, for it makes the books tiresome and gives them an artificial importance. Let us take ALICE down and dust her off and consider her critically and then give her to our children without any sermons. Let us not tell them they will be amused, or that this is a book they must like or be for ever beyond the pale. Let them discover it for themselves. They will discover it, in their own time, and re-discover it many times in the rest of their lives.

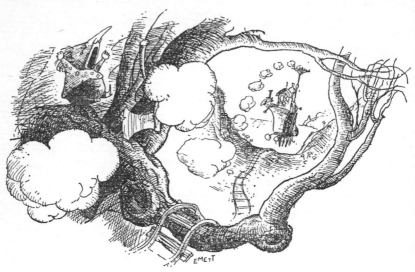

Drawing by Rowland Emett for his ANTHONY AND ANTIMACASSAR (Faber)

Reading List

*Berg, Leila. THE ADVENTURES OF CHUNKY. *O.U.P.* (1950) 1958. Illustrated by George Downs.

Berg, Leila. TRUST CHUNKY. *Brockhampton* 1954. Illustrated by Peggy Fortnum.

*Bisset, Donald. ANYTIME STORIES 1954, SOMETIME STORIES 1957. *Faber.* Illustrated by the author. (See also p. 367.)

*Bois, W. Pène du. THE GREAT GEPPY (1940 U.S.A.) 1942, THE 21 BALLOONS (1947 U.S.A.) 1949. *Robert Hale.* Illustrated by the author.

*Carroll, Lewis. ALICE IN WONDERLAND (1865), THROUGH THE LOOKING-GLASS (1872). Continuously in print in various editions, e.g. *Dent* (Children's Illustrated Classics) 1954, with original illustrations by John Tenniel.

*Coppard, A. E. PINK FURNITURE. *Cape* 1930. Illustrated by Nancy Bankart Gurney.

*Crompton, Richmal. JUST WILLIAM. *Newnes* 1922. Numerous other titles, latest WILLIAM'S TELEVISION SHOW, 1958. Illustrated by Thomas Henry.

*Egner, Thorbjørn. THE SINGING TOWN (1951 Sweden). *Methuen* 1959. Translated by Evelyn Ramsden, verses translated by Leila Berg. Illustrated by the author.

*Emett, Rowland and Mary. ANTHONY AND ANTIMACASSAR 1943, NELLIE COME HOME 1952. *Faber.* Illustrated by Rowland Emett.

*Hunter, Norman. THE INCREDIBLE ADVENTURES OF PROFESSOR BRANESTAWM (see Chap.7).

*Jansson, Tove. FINN FAMILY MOOMINTROLL (1949 Finland) 1950, COMET IN MOOMINLAND (1946 Finland) 1951, THE EXPLOITS OF MOOMINPAPPA (1950 Finland) 1952, MOOMINSUMMER MADNESS (1954 Finland) 1955, MOOMIN, MYMBLE AND LITTLE MY (1952 Finland) 1953, MOOMINLAND MIDWINTER (1957 Finland) 1958. *Benn.* First two translated by Elizabeth Portch, the rest by Thomas Warburton. Illustrated by the author. The language of the original works is Swedish.

*Jerome, Jerome K. THREE MEN IN A BOAT (1889). *Herbert Jenkins* 1953.

*Leacock, Stephen. NONSENSE NOVELS. *Bodley Head* (1911) 1921.

*Lear, Edward. THE BOOK OF NONSENSE (1846). THE COMPLETE NONSENSE OF EDWARD LEAR, edited by Holbrook Jackson. *Faber* 1947.

*Lindsay, Norman. THE MAGIC PUDDING (1931). *Angus & Robertson* 1952. *Penguin* (Puffin Story Books) 1957. Illustrated by the author.

*Linklater, Eric. THE WIND ON THE MOON 1944, illustrated by Nicolas Bentley. THE PIRATES IN THE DEEP GREEN SEA 1949, illustrated by William Reeves. *Macmillan.*

*Williams, Jay and Abrashkin, Raymond. DANNY DUNN AND THE ANTI-GRAVITY PAINT (1956 U.S.A.) 1959, THE HOMEWORK MACHINE (1958 U.S.A.) 1960. *Brockhampton.* Illustrated by E. J. Keats.

*Wilson, Yates. MORE ALICE. *Boardman* 1959. Illustrated by the author.

Chapter 10 | *Fossils and Formulas*

In one sense, all children's stories are based on fantasy; they take place in a world that is not fact, not even fictionalized fact, but a special place created out of imagination for that particular story and for no other. All the same, as we move from the younger age-groups to stories for ten-year-olds and upward, we find more demand for tales set in a normal everyday environment. Imagination must still be at work, however prosaic a story may be, but it now works in a different way. A kettle, in a story for a six-year-old, may grow legs and walk; a kettle, in a family story for a ten-year-old, will be an adjunct to boiling water. Yet it may still be the means by which a child enters a world of fantasy, a world of dreams and wishes, if it is used in a story where a girl changes her status — a school buffoon who becomes a heroine at a Guide picnic, or an unwanted orphan who becomes the central figure in a happy household. The innumerable sub-divisions of family stories and adventure stories have one thing in common. They all gratify the wishes of young people—to be richer, to be more clever, to be famous, to be in another country, to be older, to be *different*.

So fantasy and imagination are still there. But because family stories require a realistic background, they are more susceptible to the danger of second-rate writers. The writer of true fantasy makes his own world and, consequently, makes his own pace, his own atmosphere, his own conditions. Family stories are less easy to vary. Certain types of story become popular and are eagerly imitated; children, seizing upon a favourite plot, demand more of the same thing. A formula is born, and a formula, in the end, can kill life and originality for all but the genuinely talented writer.

Take school stories, for instance. How can children distinguish between the Toms, Dicks and Harrys who jostle and compete in boys' classrooms; or between innumerable madcaps of the Fourth recognizable only by the colour of their tunics or the length of their hair? How can they distinguish between one set of ink-stained desks and another? How many writers have managed to bring life to the apparently monotonous and restricted subject of school days?

It is the fashion to trace the inadequacy of boys' school stories back to writers like Talbot Baines Reed. Frank Eyre thinks that Reed brought the school story 'to a perfection of unreality from which there was no escape possible.'* George Orwell, in his celebrated essay on school stories, drew up a formidable list of their failings. They displayed, he said, an unreal world, jingoistic, Conservative, rooted in privilege, xenophobic, rabidly class-conscious and apparently denying the very existence of sex. His strictures, part and parcel of the time when they were pronounced, seem out of place nowadays, when school stories are infinitely more varied in scope and setting. Where Orwell would lump all writers of school stories together, we can look back and see them as individuals, and we can see that— as in any sphere of literature—some were genuinely creative, others were merely copying. In effect, some set a model, others worked to a formula. Certainly, if a boy of fifteen wants to know what a traditional public school is really like, he will be well advised to read an adult novel rather than a boys' school story. Vachell's THE HILL, E. F. Benson's DAVID BLAIZE, D. Wynne Wilson's EARLY CLOSING and Alec Waugh's THE LOOM OF YOUTH—any of these will give him a picture of school as a living and complete world; while, in a story written for boys, schoolmasters, adults generally, will be treated as background characters, as the natural enemies of boys. Only in STALKY AND CO. shall we find any attempt to present a school as a community in which masters and boys have the same right to personality.

There are other basic restrictions. *Competition* is the theme of most school stories, and the games-field is the customary source of drama. When we are in the classroom, lessons will never be interesting in themselves, but only because of the prizes attached to them. The Nightingale scholarship, in THE FIFTH FORM AT ST DOMINIC'S, the university scholarship in Richard Bird's THE WHARTON MEDAL, are the centre of scene after scene, but, quite rightly in the context,

*TWENTIETH CENTURY CHILDREN'S BOOKS. Longmans, Green & Co., for the British Council, 1952, p. 51.

we have no idea what books the heroes of these contests had to read. That interesting type, the scholar, has no place in school stories. The clever boy must be odd, or mischievous, or a buffoon, to earn his place. So you get the odd impression that school life consists of a series of cricket and football matches and school speech days, enlivened by petty larceny, cribbing and gang warfare.

Still, I can see no reason why a good school story should not be written within these limits, and it has often been done. The exclusion of any emotional complications between boy and boy (or boy and girl) in the pages of Talbot Baines Reed was chiefly due to the literary conventions of his day, but even today I very much doubt whether most of the boys for whom school stories are designed (that is, boys up to the age of thirteen or fourteen) will not be more interested in the drama of a cricket-match than in the drama of the head prefect or the girl next door. They do not as a rule enjoy political or social comment in their stories. The books which take a mature view of such problems—books like DAVID BLAIZE, with its tentative but honest study of homosexual love or Florence Crannell Means's SHUTTERED WINDOWS, with its striking study of the colour problem in Carolina— are outside the school story formula; and first-class books can be produced within the formula, using the day-to-day events of school life. They can be exciting events, familiar as they are: but they will only be exciting if there are strong characters.

It is characterization that makes certain writers live on, long after the boarding-school formula seems to be worked out; and I would name Talbot Baines Reed as one of them.

The most exciting event in THE FIFTH FORM AT ST DOMINIC'S is the stealing of an exam paper, but there is scope here for the clash of character, made more exciting because it takes place in a small, close community. Two boys are rivals in the Nightingale prize—the cad, Loman, and the clever, odd, unpredictable Oliver Greenfield. Loman has been consorting with a publican, who is now blackmailing him; he desperately needs the money the prize brings. Oliver is ambitious; he wants the honour of winning. When the vital paper disappears from the headmaster's study, and Oliver subsequently wins the prize, the school and staff reach the obvious conclusion. He receives his award to the sound of hissing, and an investigation begins. The scene, in essentials, is familiar enough. But few writers have matched Reed's sure direction of every detail to the one purpose of revealing character. The repercussions of the theft—Oliver's bravado and cynicism, the passionate, miserable loyalty of his young brother (a new boy), the casual support of his friend Wraysford, and the barbed, wayward encouragement of lame Tony Pembury—these are enough to make of an ordinary school story a really telling drama; and even if boys take the book up initially as a story, they will probably, as I have done from my childhood days, remember not the plot but the people.

Lesser writers have grafted on to school routine the most sensational events in order to produce excitement. But it did not help L. C. Douthwaite, a practised writer of school stories, when in THE LUCK OF ST BONIFACE he brought in a gang of crooks to steal the boxing cup, and threw in, at the end, a monastic treasure as a makeweight. His story, written twenty years after the masterpieces of Talbot Baines Reed, seems far more old-fashioned now than the lively rags and initiation ceremonies in THE COCK HOUSE AT FELLSGARTH, or the central problem of THE WILLOUGHBY CAPTAINS, which turns on the simple fact of a senior boy being taken from a good house to be head of a bad one.

Fifty years after their first appearance, Reed's stories are still real and alive, in narrative and in dialogue. They are not likely to become fossilized even by their slang—and in fact Reed uses slang far less than most writers of school stories and always dramatically. With the seniors, it is occasional and idiosyncratic; with the juniors, it is a special language, born of the younger boys' natural desire for uniformity. In the same way, slang is the badge of such lively characters in modern school stories as Specs McCann or Anthony Buckeridge's Jennings. Here are Jennings and his friend Darbishire getting ready for a cross-country run:

Darbishire had found his gym shoes by this time, but as he bent down to put them on he uttered a wail of dismay.

'Oh, fish-hooks! Some gruesome specimen has pinched my laces! I bet it was Atkinson. He broke one of his yesterday and he was snooping round my locker while . . .'

'There's no time to worry about that now. You'll just have to wear them as they are!' Jennings danced with impatience as the sound of Mr. Carter's referee whistle was wafted through the window. 'Quick, Darbi, they're starting!'

'But what about my laces? I can't go with my shoes flapping
about my ankles. They're about a hundred sizes too big for me,
anyway, and they'll fall off as soon as I try to get up speed.'

Jennings rounded on his friend with some heat. 'Now look
here, Darbishire; I'm doing you a supersonic favour by letting
you be my partner for this run, seeing that you only go as fast as
a sea-lion on its flippers.'

'Yes, I know, but . . .'

'And you heard what Old Wilkie said about getting a move on.
If we don't get going right away, he won't need a watch to time us
with—he'll need a calendar!'

Anthony Buckeridge. OUR FRIEND JENNINGS (Collins, 1955)
pp. 42–3.

The greatest achievement of Buckeridge, among other school
story writers, is to make his small boys individuals, in dialogue and in
habit, as well as giving them the typical group-character which is so
striking in any preparatory school. The same is true of William
Mayne. In his three choir-school stories the dialogue is curiously
formalized and yet so apposite that it gets nearer to the *real* talk of
boys than anything I have read later than TOM SAWYER. Here are
one or two of them nursing a dramatic secret, talking to their headmaster:

'Can we explain in a few days' time?' said Trevithic. 'We're
busy, you see, sir.'

'So long as you have a member of the staff in your confidence,
to give you leave for late meals; and you don't break rules in
front of the juniors, Trevithic, you may do what you like,' said
Mr. Ardent. 'And you must never be late for Mr. Sutton.'

'I've set one or two rules at naught,' said Trevithic. 'Will you
punish me on Monday, sir?'

'With pleasure,' said Mr. Ardent. 'And now it would be tactful
if you wiped up the crumbs and washed your plates.' Then he
asked Owen: 'When did you last have your hair cut?'

'Last term, sir,' said Owen. 'There's no one to do it at home.'

'I'd rather do it here,' said Mr. Ardent. 'As soon as you've
washed up, what about a lawn-mowing session in the senior bath-
room? You have a very wild, woolly, Welsh look.'

'Sheep-shearing, sir,' said Trevithic. 'Couldn't we make

cushions for the choir-stalls, and fill them with our own hair-clippings?'

'You'd better suggest it to the Dean and Chapter,' said Mr. Ardent.

William Mayne. A SWARM IN MAY (Oxford University Press, 1955) pp. 145–6.

From the dialogue and the narrative in Mayne's books you are always aware, too, of the extreme *concreteness* of the junior world (not an easy thing to get into a book). Mary's delight in the 'white stick' in A GRASS ROPE, the absorption of Owen in the ball and key he has found, in A SWARM IN MAY, the map on the damp wall in THE WORLD UPSIDE DOWN—all these objects are crucial to the stories, but they are also important to the children who handle or observe or find them, for their shape or texture or colour. This is one of the most important qualities of Mayne's work and links him with writers like Walter de la Mare and Elizabeth Coatsworth and Laura Ingalls Wilder, writers who have a particular faculty for reliving the life of the senses which a child cannot communicate directly to an adult. In A SWARM IN MAY the whole atmosphere of school is summarized, for me at any rate, in this little snatch of description:

> They were in their places. The organ stopped. Mr. Ardent lifted his head. 'Enter not into judgement with thy servant, O Lord; for in thy sight shall no man living be justified.'
>
> Owen found with his right hand the five small marks under the edge of the stall, where his fingernails fitted: he had been making the marks for two terms now. When they knelt he found with his left toe the crack in the flagstones that helped to hold his foot where it would not go to sleep. Silverman pushed against him and left a sticky hand-mark on the woodwork.
>
> Ibid., pp. 21–2.

When a boy reads a passage like this, he is likely to make his owe mental picture, and for this reason such descriptions can only bn given to us through the flexible medium of words which each of us can make our own. Illustrations are too restricting here, as they are, too, in the case of the dramatis personæ of a story. C. Walter Hodges, who has illustrated these three choir-school stories, has tried to draw some of the individuals in them (perhaps at the request of the publisher), but I cannot believe that anyone who enjoys these stories could want to be given someone else's impression of the features of the lordly Trevithic or the egregious Sandwell. On the other hand,

Trevithic.

when the illustrator *comments* on a scene, not reproducing it but getting at the quickening spirit of it, he is making a valuable contribution to the truth of the stories; and these are among the most spontaneous and the most living of all school stories.

But now we must come to the arch-fossil, the original fly in the ointment—Billy Bunter. Pictorially speaking, it is not correct to speak of Bunter as a fossil, for he has undergone evolutionary change. The first illustration in which the fat boy appeared, on the title-page of *The Magnet* of March 1908, is relatively normal. To be sure, Bunter is eating jam-tarts, but his figure is only that of an ordinary plump boy, his spectacles are of orthodox size. Two months later he has put on a little weight, in a picture of a picnic to which the caption is, 'It was certainly a mistake to leave Billy in charge.' And so the thing goes on. It is interesting to watch over the course of years as the artistic bicycle pump is applied and Bunter gradually

Drawing by C. Walter Hodges for William Mayne's CATHEDRAL WEDNESDAY
(O.U.P.)

becomes the gross, grotesque figure which our children know from
the pages of the last *Magnets* of 1940, from the frontispieces of the
Bunter books still continuing, and from the television screen.

It is very different, however, on the printed page. Frank Richards
conceived Bunter in 1908 as a character in a magazine story, a serial.
He has been kept alive, virtually unchanged in age and temperament, from 1908 to the present day (with a break between 1940 and
1947). The chief virtue of Greyfriars School, as of other schools in
comics of yesterday and today, is their *familiarity*. The stories rely
on a few simple formulas of plot and character, instantly recognized,

endlessly repeated. Hurree Singh's Babu English, based on the word 'terrific' and on certain self-coined abstract nouns, has never been changed; nor have the hearty ejaculations of Cherry or the mouth-ings of Bunter.

Each of Bunter's familiar characteristics was taken from real life, as Richard tells us in his autobiography. His girth came from a Fleet Street editor; his spectacles from a relation who had goggled at Richards when he was a boy; his postal order gag came from an acquaintance who was always borrowing on the expectation of a cheque; his fatuousness under cross-examination from 'an eminent public figure' of late Victorian times. Thus Bunter was born whole and immutable. At his very first appearance he was preoccupied with food, he used the onomatopœic expressions like 'Yarroo' and 'Gerumph' which shatter television valves in hundreds of homes today. To be sure, in the early days he was an incidental bit of comic relief for the trials and heartburnings of Harry Wharton, designed to be the chief character of the stories. But that 'little chatterbox', 'little Bunter', 'the smallest boy in the form' (not sarcastic, then) had soon pushed himself forward; and now that the fat boy has been given a new lease of life in full-length books, it is his name which stands for the series. They are the Bunter books, and it is his scrapes, infinitely blown up from trivial incidents, which make the stories. For Bunter's appeal must come from familiarity in childhood. Nobody could approach in middle-age paragraphs like this:

'Prime!' gurgled Billy Bunter.

Bunter did not find it easy to utter even that monosyllable. His capacious mouth was packed to capacity, with luscious, purple grapes. He gurgled happily through delicious grapes that seemed to melt in the mouth.

It was a happy fat Owl! Smithy, for once kind and sympathetic, had done the thing well. That bunch was the biggest and best that money could buy. Probably it would have pleased an invalid, —had there been an invalid, and had it reached that invalid. Certainly it pleased William George Bunter. His little round eyes were still red, and still exuded water, from the application of the onion, but otherwise, his fat face beamed . . .

Frank Richards. BILLY BUNTER'S BOLT (Cassell, 1957) p. 40.

Nostalgia, alone, can carry you through this sort of thing. Pleasure remembered is worth having; but the books to look out for are those which can be picked up and reread, with new understanding, in middle-age, or which can revive a parent's interest in school stories by a new slant. These books will never become fossilized, although they may be written well within the boarding-school formula. THE WILLOUGHBY CAPTAINS, William Mayne's CHORISTER'S CAKE and A SWARM IN MAY, Antonia Forest's AUTUMN TERM and END OF TERM—these stories, by Orwell's prescription, are all limited; but there is as much in them as in the most vigorous tale whose plot Orwell would have approved.

Antonia Forest is probably unique in the field of school stories for girls. Writing in the present day, she has boldly chosen the now old-fashioned setting of an exclusive boarding-school; she has completely cut across the silliness and triviality which resulted from half a century of Angela Brazil and her imitators; she has drawn girls who are totally feminine and yet do not tiresomely rebel against a very orthodox and restricted life. She uses the situations that would naturally develop between vigorous personalities living at close quarters. The rivalry between seventeen-year-old Rowan Marlow and Lois Sanger, in AUTUMN TERM, is displayed on the games field, in the classroom, on a Guide trek, and it is always seen as a surface tension reflecting far deeper dissatisfactions and ambitions.

Because Antonia Forest concentrates on character, I can absolutely accept her limited sphere of action. I mind very much whether Nicola Marlow or the spoilt Pomona gets the spare front desk in Form 3 Remove; but when E. Brent Dyer, a prolific writer, writes ten or twelve pages of drama concerning the dire consequences of tilting your chair while working, I cannot see the incident as she (presumably) does, for the characters involved are so shadowy and uninteresting.

In E. Brent Dyer's stories about the Chalet School, and Elsie J. Oxenham's series about the Abbey School, we have another clear case of fossilization. The appeal of these books, like the appeal of Bunter, is one of familiarity. I remember THE ABBEY GIRLS well from my own girlhood. It was in 1920 that the quaint school morris-dancing club first found its way to the Abbey and caught up in its sociable and rather absurd activities the lonely girls, Joy and Joan. I remembered nothing about the book except the vaguely medieval atmosphere and the elaborate descriptions of the Queen's dresses. Rereading this book, and pursuing the sequels up to the present day, I was astonished to find that the atmosphere in the books published in the 'fifties is almost unchanged. The same other-worldly, decorative background; the same gracious Abbey girls, grown up now but still with the sentimental vision of adolescence; the new generation of schoolgirls untouched, apparently, by the passage of time. The same may be said of the Chalet girls, who have been working for bazaars and getting into mischief continuously since 1925. Indeed, many of the later volumes are filled out with the reminiscences of Old Girls.

These are survivals, and they must eventually suffer the fate of other books, creatures and tribes that prolong existence in a world that has passed them by. The school story is keeping alive by renewing itself, as all literature must do. The boarding-school story can live now only in the hands of exceptional writers like William Mayne and Antonia Forest. It is the day-school story which has been most interesting in the past ten years or so, partly because the greater proportion of readers go to day-schools, partly because home and school can be neatly and profitably welded together.

It is a relief to escape from the wooden unrealities of Angela Brazil and her descendants to the fresh and vigorous life of a girls' day-school as some recent writers portray it. Alice Lunt's SECRET STEPMOTHER has for heroine a girl who resents her inoffensive young stepmother and refuses to admit her existence. Janet's attitude leads her into troubles large and small, as her young sister escapes from her control and gets into mischief, as the headmistress, misled by Janet's excuses, investigates what seems to be a case of parental neglect. This is a fresh, topical drama in which all the characters come to life, and JEANNETTE'S FIRST TERM, even more remarkably, fills with interest the simple theme of two friends moving up to a Secondary Modern school. Mary Harris has made a striking contribution, too, to the girls' school story. It is a sad fact that the emotions of girlhood, so often roused by unworthy causes, can be tedious to read about. There is nothing very new in the story of EMILY AND THE HEADMISTRESS, but the friendship growing between Emily and Miss Robinson in the holidays has unexpected point. A later story, SERAPHINA, goes deeper. I know few books which relate school and home life so intelligently. Seraphina is an orphan. When her beloved grandmother dies she goes to live with an aunt, a smart woman who runs a hairdressing salon and has no sympathy with moods and fancies. She packs her niece off to a boarding-hostel attached to the local grammar school. An awe-inspiring headmistress, a high standard of work, a very mixed collection of girls, these tax Seraphina and sometimes worry her; and then there is Stephanie, so fascinating, so secretive about her home. The growing friendship between these girls and their sharing of hopes and sorrows is described with real insight and the book has a quiet but impressive authenticity.

Drawing by Roger Payne for E. W. Hildick's JIM STARLING AND THE AGENCY (Chatto)

In the same way, E. W. Hildick has given a good shake to the drooping form of the boys' school story. Jim Starling is certainly a pleasant change from the usual straw-hatted hero, just as Cement Street Secondary Modern for boys, in the town of Smogbury, is a pleasant change from the ancient walls of St Boniface's. The novelty of Hildick's setting and of his working-class characters may at first distract readers from the vigour and skill of his writing. His plots are cleverly worked out, his characters fully realized, his style racy and

workmanlike. I know few school stories of any kind which give me
so completely the impression of a school from the boy's point of
view. Here is an art-lesson in progress:

> For the next ten minutes or so the boys of 3B worked away
> busily with their sticks of charcoal, sketching their ideas on large
> sheets of paper. Then, as they decided they had enough to work
> upon, they began to mix their paint. Hamer walked round,
> quietly giving advice, exploding only occasionally whenever he
> caught someone drawing too carefully. Then he would shout:
> 'Don't spend all morning drawing, lad!' or 'Fill the paper,
> don't niggle away in one corner!' or 'Use bold, free, happy
> strokes! Happy strokes! Happy strokes!' And every time he said
> 'Happy strokes' he'd fetch the unfortunate boy a clump at the
> back of the head.
>
> E. W. Hildick. JIM STARLING (Chatto & Windus, 1958) p. 34.

and here is one of those curious moments when you see the school,
as it were, from an oblique angle:

> The changing-room was up a few steps from the corridor. At
> the other side you went down another few steps and through a
> door into the gym itself. Jim had never really thought about this
> before, but now it seemed very strange that the changing-room
> should be raised up like that. In fact, everything seemed strange:
> the silence of the changing-room itself, with all the pants and shirts
> hung up, limp and bedraggled, like dish-cloths, and the shoes lying
> about as if the owners had had to leave them in a hurry and run
> for their lives (which they had, in a way, with Hilton snapping at
> them to look sharp and banging a slipper against the doorpost).
> Then the muffled clump-clumping from the gym—that sounded
> strange, too—and the commands of Hilton suddenly making the
> clumping stop or go faster. And the smell of the dust and sweat
> and rubber was strange . . .
>
> Ibid., pp. 50–1.

The books about Jim Starling are excellent, but I have not the least
doubt that Mr Hildick would have made just as much of a success
if he had chosen to write a story about a public school. Public
school or primary, Smogbury or Fellsgarth, boys and girls at home or
away from home, what does it matter so long as the book has its

own atmosphere and its own compulsion? 'School stories' are fettered by formulas; good stories about schools make use of them at their own choice.

Children will always want school stories; their appeal is universal, the appeal of sorrows and triumphs felt by any child, even if they are in an unfamiliar setting. Can the same be said of the pony book? Is its popularity over the last twenty years or so a passing fashion or is it permanent? Certainly the universal emotions of childhood can be found here, but you often have to dig deep to find them. The basic formula promises to be good—the idea of children learning a technique and winning success in it. True, it is a special technique and relatively few children come anywhere near even starting to learn it; but this does not seem to matter. Hundreds of children who have no pony, and may probably never ride, want pony books. Some, (especially town children) because of the idealized charm of country life; some just for the pleasure of learning about a technique; some because the dream formula (I WANTED A PONY, WISH FOR A PONY, GAZE AT THE MOON are typical titles) is so consoling; all, I believe, because horses make a direct appeal to the feminine need to be dominated and at the same time to be maternal (for pony books are written chiefly for girls). Above all, there is the appeal that any story has which deals with achievement. In almost every pony book success comes first and matters most; the ponies take second place. They are not animal stories. Only in a very few (Kitty Barne's moving tale of ROSINA COPPER among them) do you get to know what a horse or a pony is like.

There is one thing I do not like about pony books—their exclusiveness. It does not matter that hundreds and thousands of the girls who read them have no ponies; it *does* matter that they should be made to feel (as they are, far too often) that they could not qualify for this magic world, either, on grounds of class. In many pony books there is a distasteful feeling of clubmanship. I find myself impatiently waiting to read one in which the lower middle-class girl who comes by a pony, especially if her father is *nouveau riche*, turns out to have a perfect seat. The procession of delicately nurtured, or well-bred, children, or ordinary children adopting the current manners of the horsy fraternity, is apt to be as wearisome as a pageant produced by amateurs. Out of a hundred or so pony books (leaving out the few memorable exceptions) I can remember only a series of crash-caps and crashes, and books that must be remembered for their plots are going to have only a short life—although it must be admitted that horse-mad girls cherish this monotony, in text and in illustrations.

I think there is light on the horizon. Pony books, which must move with the times if they are to get new readers, are bound to be affected by the rise of pony clubs since the war, with their varied membership; and perhaps these same pony clubs will gradually work another necessary change. It is obvious that the young hero or heroine must succeed, must win her pony or her rosette. But the reader demands (or should demand) that success is *won*; it must not come easily. Few readers, whether they know about ponies or not, are likely to accept the situation in I WANTED A PONY, by Diana Pullein-Thompson, where Augusta discovers in a few minutes what everyone else (including the vet) has failed to deduce in months about the grey pony—that its unpleasant habit of tossing its head is *not* due to a brain-tumour but to the fact that an unusually broad forehead makes all bridles uncomfortable. This contrivance to bring the pony within Augusta's limited means is unusually bad, but there are many books far more skilfully written, among them Joanna Cannan's GAZE AT THE MOON and M. E. Atkinson's pleasant HUNTER'S MOON, where good fortune and coincidence still dominate the story, to the loss of the really important element—character.

If the gymkhana story has its improbabilities, how much more so has the pony adventure story. It is a relief to get away from the collecting ring, but the author who makes her young riders outwit crooks, sometimes quite dangerous crooks, has to be very good to win permanent belief from her readers. Here again the secret lies not in convincing detail but in character. You very seldom get anything as good as Ann Stafford's FIVE PROUD RIDERS, which triumphantly carries off a most unlikely tale about international spies in the New Forest because the children who bring them to justice— Jill, responsible and full of sense, superior Nigel, and the bumptious, resourceful little John—are so real.

Head and shoulders above other writers of the pony adventure story is Mary Treadgold. Her books will satisfy the most ardent pony-fancier, but her talent is entirely unhampered by formula. WE COULDN'T LEAVE DINAH is set in a Channel island coveted by the Nazis as an invasion base. The story is an exciting one. The Nazis come to Clerinel and are helped by the Beaumarchais family. Peter Beaumarchais is leader of a pony club, and the Templeton children are horrified to discover that his home is a centre of collaboration. Besides, Mick and Caroline should not be in Clerinel at all. In the confusion of sudden evacuation they are left behind and from their hiding-place they discover the dangerous activities of the Nazis, and the unpleasant fact that fat Nannerl, the Commandant's daughter, is riding Caroline's beloved Dinah. The spy plot is beautifully adapted to the capacities and characters of the children, and the same is true of the later story, NO PONIES, set in the South of France, where stolen ponies are used for transport in an underground railway carrying Nazi-trained agitators into other countries. In each case, a sensational plot is kept within bounds by exceptionally good character drawing (and also by exceptionally good writing).

It is character, again, which makes the stories of Monica Edwards popular with children who may or may not already love ponies. But hers are not, in the strict sense, pony books. It is true that she started well within the formula, making her first appearance with WISH FOR A PONY, where two girls on Romney Marsh lived, talked and dreamed ponies, did the worst chores at the local riding stables in the hope of rides, and ultimately, by a piece of story-book fortune, had a pony almost drop into their laps. No, it is not out of the ordinary for its plot, this book, but there is something unusually lifelike about the girls and their home background. It is not surprising to learn that the book was written to please Monica Edwards's daughter and that she and a school friend were models for the characters of Tamzin and Rissa; while the Marsh setting which appears in entrancing glimpses throughout the story had been familiar to the author from her childhood. In this simple, unostentatious story was the beginning of an attractive series in which adventures with ponies and boats rise naturally from the characters and their environment, and are pursued in a very probable manner. Smuggling at Westling, in THE SUMMER OF THE GREAT SECRET; the traffic in horse-flesh in CARGO OF HORSES; a man caught in quicksands, in HIDDEN IN A DREAM; floods on the estuary, in STORM AHEAD; foot-and-mouth disease in NO ENTRY; poaching by French fishermen in THE NIGHT-BIRD; bird protection in STRANGER TO THE MARSH when a pair of hoopoes nest in the ruined castle; oiled seabirds in OPERATION

SEABIRD; it is a wonderful list of subjects, topically and intrinsically interesting, and not one of these books has anything stilted about it. The children develop as time goes on. We know their ages and we see their capacities widening as their experience grows. In the latest story, NO GOING BACK, Meryon and Tamzin discover an adolescent love for each other which alters the happy relationship of the group; the author's sense of proportion and her sensitiveness in this matter are notable. And though ponies play their part in the stories, they are not the object of adulation or of excessive care. Sometimes they are used as casually by the girls as their boy companions in adventure use their bicycles. Monica Edwards is not setting out to please horse-obsessives. She writes stories full of common sense and with a sound knowledge of young people, and in a rare and effective way she puts these young people firmly in their environment. Their homes, the village where Tamzin's father is Vicar, the neighbours they respect and the visitors they examine with caution—everything is part of a balanced whole.

The same warm realistic atmosphere is conspicuous in her second cycle of stories, about Punchbowl Farm, which are based even more closely on her own family, and which are some of the best stories one can offer to girls of ten or so. The risk of using real life, sometimes in great detail, was worth taking. The Thorntons, learning to farm from scratch, have adventures which are perfectly credible. This is because Monica Edwards, since she is using real life, gives her young readers all of it—the disaster to the beautiful mare Moonstone as well as the romantic finding of the old diary, loss of crops or stock as well as successes, quarrels and disappointments as well as halcyon days in the country.

In these splendid, humorous, human stories, with their direct, accomplished style, we are a long way from the pony story that is written to a formula, and another kind of story shows the same wide range of accomplishment. Ballet, acting, circus-life—these, for their colour and drama, have been favourite subjects for children's stories for many years. Here is the success formula again, perhaps now better called the Footlight Formula. Hundreds of girls dream of winning public acclaim on the stage, and tales of spectacular successes are available in their hundreds to console children who feel their life is entirely drab and ordinary compared with the life of a child acrobat or a television star.

Now the disadvantage of this formula, as we have already found in the case of pony books, is that success is prescriptive. However skilfully the author mixes the rough with the smooth, it is soon obvious that the understudy is going to get the star part or that the young equestrienne is going to save the horses in the burning circus tent. A good writer, while she may accept the necessity of success, will concentrate on the clash of characters, which can be particularly interesting in the egotistical world of show business. I do not want to be too solemn about this. There are plenty of excellent stage stories where the stage atmosphere matters more than the characters. They live in the memory for less time than those where character is paramount, but they can be most agreeable to read. Pamela Brown, for instance, communicates brilliantly the feeling of crowded excitement, ups and downs, flurry and hurry of back stage, whether it is audition, rehearsal or performance. If you want to accept her books, you must accept the Footlight Formula as a whole. The six children in the Blue Door series have far more successes than failures as they pass through acting school and gain experience in repertory, cabaret, television and touring. In these books the children, lively and talented, are interchangeable, but the smell of grease-paint is authentic. Theatrical dress-shop in HARLEQUIN CORNER, Thames launch in SHOWBOAT SUMMER, greenroom in UNDERSTUDY—the atmosphere is always wonderfully real.

Real, of course, only up to a point. Children's stories about the theatre are more often than not about child actors. Too much of the danger and difficulty of real life must be left out if the subject is a girl or boy in the late teens (unless, as Pamela Brown does, you keep your character at the permanent emotional age of fourteen or so), and children of ten or twelve who want to read about the stage will naturally enjoy theatrical technique more than theatrical perils. A girl of thirteen or so will do better to read some of the best adult novels of the theatre, like Clemence Dane's BROOME STAGES, or George Moore's superb study of an opera-singer, EVELYN INNES. Margot Benary's CASTLE ON THE BORDER, written specifically for children, gives an unusually realistic view of an amateur acting company in Germany, but even this exceptionally mature writer has cast something of a rosy glow over her book to suit the young reader.

By far the most successful theatre stories for children are those which, with children as their subjects, can show rivalries and ambitions unaffected, as yet, by the awkward, sordid, bewildering adult world. Here Noel Streatfeild is outstanding. Her young actors, skaters and ballet pupils are infatuated by the theatre. They are ambitious, self-centred, as deeply obsessed by technique as any young aspirant for a jumping rosette. She even succeeds, sometimes, in conveying that intangible but unmistakable thing, star quality— in Posy, for instance, youngest of the three girls in BALLET SHOES, who, when the brilliant teacher falls ill, inquires at once what is to happen to her own career; or in Rachel in WINTLE'S WONDERS, whose talents are discovered almost by accident, but whom you recognize at once as a dedicated dancer.

Though Noel Streatfeild knows her theatre as well as Pamela Brown does, she does not put it first. She has an insatiable curiosity about people, and especially about theatrical children, with their peculiar, hard-working, rigidly organized life; and she is curious, too, about the effects of publicity and performance on young people. Her books, for all the detail and skill of their backgrounds, are primarily studies in character. Mrs Wintle's dancing-school is the battlefield for her daughter Dulcie, a conceited little girl who wants the best parts in all the shows, and the two children, Rachel and Hilary, who are taken into the family and threaten to steal some of Dulcie's thunder. The same theme, of the poor and modest child coming to the fore, is brilliantly used in WHITE BOOTS, in the rivalry of Harriet Johnson, daughter of a poor (but well-connected) green-grocer, and Lalla Moore, a well-to-do orphan whose aunt is pushing her into the limelight in the world of ice-skating. In all Noel Streat-feild's books we have portraits of the professional child, set off by the occasional brave souls who resist the dazzle of the footlights, like Petrova in BALLET SHOES, whose heart is in motor-engineering, or Hilary, in WINTLE'S WONDERS, whose attitude is entirely refreshing, when she is offered a star part:

'What do you want me for? I won't be any good.'
The producer was thoroughly amused.
'I'm sorry if I've inconvenienced you. But there's a comic robin in this new children's play which I thought would suit you.'
'Has he anything to say?'
'No, it's all mime with a little dancing.'
Hilary gave in grudgingly.

'Well, I suppose I'll have to be him.'

The producer laughed.

'Don't you want to? Most children would jump at the chance, I thought I was doing you a good turn.'

'Well, you aren't. All I want to be is just an ordinary Wonder, and look what happens to me. My first engagement is to understudy Dulcie, which nobody could like, and now I've got to be a robin. Wouldn't you rather have somebody else? There are heaps of Wonders who'd be better than me.'

The producer gave Hilary's hair an affectionate rub.

'You're a card. But no, thank you, I'm sticking to you.'

Noel Streatfeild. WINTLE'S WONDERS. (Collins, 1957) pp. 232-3.

The intrusion of such a robust point of view into the somewhat rarefied air of the theatre saves these stories, full of technical detail as they are, from becoming too specialized for the general reader. Noel Streatfeild has her feet firmly on the ground, and children who reread her books when they are older will bless her for this.

Theatrical children, of course, are not ordinary, and neither are circus children. In THE CIRCUS IS COMING, still perhaps Noel Streatfeild's most popular book, she emphasizes the oddity of circus characters by bringing into Cob's Circus a prim little hero and heroine, Peter and Santa, who have to shake down, after a suburban upbringing, in the heady atmosphere of sawdust and performance. In the same way Howard Spring, in the incomparable SAMPSON'S CIRCUS, brings real life abruptly into relation with the exotic. To Howard Spring, character is the mainspring of children's writing, and character that is recognizable—sharply, pictorially drawn. Most of his characters are outsize—like lively Charley Chaffinch, the villainous Aristide Elverdingen, and the imposing Mr Sampson himself. This is how young Jo describes him:

An extraordinary figure came down the steps with slow dignity. Through the telescope I could pick out every detail: the enormous body, so fat that it was difficult to see where the legs ended and the stomach began; the tiny feet shod in boots with brilliant toes, dove-coloured cloth uppers and buttons; the grey trousers with a broad stripe of black braid down the sides; the black frock-coat pulled so tight that it looked as though it might burst asunder, scattering a hail of buttons, at any moment. There was a white

camellia in Mr. Sampson's buttonhole. On his head was a tall
grey topper, and between the topper and the bright scarlet of his
tie was a face like an immense Dutch cheese, ornamented with
moustaches waxed to long fine points.

Howard Spring. SAMPSON'S CIRCUS. (Faber, 1936) pp. 72–3.

Like TUMBLEDOWN DICK, this is a book where good writing and
genial humour go hand in hand, without in the least falsifying the
hard knocks of the world.

Howard Spring is, of course, on good ground for the creating of
characters, for circus people are outsize. Far more difficult is the
task of those who want to present musicians as they are, present
them as ordinary people and yet indicate their particular quality.
Kitty Barne has done for the technique of concert playing much what
Noel Streatfeild has done for acting. Her stories are serious and professional, as well as entertaining. She does not let her characters win
success easily, nor does she make them larger than life. In SHE SHALL
HAVE MUSIC, for instance, we follow eight-year-old Karin Forest
through a discouraging period, when she has no piano to exercise
her talent on; we follow her as she clings to Rosalba, romantic and
tasteless in execution, because she can teach her at least something;
and because we have seen her difficulties, we can readily believe in
Karin's success on the concert platform. I think only one writer for
children has really succeeded in making you *feel* a musician's character. Elfrida Vipont's LARK IN THE MORN, with its rather sentimental sequel, THE LARK ON THE WING, really make you believe in
the special talent, as well as the dedication to music, of Kit Haverard. It is no small achievement to describe the awakening of creative
imagination in a schoolgirl without any shadow of exaggeration or
falseness. Elfrida Vipont has done just this. Kit Haverard is playing
a game of King Arthur with her friends:

> At length Elaine, cruelly forsaken, proceeded to pine away. The
> action was becoming far too slow, thought Pony. 'Buck up and
> get on to the dying part,' she urged. Elaine did not seem to hear
> her. Nowadays, Kit had a way of losing herself in the play, which
> irritated Pony very much. She seemed to be taking their games
> more seriously than ever, whereas Pony was beginning to feel a
> little self-conscious about them. None of the other girls in her

form played pretending-games. 'Can't we skip a bit of this?' she suggested.

Kit lay back on the sofa, humming to herself. The words of Elaine's song from *The Idylls of the King* were running through her mind. Somehow or other, they were fitting themselves into a kind of tune as they went along. She began to sing tentatively; her voice was uneven and uncontrolled. The others scarcely listened. They were used to Kit's oddities by now, but they did wish she would hurry up, and Pony itched to sing it for her . . . suddenly something seemed to break down in Kit. As if she had indeed been transformed into the lovelorn child of the story, she lost herself . . .

Pony and Helen stared at her. They had never heard her sing like that before. Pony pulled herself together to break the spell.

'What's up with thee, Elaine?' she began, in the fatherly tones of the Lord of Astolat. 'Art thinking of yonder knight?'

Kit said nothing. There were tears in her eyes.

'Look out!' whispered Helen. 'She's going to cry. For goodness' sake let's play something else.'

Pony nodded assent and plumped down on to the sofa. 'Cheer up!' said she. 'It was awfully nice, but don't let's do any more of it. The part where she goes down the river is a bit dull, isn't it? Let's try something else.'

Kit shook herself slightly and sat up. 'All right,' she said gruffly. 'Don't mind. Anything you like.'

'Right-o!' said Pony, taking the situation in hand. 'We'll do the last battle and you can be Arthur. You'd like that, wouldn't you? Helen can do Modred and Bedivere, and I'll be Lancelot.'

'But he wasn't there,' protested Helen.

'Can't help it,' rejoined Pony. 'And how do you know, anyway?' Elfrida Vipont. THE LARK IN THE MORN. (Oxford University Press, 1948) pp. 61–3.

There is in this book an extraordinarily easy swing of emotion, a sure sense of timing, and beyond these technical skills, an understanding of a dedicated personality. It is not often that books written for girls, even for older girls, go as deep as this story does. It is not often that you find the familiar and hackneyed success formula bursting out into fresh and pulsating life, into a book which offers as much for an adult reader as it does to girls aspiring to be adults.

Reading List

1.*School Stories* (See also p. 331.)

Allan, Mabel Esther. A SCHOOL IN DANGER 1952, OVER THE SEA TO SCHOOL
1954, AT SCHOOL IN SKYE 1957. *Blackie.* Illustrated by Constance Marshall.
Lively tales of an unorthodox school in Skye, with good characters.

*Benson, E. F. DAVID BLAIZE 1916, DAVID OF KING'S 1924. *Hodder &
Stoughton.*

*Bird, Richard. THE WHARTON MEDAL, in THE RICHARD BIRD OMNIBUS.
O.U.P. 1937.

*Buckeridge, Anthony. JENNINGS GOES TO SCHOOL 1950, ACCORDING TO
JENNINGS 1954, OUR FRIEND JENNINGS 1955. *Collins.*

*Douthwaite, L. C. THE LUCK OF ST BONIFACE. *Jarrold* 1925.

*Dyer, E. Brent. TOM TACKLES THE CHALET SCHOOL. *Chambers* 1955.
Numerous other titles, earliest THE SCHOOL AT THE CHALET 1925, latest
JOEY AND CO. IN TIROL 1960.

*Forest, Antonia. AUTUMN TERM 1948, END OF TERM 1959. *Faber.* (See also
p. 333.)

Garrard, Phyllis. NEW ZEALAND SCHOOLGIRL 1958; contains HILDA AT
SCHOOL, THE DOINGS OF HILDA, and HILDA'S ADVENTURES. Also
HILDA, FIFTEEN. *Blackie* 1944. A schoolgirl in the back-country; cheerful,
unconventional tales with a pleasing family background.

*Harris, Mary K. EMILY AND THE HEADMISTRESS 1958, SERAPHINA 1960.
Faber. Illustrated by Sheila Rose.

*Hildick, E. W. JIM STARLING 1958, JIM STARLING AND THE AGENCY 1958.
Chatto & Windus. Illustrated by Roger Payne.

*Hildick, E. W. JIM STARLING'S HOLIDAY 1960, JIM STARLING AND THE
COLONEL 1960. *Heinemann.* Illustrated by Roger Payne. (See also p. 334.)

Kästner, Erich. THE FLYING CLASSROOM (1933 Germany). *Cape* 1934.
Translated by Cyrus Brooks. Illustrated by Walter Trier. Bavarian boarding-
school, schoolboy feuds, play-acting, etc.

*Kipling, Rudyard. STALKY AND CO. *Macmillan* (1899) 1951.

Lloyd, Marjorie. ONE SUMMER TERM. *Methuen* 1959. Illustrated by Astrid
Walford. Boarding house in day school on Welsh Marches. Excellent characterization and clash of personalities.

*Lunt, Alice. SECRET STEPMOTHER 1959, illustrated by D. G. Valentine.
JEANETTE'S FIRST TERM 1960, illustrated by Dorothy Parsons. *Dent.*

*McNeill, Janet. Books about Specs McCann (see Chap. 8).

*Mayne, William. THE WORLD UPSIDE DOWN 1954, illustrated by Shirley
  Hughes. A SWARM IN MAY 1955, CHORISTER'S CAKE 1956, CATHEDRAL
  WEDNESDAY 1960, illustrated by C. Walter Hodges. *O.U.P.* (See also p. 336.)

Mayne, William. THE MEMBER FOR THE MARSH. *O.U.P.* 1956. Illustrated by
  Lynton Lamb. Somerset grammar school boys and their weekend pursuits
  in marshy country. Superb characterization, dialogue and setting.

*Means, Florence Crannell. SHUTTERED WINDOWS. *Houghton Mifflin*, New
  York 1943.

*Oxenham, Elsie J. THE ABBEY GIRLS (1920) *Collins* (Schoolgirls' Library) 1951.
  Many other titles, of which the latest is TOMBOYS AT THE ABBEY. *Collins*
  1957.

*Reed, Talbot Baines. THE FIFTH FORM AT ST DOMINIC'S (1907). *Blackie*
  1951.

*Reed, Talbot Baines. THE WILLOUGHBY CAPTAINS (1887), THE COCK
  HOUSE AT FELLSGARTH (1893), THE MASTER OF THE SHELL (1894),
  TOM, DICK AND HARRY (1894), A DOG WITH A BAD NAME (1894).
  Religious Tract Society 1931.

*Richards, Frank. BILLY BUNTER STORIES. *Magnet* 1907–1940. BILLY
  BUNTER books. *Cassell*. Latest, BUNTER THE BAD LAD 1960. Illustrated by
  C. H. Chapman.

Sterling, Dorothy. MARY JANE. (1959 U.S.A.) *Constable* 1960. Colour problem in
  Southern school; sympathetic, well-turned story.

Strong, L. A. G. WRONG FOOT FOREMOST. *Pitman* 1940. Amalgamation of two
  schools and the difficulties of an individualist.

Tring, A. Stephen. THE OLD GANG. *O.U.P.* 1947. Illustrated by John Camp.
  Small-town grammar school and its feud with Modern school; realistic without effort.

Tring, A. Stephen. PENNY DREADFUL 1949, PENNY TRIUMPHANT 1953,
  PENNY PENITENT 1953, PENNY PUZZLED 1955, PENNY DRAMATIC 1956.
  O.U.P. Illustrated by Terence Freeman. Day-school girl of dash and zeal, her
  adventures at school, at home and on holiday.

*Vachell, H. A. THE HILL. *Newnes* (1905) 1925.

*Waugh, Alec. THE LOOM OF YOUTH. *Cassell* (1917) 1929.

*Wilson, D. Wynne. EARLY CLOSING. *Constable* 1931.

Wodehouse, P. G. MIKE. *Black* 1909. Reissued as MIKE AT WRYKYN. *Herbert
  Jenkins* 1953. Conventional public-school story of some merit, with flashes
  of true Wodehouse wit.

2.*Pony Stories* (See also p. 345.)

Anderson, C. W. THE HORSE OF HURRICANE HILL (1956 U.S.A.) 1958,
AFRAID TO RIDE (1957 U.S.A.) 1959. *Brockhampton.* Illustrated by the author.
A horseman writes with understanding of people and their pleasure in horses:
excellent drawings.

*Atkinson, M. E. HUNTER'S MOON. *Bodley Head* 1952. Illustrated by Charlotte
Hough.

*Barne, Kitty. ROSINA COPPER 1954, illustrated by Alfons Purtscher. ROSINA
AND SON 1956, illustrated by Marcia Lane-Foster. *Evans.*

Baxter, Gillian. TAN AND TARMAC. *Evans* 1958. Illustrated by Anne Gordon.
South Kensington riding-school: glimpses of horses in show business, with
refreshingly professional attitude to riding.

*Cannan, Joanna. GAZE AT THE MOON. *Collins* 1957. Illustrated by Sheila Rose.

Cumming, Primrose. THE WEDNESDAY PONY. *Blackie* 1939. Illustrated by
Stanley Lloyd. Butcher's children try to improve on their pony but find him
best in the end; a lively and unusually realistic tale.

Cumming, Primrose. NO PLACE FOR PONIES. *Dent* 1954. Illustrated by M.
Tulloch. Children sent to Sussex guest-house find lack of freedom a handicap
but mystery horse adds excitement to their lives.

Cumming, Primrose. FLYING HORSEMAN. *Dent* 1959. Illustrated by Sheila Rose.
Boy kept from flying career by illness comes to terms with himself and with
the horsy family he works for. Unusually good character-drawing.

Davis, Lavinia. PONY JUNGLE. *Collins* 1944. English children in America
fraternizing over pony-express service, camps, gymkhanas and the like.

*Edwards, Monica. WISH FOR A PONY 1947, THE SUMMER OF THE GREAT
SECRET 1948, THE MIDNIGHT HORSE 1949, THE WHITE RIDERS 1950,
CARGO OF HORSES 1951, HIDDEN IN A DREAM 1952, NO ENTRY 1954,
THE NIGHTBIRD 1955, STORM AHEAD 1953, STRANGER TO THE MARSH
1957, OPERATION SEABIRD 1957, NO GOING BACK 1960. *Collins.* The
Romney Marsh stories. Illustrated by Geoffrey Whittam. (See also p. 333.)

*Edwards, Monica. NO MISTAKING CORKER 1947, BLACK HUNTING WHIP
1950, illustrated by Geoffrey Whittam. PUNCHBOWL MIDNIGHT 1951,
illustrated by Charles Tunnicliffe. THE SPIRIT OF PUNCHBOWL FARM 1952,
THE WANDERER 1953, PUNCHBOWL HARVEST 1954, illustrated by Joan
Wanklyn. FRENCHMAN'S SECRET 1956, THE COWNAPPERS 1958,
illustrated by Geoffrey Whittam. *Collins.* The Punchbowl Farm stories.

Edwards, Monica. THE UNSOUGHT FARM (Autobiography). *Michael Joseph*
1954.

Gray, Patsey. CHALLENGER (1959 U.S.A.). *Dent* 1960. Illustrated by Sam Savitt.

Girl helps grandfather to train horses and riders in California, and becomes show rider. Character and technical details equally good.

Phipson, Joan. GOOD LUCK TO THE RIDER. *Angus & Robertson* 1953. Illustrated by Margaret Horder. Australian homestead and various events with horses: cheerful, good-hearted tale.

Pullein-Thompson, Christine. A DAY TO GO HUNTING. *Collins* 1956. Illustrated by Sheila Rose. Good use of the one-day formula.

Pullein-Thompson, Christine. THE HORSE SALE. *Collins* 1960. Illustrated by Sheila Rose. One-day formula again, a number of sharply-drawn people; more mature attitude to riding and horses than in earlier books.

*Pullein-Thompson, Diana. I WANTED A PONY. *Collins* 1946. Illustrated by Anne Bullen.

*Stafford, Ann. FIVE PROUD RIDERS. *Hamish Hamilton* 1937.

Stanford, Don. THE HORSEMASTERS (1957 U.S.A.). *Harrap* 1958. Illustrated by Michael Lyne. Fascinating story of intensive training in advanced riding school: good characterization.

*Treadgold, Mary. WE COULDN'T LEAVE DINAH 1941, illustrated by Stuart Tresilian. NO PONIES 1946, illustrated by Ruth Gervis. *Cape.*

Wait, Mrs Peter. THE WANTED MAN. *Methuen* 1956. Illustrated by Mary Gernat. Escaped convict, stolen necklace, missing pony: an improbable but entirely readable tale.

West, Joyce. DROVER'S ROAD. *Dent* 1953. Illustrated by the author. The friendliest and most unorthodox horse-story I know, set on a New Zealand sheep-station.

3.*Ballet, stage, circus and music*

*Barne, Kitty. SHE SHALL HAVE MUSIC 1938, MUSICAL HONOURS 1939. *Dent.* Illustrated by Ruth Gervis.

*Benary, Margot. CASTLE ON THE BORDER. *Macmillan* 1957.

*Brown, Pamela. THE SWISH OF THE CURTAIN 1941, MADDY ALONE 1945, GOLDEN PAVEMENTS 1947, BLUE DOOR VENTURE 1949, MADDY AGAIN 1956. *Nelson.* The Blue Door Books. Illustrated by Newton Whittaker.

*Brown, Pamela. HARLEQUIN CORNER 1953, illustrated by Marcia Lane-Foster. UNDERSTUDY 1958, illustrated by Drake Brookshaw. *Nelson.*

*Brown, Pamela. SHOWBOAT SUMMER. *Brockhampton* 1957.

*Dane, Clemence. BROOME STAGES. *Heinemann* (1931) 1960.

Fitzroy, Olivia. WAGONS AND HORSES. *Collins* 1955. Illustrated by Mary Gernat. Lively story of circus families tenting about England, and in particular two children with their lions and horses.

Haskell, Arnold. FELICITY DANCES. *Nelson* 1937. An early ballet story based on fact and with emphasis on ballet technique and training.

Hewitt, Hilda. PANTOMIME CHRISTMAS. *Dent* 1955. Illustrated by Terence Freeman. An ordinary child involved in pantomime excitement but deciding not to go on the stage permanently in spite of success; refreshingly sane.

*Moore, George. EVELYN INNES (1898). *Benn* 1929.

*Spring, Howard. SAMPSON'S CIRCUS 1936, TUMBLEDOWN DICK 1939. *Faber*. Illustrated by Steven Spurrier.

*Streatfeild, Noel. BALLET SHOES. *Dent* 1936. *Penguin* (Puffin Story Books) 1949. Illustrated by Ruth Gervis. THE CIRCUS IS COMING, illustrated by Clarke Hutton. *Dent* (1938) 1948 (revised edition).

*Streatfeild, Noel. WHITE BOOTS 1951, WINTLE'S WONDERS 1957. *Collins*. Illustrated by Richard Kennedy.

Ure, Jean. DANCE FOR TWO. *Harrap* 1960. Illustrated by Richard Kennedy. Two children of different countries and social background make friends during ballet career. Interesting character studies.

*Vipont, Elfrida. THE LARK IN THE MORN 1948, THE LARK ON THE WING 1950, THE SPRING OF THE YEAR 1957, illustrated by T. R. Freeman. FLOWER-ING SPRING 1960, illustrated by Shirley Hughes. *O.U.P.*

Drawing by T. R. Freeman for Elfrida Vipont's LARK ON THE WING (O.U.P.)

Chapter 11 | *Good Chaps and Bad Chaps*

So far I have not felt it a disadvantage to be an adult commenting on children's books. In the realms of fantasy, adult and child read in the same way and look for the same things: the difference is one of degree only. The books I have discussed in the last chapter (success stories about schools or ponies or the theatrical world) perhaps offer less to adults than some other kinds, but they are interesting as a guide to what young people want and the clues they give are very definite. We come now to adventure stories, which adults must read in two different ways. If I am rereading a tale which I knew as a child, so that the suspense element is absent, or lessened, I find I am free to notice the characters and the background as I never did before; and I demand more from these than a child would. If I pick up an adventure story that is new to me, I try to read it (and am often compelled to) as a child reads, purely for the story—for 'what happens next'. The story, if it is a good one, carries me away: afterwards, I can consider the characters, the whole technique.

Obviously, action must come first. We must have a plot. We must, equally, have a background. Events must happen somewhere, and more often than not, background and plot have evolved together. Africa and KING SOLOMON'S MINES, Mississippi and HUCKLE-BERRY FINN, Arizona and Zane Grey's WILDFIRE, South America and THE TAKING OF THE GRY—you cannot separate the two elements. But what about character?

Dominating the adventure story is the formula of good chap versus bad chap. We are not to look for changes of heart, as a rule; complexity in character might slow down the action. The most interesting thing about adventure stories is the way character, persistent as weeds or woodworm, pokes up its head when you think it is dead, says its say in the middle of the banging and crashing. The force of an interesting character comes stealing upon you, making a gradual but permanent impression. Though you may have been aware only of an exciting sequence of events, you realize in the end that character has been at the bottom of it all.

It may be there for a very simple reason. Most of us, young or old, have dreams of a life more exciting than the one we lead. The gangs that children form for their own aggrandizement are repeated in another form in the stories about Bulldog Drummond, or Biggles and his pals, or the adventure-prone trio, Colt and Co., in J. Macdonnell's Australian tale. People like this do not have to look for adventure. It comes to them, and they take us with them into a world which we accept whole-heartedly in all its violent improbability. Because this is so, we can excuse the fascist outlook and the near-cruelty of the Drummond tales or the facetiousness of Biggles. They are still good yarns that carry us along. They satisfy us, whatever age we are, because, in them, action and motive are clear-cut, free from the confusions and divagations of real life. They make us feel that we too could act freely and courageously in exciting circumstances.

What happens next matters to us very much in this kind of book. In the case of a writer of Buchan's calibre it matters even when we know it already. THE THREE HOSTAGES is just as compelling at a tenth reading as it is at the first. Perhaps there is such a thing as a 'born story-teller'. It is certainly a way of saying that one writer can make you believe in the simple exploits of his characters where another, far more sensational, merely bores you. But a good narrative is a matter of craftsmanship—an adventure story particularly. You can read it again and again because when the element of surprise has gone, suspense remains, and motive, and authenticity. It is easy to parody Buchan, because the ingredients of his plots (disguise and escape) are elementary. But he wins his readers by the skill with which he holds off revelation till the last possible moment, by the vitality behind his villains and villainous places, and by the heroes he gives his readers—strong, sensitive and sensible, the unmistakable heroes of a dream-world.

The people in this dream-world are of first importance. If, in an adventure story, we see action concentrated and energized, in its characters we see people like ourselves, but larger, more upstanding, more vital. In THE SPANISH CAVE by Geoffrey Household, a really

spectacular adventure story for children, the writer leads on from
point to point, holding attention partly by the extraordinary events
he describes, partly by his characters. This is the most superbly
improbable plot I have come across for a long time, and I must not
spoil it for those who do not know it. Part of the pleasure in reading
it is in asking questions. Why is the cave on the Asturian coast
dreaded by the villagers? For how many centuries has its mystery
existed? The author lets out the secret grudgingly and expertly. All
the time he avoids too much pressure on credulity by bringing first
one character and then another into the foreground—the eager
young English boy, Dick Garland; Lolita, the young countess, brave
and tomboyish; the Basque shipwright, Echegaray, with his inheritance of magical lore; Pablo, the faithful fisherman. Lightly sketched,
but sketched in action, they are so real that they make it impossible
to doubt the adventure; only these people, you feel, would have em-
barked on such an enterprise and come out alive.

Another masterpiece of craftsmanship, which goes more deeply
into character, is Masefield's DEAD NED. This is the story of a man
who was hanged for murder and brought to life again. But this
happening is not so much the climax of the story as the resolution
of it. The climax is the murder itself, discovered only after the reader
has been almost unbearably expecting it through the events of a
long summer's day in a village near London, in the late eighteenth
century. The old Admiral who is murdered is friend and benefactor
to young Ned Mansell, a medical student near the end of his apprenticeship. The first part of the book establishes place and characters,
deliberately and with superb timing; it establishes Ned's innocence
and enlists your active sympathy for him as he tells his story. From
the Admiral's house, centre of the action, which you come to know
and to visualize in great detail, you move out to the surrounding
country, beyond that to the alleys of London town, and further still,
to glimpses of the French and English courts. The background gives
the story breadth: the foreground is established with circumstantial
detail that has great interest of its own. Every detail, every person
has a place in the slow accumulation of events. Even the minor
characters—like Jane Jollycok in her pedlar's stall at the fair, or
Dick Copshrews who has cost his father so much money, or pretty
Polly, daughter of the Admiral's housekeeper—in some way affect
the chances and catastrophes of the dreadful day that takes Ned to

Newgate. Fate is against Ned, but so is his temperament. Events follow their pattern because he has an affectionate, intuitive nature; because the Admiral is crusty and secretive; because Dennis Rackage is too mean-spirited to bear his step-brother's prosperity.

DEAD NED is a novel, an historical novel brilliantly done. But it is also very much an adventure story, and one conceived in so classic a pattern, with such a fine technique, that I would offer it to children, first because they will enjoy it, and then because they will understand, eventually, how much goes to the making of a good yarn. They will not, if they read this book at fourteen or so, see all the subtlety and wisdom of the character-drawing, but it will have been the characters, and the way they are integrated with the action, that has held them through the compelling story.

Most writers of adventure stories are content with a rather more simple combination of character and action than this. Certain subjects, indeed, may seem to demand the good chap/bad chap formula and nothing more. E. S. Turner has put it in a nutshell. In his splendid history of boys' literature, BOYS WILL BE BOYS, discussing the scient fic magazine story, he says:

> That attempt by Venus to steal the Moon was only one illustration of a failing which characterized the inhabitants of other planets: they were not sporting. Time after time, in stories of planetary adventure, this deficiency was stressed. The dwellers on alien stars might be, and usually were, ahead of us technically; they might have robots working for them as slaves; they might have attained the twin goals of perpetual motion and perpetual life; but they had no more sense of fair play than Neanderthal Man.
> E. S. Turner. BOYS WILL BE BOYS (Michael Joseph, 1948) p. 189.

Scientific tales are a special case, of course. For one thing, while scientific teaching lags behind in girls' schools, they will be less interested in technical plots, and if a writer can ignore girls when he is writing, he will have less need to allow for flexibility of character. But do the science stories of the last three decades offer enough even for boys, who are more ready to accept broadly drawn characters? I think not.

Space is the stage for science stories. As a subject it is superb, but few books nowadays have the force and excitement of those old-fashioned practitioners, Jules Verne and H. G. Wells. Inspiration is notably lacking, and so is enterprise. Curious limitations seem to have been imposed. In a great many space stories, the writer concentrates on the *journey*, which is easier to describe than worlds different from our own. Certainly there should be as much scope for drama in the preparation for a journey into space as in the actual arrival; but, again, many writers concentrate on technical detail and leave out the clash of character which alone could enliven it.

Many space stories, in fact, are stories about machinery. The monotonous exploits of Dan Dare are varied only by changes in technique, and the popular Kemlo books of E. C. Eliott often give me the same impression. In KEMLO AND THE END OF TIME, for instance, the theme is the discovery of a Sphere of Sound where radio programmes and conversations from Earth have been trapped and frozen, forming a rich historical deposit for the people of outer space to study. People from space finding a vessel preserved in space from centuries back—what might they not feel about the past, what might they not be allowed to discover? But no; Kemlo and his friend Kerowski, two space-boys, are impressed, momentarily, but soon rush on to more exciting things—and things, incidentally, which are far easier to describe. When they make contact with space-officers on Earth, you can almost hear the sigh of relief as the author steps back on to known ground. Small wonder that he gives far too many pages to a description of a meteoric storm in space from which the boys rescue a fleet of earth-vessels. The storm itself, the explanation of it, the squaring up for the rescue of the vessels, all take up a good many words. When at last we reach the crisis, what noise, what agitation—and what complete lack of excitement:

The first two ships were about to hit the holding rays when Kemlo yelled:

'Calling all centre ships in formation! Lower holding rays to half distance!'

As Kemlo gave this order, Kerowski manipulated their own holding rays, and at the same moment all the ships around them, except those on the outside edges, brought down their holding rays. In this way the first two of the nine ships were lowered; then the next three, and before the last four could descend farther but were below the height of the outside circle of rays Kemlo almost screamed into the speaker pad, so tense was he:

'They're gathered! Now sweep them away! Full power—twenty degrees right—forty degrees hull incline. Full blast—NOW!' He shouted the last word urgently because no mistake must occur at this moment.

E. C. Eliott. KEMLO AND THE END OF TIME (Nelson, 1957) pp. 166–7.

You have only to compare this passage with one of the really fine descriptions of urgent action (for instance, the dismasting of the *Hurrying Angel* in Masefield's VICTORIOUS TROY, or the fight between Curtis and Twala in KING SOLOMON'S MINES) to see where the trouble lies. Imagination is lacking, and the action never comes to life.

Without imagination—strong, vigorous, free-ranging imagination—it is no use writing space-stories for children except for their very temporary enjoyment, and there the field has been fully exploited. No boys' comic or magazine is complete without its space story. No publisher's list is complete without at least one writer who knows how to get into a space-suit. But the really vital writers for children in this sphere are as scarce as inhabited planets. If boys over twelve really want to be stirred by exploration in space, by the feeling of alien worlds, I can only suggest they give up children's books at once and turn to writers like Arthur Clarke and James Blish. Let these guide them into space and the mysteries of science, for their speculation, conceived in adult terms, has the force of questioning youth. No writer of space stories can afford to be limited by what young readers can understand. Which of us can, after all, understand space? But we want, and children want, the feeling of the unknown. No writer who is still mentally tied to the quadrangle and the officer's mess can give us this.

So we come back to the good chaps and bad chaps. Take Dan Dare, for instance. How monotonous, how mechanical, how limited the adventures of this big, bronzed tailor's dummy of a hero! What matters in the Dan Dare stories? First, the machinery—but does it matter? These gravity rays, these streamlined vessels, these mysterious gases—are they really very new? Or does it matter that Dan should conquer all the planets whose inhabitants are so suspiciously like the nigs and wogs of adventure stories forty years back? No, there is nothing stimulating here. This is where we came in:

Once more Dan made a tour of the area . . . The skeleton
defences of Tony's battle patrol were thickened and deepened;
outposts and O.P.s were set up miles out in the Martian desert, to
control the long-range atomic artillery and the batteries of guided
H-missiles; the latest forms of anti-spacecraft defence, borrowed
from Treens and Therons, were sited in the area, and all around it.
When the operation was complete, the helenium mines were
powerfully defended on all sides. And when Dan finally handed
over command and responsibility to Major Crawford he was
satisfied that the area was as near impregnable as human resources
could make it.
Basil Dawson. DAN DARE ON MARS (Hulton Eagle Novels, 1956)
pp. 83-4.

The books about Dan Dare and the similar space stories by W. E.
Johns are full of this brashly imperialistic flavour, this crude reduc-
tion of human beings to two camps. Of course every good adventure
story has in it the element of conflict as well as of discovery. But
even if a space story is conceived in the all too familiar terms of
warfare, need it be confined to the struggle of two earth powers to
dominate space, or the equally distasteful theme of imperialist
conquest? Will no writer go deep enough to show children a conflict with worlds that are really different—as Donald Suddaby almost
does in his unusually enterprising PRISONERS OF SATURN? There
seems no reason why boys should not be asked to make some imaginative effort, to try to appreciate the possible existence of points of
view other than their own; yet in book after book the author makes
his space people no more than physically modified versions of ourselves, bad chaps for our good chaps to fight, or good chaps to be
taken on the strength.

Of course it is natural that bad chaps, in outer space, should be
seen as power-mad, tyrannical, rigid in mind—natural that they
should reflect our own present fears.

Equally, the nobler races from other planets can be used to comment on the problems of our times. In TO WORLDS UNKNOWN,
by Captain Johns, Rolto, a space-pilot, feels that Earth should be
destroyed before her inhabitants have wrecked the universe by their
war-mongering, and there are other writers who make this a subject
for interplanetary discussion. The idea of an international spy-

satellite, put forward by the Americans in October of 1959, may
be found in Patrick Moore's WHEEL IN SPACE, published in 1956.
E. C. Eliott's KEMLO AND THE CRAZY PLANET contains a moving
plea that the race of Zanians, still not fully evolved as humans from
their web-footed ancestors, should be left alone by men of Earth
and Space to work out their own destiny.

In discussing such moral questions, writers of space-fiction have
been more, or less, successful according to the force of their imagination.

Donald Suddaby's PRISONER OF SATURN (like many other stories)
is based on fear of oppression; but he has really tried to imagine
personality and power in extra-human terms. The Will of the
Saturnians is expressed, as far as the visiting Earthmen are concerned,
in terms of cosmic rays allied to an invincible intelligence. For the
benefit of men, a physical appearance is formed to communicate
with them. This being, built up rather lumpily of congealed cloud, they
nickname Alpha, and it is presented at first in a partly humorous way:

Eyes and mouth might have been playfully designed with a pair
of compasses; the nose was beaked, he had no finger-nails, no
hair on the fuzzy head, and his chest and back and arms and legs
looked as though they were made of discoloured wheat-husks.

'Here!' exclaimed Jonah after a time, somewhat nobly strip-
ping himself of his jacket. 'Put this on.'

In spite of himself he had kept glancing back at the worrying
figure and suddenly decided to humanize it a little more. Alpha,
of course, had no notion of how to wear clothes, so plain Fred
Jones and I had to dress him—lifting the queer, heavy arms and
thrusting them into sleeves, buttoning him across the chest,
pulling the tweed down properly behind.

'I'll be hanged if I'm giving him my trousers,' said Jonah,
standing back half angry, half laughing, to gauge the general effect.
'But you look a trifle better now.'

'*It is an act of what you call kindness*,' the eerie figure pronounced, and we all noticed that his intonation was much more
human, a proof of quick learning. '*Spasíbo. Thank you. If it
causes you to accept me more easily, it is good.*'

Donald Suddaby. PRISONERS OF SATURN (Bodley Head, 1957)
p. 115.

But in later descriptions of this being, and of the glass cities where thought has a local habitation, there is real force and originality. The author has tried to take us to Saturn, not only geographically, but also psychologically. Patrick Moore, from whom we are surely entitled to expect a great deal, has somehow failed to do either. With all the energy and skill he has spent on the invention of supremely terrifying death-rays and ultra-ingenious machines, the planets he describes are really only the same old pantomime backcloth that comes out each year for the next conflict of Demon King and Fairy Queen. There is no feeling that we are in a mysterious unknown world. The characters are almost always men of the familiar pattern, representing either the good British or the evil foreigners. There are, it is true, some Martians, but their thought-processes seem very much like our own: they are out to win land, power, or wealth of some kind and to do down their rivals. Patrick Moore's stories are most exciting, but children will be more permanently satisfied, I am sure, with something like David Craigie's artless tale, THE VOYAGE OF THE LUNA I, where he tells of a boy and girl unexpectedly rocketed to the Moon; for here, together with a generous allowance of bat-like, spider-like and jelly-like creatures (which are *really* frightening), the young reader can follow the adventures of a hero and heroine who are not hard-boiled and invincible, but timorous and brave by turns, sensible and then frantic, one minute longing for Earth and the next minute observing eagerly an entirely new world.

What I miss more than anything else in children's space stories is the element of discovery, that priceless element in any adventure story. What other real excuse can there be for using space as a setting?

In the long run, no child demands that other worlds should be *described*. We have to be made to believe in them by the force of suggestion, by arrangement of significant details; by the glancing, poetic descriptions, for instance, in Paul Berna's THRESHOLD OF THE STARS and its sequel CONTINENT IN THE SKY. His standpoint is expressed by M. Wertz, a school teacher in the sealed experimental station where space-vessels are launched to circle the Moon:

'The Moon may well seem to you to be another living, friendly planet like our Earth. Do not believe it: it is a dangerous world burnt out alternately by roasting heat and freezing cold, in which nothing is on a human scale. My first lesson in lunar geography may perhaps disabuse you of that inclination towards the marvellous which is only natural at your age. You have this consolation, children—soon you will come to agree with me that scientific fact is just as enthralling as legendary fiction.'

What followed swept from our heads all the pretty pictures that had amused past generations. None the less this strictly scientific viewpoint which he substituted left a door through which the imagination could range, and I think many of us felt the poetry that shone from the dead planet.

Paul Berna. THRESHOLD OF THE STARS. Translated by John Buchanan-Brown. (Bodley Head, 1958) pp. 32–3.

And what child would not find his mind suddenly racing after reading the test-pilot's description of the crystalline formations on Copernicus which, when the sun catches them, look like 'fields of dazzling roses', or the impressionist picture of a journey through a canyon on the Moon (in CONTINENT IN THE SKY) where a 'sheer wall of delicately tinted lava, like an immense stained-glass window . . . glowed an instant and then was swallowed up in darkness behind us.'

Ultimately, though, Paul Berna's space stories are valuable for their characters. The details of the use of space ships, for instance, which can be wearisome even to the most scientifically-minded boy, are floated from time to time on an agreeable personal humour, as in Dimoto's description of the flight of the *Agnes*:

'The newspaper men who were there . . . got together straight away and called the new craft the *flying saucepan* and declared that its first flight would be its last! I gave them forty seconds to laugh their fill and then took off with all eight jets at full power. The roar soon stopped their chatter! I was ordered to go through some set manœuvres at high altitude; that was a piece of cake, then I treated myself to a few low level aerobatics right under the noses of the stupid asses, finishing with a burst of speed that nearly blew out their eardrums . . . Then I brought my flying saucepan down plumb on the launching platform, two hundred yards from the observation post, as neatly as an egg in an egg-cup. The observers who weren't flat on their faces with their hands over their ears fell over backwards to see ten tons of deadweight touch down as gently as a toy balloon.' Ibid., p. 15.

More deeply, the books are concerned with the *effect* of discovery—on the boy Michael Jouffre (who tells the stories), on Captain Bouscart the bully and the mutinous lieutenant Yves, and the Commander himself, who wants power and achievement for his country's sake but who wants scientific discovery far more. There are good chaps and bad chaps here, but something more besides.

Children have a right to that 'something more', and this brings me to the question of the hero in adventure stories. Who is he? And who should he be?

Now adventure—danger and discovery, national or personal conflict—must to some extent be adapted for children. They should be given real dangers, real wounds, but, for them, dead bodies should not lie in the horrifying and soul-cringing postures of bodies in police photographs. There is no room for the sordid in adventure stories, though plenty of room for the disgraceful. Crooks must be wicked: they should not be perverted. Heroes, even if they show cynicism or self-doubt, must have the brightness of the stars somewhere about them. Adventure stories are a form of romance. To this extent they are limited, but they need not be unreal. They must reflect an active world, even if it is a world that no longer exists (like Rider Haggard's Africa, or Masefield's oceans crowded with clipper ships).

This is primarily an adult world, and is best presented, as a rule, with adult or near-adult heroes. The scuffling investigations of children can rarely hold up a tale of great danger, great disaster, great enterprise. That is why the great adventure stories of the past, like ROBBERY UNDER ARMS or LORNA DOONE or KING SOLOMON'S MINES, go on flowering while lesser and more recent books have wilted away; and that is why children have appropriated many modern writers who do not write for them—among the most obvious, Buchan, Masefield, Hammond Innes, C. S. Forester and Nevil Shute.

We have our hero, then, an ardent youth or an active pioneer keeping middle age at bay. What are his adventures to be? Above all, they must have an ideal behind them. The hero must be concerned for a cause, a great love, a treasure-hunt whose end is mystery as well as gain. When we read adventure stories, at any age, we want the power to disengage ourselves from the affairs of this world and to follow by proxy a course of action not wholly materialistic. Allan Quatermain is paid a salary for some of his exploits, but even for a child reader his desiccated and matter-of-fact exterior conceals a romantic heart. Quatermain is a complex character. His superb skill as a hunter is enough for children at their first reading. It is later that they will notice the fears and doubts behind that skill. As a hero, he probably appeals to boys more for what he does than what he is, and yet, rereading the Quatermain stories, I am struck by the way his character dominates these brilliant, exciting tales of elephants and witches, treasure and betrayal.

In much the same way Andrew Balfour's magnificent African travelogue, THE GOLDEN KINGDOM,* can be read simply for such dramatic scenes as the crossing of the perilous swamp or the shooting at the papegai, but in fact the book stands and falls by the character of Corkran the Coxswain, who drags the unwilling narrator, Doctor Mortimer, from his comfortable village practice with the lure of untold riches. Here, as with Alan Quatermain, we have, not a good chap nor a bad chap, but a fascinating amalgam of worthy and unworthy, heroic and unheroic.

Africa, that secret and fabulous land, has always been a mine for adventure stories, most of them conceived as adult novels. There is Buchan's PRESTER JOHN, with its earnest, determined young hero, and its fantastic treasure-house. There is Masefield's LIVE AND KICKING NED, with its vivid descriptions of attack and defence in a Guinea village. There is FLAMINGO FEATHER, by Laurens van der Post, a thriller so compelling that you seem to tread in the footsteps of fugitive and tracker. Against these adult stories, how does the boy hero look, in the story written for boys?

Such stories are most likely to be good if they accept and exploit their limitations; almost certain to fail if they try to pretend that they are not limited. Obviously children can be brave and their adventures can be exciting and dangerous; but they do not often, in real life, meet a villain on his own terms and defeat him, and it is not easy to believe in a story that makes them do this. Nor is the attitude of children to danger usually romantic. It is desperate and direction-

---

* (THE GOLDEN KINGDOM, first published in 1903, has been out of print for many years. It is long-winded in parts, occasionally tedious, but it is still one of the best African adventure stories ever written.)

less, sometimes cunning, sometimes futile and mistaken. So that a writer who embroils a hero of twelve in a serious matter like a native uprising, as Frances Greenall does, for instance, in THE ULENDO DETECTIVES, is asking for trouble. It is true that this author does confine the activities of her young characters to nosing around, tracking and other matters suitable to their years, and keeps them a longish way away from danger. All the same, the telegram that comes to them as a reward for their detective work does suggest what dangerous ground she is treading. It reads like an abstract of a whole class of adventure stories:

'The Brightstones Diamond Corporation expresses its sincere thanks to four young detectives who exposed illicit diamond route from Tanganyika. Present successful operations against smugglers entirely due to information received from you stop. Brightstones arranging one hundred and fifty pounds reward to each detective whose aid they hope to enlist again in future.'
Frances Greenall. THE ULENDO DETECTIVES (Bell, 1956) p. 188.

Far better, I believe, to put your young hero and heroine a little off centre, and give them attendant adults who can at moments of crisis produce commonsense or pistols as required, while the children face danger in their own way. In Masefield's boys' story MARTIN HYDE, a woman spy (who has been outwitted by the young hero) remarks 'a boy is so unexpected, there's no beating a boy, except with a good birch rod.' Any writer who wants to make the best of a boy hero would do well to take this as his motto.

Patrick O'Brian has done so in THE ROAD TO SAMARCAND, a superb picaresque story. Young Derrick does the fantastic journey across the Gobi desert and through Himalayan passes with the support of his tough uncle and the tougher Mr Ross, of Professor Ayrton, whose absent-mindedness is more apparent than real, of Li-Han the Chinese cook and Olaf, the thick-headed Swedish sailor. A good deal of what he does, in fact, is planned for him; but his wits and his powers of endurance are often called upon, and he comes out of the adventure older and wiser. The magnificent adventure story, BIG TIGER AND CHRISTIAN, by Fritz Mühlenweg, has this same plan. The two boys, one English and one Oriental, are mixed up in Chinese guerilla warfare and they survive because of good luck, because of the kindness of adults, and, often, because of their own resourcefulness, and their boyish talent for turning up unexpectedly at the wrong moment for the villain.

The story-telling magic works best, of course, when the reader can identify himself with the hero, and this may sometimes be easier (though not always so satisfying) when that hero is a boy. One of the best African stories written for children is Roy Fuller's SAVAGE GOLD, a casual, sophisticated tale about the clash of rival mining interests in Kenya, with two boy heroes and two adult supporters. The adults (Mr Craig the District Commissioner and Mr Brown the anthropologist) are pleasantly lazy and like to keep out of danger. The two boys, Charles Craig and Robert Brown, are presented crisply as interesting individuals, Robert with his know-all front, Charles with his affectation of insouciance. Conversations like these are not easy to find in children's stories:

'Makala is boring,' said Charles, as they prepared for bed the first night, 'but if you really want to see them I'll take you round and show you the sights—such as they are.'

'After my experiences on the ship and in Mombasa,' said Robert, a little sententiously, 'I should hesitate before I called anywhere boring.'

'Yes,' said Charles, with a lethargic air, 'I must say you have been involved in a bit of blood and thunder. But nothing like that ever happens to me. I don't think I want it to.'

'Well, then,' asked Robert, with the seriousness of one who imagines he is just beginning to see what life is about, 'what do you want out of existence?'

Charles turned round from an experiment he was conducting at the mirror of introducing carbolic soap with a needle into a pimple on his chin. 'Detachment,' he said. 'The opportunity to observe. To make scientific observations like this.' He wagged the needle.

Robert laughed amiably. The ice between them was broken.

'I must say, Brown,' said Charles, with interest, 'you are one of a very few persons who laugh at me.'

Roy Fuller. SAVAGE GOLD (Penguin, 1957. First published 1946) p. 32.

This naturalness, and the refreshing attitude to adventure, make it easy to believe in the way the boys tackle situations of real danger, as boys and not as imitation adults. Robert, when he is kidnapped

Frontispiece by Robert Medley for Roy Fuller's SAVAGE GOLD (Penguin).
Sets the sophisticated tone of the story

in a brutal fashion, is worried, alarmed, despondent, even tearful.
His plot to circumvent the villain by pouring away all the whisky
intended to bribe the native king is more a hindrance than a help.
The boys react to the war between the king and his usurping half-
brother in a typical way. Charles comments at one point:

> 'There seemed to be so few of them . . . And the villages were
> burning so casually. And then we came along so accidentally. I
> had imagined a war to be very different. There is such a lot of
> space where the war *isn't*.'
> Ibid., p. 123.

And after William, their negro servant, is killed by the enemy, the
author touches the event with delicacy and truth:

> 'The poor fellow's dead.' The Major's hat was in his hand, and
> he did not know where to look.
> 'Oh, Father!' said Robert, turning aside and wanting to run
> away over the huge green country which lay before him, from the
> ugly body and the warriors standing silently round it. But it was
> not until William was lifted and being borne back to the guest
> huts and he saw the dangling arms and the lightish undersides
> of the bare feet that the full sense of loss was brought home to
> him. He started painfully and silently to cry.
> Ibid., p. 170.

In fact, Roy Fuller has had the courage to show a boy behaving in
adventure as we can believe he really might behave, skirting danger
and not at all sure if he likes it. Stories like this say something about
their characters which is well worth saying.

Adventure flourishes at its simplest and most striking in tales of
the sea. An apprenticeship in sail or in steam has always given
opportunity for the young to show their gifts, though these have
more often been gifts of endurance and patience than anything more
dramatic. Here we have a special version of the hero, the apprentice
seaman or junior officer of seventeen or eighteen, a boy free from the
dependencies of schooldays but not yet cast in the mould of a man;
a boy with plenty to learn but with the right equipment for learning,
with the ardour and curiosity and energy of his age. Such heroes
we find in Masefield's VICTORIOUS TROY and THE BIRD OF
DAWNING. These are not children's books—that is, they are not
sold by the publisher for children, and they present adventure in a
serious adult manner. All the same, no child with any feeling for
adventure can afford to miss them. In both stories (they are founded
on fact) a young man is suddenly burdened with overwhelming
responsibility. 'Cruiser' Trewsbury, a young officer, hero of THE
BIRD OF DAWNING, is twenty-two when he meets with the adventure
of the drifting, mysteriously empty clipper ship. We can well believe
in his skill and enterprise and we are chiefly interested in how he will
use his experience. But in VICTORIOUS TROY we are dealing with a
lad, Dick Pomfret, senior apprentice of the *Hurrying Angel*. When
the ship is caught in a cyclone in the South Pacific, with Mate and

Second Mate dead and the Captain disabled, Dick is taken unawares. He is a worrier, a boy who likes to chew over dangers and approach them slowly. Somehow, with a courage that is blind and muddled and infinitely touching, he collects his thoughts and makes plans for putting over a sea-anchor, cutting away the wreckage of the masts, rigging emergency sails. Some of his plans succeed, others fail. At the burial of the elderly Mate, whom he had liked in an exasperated fashion, he blunders through the few words he can remember of the service, confusedly and in misery, Always, at the back of his mind, he thinks about the support of someone older:

> Crawling away from where he was he thought, 'Why, the officers may be in the half-deck. They may have been swept down here . . . They may have brought Newbarn here . . . Of course: why haven't I thought of that before? That is where they will be . . . waiting for someone to help—Captain Cobb, old Duck, and good old Dudley Mac, that glorious Scot, and Newbarn, saddle-sore from the boom.' Dick was still a boy. Though the sea had given him manhood before his years, he still hoped as a boy. 'Oh God,' he prayed, 'please let them all be there.'
> John Masefield. VICTORIOUS TROY (Heinemann, 1935) p. 97.

Yet, as the storm rages on, Dick changes. Confidence comes, slowly: he takes courage to assert himself with the Old Man, and even, in a burst of fury at the fate of his fellows, to criticize him. When they are hailed at last by a passing steamer, Dick speaks to its captain as a man. He knows that if he can borrow tools and supplies he can rig the ship and get her to a Cape port. Courage in him has met and responded to the endeavour of the old ship. The spirit of courage and endeavour, victorious Troy, the defeated rising again, this is the theme of the book, expressed in the behaviour of a boy in time of danger; a boy in years and a boy in temperament, so that no young person reading the book could fail to understand and follow his feelings and actions.

With Masefield, as with Conrad, it is endeavour that matters, the motives and the potentialities of the people who behave heroically. The hero is a symbol of the best in man, as well as an individual meeting danger in his own way and in nobody else's. This splendid theme is not easy to use in children's books, where heroism is taken for granted, not analysed. In adult stories, adventure is something

that can be real and strong and impressive and yet suffer the indigni-
ties and malignities of real life. We can see a hero in the making,
whereas, in stories for children, the boy hero usually has his courage
already, as an accepted quality, at the outset of the story. Adventure
shapes him: he does not shape adventure.

Armstrong Sperry's THE BOY WHO WAS AFRAID is a notable
exception. It tells briefly and lyrically the story of a Polynesian boy,
Mafatu, who was wrecked as a baby and is haunted by fear of the
sea. It is with a boy's limitations that he takes a canoe and pushes
off into unknown waters, sails through a storm and lives for a time,
in some danger, on a *tapu* island. The theme, the conquest of fear, is
studied seriously, in regard to this particular boy. But in another of
Sperry's stories, DANGER TO WINDWARD, we have the more
familiar externalized adventure story. Our young hero, Hugh
Dewar, involved in a family feud, is impressed on to the whaler *Good
Intent*. In his adventures on shipboard and on the island of Tonga-
reva he is supported by the young ship's doctor; and in the end he
defeats his enemies, white and black, and wins back his inheritance.
This is a good adventure story, tough, thrilling, vivid and fast, but it is
limited. Action comes first, character second. The two are never,
really, interdependent. The majority of children's adventure tales are
externalized, and use the formal distinction between good chaps and
bad chaps. Given a good story (which is not as easy to find as you
would think), these simple characters will do very well; but the
story must be especially convincing. Among sea stories, Captain
Frank Knight's tales of the great age of sailing ships are outstanding
in this respect. THE GOLDEN MONKEY has a boy as hero, seeking for
a father lost in the early Australian gold-rush. VOYAGE TO BENGAL
has for nominal hero a lad of seventeen working as a foremast hand
on an East Indiaman; but in fact this is a spirited contest of good
chaps and knaves, rounded off by a romance with the captain's
daughter. CLIPPERS TO CHINA, with its tea-race plot, is a straight
fight between the ship's apprentice and the sinister First Officer
Pengold. Background and action carry these stories through; only
the simplest typed characters are needed.

It is no accident that the best stories of adventure at sea are
historical in setting and subject. It is far more difficult to make a
successful story out of a trawler, a steamship or a dinghy with an
outboard motor. The bad chaps of a century ago can be dressed up

to suit the author's needs. Their evil deeds wear the gloss of antiquity. But let the writer move from the deck of a sailing ship to a modern steam yacht and he moves at once into hazard. He has got to create modern crooks and here we shall be hampered by reality—for, however imperfectly they understand, his younger readers do study newspapers and have their own ideas about crime. Besides, modern communications have affected the sea story. Anything might happen on a voyage of five or ten weeks; but today, ships being as accessible as any other environment, crooks are merely visitors or refugees— no longer inhabitants of an enclosed and extraordinary world. The sea itself has become a mere background, having no effect on character, mood or action.

Not for all writers, luckily. Allan McLean has sited the adventure of THE MASTER OF MORGANA, most successfully, in a working trawler; and Richard Armstrong, in SEA CHANGE, THE LAME DUCK and NO TIME FOR TANKERS, presents his dirty modern vessels in as exciting a light as even Masefield shed on clipper ships. I was stirred by Armstrong's books, not because Cam Renton's adventures in South America or Greg Harris's in the Persian Gulf were particularly original, but because the purpose of the stories was not, ultimately, adventure. They are stories full of thrills and surprises and chases, but what matters all the way through is the development of character, the making of a man out of the changeable, uncouth elements of a boy.

It is obvious, of course, that a story of adventure *can* only last because of its characters, and this is not contradicted by the paramount necessity of a good story. For it is the characters who make the story move. It is Allan Quatermain who makes KING SOLOMON'S MINES outstanding among innumerable searches for lost tribes and treasure in the African interior. It is the perplexities of Armstrong's young heroes which light up his stories, unoriginal as to plot, of crooks at sea. There are only a few stock adventures on which the writer must exercise his ingenuity—and the illustrator, too, though I myself often find him out of place. Certainly no boy who is eagerly following a fight in his imagination wishes to see one moment of it frozen in a drawing on the opposite page. Scenes of action could only be adequately illustrated by *moving* pictures. Failing these, the author can only hope that his illustrator will try to interpret the mood of his story and create the right atmosphere for him. One

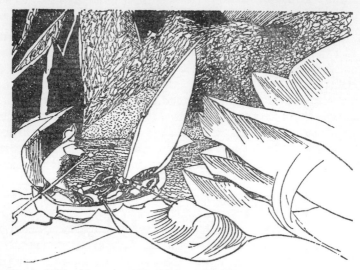

Drawing by Michael Leszczynski for Richard Armstrong's DANGER ROCK (Dent)
Below: Drawing by Edward Osmond for Richard Armstrong's THE LOST SHIP
(Dent)

sailing ship, one tanker, is much like another, but an artist with a sure line and a personal vision can make it seem the one and only; and since at the present time illustration seems to be the rule in adventure stories, this is what we must look for.

But the sea is not only a place of transit for crooks and would-be heroes. It is the road to that most romantic subject of adventure stories—buried treasure.

There are few of us who are unmoved by the lure of a desert island which offers privacy and adventure at the same time, few of us who do not feel excited at the thought of hidden treasure. In TREASURE ISLAND, Stevenson welded the Robinsonnade and the treasure hunt together once and for all. This splendid adventure story, written to please his thirteen-year-old stepson, first serialized in a boys' magazine, is built upon *character*; on the opportunism, the sheer nosiness of Jim Hawkins, a boy meeting danger as a boy; and on the bad chap with a heart of gold, Long John Silver, loud-mouthed, sinister, with an intermittent yearning for the good. Barrie's caricature of him, in Captain Hook, only emphasized what children have been discovering for more than a century, that Long John Silver is the most convincing, as well as the most exaggerated, of all story book villains.* The ambivalence of his character is not allowed to upset the balance of the story. Stevenson accepted, like all his descendants, the formula of good chaps and bad chaps. The good chap, by definition, is the chap who has a right to the treasure; the bad chap is trying to take it from him or to get there first. The good chap's right may only be in fact a priority. It may be a matter of sheer good luck, the fact that he is the first to see the map or hear the legend. But we know from the start which side we are on. Just as, in a space story, we accept the author's assumption (not always cheerfully and easily) that Earthmen have a right to colonize Mars or Saturn, regard-

---

* In 1936 Black's of London published a sequel to TREASURE ISLAND by H. A. Calhoun, BACK TO TREASURE ISLAND, which follows up hints for a sequel which the author believes were left deliberately by Stevenson. It is a good swashbuckling tale, with Jim Hawkins and Silver once more opposed on the beach and in the stockade; the language is a tolerably good imitation of Stevenson's; what is missing is the subtlety of character, especially in the case of Silver, who has become an out-and-out villain.

Mention must also be made of THE ADVENTURES OF BENN GUNN by R. F. Delderfield (Hodder & Stoughton, 1956), an ingenious attempt to explain Gunn's presence on the island.

less of the wishes of the inhabitants, so in treasure tales we turn a
deaf ear to any possible claim the bad chaps may have.

In a good yarn by Richard Armstrong, THE LOST SHIP, two boys
feel it their duty to beat Bull and Mac to the gold on the wrecked
Drachenfels. The author makes it clear that Shorty and Nick are
good chaps and that Bull and Mac are a couple of crooks, and yet it is
Bull and Mac who first knew of the treasure and nobody has more
right to it than they have. Of course no one is going to question the
author, because this is a story, and everybody expects the good
chaps to get the treasure. The claim of young David and his uncle is
just as dubious in Ian Serraillier's South Sea tale, THEY RACED FOR
TREASURE; and in THE TAMBAI TREASURE by R. S. Porteous, the
thirteen-year-old hero learns by eavesdropping the secret of a syndicate of Australian businessmen who are after a sunk Spanish galleon.

In a book that turned on character, all this would matter very
much. But these are stories of action which, based on apparently
concrete facts of place and time and event, belong, really, to an
unreal world governed by the strictest conventions. The traditional
morality of the cowboy tale sometimes cuts right across the morals
of civilized communities. It grows from an environment where
violent means may be justified by their ends. It prescribes that the
good chap shall always win, no matter what he does in the process.
Now this is fair enough so long as we *are* dealing with good *chaps*
and not with good *boys*. In the true cowboy story, it is a case of
'children (and women) should be seen and not heard'. This is probably, in part, because the Western story grew up alongside the
Western film. Tom Mix and Buck Jones, those cowboy heroes of the
'twenties, belong to the Zane Grey period. Hopalong Cassidy rose to
international fame simultaneously in print and on the screen. The
exploits of Buffalo Bill and Wyatt Earp were always chronicled
both in comics and in films. Where our eyes, as well as our minds,
are filled with the picture of a young man leaping on to his horse,
we are affronted by the sight of a lad in cut-down breeches doing the
same.

This is why Rex Dixon has failed in his attempt to introduce a boy
into a man's world. Pocomoto, hero of a series of boys' stories, is an
orphan brought up by two old-timers and admirably equipped for
outdoor adventure; but he invariably stands on one side of the
action. In POCOMOTO—BUFFALO HUNTER, the action is almost all

in flash-back, with the boy a ready listener. In POCOMOTO—
PONY-EXPRESS RIDER, he has one exciting ride in dangerous
circumstances, but he rides as an imitation cowboy, and he is far
more interesting as a boy trying to settle down in a respectable household. I would rather prescribe for boys the rattling yarns of John
Robb, like SIOUX ARROW and TEN GUNS FOR SHELBY, where the
central character is a man. Young Ray Milroy plays a useful part in
the stories, but any boy reader will at once identify himself with the
enigmatic, tough Captain Shelby. Again, Rutherford Montgomery's
Golden Stallion stories have a young hero, still at school though
he enters fully into the life of his father's ranch. But although the
Golden Stallion's adventures involve men—stockmen, oil-prospec-
tors, dudes visiting the ranch, bad chaps of various kinds—it is really
the band of wild horses that chiefly concerns us, and the tang of the
open air, in blinding sun or whirling snow, is more impressive than
the rather limited clashes of character, the rather perfunctory plots.

In Rutherford Montgomery's tales we are still out West, but the
cowboy of today is moving his range, and perhaps in the future the
climate of Australia may suit him better than that of Texas or
Arizona. Frank Dalby Davison's fine story of a red calf, MAN-SHY,
has its cowboys, but they resemble the traditional cowboy only in
their monosyllabic names. They are drawn from the life—tough,
enduring, speaking only when they have to and then little. This is
not a story of conflict between men. Theirs is a geographical problem. How are they to keep their herds separate from the scrubber
gangs that roam the waste lands, the rogues and outlaws and escaped
beasts whose brands have grown over?

The old energetic life of the Westerns seems to have been trans-
ferred. Perhaps the Western as such is finished. Certainly it has
dwindled, except in the hands of a few writers, to a meaningless
series of fights. These are not in themselves bad for children, in my
opinion. They are entirely formalized. The hero and the villain will
settle their differences with stereotyped punches, one-two-one-two,
and the hero always wins; or there will be a shooting match in which,
even if the good chaps and bad chaps get mixed in the reader's mind,
he has the comfortable certainty that the good chaps are bound to
come out best. There can be nothing either frightening nor misleading in a morality so absolute. What *is* wrong is that the motives
of violence, in cowboy stories and in films of today, are so often

superficial. The writer will put his best efforts into the action of a story, letting character take its chance. The child reader is bound to gather that cowboys only fight over money or water-holes or such material objects, that personal enmity counts for nothing. There is no room for the real conflict of character which is what he should be persuaded, now and then, to contemplate.

I am sure, anyhow, that every boy and girl should know the traditional cowboy as he once was, and for this he must go to the adult bookshelf. Here he will find stories where men are men and yet may also be mixed, interesting human beings. Among modern writers, there is H. L. Davis, difficult to read, but infinitely rewarding, with pioneer tales like WINDS OF MORNING and THE DISTANT MUSIC. There is Jack Schaefer, with stories like THE BIG RANGE and, above all, SHANE; for Schaefer can put across the man of mystery, the outlaw with a secret, the cryptic hero, as nobody else can at the present time. There is Max Brand's DESTRY RIDES AGAIN, with its magnificent hero-villain. And there is Zane Grey, with his gallery of heroes as dashing as Rupert Rassendyll himself, as tormented as Captain Nemo, as adult as you could wish but with a youthful flame of courage and idealism burning in them.

Nothing is ever simple with Zane Grey. The arresting, brooding peculiarities of the Mormons make gang-warfare seem quite new in THE HERITAGE OF THE DESERT and the superb RIDERS OF THE PURPLE SAGE, and, in this last book, there is Lassiter, one of the most mysterious and compelling of all adventure heroes. There is the historical, pioneering background of FIGHTING CARAVANS or THE THUNDERING HERD. There is the fascinatio of horse-breaking, the pure breath of the open spaces, in W ILDI RE, and, besides, the romantic force of the character of Slone. The e is everything here for the boy or girl who will take a chance on occasionally wearisome passages. For, if Zane Grey's style is sometimes slow, at other times it moves faster than a wild mustang. He has the two priceless gifts for a writer of adventure stories—he can describe action and he can create character. It is the duty of the writer to isolate the moment of action from the hours of inaction, to prove that life is exciting. And he can only do this if, even as he sweeps his reader right away from the ordinary world, he takes with him into the unknown parts of sea or land or air, not good chaps and bad chaps, but men.

Reading List

1.*Space stories*

*Berna, Paul. THRESHOLD OF THE STARS (1954 France) 1958, illustrated
   by Geraldine Spence. CONTINENT IN THE SKY (1955 France) 1959,
   illustrated by Janet Duchesne. *Bodley Head.* Translated by John
   Buchanan-Brown.

*Craigie, David. THE VOYAGE OF THE 'LUNA I'. *Eyre & Spottiswoode* 1948.
   Illustrated by Dorothy Craigie.

Cross, John Keir. THE ANGRY PLANET 1945, S.O.S. FROM MARS 1954. *Hutchinson.* Mock-veracious accounts of expeditions, startling and exciting.

*Dawson, Basil. DAN DARE ON MARS. *Hulton* (Eagle Novel) 1956.

*Ellott, E. C. KEMLO AND THE CRAZY PLANET 1954, KEMLO AND THE END
   OF TIME 1957. *Nelson.* Many other titles. Illustrated by Bruce Cornwall.

*Johns, Capt. W. E. TO WORLDS UNKNOWN. *Hodder & Stoughton* 1960.
   Illustrated by Stead.

*Moore, Patrick. THE MASTER OF THE MOON 1952, THE FROZEN PLANET
   1954. *Museum Press.* WHEEL IN SPACE. *Lutterworth* 1956. RAIDERS OF
   MARS 1959, CAPTIVES OF THE MOON 1960. *Burke.*

*Suddaby, Donald. PRISONERS OF SATURN. *Bodley Head* 1957. Illustrated
   by Harold Jones.

Walters, Hugh. BLAST OFF AT WOOMERA 1957, THE DOMES OF PICO 1958,
   OPERATION COLUMBUS 1960. *Faber.* Contest of British and an enemy power
   on the Moon. Good example of imperialistic type of space-story, with little
   time for describing space and rather bloodthirsty emphasis on violence and
   physical suffering.

2.*African adventure*

*Balfour, Andrew. THE GOLDEN KINGDOM (1903). *Nelson* (1916) 1920.

*Buchan, John. PRESTER JOHN. *Nelson* 1910. *Penguin* 1956.

*Fuller, Roy. SAVAGE GOLD. *John Lehmann* 1946. *Penguin* (Puffin Story Books)
   1957. Illustrated by Robert Medley.

*Greenall, Frances. THE ULENDO DETECTIVES. *Bell* 1956. Illustrated by Michael
   Ross.

Guillot, René. ELEPHANT ROAD (1957 France). *Bodley Head* 1959. Translated
   by Richard Graves. Illustrated by Don Higgins. Ivory Coast, boy seeking
   father in the jungle; background of film-making among animals in the wild.

Guillot, René. THE WHITE SHADOW (1948 France). *O.U.P.* 1959. Translated by Brian Rhys. Illustrated by Faith Jaques. French West Africa, mysterious bond between French girl and African orphan. Wonderful atmosphere and background.

*Haggard, H. Rider. KING SOLOMON'S MINES (1885). *Penguin* (Puffin Story Books) 1958. ALLAN QUATERMAIN (1887). *Macdonald* 1949. NADA THE LILY (1892). *Dent* (1933) 1959. THE IVORY CHILD (1916) *Cassell* 1926. THE HOLY FLOWER (1915). *Macdonald* 1954. ALLAN AND THE ICE GODS. *Hutchinson* 1927. ALLAN'S WIFE AND OTHER TALES (1889). *Macdonald* 1951.

*Masefield, John. LIVE AND KICKING NED. *Heinemann* 1939.

*Post, Laurens van der. FLAMINGO FEATHER. *Hogarth Press* 1955.

3.The Sea and Treasure Islands

*Armstrong, Richard. SEA CHANGE 1948, DANGER ROCK 1955, illustrated by Michel Leszczynski. THE LOST SHIP 1956, illustrated by Edward Osmond. NO TIME FOR TANKERS 1958, illustrated by Reginald Gray. THE LAME DUCK 1959, illustrated by D. G. Valentine. *Dent.* (See also p. 331.)

Armstrong, Richard. HORSESHOE REEF. *Dent* 1960. Illustrated by D. G. Valentine. Wrecking on remote island in North Sea: two boy heroes.

Catherall, Arthur. DANGEROUS CARGO. *Dent* 1960. Illustrated by Geoffrey Whittam. Contest between honest and crooked tug-masters over wrecked ship in Java Sea which carried illicit arms.

*Knight, Captain F. THE GOLDEN MONKEY 1953, illustrated by J. S. Goodall. VOYAGE TO BENGAL 1954, CLIPPERS TO CHINA 1955, illustrated by Patrick Jobson. *Macmillan.*

*Masefield, John. THE BIRD OF DAWNING 1933, VICTORIOUS TROY 1935. *Heinemann.*

Masefield, John. THE TAKING OF THE GRY. *Heinemann* 1934. Two young men stealing Dutch ship from Santa Barbara harbour in time of revolution; incomparable mixture of meticulous detail and suspense.

*McLean, Allan. THE MASTER OF THE MORGANA. *Collins* 1960.

*Porteous, R. S. THE TAMBAI TREASURE. *Angus & Robertson* 1958. Illustrated by Wal Stackpool.

*Serraillier, Ian. THEY RACED FOR TREASURE. *Cape* 1946. Illustrated by C. Walter Hodges.

*Sperry, Armstrong. THE BOY WHO WAS AFRAID. *Bodley Head* 1942. Illustrated by the author. Published in U.S.A. in 1940 as CALL IT COURAGE.

*Sperry, Armstrong. DANGER TO WINDWARD (1947 U.S.A.). *Bodley Head* 1952. Illustrated by the author.

*Stevenson, R. L. TREASURE ISLAND (1883). *Dent* (Children's Illustrated
   Classics) 1948. Illustrated by S. Van Abbé. *Penguin* (Puffin Story Books) 1946.

4.*Cowboy stories*

*Brand, Max. DESTRY RIDES AGAIN (1930). *Pan* 1950.

*Davis, H. L. WINDS OF MORNING. *Cassell* 1952. THE DISTANT MUSIC. *Gollancz*
   1957.

*Davison, Frank Dalby. MAN-SHY : A STORY OF MEN AND CATTLE. *Angus
   & Robertson* (1931) 1947. *Penguin* (Puffin Story Books) 1956. Also published
   as THE RED HEIFER. *Eyre & Spottiswoode* 1949.

*Dixon, Rex. POCOMOTO—PONY-EXPRESS RIDER 1953, POCOMOTO—
   BUFFALO-HUNTER 1954. *Nelson*. Many other titles. Illustrated by
   Jack Harman.

*Grey, Zane. RIDERS OF THE PURPLE SAGE (1912 U.S.A.) 1954, THE HERIT-
   AGE OF THE DESERT (1910 U.S.A.) 1956, WILDFIRE (1917 U.S.A.) 1920.
   Nelson.

Grey, Zane. THE THUNDERING HERD (1925 U.S.A.) 1958, FIGHTING
   CARAVANS (1929 U.S.A.) 1930. *Hodder & Stoughton*. Many other titles
   available in paper-back editions.

*Montgomery, Rutherford. THE CAPTURE OF THE GOLDEN STALLION 1954.
   THE GOLDEN STALLION'S REVENGE 1955, THE GOLDEN STALLION TO
   THE RESCUE 1956. *Hodder & Stoughton*. Illustrated by George Giguere.

*Robb, John. SIOUX ARROW 1956, TEN GUNS FOR SHELBY 1958. *Hutchinson*.

*Schaefer, Jack. SHANE 1954, THE BIG RANGE 1955. *Deutsch*. (See also p. 365.)

5.*Miscellaneous adventure stories* (See also p. 365.)

*Buchan, John. THE THREE HOSTAGES. *Hodder & Stoughton* 1924. *Penguin*
   1953.

Catherall, Arthur. LAPLAND OUTLAW. *Dent* 1960. Illustrated by Fred Wood.
   Threat to private herd by crooked syndicate: fine action and local colour.

Dillon, Eilís. THE SAN SEBASTIAN. *Faber* 1951. Illustrated by Richard Kennedy.
   Boy discovers galleon off Connemara coast: adventures with Norwegian
   sailors and discovery of treasure.

Durrell, Lawrence. WHITE EAGLES OVER SERBIA. *Faber* 1957. Secret service
   agent in Yugoslavian mountains. The effort, boredom and fatigue of guerilla
   warfare are excellently conveyed.

*Household, Geoffrey. THE SPANISH CAVE (1936). *Bodley Head* 1960.

*Johns, Capt. W. E. BIGGLES SWEEPS THE DESERT 1942 (Sahara) BIGGLES

BREAKS SILENCE 1949 (Antarctic), BIGGLES GOES HOME 1960 (India).
Hodder & Stoughton. Illustrated by Stead.

Johns, Capt. W. E. BIGGLES TAKES CHARGE 1956 (Southern France), BIGGLES
BURIES A HATCHET (N. Russia). *Brockhampton* 1958. Illustrated by Stead.
A selection from innumerable titles.

*Macdonnell, J. COLT AND CO. IN THE VALLEY OF GOLD. *Dent* 1960.

*Masefield, John. DEAD NED. *Heinemann* 1938.

*Mühlenweg. Fritz. BIG TIGER AND CHRISTIAN (1950 Germany). *Cape* 1954.
Translated by Isabel and Florence McHugh. Illustrated by Rafaello Busoni.

*O'Brian, Patrick. THE ROAD TO SAMARCAND. *Hart-Davis* 1954.

'Sapper'. BULLDOG DRUMMOND. *Hodder & Stoughton* (1920) 1953. Many
other titles about this hero.

Drawing by Faith Jaques for René Guillot's THE WHITE SHADOW (*O.U.P.*)

Chapter 12 | *Truth and Ginger-bread Dragoons*

Adventure here and now, adventure in the past—whichever we are dealing with, problems of balance will have to be faced. Character, setting, plot—the importance of each must be decided. But when we come to the historical story we must ask another question. How is fact to be balanced with fiction? The journey into the past gives an *impression*, whole and vivid; it depends on atmosphere; fact is subordinated to fantasy. The writer of a straight historical story has got to deal far more directly with the stuff of history, and here lies his difficulty.

For the more fact he has to deal with, the more imagination he will need to carry it off. It is not enough to be a scholar, essential though this is. Without imagination and enthusiasm, the most learned and well-documented story will leave the young reader cold, where it should set him on fire. Stevenson, writing of a child's imagination,* says that 'he cares no more for what you call truth, than you for a ginger-bread dragoon.' As adults, if we do not care for ginger-bread dragoons, we enjoy them in fancy-dress very much; but we read historical stories with a conscious suspension of belief, aware all the time that we are reading a story. With children, fact and fiction fuse, or should fuse, into a warm, exciting whole. Historical fact should not strike them as fact at all; it should live in the story.

How many people of my generation must have had the historical sense stirred in them for the first time by stories like Kipling's THE KNIGHTS OF THE JOYOUS VENTURE, or by the superb purple passages in Van Loon's HISTORY OF MANKIND, or by the dashing romances of Dumas? Now it would not be possible to write an essay on early explorations of Africa based on Kipling's story; to rely on

* R. L. Stevenson. TRAVELS AND ESSAYS (Scribner, New York, 1898) vol. 3, pp. 147–8.

Van Loon's prehistory today would be to make many false statements; to take Dumas's Buckingham as the whole man, or even as a
reasonably accurate portrait, would be a mistake. Yet these books
gave us a priceless feeling of the past. They may have taught us
very little accurate history; but they made us *want* to learn more.
Imagination must come first. This is not to say that we do not,
always, need accuracy. But we need boldness as well, and better a
few mistakes made in the heat of writing, a few omissions, a few
prejudices, than a book that is still-born in a superfluity of facts.

Thirty-four years ago M. G. Bonner, in a critical book on
children's reading,* said that once you had mentioned Buchan and
Masefield, 'the forecast for historical romances is not very bright.'
Today, historical stories for children are sure sellers from any publishing house and the standard of style, documentation and narrative is very high. Still, there are relatively few stories that will swing
and startle and electrify a child into real imaginative experience;
we must find and hold fast those writers, past and present, who can
provide such stories.

A child's imagination will often be more easily roused if he is
reading about a character like himself, whose feelings and actions
he can understand even if they are conspicuously different from his
own. Historical writers of today often present their story in terms of
the modern world, as an eye-witness account, often a first person
account. The modernization of history can be successful even at its
most extreme. Roger Lancelyn Green used mythological history
boldly in MYSTERY AT MYCENAE, when he told the story of Helen
of Troy as a modern detective-story, with Ulysses (naturally) as chief
detective. His vivid story of the Argonauts and their journey from
Colchis with the Golden Fleece, THE LAND BEYOND THE NORTH,
reads like a thriller by Hammond Innes. John Masefield's two
stories of the Eastern Roman Empire, BASILISSA and CONQUER,
with their pattern of social revolution, their colloquial dialogue
and wholly contemporary feeling, achieve a special liveliness by this
kind of presentation. (These last two are adult novels, but I warmly
recommend them to older schoolchildren.)

It is in dialogue that we see most clearly the way historical stories
have changed during the present century. You can write historical
dialogue in two ways. You can work out an approximation of the

* M. G. Bonner. PARENTS' GUIDE (Funk & Wagnall, 1926) pp. 64–5.

language of your period. At its worst this method degenerates into a ludicrous pishtushery, and those writers are fortunate who have chosen a period for which an approximation is impossible. At its best, archaic or antique idiom is supremely well suited to moments of lofty importance, and many present-day writers use it like this, occasionally and with effect—among them Hilda Lewis and Jane Oliver. This is a welcome change from the clotted and jewelled language which was in vogue two generations ago, and the tense or dramatic moments of history stand out in relief if the rest of the dialogue is simple and everyday, as we know it. In Pauline Clarke's novel of Henry V's times, THE BOY WITH THE ERPINGHAM HOOD, we have, as it were, an eye-witness account, not only of Norwich with its monastic houses, its markets and festivities, but also of Harfleur and Agincourt. The Londoners discuss the war which they can fore-tell from the piling up of supplies and the building of new ships. The dialogue is colloquial, designed to give an immediate, vivid picture; for instance, in this description of the Norwich wrestlers waiting to perform at Windsor before the King:

> A man in motley leaped out of a tree into the middle of the nervous men, making them jump and curse before they laughed.
> 'Scram! Scatter! Pass along from the clearing please! No standing about 'ere, his Grace is to watch some half-baked, rough wrestlers from a little village called Norridge who will tear each other to pieces with their Norfolk outplay.'
> He laid about him with a blown-up bladder on the end of a stick, hitting whoever was in his way.
> 'You fool, we *are* the wrestlers,' William Thweyt snapped. 'From the city of Norwich.'
> The fool smiled slyly, he knew this perfectly well. He somersaulted out of the way, making faces at them through his legs each time and tripping over his balloon. They roared with laughter, and felt better.
> Pauline Clarke. THE BOY WITH THE ERPINGHAM HOOD (Faber, 1956) p. 37.

The battle of Agincourt is dealt with in the same practical vein. We are conscious of the weather, the men's fatigue and hopelessness, the details of strategy, the camp-fire and the tending of weapons. But there is a slight heightening of tension, an echo of Shakespeare's grand manner, to isolate the end of the description of Agincourt:

> The king had raised his hand. He looked pale and exhausted, but his eyes glittered with triumph. It had begun to rain again.
> 'Fellows,' he said. 'We thank you. England thanks you. To-day is the feast of Saints Crispin and Crispian. It will never dawn, but Englishmen will remember this field. Now let not any man take himself the glory which is God's alone. Sing you therefore his praises and keep you yourselves in his grace, through whom he has laid this host in the dust.'
> Ibid., p. 127.

Some writers today compromise by using a neutral style, with a sprinkling of period words—as indeed did Scott and Charles Reade a long time ago. Rhoda Power carries her scholarship easily in the language of REDCAP RUNS AWAY, a story of the late Middle Ages. Cynthia Harnett uses historical technical terms with great skill, but she has given herself an extra aid by using line-drawings to do some of the work for her. Carola Oman, a better historian than any of these, is defeated by erudition. Here are two children discussing a troupe of wandering jongleurs, in the time of King John:

> 'Like those that came and performed in the Great Hall last Martinmas,' agreed Ferry. 'There was a singing damsel with them no taller than you, though, judging by her face, a little older mayhap. She was a jocund little piece, as rosy and brown as a robin. I saw her afterwards in the stables, together with a whole parcel of our fellows, very merry, slaying fleas and drinking ale. One of our fellows accollared her and kissed her, whereat one of the fellows that had come with her smacked her face and knocked him down. There was a great bru all amongst the burning straw (for they had overturned a torch), some of our hounds joining in . . .'
> Carola Oman. FERRY THE FEARLESS (Penguin, 1945) p. 38.

This is a stilted way of describing a domestic episode.

If you can modernize historical dialogue, you can also, of course, modernize characters. What boy or girl could not find a parallel among their acquaintance for Sir Fulk de Grandmesnil, one of the knights in Ronald Welch's KNIGHT CRUSADER? Here he is holding forth about the iniquity of an Arab doctor:

> 'Do you know what he had the infernal impudence to tell me? . . .

Told me that the best treatment for sword wounds was clean bandages and fresh air. To me, who've been wounded scores of times! Everyone knows the only thing to do is to tie the wound up, keep the air out, and let the blood and pus sort themselves out. If they don't, then it shows your blood is unhealthy, and that's the end of you.'
Ronald Welch. KNIGHT CRUSADER (O.U.P., 1954) p. 47.

Jack Lindsay used this method of presenting character a quarter of a century ago, when, in RUNAWAY, he told simply and racily the story of Brennos, a Britain, and Maron from Thrace, slaves who escaped from their master and joined in the rebellion of Spartacus against the Roman legions. We might easily meet the kind of people he puts into this book, just as we might meet the characters in Geoffrey Trease's more recent WORD TO CAESAR, set in the second century A.D. Calvus, king of the Roman underworld, with spies operating all over the Empire, is the modern gangster in fancy-dress. For roadside cafés we have wayside taverns, for chases in car and aeroplane, wild horseback rides. The racy dialogue reflects easily, but in a scholarly fashion, the Roman scene. Here is Manlius, the chariot-racer, talking to young Paul on their arrival at Ostia:

'Somewhere to stay?' he echoed, looking thoughtful. 'I'd steer clear of the inns if I were you—Roman inns are no place for a decent boy to sleep in. Why not get a room for the time being, and buy your food as you want it?'
'I'd sooner do that.'
'Rooms take some finding. The city's shockingly overcrowded, and you don't want to land yourself in a slum. Let me see now . . . I know—' He frowned, then gave me a name and address in the Clivus Palatinus. 'They're a very respectable family—one of our drivers, retired now. Mention my name, and they'll let you have one of their rooms. Top floor, I'm afraid, but you won't mind the stairs at your age. Anyhow, it's a good solid building, it won't collapse under you in the middle of the night.'
'Is that usual?' I laughed.
'Happens more often than you think! Too much cheap building —and they stick on too many storeys for the foundations to carry. But this block is sound enough. You needn't worry.'
Geoffrey Trease. WORD TO CAESAR (Macmillan, 1955) p. 163.

How does this work when we leave fictitious characters for historical figures? Understatement is the prevailing tone today. Familiar
characters are treated in a deliberately off-hand manner, for the
author tries to get behind their historical reputation to see them as
ordinary men and women of their time. This, again, has to be carefully done.

In COLUMBUS SAILS, Walter Hodges looks at the explorer's
career first through the eyes of an old monk who had seen him
when he was a novice, secondly through the eyes of one of
Columbus's own seamen. The explorer is presented casually, as a
contemporary *would* present him. His ambitions are summarized
when a group of sailors sign on for a voyage and are brought up
short by the forceful criticism of an old salt:

> 'All right, then, here's what you don't know. Along comes this
> Admiral Christopher Columbus that nobody's ever heard of, and
> he enlists a crew for an expedition. He doesn't say where he's
> going, but he says we'll find gold, and he offers four months' pay
> in advance, so all we here sign on. And then what do we find? . . .
> Believe it or not, he says he's going to sail that way, Westwards,
> to India! India, if you please! When every man with a sound head
> on his shoulders knows that India lies East, and always will!
> And that, my lads, . . . is the voyage you've signed on for, and I
> hope you like it.'
>
> C. Walter Hodges. COLUMBUS SAILS (Bell, 1939) p. 44.

Again, in RED MAN'S COUNTRY, Philip Rush draws a fine picture
of Captain John Smith of Virginia. We first see the Captain when he
rescues the young Lincolnshire boy who becomes his protégé; we
see Smith not with foreknowledge but as simply as young John
Brookes did:

> If he was a Willoughby man, he could be trusted and John said
> he would tell a secret. 'I am running away. It was my school
> satchel and books I sold.'
>
> The response was unexpected. The gentleman doubled up and
> slapped his bulky thighs in delight.
>
> John saw nothing to laugh at. 'My aunt says it's vulgar to slap
> your thighs when you laugh!' he said sharply.
>
> 'Is that why you're running away? No, boy, I'm not laughing

at you, but do you know I did the self-same thing as a boy?'

'Did you now! What luck did it bring you?'

'They tied me to a desk at Lynn! But they couldn't lime me for long. I got clear and jogged around the world a little. I'm not much older than yourself. I was born in 1580, the year Frankie Drake sailed round the world.'

Philip Rush. RED MAN'S COUNTRY (Collins, 1957) p. 27.

Sensible writers use this device sparingly, for it can easily become absurd—as I think it is in this extract from the adventures of a girl in eighteenth-century London:

Prue was not offended. 'Oh please, Mr Johnson', she exclaimed, 'may I see The Dictionary?' She contrived to give it capital letters as if she had been Great-Aunt Penelope.

Johnson looked flattered. 'But that is dull matter for young eyes', he objected half-heartedly.

'No, really, sir, I do want to see how you do it, for I can't imagine how it's possible', said Prue in awestruck tones. 'To list all the words in the English language! And to give their meaning! I hope it will be ready soon, for father has promised to buy a copy, and it will be such a help with my spelling.'

'Females', pronounced Mr Johnson, 'seldom possess the ability to spell or the knowledge of what words to use if they had the power of spelling them!'

Joyce Reason. TO CAPTURE THE KING! (Phoenix House, 1956) p. 125.

All the same, it is sound sense to create a fictitious boy or girl and involve them in affairs of state or with historical characters, so long as the young reader can really believe in this involvement. Philip Rush is particularly ingenious and successful here. In QUEEN'S TREASON, for example, he very naturally combines the story of Edward II, his favourites and his embittered Queen with the fortunes of two boys—Alan Blount, son of a warder in the Tower, and Nicolas, a journeyman stone-mason. Alan is training as a surgeon with John Arderne, himself a servant of Hugh Despenser, the current favourite, so the boy is brought up against matters of state most convincingly; at the same time the real meat of the story lies in the domestic and social background, the London homes of the boys, their work and their play. You can find the same ease of manner in KING OF THE CASTLE, which puts a young squire in the thick of Wat Tyler's rebellion, and in A CAGE OF FALCONS, where Roger Crispin, son of a shoemaker, and an aspiring artist, watches as a Londoner the contest between Henry VI and the Yorkist rival Edward. This is an author who can always make history live for his readers, especially when he is writing of London and Westminster, whose medieval streets and buildings and customs are obviously as real to him as the city of today.

It is easy for children to identify themselves with the past while they are reading Philip Rush's stories. He chooses the kind of situation which they can appreciate—spying, overhearing, fighting—and his details of food, clothes, games, weapons and so on are congenial and interesting. His books are, however, rather light emotionally. He only occasionally shows what adventure *means* to his heroes in terms of emotional strain and inspiration. Children who want to go deeper will appreciate Masefield's stories for boys, JIM DAVIS and MARTIN HYDE, written many years ago, which combine lucid and exciting plots with some fine character drawing. Young Martin Hyde does not like adventure, although at the outset of the story he thinks he does, and all through the West Country campaign of Monmouth against James II, in which Martin acts as messenger for the rebels, we see how events change his attitude. There is a sad note of expected failure in the book which comes from the gradual opening of his eyes to the unromantic side of great causes.

The story starts in a fine, open, active style. Martin, newly come to London from Suffolk to live with his uncle, is leaning on a parapet, looking at the river, when he notices an intriguing passenger being rowed past, intriguing because a sudden puff of wind reveals that he has a false beard. The passenger is an agent for Monmouth and, through his inquisitiveness, Martin is drawn into treasonable activities. Offered far more kicks than ha'pence in the plotting trade, he begins to see adventure less like a heedless boy and more like a sensible youth. His first thought, that he would soon become a General and return to his uncle splendidly dressed ('I thought that life was always like that to the adventurous man') gives place to this view:

You don't know what an adventurous life is. I will tell you. It is a life of sordid unquiet, pursued without plan, like the life of an animal. Have you seen a dog trying to cross a busy street? There is the adventurer. Or the rabbit on the cliff, in his state of continual panic; he, too, lives the adventurous life.

John Masefield. MARTIN HYDE (Wells Gardner, Darton, 1949) p. 106. (First published 1910).

And through Martin we see, too, exactly what happens in history (or what might be reasonably assumed to have happened). What child does not long to be told exactly what a battle or a siege was like; but how seldom does a writer go beyond the obvious details. Here is Martin's impression of the battle of Sedgemoor:

That morning's work is all very confused to me. I remember seeing men cut down as they ran. I remember a fine horse coming past me lurching, clattering his stirrups, before leaping into the river. I remember the stink of powder over all the field; the strange look on the faces of the dead; the body of a trumpeter, kneeling against a gorse bush, shot through the heart, with his trumpet raised to his lips, the litter everywhere, burnt cartridges, clothes, belts, shot, all the waste of war.

Ibid., p. 187.

The tension and confusion of battle, the different tension of single combat—these are extraordinarily real in Masefield's books.

Present-day writers are doing nothing new, of course, when they cut the cloth of history to fit the form of their own time. Shakespeare's view of Richard III was essentially a Tudor view. Scott wrote in the mood of eighteenth-century Gothic romanticism. Geoffrey Trease, in BOWS AGAINST THE BARONS (published in 1934), presented Robin Hood under the shadow of hammer and sickle, as a revolutionary trying to inspire an oppressed and stupefied peasantry. His book was written in the spirit of the 'thirties and now seems an exaggerated piece of propaganda, as he would be the first to admit.* L. A. G. Strong's study of Wat Tyler's

---

* In an article, 'Why write for children?' (in *The School Librarian*, Vol. 10, No. 2, July 1960, p. 107), he says: '*Silver Guard* was an attempt to correct the romantic royalist vision most children have of the Civil War: if I had written it ten years earlier it would have been a fervent piece of Roundhead propaganda, but by 1947 I was attempting a more objective approach.'

rebellion, KING RICHARD'S LAND, published three years after BOWS AGAINST THE BARONS, gave a more all-round picture of feudal tyranny. Nor was Trease the first to present the case for the ordinary man. Scott had been aware of it and so had Marjorie Bowen and Herbert Strang in the 'twenties. Trease's effect upon children, and upon the course of historical writing for children, has all the same been far greater than that of earlier writers, because of his gift for choosing his subject so as to show that past and present are comparable, interacting, interdependent. Particularly for boys and girls awake to the world around them, this can be very exciting. In THE HILLS OF VARNA, which is set in the early sixteenth century, he links the Renaissance with the atmosphere of discovery in our own times, and CUE FOR TREASON, a spy story of Tudor times, draws a parallel with modern secret service methods.

Interpretation of history has somehow to be reconciled with historical truth, if, indeed, there is such a thing. Obviously it must always be partial truth. We cannot know, even with the fullest use of contemporary documents, just what a past age was like or how its people thought and felt. We can only feel towards an approximation of the truth. This is no reason to condemn historical stories, either for adults or for children, even if they are prejudiced by the writer's own ideas. Children's stories in particular must be prejudiced, as a rule, so that they may be simple. Academic history is a matter of adjustment, of reservations, of constant parenthesis; but in a story for children the issues must be clear-cut. A sensible child adjusts his ideas of history as he grows older, discarding parts of stories he has read, keeping others. In a book like Hilda Lewis's HERE COMES HARRY, he may find all kinds of hints which will mean more to him later—hints about Gloucester's character, his heroic and his ignoble side, hints about the mental instability of the young Henry VI; but he will be caught first by the sympathetic portrait of the boy king and, by contrast, the enmity and ambition of Gloucester (no Crookback but, for the purposes of the story, a villain). The author has decided on an interpretation of historical fact, and her young readers are all the better for this.

An historical story must have a point of view, though this may sometimes become a prejudice. Geoffrey Trease recalls how the BBC declined to serialize one of his stories in Children's Hour because it was 'anti-Cavalier.' He comments:

. . . it was an attempt to present my own belief that, in every ten
people during the Civil War, there were approximately one Cavalier,
one Roundhead, and eight others just longing for it to stop.
Geoffrey Trease. 'The Problems of the Historical Story Teller.'
Junior Bookshelf, vol. 15, 1951; pp. 263-4.

True as this may be, children expect to be on one side or the other.
An impartial tale of the Civil War might well be confusing and it
would certainly be dull. Trease's own series about this period
(SILVER GUARD, THE GREY ADVENTURER and TRUMPETS IN
THE WEST) is written from the Puritan point of view, though he
deals fairly with the Cavaliers. By contrast, in THE CHILDREN OF
THE NEW FOREST, Marryat endears the Cavalier Beverlys to readers
of all time, whether they live in a reactionary or a progressive age;
all the same, the Roundheads in his story are ordinary, unexaggerated people with their own rights. Rosemary Sutcliff's SIMON has
two heroes, one on each side of the war, friends divided by politics
but not in heart. This conflict of loyalties makes the book moving
and mature, but, in the long run, most readers will plump for the
Roundheads, because the author is chiefly interested in them. There
is still room, too, for the romantic point of view, if it is fresh and
original. Two writers have used brilliantly the story of Charles II's
flight after the battle of Worcester. In HUNT ROYAL, David Scott
Daniell concentrates on the chase itself; this is a rousing adventure
story in which we are on the king's side as a matter of course, not
because we really see him as a person at all. Laurence Meynell has
taken a more interesting line. Charles's flight, in THE HUNTED
KING, is not a national but a local event. In a preface, Meynell
explains:

> Shortly after World War I when I was an articled pupil in land
> agency (the Giffards' estate at Chillington was amongst the ones
> we managed) a man came into the office and said without explan-
> ation or preamble: 'My name is John Penderel and I have come
> for the money for saving the King.' He was in fact a lineal descen-
> dant of the Penderels who befriended Charles, and I paid out the
> requisite annuity to him.
>
> That incident, a piece of live history if ever there was one,
> started my interest in the astonishing story of Boscobel and the
> King's secret journey to the coast.

In my version of it the only real invention is the one character Philip; apart from him it is historically true, and it will always surely remain the most colourful and romantic episode in England's long story.

Laurence Meynell. THE HUNTED KING (Bodley Head, 1959).

Philip, the only fictional character, is most important; he and the king are young men in company with older and more experienced people, and this contrast helps to throw into relief the character of the king—innately melancholy, courageous and debonair—and to make history most moving.

We need not be too much afraid of a partisan approach to history. We must allow children some intelligence in these matters. If they read IVANHOE and feel a fine sympathy for the poor Saxons persecuted by the brutish Normans, they will redress the balance by reading a story like Meriol Trevor's MERLIN'S RING, where it is the Romanized Britons who are persecuted by the brutish Saxons. Against a picture of marauding Norsemen they can set Joyce Reason's THE SECRET FORTRESS or Rosemary Sutcliff's THE SHIELD RING, where the Norsemen in Cumberland make a wonderful stand against the settled invaders, the Normans. The invader of today becomes the besieged of tomorrow. The author must choose a period and a point of view and make an honest job of it. This is specially necessary in the case of ancient history, where the background is less familiar to most of us. Here, too, if anywhere, an author must have an imagination well stored and well exercised. This is the moment to speak in detail of Rosemary Sutcliff, whose books are waking as many children to the special delight of Roman Britain as Kipling's did in my day.

The feelings and thoughts of her characters are universal. The hero of OUTCAST is Beric, Roman-born but brought up by Britons, sold as a slave to a Roman senator, serving a spell in a galley, finally returning to Britain to work on the draining of Romney Marsh. The feeling of exile is common to any period, but in this book it is always expressed in terms of a Roman, not of a young man of the present day. The Roman strength, reticence, lack of imagination—all are here. There is no introspection, no sentimentality, no over-subtle motives. The same is true of THE EAGLE OF THE NINTH and THE LANTERN BEARERS, the first dealing with the last years of Roman

rule in Britain, the second with the vexed days of Arthur and Vorti-
gern. There is nothing in these books that is incompatible with
known fact, historical or archæological, but no detail, likewise, that
is not illuminated by a passionate, tense realization of the past,
communicated in a very pictorial manner. This glimpse of Arthur in
battle is a characteristic example:

> It was like Artos to sweep his men into action with the gay notes
> of a hunting-horn. The sound rose above the battle din, high and
> sweet and shining as the song of the storm-cock in the white-
> thorn tree. A great warning cry went up from the nearest ranks of
> the enemy, and snatching one glance over his shoulder, Aquila saw
> the flower of the British cavalry sweeping towards them along
> the tawny slope. There was a swelling thunder of hooves in his
> ears, and the wild, high song of the hunting horn as the great
> arrow-head of wild riders hurtled down upon the battle. At the
> shining point of the arrow-head, Artos swept by, his great white
> horse turned for a flashing moment to silver by the burst of sun-
> light that came scudding down the valley to meet him, the silver
> mane streaming over his bridle arm, and the sods flying like birds
> from the great round hooves.
> Rosemary Sutcliff. THE LANTERN BEARERS (O.U.P., 1959) p. 216.

Rosemary Sutcliff shows a Britain completely unlike anything we
know now, small, claustrophobic, dark, lit up with passionate conflict and passionate loyalties; and the illustrations of her books,

Drawing by Charles Keeping for Rosemary Sutcliff's THE LANTERN BEARERS
(O.U.P.)

particularly Charles Keeping's strange drawings for THE LANTERN BEARERS, with their hatching of thick lines, echo this impression.

Very far from our own times, yet all these books will take children back to the past easily because of their vividness. Prehistoric times present greater difficulty. It is by no means easy for anyone to put himself in the place of a tribesman of the New Stone Age, for instance, when that tribesman (as Henry Treece points out) is probably nearer to the natives of Australia or New Guinea than to us. To bring prehistoric times to life, the writer must make a bold attempt to give his characters something to say, something to ponder over, although their processes of thought can only really be guessed at. But most of all, he must interpret history in a rather special way, by the careful selection of details; for in early times it was the means of existence (fire, food, predators, weather) that determined tribal rules and patterns of thought. Henry Treece's MEN OF THE HILLS, a study of the Cattle Folk of the Bronze Age moving in on the Stone Age natives of Britain, is distinguished by this synthesis of domestic life and thought. Here is a description of the men of the flint settlement going out on a wolf hunt:

> The twenty warriors loped on, their thin, delicately featured brown faces streaked with white ochre in a tribal sign, the bear-claw necklaces clacking about their necks, their shiny black hair knotted with bone pins on top of their long heads, or pushed down into white tubes of bone from which the marrow had been sucked. They were in quest of their enemy and must take no chances; so each man wore a broad belt of tough cowhide about his middle and wide bracelets of leather up to his elbows. Old Hair the wolf must not be allowed to sink his yellow fangs into body or arm, for the wounds he made seldom healed, however carefully one covered them with cobwebs or let the good cow milk curdle into them, however many times the Old Man of the tribe, the chieftain, said his spells. Old Hair was a dangerous one to hunt, and a man must be ready for him, always.
>
> Henry Treece. MEN OF THE HILLS (Bodley Head, 1957) p. 10.

Christine Price has drawn for this story pictures which with their bold, simple lines emphasize the contrast between the two races.

Archæological research in the last decade has opened new sources of material for illustrators, and in many of the best stories of early

Drawing by Malcolm Pride for Jane Oliver's THE EAGLET AND THE ANGRY
DOVE (Macmillan)

communities (like Kurt Schmeltzer's THE AXE OF BRONZE and
Rosemary Sutcliff's WARRIOR SCARLET) verbal descriptions and
drawings complement each other admirably. Action is still best
described in words; but pictures can give the *feel* of action, its
emotional content. The description of the king-making in WARRIOR
SCARLET, extremely vivid in the text, is completed by Charles
Keeping's magnificent decoration. Again, THE EAGLET AND THE
ANGRY DOVE contrasts Druidical belief with Columba's early
Christian teaching. Jane Oliver's dramatic analysis of these beliefs is
helped by Malcolm Pride's drawings. For periods remote from our
own, this impressionistic, poetic method of illustration is supremely
well suited.

A more practical, informative style is more often used for stories
which are concerned with a technique—a good basis for an historical
study of any period. What child ever forgets the detail of how the
Beverlys made the stockade, in THE CHILDREN OF THE NEW
FOREST. That glorious, multi-coloured jumble, THE CLOISTER AND
THE HEARTH, is fascinating most of all because it tells you *how*
people do things. In THE BOMBARD, Henry Treece makes the invention of the first cannon the centre of a rousing story of Crécy and its
aftermath. Patrick O'Brian's matchless tale, THE GOLDEN OCEAN,
is completely instructive, in the most readable way, about the way
sailors worked on Anson's frigate in the eighteenth century. Ursula
Moray Williams bases THE NOBLE HAWKS on falconry in the
fourteenth century, and her book shows what can be done with a
domestic subject. Details of a craft must necessarily lead to questions
of rank and status, and there is a chance here to cover the social
ground without bringing in any political bias. THE NOBLE HAWKS
offers not an adventure but a situation—the rivalry between Dickon
(who, as a yeoman's son, has the right only to a goshawk) and young
Gareth, heir to a Welsh earl, whose skill falls short of his birth.

Cynthia Harnett's domestic stories give the same clear, precise
social picture. THE LOAD OF UNICORN, for instance (an uncom-
monly good story), has for its theme the introduction of printing.
Bendy, the boy hero, is the son of a scrivener, who sits in St Paul's
writing letters for his fellow-citizens while his sons run the family
business of manuscript chapbooks. Bendy, with his father's consent
—for John Goodrich feels and responds to the renaissance in learning—goes as apprentice to Caxton, who is newly arrived in London,

and it is Bendy who tracks down the paper thieves who are trying
to put his master out of business, secures for Caxton an unknown
Malory manuscript, and, to crown his efforts, reveals a spy-ring
sending information out of England to Henry Tudor. Exciting this
plot may be, but behind adventures with spies and robbers, the daily
life of Bendy's family is meticulously described. The spy-plot of
RING OUT BOW BELLS, set in the reign of Henry V, has the same
mercantile setting, while in THE WOOL-PACK (a Carnegie medal
award, and deservedly so) we are in the middle of the Cotswold
wool trade in the time of Chaucer. Major historical events are kept
in the distance in these books. There is no probing of character
and only the simplest statements about motives. But there is a sure
handling of innumerable details which, like pieces in a mosaic, add
up to an accurate and lively panorama of everyday history.

This panorama is mirrored in the author's
representational drawings. As a rule she is concerned less with illustrating actual scenes in her
story than with annotating it with insets
of clothes and weapons, buildings, ships,
anything germane to her period. But there
is no suggestion of the textbook here, for
each object she draws has its place in the
story. Bendy's doings, in THE LOAD OF
UNICORN, are all the more real because
we can see his father's desk and ink-well,
the composing-frame he learns to use, and
many other tools of his trade.

Costume is one of the easiest ways of setting
an historical period on paper, but many artists
allow it to become an end in itself. Those of
us who first met Jane Austen's characters in the
edition illustrated by Hugh Thomson will remember how disappointing were those insipid
faces which looked out above the carefully drawn
Regency clothes. No illustrator can afford to use his characters as
tailor's dummies. If he is going to draw people, they must be people.
William Stobbs's gallery of late eighteenth-century types, in Frederick
Grice's AIDAN AND THE STROLLERS, shows how faces can be used
to bring out points from the text, and in David Scott Daniell's

HIDEAWAY JOHNNY, a Regency story for younger children, Biro's
slighter portraits similarly echo the period language.

Clothes, utensils, dwellings—the background of life at any point
of historical time—are more interesting as we approach our own
times and can better appreciate details of domestic life. Here the
keynote is familiarity, and writers and illustrators alike play upon
it. Domestic stories written from living memory—Tales of a Grandfather, you might call them—have a particular authenticity and
charm, and I am always surprised that more writers do not exploit
the tales that are current in their own locality. John Niven's GYPSY
IN SCARLET tells of a young man who learns the logging trade on an
East Scottish river and then leaves his home to fight in the Crimean
War. This does not read like a tale invented or reconstructed. It has
the sound of hearsay, almost of gossip. It might have been passed
on to the author by an aged relative. Henry Garnett's stories of the
Severn barge traffic at the same period (ROUGH WATER BROWN
and SECRET OF THE ROCKS) also have the special vividness of
localized history.

Barbara Ker Wilson's novels of the recent past gain much from
their illustrations. In PATH-THROUGH-THE-WOODS, the story of
a girl fighting her way to a medical career in the late Victorian era,
each section of the story is marked by a vignette with a family-
album flavour, by Charles Stewart, and THE LOVELY SUMMER,
a tale of the suffragette movement, is decorated by Marina Hoffer
with daintily framed idealizations of the time. The key to these
drawings is the phrase 'family album'; they tantalize the memory
as well as the imagination.

Among American writers, Lois Lenski is most important as a
recorder of social history. To collect material for tales like CORN-
FARM BOY, BOOM-TOWN BOY, BAYOU SUZETTE and STRAW-
BERRY GIRL, she visited isolated communities in Iowa, Oklahoma,
Louisiana and Florida, she talked to old people and noted their
idiom, looked at family documents, got the feel of localities whose
special character may well be wiped out soon by the standardizing
of civilization.

Most vivid of all American tales of this kind are those by Laura
Ingalls Wilder, in which she relives her childhood in pioneering days.
Her books reflect sincerely the point of view of a child living through
difficult and dangerous times, protected by trust in her parents,

understanding part of what she sees and observing much more. Here
is Laura's impression of her first night on the great Kansas plain:

> On the other side of the canvas, Pet and Patty were eating their
> corn. When Patty whooshed into the feed-box, the whoosh was
> right at Laura's ear. There were little scurrying sounds in the
> grass. In the trees by the creek an owl called, 'Who-oo? who-oo?'
> Farther away another owl answered, 'Oo-oo, oo-oo.' Far away
> on the prairie the wolves howled, and under the wagon Jack
> growled low in his chest. In the wagon everything was safe and
> snug.
> Thickly in front of the open wagon-top hung the large, glittering
> stars. Pa could reach them, Laura thought. She wished he would
> pick the largest one from the thread on which it hung from the
> sky, and give it to her. She was wide awake, she was not sleepy
> at all, but suddenly she was very much surprised. The large star
> winked at her!
> Then she was waking up, next morning.
> Laura Ingalls Wilder. LITTLE HOUSE ON THE PRAIRIE
> (Methuen, 1957) p. 24.

And here is a deeper note out of the memory of the past:

> Laura was not exactly scared, but that sound made her feel funny.
> It was the sound of quite a lot of Indians, chopping with their
> voices. It was something like the sound of an axe chopping, and
> something like a dog barking, and it was something like a song,
> but not like any song that Laura had ever heard. It was a wild,
> fierce sound, but it didn't seem angry.
> Ibid., p. 164.

For a thoughtful child, history personalized in this way has an
irresistible attraction, and there is great scope here for British
writers.

Fact used imaginatively—this is what children look for in historical
stories—a good story and a full, even a crowded background. A
quarter of a century ago we used to get these things, in profusion,
from historical romances which were not, in fact, intended for
children. They suited the taste of older schoolgirls, in particular,
very well. Perhaps they still do, those glorious, long-winded, partisan tales of the French Revolution and the Regency. But though

Baroness Orczy and Georgette Heyer are still read and enjoyed by girls (and Jeffery Farnol, Rafael Sabatini and Stanley Weyman could be, too, if they knew about them), the wind has changed. Our children cannot think only in terms of the dashing Scaramouche or the intrepid Pimpernel. They know too much about the other side. Their eyes have been opened to the less romantic side of these periods of history by C. S. Forester's tales of Captain Hornblower, with their subtle deflating of the pomp and circumstance of war, or by David Scott Daniell's matter-of-fact dealings with the Napoleonic wars through that lively couple, Polly and Oliver. L. A. G. Strong's vigorous story, MR SHERIDAN'S UMBRELLA, has taken them out of the stuffy atmosphere of court life to the Regency Brighton the ordinary tradesman saw.

Those bygone romances may be collecting dust on our shelves now, but many other historical novels will be borrowed from us by our children, for different generations may easily share them. The themes of history are ageless and for no special age. Lost causes, the din of battle, the breaking and making of laws, the founding of dynasties and the tribulations of the common man—all these subjects can be appreciated by children in their full strength. They will pick up their parents' books and have no feeling of inadequacy if the writers who cater specially for them have given them the right diet beforehand. The transition from junior to adult novels will be easy if history has been presented to them, in stories strong rather than sentimental, pictorial and not vague, pointed and not trivial. The best historical stories for children have little or nothing of the juvenile in them.

Reading List

Ashton, Agnes. WATER FOR LONDON. *Epworth* 1956. Illustrated by Monica Walker. Sir Hugh Middleton's scheme of 1609: clever combination of fact and fictional adventure.

Baumann, Hans. THE BARQUE OF THE BROTHERS (1956 Germany). *O.U.P.* 1958. Translated by Isabel and Florence McHugh. Illustrated by Ulrik Schramm. Two brothers exploring west coast of Africa with Henry the Navigator. Distinguished style, packed with interesting detail.

Brink, Carol Ryrie. CADDIE WOODLAWN. *Macmillan of New York* 1947.
Illustrated by Kate Seredy. A child in Wisconsin in the 1860's: Indians,
school and the delights of home life.

*Clarke, Pauline. THE BOY WITH THE ERPINGHAM HOOD. *Faber* 1956.
Illustrated by Cecil Leslie.

Dallow, Mark. THE HEIR OF CHARLECOTE. *Cassell* 1938. *Penguin* (Puffin
Story Books) 1955. Illustrated by Arthur Hall. Two boys travel from
Stratford to London, ending in Burbage's company. Free, natural narrative
suitable for younger children.

Daniell, David Scott. THE BOY THEY MADE KING. *Cape* 1959. Illustrated by
William Stobbs. Perkin Warbeck's tale told in domestic vein, chiefly set in
Oxford. Class differences especially well done.

*Daniell, David Scott. MISSION FOR OLIVER 1953, POLLY AND OLIVER 1954,
POLLY AND OLIVER AT SEA 1960. *Cape*. Illustrated by William Stobbs.
(See also p. 369.)

*Daniell, David Scott. HUNT ROYAL. *Cape* 1958. Illustrated by William Stobbs.

*Daniell, David Scott. HIDEAWAY JOHNNY. *Brockhampton* 1959. Illustrated
by Biro.

Fabricius, Johan. JAVA HO! (1926 Holland). *Methuen* 1933. Abridged and
translated by M. C. Darnton. Rousing tale of four boys on voyage to the East
in the seventeenth century; uncompromising attitude to danger and death.

Forbes, Esther. JOHNNY TREMAIN (1943 U.S.A.). *Constable* 1958. Illustrated
by Lynd Ward. Boston at opening of War of Independence: one of the most
human and interesting stories about this period.

*Forester, C. S. THE HAPPY RETURN 1937, FLYING COLOURS 1938, A SHIP OF
THE LINE 1938, LORD HORNBLOWER 1946, MR MIDSHIPMAN HORN-
BLOWER 1950, LIEUTENANT HORNBLOWER 1952, HORNBLOWER AND
THE ATROPOS 1953. *Michael Joseph*. Cadet editions, selected by G. P. Griggs.
Michael Joseph 1954. Illustrated by Geoffrey Whittam.

*Garnett, Henry. THIRTEEN BANNERS. *Bodley Head* 1956. Illustrated by Peter
Jackson. Rebellion of Simon de Montfort: emphasis on feudal system.

*Garnett, Henry. ROUGH WATER BROWN 1955, illustrated by Sheila Findlay.
SECRET OF THE ROCKS 1958, illustrated by Peter Jackson. *Bodley Head*.

Gray, Elizabeth Janet. ADAM OF THE ROAD. *Black* 1943. Illustrated by
Robert Lawson. Journey of minstrel's son from London to Winchester and
back; panorama of English medieval life.

*Green, Roger Lancelyn. MYSTERY AT MYCENAE 1957, illustrated by Margery
Gill. THE LAND BEYOND THE NORTH 1958, illustrated by Douglas Hall.
Bodley Head.

*Grice, Frederick. AIDAN AND THE STROLLERS. *Cape* 1960. Illustrated by William Stobbs.

Grice, Frederick. THE BONNY PIT LADDIE. *O.U.P.* 1960. Illustrated by Brian Wildsmith. Brilliant evocation of Durham mining village a century ago: fine characterization and a sturdy narrative style.

Guillot, René. RIDERS OF THE WIND (1953 France). *Methuen* 1960. Translated by Geo. H. Bell. Illustrated by Richard Kennedy. Boy from river gang, seventeenth century, and his adventures in North Africa. Superb feeling for place and event.

*Harnett, Cynthia. THE WOOL-PACK 1951, RING OUT BOW BELLS! 1953, THE LOAD OF UNICORN 1959. *Methuen*. Illustrated by the author.

*Hodges, C. Walter. COLUMBUS SAILS. *Bell* 1939. Illustrated by the author.

Howard, Elizabeth. NORTH WINDS BLOW FREE (1949 U.S.A.). *Bodley Head* 1953. Michigan in time of Fugitive Slave Law: family helping with underground railway and Freedom Settlement in Canada.

Keith, Harold. RIFLES FOR WATIE (1957 U.S.A.). *O.U.P.* 1960. Civil War in Oklahoma and neighbouring states: Northern point of view. A vigorous and varied tale.

*Kipling, Rudyard. PUCK OF POOK'S HILL, REWARDS AND FAIRIES. (see Chap. 6).

*Lenski, Lois. BAYOU SUZETTE 1943, STRAWBERRY GIRL 1945, BOOM-TOWN BOY 1948, CORN-FARM BOY 1954. *J. B. Lippincott*, Philadelphia and New York. Illustrated by the author.

Lenski, Lois. PRAIRIE SCHOOL (1951 U.S.A.). *O.U.P.* 1959. Illustrated by the author. Based on facts of winters 1948–9 and 1949–50, in South Dakota: a fine example of living history and a good story.

*Lewis, Hilda. HERE COMES HARRY. *O.U.P.* 1960. Illustrated by William Stobbs.

Lewis, Hilda. THE GENTLE FALCON. *O.U.P.* 1952. Illustrated by Evelyn Gibbs. Richard II and Isabella of France: a touching story told by a woman.

*Lindsay, Jack. RUNAWAY. *O.U.P.* 1935.

Lowndes, Joan Selby. MAIL COACH. *Collins* 1945. Illustrated by the author. Light-hearted tale of two children adventuring to London: glimpses of Astley's Circus.

Lowndes, Joan Selby. ROYAL CHASE. *Collins* 1947. Illustrated by the author. Dissolution of monasteries. Set in North Bucks. Excellent background and detail.

Manning-Sanders, Ruth. CIRCUS BOY. *O.U.P.* 1960. Illustrated by Annette Macarthur-Onslow. Boy training with Bright's Circus, tenting through Ireland during Orangeman troubles. Lively mixture of adventure and period detail.

*Marryat, Captain. THE CHILDREN OF THE NEW FOREST (1847). *Dent* (Children's Illustrated Classics) 1955. Illustrated by Lionel Edwards.

*Masefield, John. MARTIN HYDE 1910, JIM DAVIS 1911. *Wells Gardner.*

*Masefield, John. BASILISSA 1940, CONQUER 1941. *Heinemann.*

Masefield, John. LOST ENDEAVOUR. *Nelson* (1910) 1923. Pirates and treasure in Virginia, late seventeenth century.

*Meynell, Laurence. THE HUNTED KING. *Bodley Head* 1959.

Mitchison, Naomi. THE LAND THE RAVENS FOUND. *Collins* 1955. Illustrated by Brian Allderidge. Practical and moving story of colonization of Iceland by the Vikings, ninth and tenth centuries.

*Niven, John. GYPSY IN SCARLET. *Faber* 1954. Illustrated by Richard Kennedy.

*O'Brian, Patrick. THE GOLDEN OCEAN. *Hart-Davis* 1956.

O'Faoláin, Eileen. HIGH SANG THE SWORD. *O.U.P.* 1959. Illustrated by Brian Wildsmith. Eleventh century, Brian Boru and his attempt to unite Ireland against the Norsemen. Exciting and carefully documented with fascinating drawings.

*Oliver, Jane. THE EAGLET AND THE ANGRY DOVE. *Macmillan* 1957. Illustrated by Malcolm Pride.

*Oman, Carola. FERRY THE FEARLESS. *Pitman* 1935.

Parker, Richard. THE THREE PEBBLES. *Collins* 1954. Illustrated by Prudence Seward. Three French boys in new settlement in Florida, sixteenth century: practical and realistic.

Polland, Madeline. CHILDREN OF THE RED KING. *Constable* 1959. Illustrated by Annette Macarthur-Onslow. Thirteenth century, guerilla war against Norman castles in Ireland, with boy and girl heroes.

*Power, Rhoda. REDCAP RUNS AWAY. *Cape* 1952. Illustrated by C. Walter Hodges.

*Reade, Charles. THE CLOISTER AND THE HEARTH (1861). *Dent* (Everyman) 1955.

*Reason, Joyce. TO CAPTURE THE KING! *Phoenix House* 1956. Illustrated by David Walsh.

*Reason, Joyce. THE SECRET FORTRESS. *Dent* (1946) 1950. Illustrated by S. van Abbé.

*Rush, Philip. QUEEN'S TREASON 1954, A CAGE OF FALCONS 1954, KING OF THE CASTLE 1956, illustrated by Martin Thomas. RED MAN'S COUNTRY 1957, illustrated by Brian Keogh. *Collins.*

Rush, Philip. APPRENTICE AT ARMS. *Collins* 1960. Illustrated by Christopher Brooker. Rising of Sir Thomas Wyatt seen by a boy who joined him in march from Kent to London.

*Schmeltzer, Kurt. THE AXE OF BRONZE. *Constable* 1958. Illustrated by M. A. Charlton.

Snell, J. B. JENNIE. *Nelson* 1958. Illustrated by G. K. Sewell. Story of a narrow-gauge railway in Wales and the life of a nineteenth-century family that ran parallel with it.

Sperry, Armstrong. WAGONS WESTWARD (1936 U.S.A.). *Bodley Head* 1948. Illustrated by the author. Vivid tale of pioneering in America in the 1840's.

Strang, Herbert. DICKON OF THE CHASE. *O.U.P.* 1931. Local Robin Hood at end of Wars of the Roses.

*Strong, L. A. G. KING RICHARD'S LAND. *Dent* 1938.

Strong, L. A. G. MR SHERIDAN'S UMBRELLA 1935. *Penguin* (Puffin Story Books) 1949.

*Sutcliff, Rosemary. SIMON 1953, illustrated by Richard Kennedy. THE EAGLE OF THE NINTH 1954, illustrated by C. Walter Hodges. OUTCAST 1955, illustrated by Richard Kennedy. THE SHIELD RING 1956, illustrated by C. Walter Hodges. WARRIOR SCARLET 1958, THE LANTERN BEARERS 1959, KNIGHT'S FEE 1960, illustrated by Charles Keeping. *O.U.P.*

Sutcliff, Rosemary. BROTHER DUSTY-FEET. *O.U.P.* 1952. Illustrated by C. Walter Hodges. Boy travelling South Country with strolling players in reign of Elizabeth.

Swift, Hildegard Hoyt. THE RAILROAD TO FREEDOM (1932 U.S.A.). *Bodley Head* 1960. Illustrated by James Daugherty. Fictional version of story of Harriet Tubman, negro slave and indefatigable rescuer of slaves from South. A sincere and moving book.

Syme, Ronald. RIVER OF NO RETURN. *Hodder & Stoughton* 1958. Illustrated by William Stobbs. Spanish exploration of Amazon after Pizarro's expedition: detailed picture of a terrible journey.

Syme, Ronald. THE FOREST FIGHTERS. *Hodder & Stoughton* 1958. Illustrated by William Stobbs. Two English boys involved in War of Independence. Local interest, a very immediate picture of war.

*Trease, Geoffrey. BOWS AGAINST THE BARONS. *Martin Lawrence* (1934) 1948.

*Trease, Geoffrey. CUE FOR TREASON 1940, THE GREY ADVENTURER 1942, illustrated by Beatrice Goldsmith. TRUMPETS IN THE WEST 1947, SILVER GUARD 1948, illustrated by Alan Blyth. *Blackwell.*

*Trease, Geoffrey. THE HILLS OF VARNA 1948, illustrated by Treyer Evans WORD TO CAESAR 1955, illustrated by Geoffrey Whittam. *Macmillan.*

Trease, Geoffrey. COMRADES FOR THE CHARTER. *Martin Lawrence* 1934. Vigorous story of the Chartists with strong social moral.

*Treece, Henry. MEN OF THE HILLS 1957, THE BOMBARD 1959. *Bodley Head.*
Illustrated by Christine Price.

Treece, Henry. THE EAGLES HAVE FLOWN. *Bodley Head* 1954. Illustrated by
Christine Price. Britain after departure of the Romans: study of Arthur.

Treece, Henry. LEGIONS OF THE EAGLES. *Bodley Head* 1954. Illustrated by
Christine Price. Roman invasion of Britain; leadership of Caratacus.

*Trevor, Meriol. MERLIN'S RING. *Collins* 1957. Illustrated by Martin Thomas.

*Welch, Ronald. KNIGHT CRUSADER. *O.U.P.* 1954. Illustrated by William
Stobbs.

Wibberley, Leonard. THE WOUND OF PETER WAYNE (1955 U.S.A.). *Faber*
1957. Illustrated by Douglas Gorsline. Southern point of view in Civil War:
boy trying to recover and run his estate after war is over.

*Wilder, Laura Ingalls. LITTLE HOUSE IN THE BIG WOODS (1932 U.S.A.) 1956,
LITTLE HOUSE ON THE PRAIRIE (1935 U.S.A.) 1957, ON THE BANKS OF
PLUM CREEK (1937 U.S.A.) 1958. *Methuen.* BY THE SHORES OF SILVER
LAKE (1939 U.S.A.) 1953, THE LONG WINTER (1940 U.S.A.) 1953, LITTLE
TOWN ON THE PRAIRIE (1941 U.S.A.) 1953, THESE HAPPY GOLDEN YEARS
(1943 U.S.A.) 1953. *Harper,* New York. Illustrated by Garth Williams.

*Williams, Ursula Moray. THE NOBLE HAWKS. *Hamish Hamilton* 1959.

*Wilson, Barbara Ker. PATH-THROUGH-THE-WOODS 1958, illustrated by
Charles Stewart. THE LOVELY SUMMER 1960, illustrated by Marina Hoffer.
Constable.

Worth, Kathryn. THEY LOVED TO LAUGH. *Doubleday,* New York 1942.
Illustrated by Marguerite De Angeli. North Carolina in the 1830's,
Quaker family and their pioneering life.

Worth, Kathryn. THE MIDDLE BUTTON. *Doubleday,* New York 1950. Illustrated
by Dorothy Bayley. North Carolina in the 1880's: girl fighting for the right to
study medicine.

(See also p. 369.)

Adult Historical Fiction recommended for older children

Bowen, Marjorie. DICKON. *Hodder & Stoughton* 1929. Still the best sympathetic
study of Richard III.

Bullett, Gerald. THE ALDERMAN'S SON. *Michael Joseph* 1954. Sensible and
lively version of Shakespeare's early life at Stratford.

Daniell, David Scott. FIFTY POUNDS FOR A DEAD PARSON. *Cape* 1960. Napoleonic period, 1806, in an English village.

Duggan, Alfred. KNIGHT WITH ARMOUR 1950. *Penguin* 1959. First Crusade.

Duggan, Alfred. LEOPARDS AND LILIES. *Faber* 1954. Thirteenth century. Noble lady marries mercenary captain under King John and follows the army.

Duggan Alfred. WINTER QUARTERS. *Faber* 1956. Late Roman Empire. All Duggan's books are distinguished by his dry sense of humour and extraordinarily actual presentations of the ordinary in the past.

Garnett, David. POCAHONTAS. *Chatto* 1933. Captain John Smith in Virginia, seventeenth century. Beautifully written and a fascinating story.

Graves, Ralph. THE LOST EAGLES. *Faber* 1956. Roman Legions in Germany.

Graves, Robert. I CLAUDIUS (1934) 1941, CLAUDIUS THE GOD (1934) 1954. *Penguin*. Classic study of Roman Imperial rule from the inside.

Heyer, Georgette, THE TOLLGATE. *Heinemann* 1954. Regency adventure, romantic and exciting.

Irwin, Margaret. ROYAL FLUSH. *Chatto* 1932. Story of Minette, daughter of Charles I. Touching and wonderfully thorough study of royal family.

Jefferis, Barbara. BELOVED LADY. *Dent* 1956. Masterly use of Paston Letters to show ordinary people in Wars of the Roses.

Le May, Alan. THE SEARCHERS. *Collins* 1955. American frontier, Texas. Moving and vivid.

Lofts, Norah. SCENT OF CLOVES. *Hutchinson* 1959. Indonesia, seventeenth century. Exotic and romantic.

Lofts, Norah. THE TOWN HOUSE. *Hutchinson* 1959. Story of a family and a house fourteenth and fifteenth centuries.

Masefield, John. BADON PARCHMENTS. *Heinemann* 1947. Superb version of story of King Arthur and battle of Mount Badon.

O'Brian, Patrick. THE UNKNOWN SHORE. *Hart-Davis* 1959. Long account of the disastrous experiences of the crew of *Wager*, separated from Anson's squadron, late eighteenth century, struggling round Cape Horn and to Chile.

Oldenbourg, Zöe. THE CORNERSTONE. *Gollancz* 1954. Long, intricate, fascinating study of Crusades in Europe.

Onions, Oliver. THE STORY OF RAGGED ROBYN 1945. *Penguin* 1954. Seventeenth-century panorama, domestic.

Prescott, H. F. M. THE MAN WITH THE DONKEY. *Eyre & Spottiswoode* (1952) 1956. Henry VIII and the dissolution of the monasteries.

Sutcliff, Rosemary. THE RIDER OF THE WHITE HORSE. *Hodder & Stoughton* 1959. Civil War from the point of view of Fairfax.

Chapter *13* | *Innocents in the Underworld*

Adventure stories rest on a delicate balance of fantasy with circumstantial detail, and I am never quite sure how far children notice
this balance. From good nature, laziness, ignorance or the pure joy
of reading, they may accept story after story without question, but
now and then something will stir their critical sense; and this is most
likely to be when they are reading about children running into danger
in a contemporary setting.

Even then it is probably some factual detail they will question,
rather than the general concept of the happy ending, the young hero
triumphing against the crook, penknife against pistol, innocent
curiosity against experienced lawlessness. They like this formula because it offers them a preview of what they feel sure life is like. It is up to
the writer to make up his mind, every time he begins a story, whether
it is to be reasonable or not. In this kind of writing, I believe that adult
criticism must give a lead to the hit-and-miss opinions of children.

Every author has his own way of approaching this business of
probability. Some, like E. W. Hildick and Erich Kästner, choose
plots which are easily related to everyday life. Others, like Mary
Fitt, put over tall stories by sheer virtuosity. Others, like J. M.
Scott and John Verney, carry their readers along because of the liveliness of their characters. Others, like Eilís Dillon and Elisabeth
Kyle, rely on authentic backgrounds to carry off their mysteries.
One of the best methods, perhaps, is to give your adventure to a gang
of children, for hazard will then be shared, wits and resources pooled
and the chances of success multiplied.

The ancestor of the gang-story is probably Erich Kästner's EMIL
AND THE DETECTIVES, which reached England in translation in
1931 (it was published in Germany in 1929). It did not set a fashion
straightaway. In fact it was not for nearly twenty years that the same

relaxed, slangy, casual note was heard again in this country, in Cecil Day Lewis's masterpiece, THE OTTERBURY INCIDENT. A few of the episodes in this book were modelled on the film *Nous les Gosses*, and the general idea of making money to pay for damage was taken from it. The characters have little or no relation to those in the film, and the dialogue is the author's own. Kästner had the advantage of an unselfconscious approach to class-distinction. At a time when, in England, adventure stories were still largely middle-class, Kästner could write as a matter of course of a very mixed Berlin street-gang, in which one member has a father working as night-watchman in an hotel and another belongs to a professional family; while Emil, whose journey to the city to stay with his grandmother sparks off the whole comical business, lives with a widowed mother who is a hairdresser. The adventure rises naturally out of this very background. Emil goes to Berlin by train, with an envelope in his pocket containing his money. For safety he pins the notes to his jacket, and it is the pin-marks which finally convict smooth Mr Grundeis, who has stolen the notes while Emil is asleep in the carriage. Nothing was ever more convincing than that Emil should awake just in time to see his chatty companion hurriedly leaving a station, and should be able to keep him in sight until the happy accident of his meeting with the gang of street boys. Nothing was ever more utterly lifelike than the swift, efficient deploying of the gang—one to stand by for telephone reports, one to lurk in the hotel where Grundeis has taken refuge, others to shadow him until the triumphant moment when they all close in on him at the bank with the cry, 'Stop him. That is stolen money.' Kästner has not once had to go beyond probability, and yet here are all the requirements of the adventure-story—tension, speed, surprise.

The course of such stories in England might have been happier if more writers had taken note of Kästner's technique; his brilliant selection of detail, his crisp, utterly unpadded narrative, broken up with racy dialogue; his strict attention to character. For if his crook, shady and meagre, is horrifyingly real, his boys are too, each one set in his proper environment. We know who they were, what they were like, where they lived and how they lived. The crowning touch of realism comes with the reaction of Emil's mother to the publicity the 'boy-detective' receives. I would have her words learnt by heart by anyone who wants to write crook stories for children:

'Emil's a clever boy, and works hard. He's always top of his class. But supposing something had gone wrong! It makes my hair stand on end to think of it, though I know it is all over now, and everything has really turned out all right. I'll never let him go away alone again, that's certain. I'd die of fright, wondering what was happening to him.'

Erich Kästner. EMIL AND THE DETECTIVES. Translated by Eileen Hall. (Penguin, 1959) p. 121.

together with Grandma's trenchant reminder of the lesson *she* has learned from all the fuss—'Money should always be sent through the post.'

Kästner, then, chose a probable plot and a probable crook. In THE OTTERBURY INCIDENT the gang is up against a tougher proposition, black marketeers who have also tried and abandoned the idea of coining. We are led towards this by such gradual stages that it is impossible even to consider doubting whether it could all have happened. The setting, a country town, is superbly described, not in set pieces but emerging through the activities of Ted's gang and Toppy's gang as they carry on a sporadic war on the bomb site known as The Incident. When the story begins a campaign is in progress:

Just then, Toppy blew his whistle, and all his men who weren't casualties began streaming back towards the tank. In the heat of the battle, the enemy hadn't yet realised that their tank was captured. As they shot past behind the tank, Nick leant out and bopped one after another of them on the head with his football, yelling out: 'You're dead! *You're* dead! *You're* dead!' He got four of them like that, and at last he got Toppy himself.

'What the hell are you playing at?' shouted Toppy.

'Lie down,' I said. 'Don't you know when you're dead?'

'*And* we've destroyed the tank,' said Charlie. 'We've put five sticky bombs on it, honest. Look.'

'Oh, you have, have you?' Toppy said, when he'd examined the side of the tank, and underneath it. 'Yes, that's O.K. Five bombs. The tank's blown to smithereens. And so are you two fools in it. And therefore Nick couldn't have conked anyone with his football. And *therefore* I'm *not* dead.'

C. Day Lewis. THE OTTERBURY INCIDENT (Putnam, 1948) pp. 12–13.

But a treaty drawn up by the narrator (one of those brainy boys who can usually be found in a gang) gives them space to plan a more useful campaign, for they have to earn enough money to pay for a window broken in the fight. Ted keeps the money in a box; it disappears; the gang is divided into those who suspect Ted and those who want to investigate the unsavoury Johnny Sharp, a local lounger. And so we move naturally from the streets to Skinner's yard and then into his cellar. The boys have no easy job when they tackle Skinner and his associates. Ted, who is caught in the cellar, is in real danger and is rescued by the police only just in time. And the police, far from congratulating the boys on their detective skill, as many inferior authors would have allowed them to do, temper their praise with severe warnings against interfering with police routine.

It is in the relation of boys to grown-ups that the author shows his quality. The boys succeed because of virtues typically their own—blind courage, inquisitiveness, intelligence—plus a certain amount of luck. When they learn that Ted is caught in the cellar, they send a message to the police and wade in at once to attack the warehouse:

> An odd thing, worth recording, is that it never occurred to any of them to enlist the aid of one or two grown-ups who came along the lane while they were making their plans. Rickie had to admit, though, when we told him the whole story later, that they were probably right: either these passers-by wouldn't have believed them, or else they'd have said, 'Wait for the police,' grown-ups being a bit windy about winkling out gangs of desperate criminals.
> Ibid., p. 130.

and when they are chasing the wounded Johnny Sharp through the town, their status as tiresome boys is unchanged:

> The rest of them passed on down the street, and spread out across the allotments, where one ancient man leant on a fork and shook his fist at them for treading all over his vegetables.
> Ibid., p. 139.

A beautiful sense of proportion, allied to a smooth, flexible style, make this a jewel among children's stories.

This is, above all, a story of action. The characters are neatly sketched, not complex; for you see them all, in action and in talk, through the eyes of George, who is one of them. But two stories by Richard Church are written first and foremost as studies of character. At the beginning of THE CAVE we are introduced formally to the members of the Tomahawk Club. There is John Walters, on holiday with an uncle and aunt; Meaty, son of a butcher, oafish and good-hearted; Harold Soames, called Lightning, 'a tiny little chap who was always in front of time and in a desperate hurry'; Alan Hobbs, self-appointed leader, and George Reynolds, quiet and reserved because of an unhappy home. The story is a simple one. John finds by accident the entrance to a limestone cave. The boys decide to explore it, prepare systematically for the expedition, venture into a network of passages and vaults, and, in circumstances of some doubt and danger, get out again by way of an underground river. What happens in the cave is far less important (and even less exciting) than what happens to the boys themselves. They do not come out just as they went in. John overcomes some fear of the dark; Alan loses his ascendancy and is revealed as a coward; George, in a crisis, accepts responsibility and deserves it. The author is quite unconcerned with what his readers can or cannot appreciate in the realm of human feelings, and this is as it should be. Everything he says in this and in the vigorous sequel, DOWN RIVER, is genuine, straightforward, undiluted.

Here is an author who can describe a fight so that it can be followed blow by blow. It is not this that will keep his readers, though, but his psychology, and the same is true of Paul Berna, whose plots, unlike Church's, are pretty unlikely. A HUNDRED MILLION FRANCS, one of the liveliest children's stories I know, supposes that a gang of children in a French suburb could really, behind the backs of long-suffering and overworked policemen, round up several thieves and recover a huge sum of money stolen from the Paris-Ventimiglia express. I defy anyone to disbelieve one detail of this logical craziness, from the moment we meet the children riding their headless horse perilously down the hill to the moment when, with the cockiness of children who have got more than they deserve, they bid farewell to weary Inspector Sinet, with an offer of a turn on their battered steed. Their characters show in every word they say, every drawing of their exploits. At one point we see them engaging in a pitched battle with the crooks in a factory full of carnival novelties; but their barricading is a matter of hasty discipline, and they have first of all been behaving with the wild irresponsibility of their age:

> The younger ones were calmly trying on wigs and false beards
> in the store-room at the end, standing round Zidore, who was
> dressed up as a demon; Tatave had already broken a dozen
> gazookas; Berthe and Mélie were hurling paper streamers furi-
> ously at each other; and Criquet, decked out in a three-cornered
> hat, was having a row of medals pinned on his chest . . .
>
> Paul Berna. A HUNDRED MILLION FRANCS. Translated by
> John Buchanan-Brown (Bodley Head, 1957) pp. 113–4.

We know these children—Monica, the tomboy, with her attendant
dogs collected from all over the town; Gaby, terrified of growing
out of the gang; Criquet, the negro boy, grinning and alert; Bonbon,
the youngest, who serves as mascot; and all the rest of the crew.
Their appearance, their talk, their homes and their hide-outs, all are
as real as they can be, and they are just as much so in a sequel, THE
STREET MUSICIAN.

Authenticity, that is the secret, as in Anne Barrett's SONGBERD'S
GROVE. Here is a story which turns out pat, involving half a dozen
startling coincidences by which the Singer family is left in peace to
enjoy a new home, a spiv is given new hope for the future, an ageing
dancer is restored to slimness, and a row of Georgian houses is
revealed in its former elegance. An improbable plot, but in every
other respect the book is so real that most children will accept
what happens without question. You can imagine right from the
start the slummy London street, and Number Seven, and the
Singers as they move in—quiet father, a factory worker, and his
plump wife, relaxing after a trying stay with her sister-in-law;
and spectacled, determined Martin:

> Clutching his parcels to him and glaring at them from behind the
> blinding shields of his glasses, on which the afternoon sun was now
> shining, Martin strode past them and up to the front door, where
> his mother had already rung the appropriate bell. The paint had
> once been red but was now darkened and peeling; there was a
> fanlight above with the number seven painted on it in black, with
> a thin gold edge. For the first time a touch of sympathy with the
> house stirred in Martin. It was a good seven.
>
> Footsteps sounded from inside and an old man, frail and

pinkish, stood blinking in front of them, as though he had suddenly been recalled from very far away. He was in his shirt-
sleeves and slippers and wore a curious sort of tapestry waistcoat,
from whose pocket the end of a measure-tape was trailing; all
over him, as though he had been sleeping inside a mattress, small
bits of cloth and thread and horsehair were clinging, and a pad
stuck full of pins was attached to one of his wrists.
Anne Barrett. SONGBERD'S GROVE (Collins, 1957) p. 8.

The author wisely spends a long time establishing the scene, describing the down-at-heel houses and the urchins, loitering and spiteful,
and the spoiled only child, Lennie, Number One of the street gang.

As a gang leader, Lennie is a failure. He soon collapses under the
practical opposition of Martin and his ally, and the sensible way the
author shows up this petty spiv and explains his background makes
up for the sensational happy ending. Lennie is the kind of boy who
does develop into a crook, and who can very suitably be used in a
story, and so is Red Hendy, the young spiv in JO AND THE SKIFFLE

Drawing by Richard Kennedy for Paul Berna's A HUNDRED MILLION
FRANCS (Bodley Head)

GROUP by Valerie Hastings, another story with the true atmosphere
of London back streets. The crooks are kept in proportion; here is an
impression of one of them, delivered with scorn by the sensible Don:

> Monkey approached the place with exaggerated caution. Then
> he flattened himself against a wall, with his hands thrust in his
> pockets, and looked both ways along the street. Satisfied that he
> wasn't observed, he made a dash for the door, stumbling up the
> low step in his haste.
>
> Don chuckled. 'Not so hot at the cloak and dagger stuff, is he?
> Sticks out a mile that he's up to no good. You know, if it wasn't
> for their outbreaks of real viciousness Red's gang could be dis-
> missed with a good laugh. They're a ham bunch.'
>
> Valerie Hastings. JO AND THE SKIFFLE GROUP (Parrish, 1958)
> p. 86.

This is salutary, I suppose, from the moral point of view, and it is
certainly a more satisfactory basis for a story than the idea that a
crook with an international connection can be floored by a pack of
kids. It is perfectly likely, in fact, that children on their own ground,
in streets or fields which they know inside-out, should be able to run
rings round crooks who underestimate the opposition out of sheer
stupidity. From this point of view the crook story of today, set as a
rule in a familiar background, has a chance of being more convincing
than the spy and treasure tales of the 'twenties, with their exotic
backgrounds in Egypt, South America or Afghanistan. If you use a
background which your readers are likely to know, you have to be
scrupulous about detail and the balance of your story must be
absolutely true. What Peter Fleming calls 'with-Harry-it-was-the-
work-of-a-moment adventure stories', are far less common today,
thank goodness, than they used to be; in their place we have tales
like E. W. Hildick's recent thriller, THE BOY AT THE WINDOW,
where a crime is attempted, and stopped by a bedridden boy and his
two friends—an idea handled by the author composedly and with
absolute success.

Amateur detection, too, is all the better for a familiar setting and
for situations which boys and girls could naturally cope with.
Anthony Wilson's clever pair, Norman and Henry Bones, for example,
solve all their cases by fair means, by pertinacity or simple deduction
or observation or memory, and they tackle nothing outside their

range. If these are not stories to read often, they provide for younger readers (say from eight or nine) an introduction to the traditions and formulas of the detective story which will probably remain a permanent part of their diet; and Malcolm Saville's clever tales of Susan and Bill serve the same purpose. These children (they are nine and eleven and not particularly clever or precocious) solve mysteries suitable to their capacity, tracing a long-lost legacy for an old lady, stopping a back-door snooper from taking the farmer's wife's treasures, disclosing the secrets of some fairly innocuous smugglers.

In fact, the amateur detective had better not be up against anything too tough. Linda Carroll, Winifred Donald's schoolgirl detective, who is consulted officially even by adults, is far more convincing when she is following up clues leading to a legacy (in LINDA IN CAMBRIDGE) than when she is hunting down, with foolhardy courage, an American kidnapper (LINDA IN NEW YORK) or a seller of national secrets (LINDA AND THE SILVER GREYHOUNDS). She is sixteen when she goes in for this kind of case, and when you get to this point I should have thought it was better to go over to adventures where adults take control and the young merely stand by. Stories like P. H. Newby's THE LOOT RUNNERS, or Rex Warner's drug-smuggling thriller, THE KITE, or Henry Treece's brilliant series ASK FOR KING BILLY, HUNTER HUNTED, and DON'T EXPECT ANY MERCY, deal with serious crime in a suitably serious manner.

You can't have it both ways, in fact. If you want to write about real danger, you can't really have children as your main characters. If you want children, your plot must be cut to fit them, or you get an awkward compromise that satisfies nobody. Yet how many children in fiction launch themselves into the country, on to the moors, to the seaside, to old ruined mansions, meeting on their arrival (or even on the journey) some ferocious challenge from the underworld. The formula is easily recognized:

A lively family rather reluctantly go to spend the Easter holidays with a hitherto unknown grandfather. The prospect of any fun coming their way seems slim; but even before they leave London they find they have become involved in a mystery.
Blurb for SECRET OF THE SANDHILLS by Kitty Barne. (Nelson, 1955).

Suppose we accept the premise that children on holiday are likely to stumble on a spy, a smuggler or a jewel thief—what follows? Another premise, that the grown-ups will allow them to run their heads into danger. In R. J. McGregor's story, THE SECRET OF DEAD MAN'S COVE, Mr Mackenzie remarks that he hopes his children will allow *this* holiday to be peaceful; the year before he had been recalled from Scotland to Cornwall to learn that they had stopped a gang from stealing a new, secret explosive (see THE YOUNG DETECTIVES). This understandable attitude lasts for two chapters; after that he cheerfully backs up the recommendation of the local police inspector that they should 'watch out for a little man with very ruddy cheeks who has a glass eye' and pass on all they see. Mr Mackenzie is in fact working for the government and has, rather casually, brought a top secret paper down to work at. It is true that he has taken the precaution of bolting down the window-seat which conceals a secret way to the beach, but this year's batch of crooks manages very well elsewhere.

It is obviously best to ditch the parents at the start, and most fiction writers do this expertly. I am always prepared to accept a major operation on Mother or a sudden business trip to China, other things being equal; among these 'other things' are character-drawing and a good setting. It is hard to accept literally the coincidences and convenient endings in Elisabeth Kyle's stories, but nobody draws old cities as well as she does, nobody can suggest as she does the mystery of a small object (a musical-box or a model ship or a jewel) which crystallizes the feeling of past and present. Edinburgh in the incomparable story, THE HOUSE OF THE PELICAN; Glasgow in CAROLINE HOUSE; London in THE SEVEN SAPPHIRES and RUN TO EARTH; the Outer Isles in VANISHING ISLAND; all these places *make* the story.

Elisabeth Kyle stands head and shoulders above most writers of this kind of topographical thriller because her characters are as variable and interesting as her backgrounds. Two other writers must be mentioned who dig deep into motive and whose criminals, such as they are, are fallible human beings, not just lay figures providing a focal point for action. Allan McLean's three excellent stories for boys are set in Skye. The first (perhaps the best), THE HILL OF THE RED FOX, with its Buchanesque crypto-villain, its plot of the kidnapping of scientists by foreign powers, has a firm domestic basis.

The hero, young Alastair Cameron, is not in fact a hero; he is a boy, at first intrigued by an odd encounter in the train, then frightened when he realizes he is out of his depth in villainy:

> I had read many adventure stories, and I used to play a game, imagining myself to be the hero facing dreadful perils with cool courage. But this was no game, and now that I knew my life to be in danger I was afraid. None of the heroes in my stories was ever afraid. Sword in hand, they fought off half a score of attackers with a smile on their lips. But this was different. A whispered word, spoken in the darkness of the night, could be far more frightening than a dozen sword blades.
> Allan McLean. THE HILL OF THE RED FOX (Collins, 1955) pp. 81–2.

Alastair and the solitary crofter, Duncan Mor, who helps him, blunder to success through a number of mistakes (one of which costs Duncan his life) and the head of M.I.5 makes a familiar but appropriate remark at the end—'it has always been the amateurs who have pulled us through.' In other words, Alastair is an ordinary boy who fights with the weapons at his disposal, who is often in extreme danger, whose ultimate fate you can't take for granted, although you can be sure he will fight to the last gasp. THE MAN OF THE HOUSE, with its tale of theft and intrigue, and THE MASTER OF MORGANA, which skilfully mixes salmon-fishing and the search for a wrecked galleon, offer, too, so much that is sound and real about ordinary people that their melodramatic scenes seem entirely natural too.

What Allan McLean has done for Skye, Eilís Dillon is doing for remote Irish seaboards. Here are no crooks in the story-book sense, but people gone wrong. In THE ISLAND OF HORSES it is a local dealer who has turned thief to bolster up his self-importance. In THE SINGING CAVE it is an egotistical recluse who covets the Viking found in the sand. In THE HOUSE ON THE SHORE it is an old man warped by his wife's death. With the free emotional swing of Irish tales, the motives of these very individual criminals are laid bare to us. Here is Jim O'Malley's Uncle Martin gloating over the church plate which he has kept hidden in his derelict house for years:

'I was a young man when I found them first. They have been wife
and child to me ever since. I never wanted to leave them. I never
went away from my house without taking leave of them first. I have
loved them and watched over them for twenty years. See how they
gleam in the light. That's because I always kept them polished—'

'God save us from such a curse!' said Roddy in my ear.
'Look at the miserly face of him! Look at the greedy paws of
him! The devil has a hold of that man, for certain sure!'

Uncle Martin's hands were opening and shutting and rubbing
each other, over the gold vessels, as if they had a life of their own.
He certainly looked like a man that had an evil spirit in him, which
now seemed to fill the little house to suffocation.

Eilís Dillon. THE HOUSE ON THE SHORE (Faber, 1955) p. 173.

And behind the people is the Irish scene, superbly described; the
hidden valley where the wild horses wheel and stamp, the cave with
the pieces of the wolf-game lying beside the Viking skeleton, old
Martin's tree-house, peat bogs and mountains and crofts. To find
crime in everyday life, to find real motives for it, and to fuse detail
into an imaginative whole—Eilís Dillon has done this, and has raised
the standard of the adventure story in doing it.

Oddly enough, the most fantastic kind of plot may also be the
nearest to the events of real life. The adventures of a spy are as exciting in fact as in fiction, and can provide excellent plots. Unfortunately, writers for children often leave out the essential element, the
reasons for spying. John Buchan, ancestor of the spy-story writers,
knew better than this. His international agents, his monomaniacs
seeking world power, are formidable indeed, yet nothing in their
motives or their circumstances is beyond the understanding of a
schoolboy. Though Buchan did not write for children, he is still, and
always will be, popular with them, because he gives them character
as well as action, whereas many writers today, realizing the complexity of the spy or the traitor, take him for granted and concentrate on
the adventure. M. Pardoe's Bunkle, chattering his way past enemy
agents of all nationalities, Bertram Edwards's schoolboys tackling
enemy agents during a half-term holiday, John Pudney's boy heroes
helping or hindering Uncle George—none of these youthful heroes
has much idea of what is going on in the minds of their adversaries,
or, indeed, what they are really trying to do. It is true that John

Verney's children, in FRIDAY'S TUNNEL, have some idea what they are up against, but their father is a roving correspondent who detects in his spare time, and they know enough about the secret mineral of Capria to make themselves useful in his absence. In J. M. Scott's romantic adventure, THE BRIGHT EYES OF DANGER, the children who foil Communist elements on a Ruritanian island in the Aegean have been brought up in diplomatic circles and make the most of what they have picked up. But I know only one story, written for children, which really examines the mind of a spy. THE MARLOWS AND THE TRAITOR, by Antonia Forest, involves the twins, Nicola and Lawrie (whom we have already met in two first-class school-stories) and their brother Peter, with Ralph Foley, one of Peter's instructors at Dartmouth, who is selling secrets to the Germans in wartime. To the end of the story, the children are not sure what they think of Foley. They like him, a good deal of the time, even when he has given them a bad time in a lonely lighthouse; they are puzzled by his behaviour and by his odd lack of apology for being a traitor; they hover uneasily between the accidental perceptiveness of children and the orthodox views they have learned from grown-up people. This story, with its warmth, its courage in character-drawing, its narrative skill, deserves to outlast hundreds of tales which may seem, at first reading, to be just as exciting.

It is not easy to put spies into stories for children because of the complexity of their motives and of political and national affairs as a whole. Geoffrey Trease was one of the first to try to give children an honest version of war. THE CALL TO ARMS, which was published twenty-five years ago, is no tale of honour and glory; it is a business of secret arrangements, vested interests, confusion, discomfort and death. This is very much a book of the 'thirties, and parts of it (like the strike in the South American town, and the triumph of the People's Army) are more doctrinaire than anything this author is writing today; his theories stand out like gaunt signposts pointing to a new world, rather than being related to the characters. He must be respected always for his consistent belief that children are not given enough of the truth in their stories.

Writers who have an axe to grind must often be blamed unfairly for deafening us with the sound. Certainly reviewers will be on the look-out for tendentiousness in a writer whose political views are well known. In any case, children will not stand for principle if it holds up action. It is all the more to the credit of Naomi Mitchison that she has kept a well-informed and progressive point of view in the forefront of stories which are exceptionally readable, for old or young. JUDY AND LAKSHMI, a story of modern India, has a good deal of political theory in it, but it is primarily a touching story of the friendship of two girls with dissimilar backgrounds. THE FAR HARBOUR, with its uncompromising picture of fishermen in the Western Highlands, stands and falls by its characters, and so does THE RIB OF THE GREEN UMBRELLA, which is set in an Italian town in the Second World War. All the dangers of the underground movement are here, all the social structures of the place, but what we shall remember is the two lively boys who carry messages, laughing and playing through danger. Again, among many recent stories for children which touch on African problems, the one that impressed me most was ASHANTI BOY by Akosua Abbs, because its knowledgeable picture of Ghana on the eve of independence was enlivened by the brilliant characters of schoolboys, boys aspiring to school life, teachers, preachers, native chiefs and many others.

Perhaps it is not surprising that books like these are in the minority, for they have cut loose from the prevailing belief that stories for children must adopt a youthful tone. For every book of the calibre of THE SILVER SWORD, Ian Serraillier's story of children in war-shattered Poland, with its crystal-clear sincerity, there are half-a-dozen which romanticize war into a matter of chases and excitement, with danger nothing more than a word. Until we return to the Victorian custom of treating children as embryo adults (at least in their reading matter), they are not likely to get many books which give them enough to think about without being laboured or priggish. We are not likely, for this and other reasons, to get many books like DOG TOBY, Richard Church's clear-headed, sympathetic story showing up the causes of war.

Here we are in a Central European country, looking over the frontier into another country on the brink of war. Between the two a tunnel carries a railway, through which patrol-trains run, their staff keyed-up and nervous. The Brown children, Maria and Jan, and their friend Fritz, plan an all-day outing to the frontier, to the delectable hillsides where they have been forbidden to play. In the sunshine, they relax and wonder about the tension among the grown-ups. Then their puppy runs into the tunnel. They follow, are caught by the guards, help to avert a collision with an international express, and the whole stupid, inevitable, indefensible deadlock is summed up in the farewell of the rival parties, now on friendly terms after the homely incident:

> Dog Toby shook a paw with him, and accepted a biscuit from another of the Northern Guards. Mitzi also came forward and was suitably rewarded for the part she had played in the tunnel; not a very heroic part but worth a biscuit.
>
> 'Well!' said the once-grumpy Northern officer, when all the fraternizing was complete and people had begun to look at each other with that 'what comes next?' shyness in their eyes. 'Time we got going! What do we do with the prisoners?'
>
> This was indeed a problem, almost an international situation. 'Hang 'em!' said a voice, the kindest voice in the whole party. 'Hang 'em from that strand of ivy over the tunnel-mouth.'
>
> Laughter! Slapping of backs, patting of dogs; handing round of biscuits and cigarettes.
>
> 'You can't do that. It is strung with bells,' said another.
>
> More laughter, more congratulations, as though a heavy weight had been lifted from all hearts; as though a good spirit had come down out of the Northern and the Southern sky and whispered to these men: 'No more suspicions; no more barbed wire! Let the Transcontinental run; let the children wander over the hills where their fathers used to wander when *they* were children!'
>
> And so it was. The guards shook hands once more, but surely not for the last time; shook hands and separated into their two patrols, making for the trains, mounting the trucks, blowing the whistles, and setting off.
>
> Richard Church. DOG TOBY: a frontier tale (Hutchinson, 1954) pp. 170–1.

This is a fine book, humorous and moving. Aiming at the truth, because he believes children should have no less, Richard Church has climbed the heights, leaving most of his fellow-writers panting on the foothills.

Reading List

1.*Children and Crooks* (See also p. 342.)

Aldous, Allan. THE TENDRILLS IN AUSTRALIA. *Chatto* 1959. Nuclear physics and cattle-rustling combine in a good story.

Ballantyne, Joan. KIDNAPPERS AT COOMBE. *Nelson* 1960. Illustrated by Edward Ardizzone. Children of Balkan Prime Minister, at holiday home, threatened by kidnappers; older children do some effective and convincing detective work.

*Barne, Kitty. THE SECRET OF THE SANDHILLS. *Nelson* 1955. Previously published as THE EASTER HOLIDAYS. *Heinemann* 1935. Illustrated by Joan Kiddell-Monroe.

*Barrett, Anne. SONGBERD'S GROVE. *Collins* 1957. Illustrated by David Knight.

*Berna, Paul. A HUNDRED MILLION FRANCS (1955 France) 1957, THE STREET MUSICIAN (1956 France) 1960. *Bodley Head*. Translated by John Buchanan-Brown. Illustrated by Richard Kennedy. (See also p. 342.)

*Church, Richard. THE CAVE. *Dent* (1950) 1953 (revised edition). Illustrated by Geoffrey Whittam.

Church, Richard, DOWN RIVER. *Heinemann* 1958. Illustrated by Laurence Irving.

Clarke, Pauline. THE WHITE ELEPHANT. *Faber* 1952. Illustrated by Richard Kennedy. Jewel-thieves in London streets: convincing because of speed and authentic background.

Clarke, Pauline. SMITH'S HOARD. *Faber* 1955. Illustrated by Cecil Leslie. Sophisticated tale of children in East Anglia saving Iron Age hoard from thieves.

Cross, John Keir. THE SIXPENNY YEAR. *Hutchinson* 1957. Agreeably adult and sensible tale of town children staying on Devon farm, involved with sheep stealer.

*Dillon, Eilís. THE SAN SEBASTIAN 1953 (see also Chap. 11), THE HOUSE ON THE SHORE 1955, THE ISLAND OF HORSES 1956, THE SINGING CAVE 1959. *Faber*. Illustrated by Richard Kennedy. (See also p. 342.)

*Donald, Winifred. LINDA AND THE SILVER GREYHOUNDS 1952, LINDA IN CAMBRIDGE 1955, LINDA IN NEW YORK 1956. *Hutchinson*.

*Edwards, Bertram. MIDNIGHT ON BARROWMEAD HILL 1957, STRANGE TRAFFIC 1959. *Brockhampton*. Illustrated by Richard Kennedy.

Finlay, Winifred. PERIL IN LAKELAND 1953, COTSWOLD HOLIDAY 1954, STORM OVER CHEVIOT 1955, THE LOST SILVER OF LANGDON 1955, CANAL

HOLIDAY 1957, THE CRUISE OF THE 'SUSAN' 1958. *Harrap.* Adventure
stories, with crooks or treasure or both, unusually convincing because rational
and unexaggerated. Excellent backgrounds in Border country, the Lakes,
the Cotswolds and Northamptonshire.

*Fitt, Mary. THE ISLAND CASTLE 1953, ANNABELLA AT THE LIGHTHOUSE
1955, POMEROY'S POSTSCRIPT 1955, THE TURNIP WATCH 1956, THE
SHIFTING SANDS 1958. *Nelson.*

*Forest, Antonia. THE MARLOWS AND THE TRAITOR. *Faber* 1953. Illustrated
by Doritie Kettlewell. (See also p. 333.)

Gunn, John. THE HUMPY IN THE HILLS. *Lutterworth* 1960. Illustrated by
Noella Young. Australian setting: boys join with educated tramp to foil the
last member of a gang of thieves.

*Hastings, Valerie. JO AND THE SKIFFLE GROUP 1958, JO AND CONEY'S
CAVERN 1959. *Parrish.*

*Hildick, E. W. THE BOY AT THE WINDOW. *Chatto* 1960.

*Kästner, Erich. EMIL AND THE DETECTIVES (1929 Germany). *Cape* 1931.
Translated by Eileen Hall. *Penguin* (Puffin Story Books) 1959. Also EMIL,
comprising EMIL AND THE DETECTIVES, EMIL AND THE THREE TWINS and
THE THIRTY-FIFTH OF MAY. *Cape* 1949. Illustrated by Walter Trier.

*Kyle, Elisabeth. THE HOUSE OF THE PELICAN 1954, illustrated by Peggy
Fortnum. CAROLINE HOUSE 1955, illustrated by Robert Hodgson. VANISH-
ING ISLAND (1942) 1956, THE SEVEN SAPPHIRES (1944) 1957, illustrated
by Leslie Atkinson. RUN TO EARTH 1957, illustrated by Mary Shillabeer.
Nelson.

*Lewis, C. Day. THE OTTERBURY INCIDENT. *Putman* (1948) 1958. Illustrated
by Edward Ardizzone.

*McGregor, R. J. THE YOUNG DETECTIVES 1934, THE SECRET OF DEAD
MAN'S COVE 1937. *Burns Oates.*

*McLean, Allan. THE HILL OF THE RED FOX 1955, THE MAN OF THE HOUSE
1956, THE MASTER OF MORGANA (see Chap. 11). *Collins.*

*Newby, P. H. THE LOOT RUNNERS. *John Lehmann* 1949.

*Pardoe, M. FOUR PLUS BUNKLE. *Routledge* 1939. And many other titles.

*Pudney, John. SATURDAY ADVENTURE 1950, SUNDAY ADVENTURE 1951.
Bodley Head. Illustrated by Ley Kenyon.

*Pudney, John. MONDAY ADVENTURE 1952, TUESDAY ADVENTURE 1953,
WEDNESDAY ADVENTURE 1954, THURSDAY ADVENTURE 1955. *Evans.*
Illustrated by Ley Kenyon.

*Saville, Malcolm. SUSAN, BILL AND THE WOLF DOG 1954, SUSAN, BILL AND
THE IVY-CLAD OAK 1954, SUSAN, BILL AND THE VANISHING BOY 1955,

SUSAN, BILL AND THE GOLDEN CLOCK 1955, SUSAN, BILL AND THE DARK
STRANGER 1956, SUSAN, BILL AND THE SAUCY KATE 1956, illustrated by
Ernest Shepard. SUSAN, BILL AND THE BRIGHT STAR CIRCUS 1960,
illustrated by T. R. Freeman. *Nelson.*

*Scott, J. M. THE BRIGHT EYES OF DANGER. *Hodder & Stoughton* 1950.

Treadgold, Mary. THE POLLY HARRIS. *Cape* 1949. Illustrated by Pat Marriott.
London riverside adventure with smugglers: good characterization.

*Treece, Henry. ASK FOR KING BILLY 1955, HUNTER HUNTED 1957, DON'T
EXPECT ANY MERCY 1958. *Faber.* Illustrated by Richard Kennedy.

*Verney, John. FRIDAY'S TUNNEL. *Collins* 1959. Illustrated by the author.
(See also p. 344.)

*Warner, Rex. THE KITE. *Blackwell* 1936.

Westlake, Veronica. THE INTRUDERS. *Routledge* 1954. Illustrated by Sheila
Rose. Schoolboy inherits manor and comes up against crooked lawyer:
natural, easy style and convincing direction of story.

*Wilson, Anthony. NORMAN BONES, DETECTIVE 1949, NORMAN AND HENRY
BONES, THE BOY DETECTIVES 1952, NORMAN AND HENRY BONES INVES-
TIGATE 1953, illustrated by Kenneth Beauchamp. NORMAN AND HENRY
SOLVE THE PROBLEM 1957, illustrated by Elizabeth Andrewes. NORMAN AND
HENRY FOLLOW THE TRAIL 1959, illustrated by Margery Gill. *Methuen.*

*Wilson, Anthony. FOUR MYSTERIES SOLVED BY NORMAN AND HENRY
BONES. *Penguin* (Puffin Story Books) 1957. Illustrated by Elizabeth Andrewes.

2.*War and its aftermath* (See also p. 365.)

*Abbs, Akosua. ASHANTI BOY. *Collins* 1959.

Barne, Kitty. WE'LL MEET IN ENGLAND. *Hamish Hamilton* 1942. Illustrated
by Steven Spurrier. Norwegian family escaping from Nazi occupation.

Barne, Kitty. VISITORS FROM LONDON. *Dent* 1940. Illustrated by Ruth Gervis.
Good-humoured and realistic tale of evacuees.

Benary, Margot. THE ARK 1954, ROWAN FARM 1955. *Macmillan.* German
family fighting back to reasonable life after Second World War.

Benary, Margot. THE LONG WAY HOME. *Macmillan* 1960. Orphan in Eastern
Zone escapes to new life in America: a distinguished and mature book for
older children.

*Church, Richard. DOG TOBY. *Hutchinson* 1954. Illustrated by Laurence Irving.

Gleit, Maria. CHILD OF CHINA (1948 Germany). *O.U.P.* 1960. Translated by
E. F. Peeler. Illustrated by Walter Holtz. Girl sold into slavery, her courage
in Japanese attack on Chinese city: superbly real and moving.

Jong, Meindert De. THE HOUSE OF SIXTY FATHERS (1956 U.S.A.). *Lutterworth*

1958. Illustrated by Maurice Sendak. Chinese boy and family pig hiding from Japanese and helping American airman.

Kemp, Rouse. YOU CAN'T FIGHT WITH CATTIES. *Methuen* 1959. Illustrated by William Randell. Kenya before Mau-Mau riots: unrest seen through adventures of a group of children camping. Simple, direct and vigorous.

Loeff, Rutgers van der. AVALANCHE (1954 Holland). *U.L.P.* 1957. Translated by Dora Round. Illustrated by Alie Evers. Exciting and human story of a village in danger: aspects of Pestalozzi international village.

*Mitchison, Naomi. THE FAR HARBOUR 1957, illustrated by Martin Thomas. JUDY AND LAKSHMI 1959, illustrated by Arinash Chandra. THE RIB OF THE GREEN UMBRELLA 1960, illustrated by Edward Ardizzone. *Collins.*

*Serraillier, Ian. THE SILVER SWORD. *Cape* 1956. Illustrated by C. Walter Hodges.

*Trease, Geoffrey. THE CALL TO ARMS. *Martin Lawrence* 1935.

Watson, Sally. TO BUILD A LAND. *Hutchinson* 1959. Jewish refugee children settling in a new community in Israel.

Chapter *14* | *Little Birds in their Nests Agree*

When the sandhills and the moors are deserted, when the streets are empty and the children of fiction are safe at home, we might then expect a greater measure of realism in stories; but family stories are often as unreal as the most far-fetched adventure yarn. The convenient label turns out to be misleading, for, far from being in a family, children are left on their own quite as much as they are in stories of gangsters and smugglers. Their parents are barely glimpsed in the background.

There is one type of story where this is essential, the story about the solitary child, where everything and everybody else becomes background, to be seen through her eyes. We are concerned here with the poetry of living, a single, private affair. Among the riotous family chronicles of Elizabeth Enright, two books stand out for their concentration of atmosphere. THIMBLE SUMMER is the story of a few months in the life of Garnet Linden, a nine-year-old girl on a farm in the Middle West. Garnet is not a recluse. She works in the harvest field, she goes to a country fair, she helps in the house and the farmyard. All the same, the book is a record of private pleasures, of an enchanted summer. Here is a child seeing familiar surroundings with the fresh vision of her age. In THE SEA IS ALL AROUND, Mab Kendall opens sharp eyes and ears to an unfamiliar world, an island she is visiting off the New England coast, with the noise of the sea, the oddness of the people, the delight of new objects, all to discover. This kind of story cannot be written to order. It must come from a mind recollecting in tranquillity the joys of childhood. This is the impetus behind that exquisite, sharp picture of the English countryside, THE TRUANTS by J. C. Badcock, with its lovely decorative drawings, and behind a good deal of Elizabeth Coatsworth's work. ALICE-ALL-BY-HERSELF, for instance, sets a little girl plumb in the middle of her home in Maine, observing, listening, saying very little; watching old Miss Abby in her house full of pot-plants, watching an old man making figureheads, watching the stall-holders at the fair, always watching, and reflecting on her impressions, as she does about the wonderful fair:

> Alice drank root beer. A man went by quarrelling with his wife. When Alice stopped near the booths she could not help seeing how worn and dirty the cloth was, though it looked so gay at a distance. And hardly any of the people in them had nice eyes.
> ... But that night as she lay quietly in bed, with the square of moonlight showing in her open window and the smell of salt water drifting to her from the river, she saw the fair again in her mind's eye. She was standing watching Mr Dunbar and his big oxen, and the bright horses flashing by in the outer ring, and beyond them were the roundabouts, foreign-feeling and mysterious in spite of their shabbiness. Where would they all be to-morrow? How did they live? She felt again her first excitement in the crowd; her sense of the known and the unknown all stirring together, of eyes that looked at her which had come from far-away places, of the music beating and beating, and the balloon which had floated up against the blue sky.

Elizabeth Coatsworth. ALICE-ALL-BY-HERSELF (Harrap, 1959. First published 1938) pp. 69–70.

Stories like this do not challenge the attention with action; their characters have, at first sight, little definition, there is no 'story'. Adults will read them for their nostalgic quality: children, more often, for the details of childhood pleasures. The feeling of getting inside a child's mind, the imaginative reconstruction, will steal on a thoughtful young reader unawares.

Children hardly analyse their own desire for privacy, but they recognize it in fictional children, and they recognize, too, their natural desire for independence. This accounts for the popularity of stories about running away—about children on their own. We do not want realism here, in the strict sense. After his wanderings, the child must get home again. The place for the lost child, the homeless, the unwanted, is in adult fiction, through which older boys and girls may widen their experience; not in stories for schoolchildren, which must assure their readers of safety in the end, no matter what hazards they describe first.

But we should demand realism in one way. It is no fun reading about a child on his own unless you feel he really *is* on his own, unless he meets some difficulties and has some doubts in the course of his adventure. Every writer has his own kind of probability. When I first read THE JOURNEY OF JOHNNY REW, I felt things were made too easy for the hero. Anne Barrett sends him off from London to the West Country in search of his long-lost father with no better clue than his surname and a letter with two geographical details. Certainly Johnny is taken for a burglar, early in his travels, but before this can worry him too much, he wanders to Miss Merrament's house and has her kindness and good sense to rely on. When I reread the story, I forgot these niggling doubts because I was interested in the characters, in Johnny himself, reflective and determined, and in the odd and exciting people he met.

This is one way of establishing the veracity of a story. Another is to accumulate domestic detail, to make the journey, wherever or whatever it is, seem exact in every particular. This is what Marjorie Fischer does in STREET FAIR, a gay and utterly believable story about two American children, Anna and John, on holiday in Paris, who are whisked away by accident in a train to the Riviera. You know exactly how much money they had between them and what they spent it on, what they eat, where they sleep and who they talk to. Above all, you know how they feel; you realize how irresponsible they are, as they casually plan that sometime they will try to get in touch with Mother (who is at Cannes); you notice when they begin to find independence a little frightening. They deal with emergencies as they arise. When John splits his shorts, they bribe a small English girl (with ice-cream) to steal a pair of her brother's trousers for him:

> At last they saw the little girl turn the corner and John stood up to see what she was carrying over her arm, and it was plainly long trousers. He was so excited that he told Anna.
> 'She's got longs!' he said.
> 'Something like mine, I expect,' said Anna. 'Only not sailor.'
> 'Of course not,' said John. 'Regular long trousers.'
> 'Well, I don't see anything to get so excited about,' said Anna.

'And you'd better sit down till she comes. You look funny.'
Marjorie Fischer. STREET FAIR (Penguin, 1949. First published
1935) pp. 150-51.

The whole essence of a child's view of life is summed up in this small
exchange. Richard Parker's story, MORE SNAKES THAN LADDERS,
has the same glancing eye over a child's world, the same telling use
of small details; and his tale of a boy and girl making their way
(again, quite without plan) from Kent to Weymouth fulfils its title,
for nothing is as easy as the two of them had expected.

Beside children travelling, there are the equally popular young
heroes and heroines who escape from parental control and establish
a home of their own. A story like Eleanor Graham's THE CHILDREN
WHO LIVED IN A BARN is the logical extension of all the books for
small children about dolls' houses and rabbit burrows, the older
child's version of the housekeeping of Golliwogg and his Dutch
dolls, or of the bachelor life of Pooh. The reader is ready now for
a sterner view of responsibility than Pooh's. Eleanor Graham has
not made housekeeping easy or romantic for Sue and her family.
Removing their parents (rather violently, in a air-crash), she then
leaves them in a serious dilemma, for their unpleasant landlord has
decided to terminate their lease, and the only shelter that offers is
Farmer Pearl's barn. Picnic delights soon pall—at least for thirteen-
year-old Sue, who feels she must keep the twins and little Alice clean
and well-fed, but does not know how to set about it or how to persuade Bob to pull his weight. Bad weather, an interfering District-
Visitor, Alice's tantrums, problems of washing and cooking and
funds—all these are faced squarely, and not always cheerfully, until
the wonderful moment when the parents are found to be alive after
all, and the children realize what home really means to them.

The children in Nan Chauncy's THEY FOUND A CAVE have the
same lesson to learn, though they start with a better understanding
of what it means to be homeless. Their extended picnic in a cave on a
Tasmanian hillside begins on a sensible note:

'We've decided everything, but first we're going to make one rule.
We won't grumble. However things turn out we won't grumble,
but we will work hard. Is that agreed, you blokes? We don't expect
it to be all jam, do we? There won't be any jam as a matter of
fact . . .'

Nan Chauncy. THEY FOUND A CAVE. (Oxford University Press, 1948) p. 49.

For all their common-sense, they have not been able to foresee bore-dom and the exasperating effect of continued lack of comfort; and for Cherry at least the responsibility becomes very hard before their aunt comes back from hospital to rescue them from the un-pleasant married couple who are trying to persuade them from their eyrie.

There is something more in these two books than an adventure, entertaining and spiced with discomfort; there is something more than the entrancing details of housekeeping with a difference. There is a feeling for character, for the behaviour of the various members of a family when faced by a crisis. Let children enjoy the ninety-nine readable but undistinguished holiday adventures which merge into one jumble of caravanning, toffee-making and stamp-collecting. The story with characters in it, the hundredth story, is the one I am concerned with; the book that children will read till its pages fall out. And that hundredth book may well be by the pioneer in the field of holiday stories, Arthur Ransome.

Now with Ransome the rule is 'Grown-ups not admitted unless accompanied by a child.' The Blackett and Walker parents know their place; they stay tactfully at home and act as ship's chandlers. Uncle Jim can approach a little nearer when he is needed as a pirate or a mining expert or a ship's captain, but even he is some distance away from the centre of action—like Ransome himself, who watches, with evident delight, the important exploits of his creations, and lets them express themselves (even in the illustrations).

And they *are* important. Ransome's children always have some-thing on hand—bird-watching, gold-mining, astronomy, tracking, innumerable outdoor projects, involving (usually) no serious ex-pense of emotion but a great deal of energy and technical skill. As he never writes about anything unless he knows it from A to Z, his books have an accuracy and precision much appreciated by his readers. If they followed his clear indications they could probably become as accomplished as the Swallows and Amazons. And they will want to imitate Ransome's children all the more because he never cheats. He never makes things too easy. When, in PIGEON POST, Dick has built his kiln to extract gold (as he hopes) from the pile of stone they have collected, he feels triumphant, but then comes the reaction:

> The miners looked at each other and at the stone furnace that was far too hot to touch. They were suddenly tired. It was as if the string of a necklace had snapped and the beads were rolling all ways on the floor. The work that had kept them all awake was at an end. With no bellows to work or furnace to feed they were no longer a team, and each one separately was wondering how it had been possible to keep awake so long.

Arthur Ransome. PIGEON POST. (Cape, 1936) p. 32.

It is the writer who understands children who thus alters the pace of their schemes and their achievements. The stories of Lois Lamplugh and Tyler Whittle, two authors who write in the Ransome tradition, are immensely spirited and readable, but they have this flaw, that the children are seldom anything but energetic and successful. Certainly these writers communicate the enthusiasm of the young and their casual erudition on subjects that interest them, and these subjects (bird-watching, archæology, amateur building) are highly topical. All this is worth a great deal. But it is interesting to compare their versions of young adventure with books written by young holiday adventurers themselves.

In the remarkable stories written by Katharine Hull and Pamela Whitlock (the first of them, THE FAR-DISTANT OXUS, when they were schoolgirls of fifteen and sixteen respectively), there is a convincing variety of pace. These are outdoor stories, set on Exmoor, and the children are on their own by choice (as one title, ESCAPE TO PERSIA, emphatically suggests). They camp in their own log-hut very much as children would. They get bored from time to time because meals do not produce themselves, though they will put endless effort into a special feast. There are moments of slackness, even moments when they feel uneasy at the absence of authority. All these off-moments are faithfully recorded, and so are the moments of pleasure, comradeship and pure joy. These two authors have put into a public and coherent form a body of intense private emotion which will be recognized at once as superbly true by all children with like tastes. It is this truth of youthful enjoyment which can so easily be missed, or distorted, in stories of this kind by adults.

Few schoolgirls would have the capacity to put their dreams so

finely into words. These books are manufactured from the unexaggerated stuff of real life. They are not derivative, even though the
well-worn scenes of gymkhana and camp are used. Their freshness
can be seen if they are compared with SANDAL ASH, a family adventure story written by Patricia Ann Cox when she was sixteen. Beginning with a lifelike presentation of children in a village, engaged in a
war of bows and arrows and ambushes, this pleasing tale soon edges
off into a sub-plot of burglars and midnight activities which reflects
wishful reading rather than wishful thinking.

To read the Oxus stories, adults must accept a certain amateur-
ishness. This does not matter in the drawings, which have the feel of
young and energetic busyness. It does not matter much in the style,
though this is prolix. Nothing has been left out because, to the
authors, all details have the same importance. There is none of Ransome's careful selection of detail. The conversations go on and on,
very entertaining, absolutely real, but, again, full of irrelevant
shoots which an adult writer would not leave unpruned.

This is adventure as girls would write it, superbly conceived, with
moments of touching truth beyond the scope of an adult writer,
and with a mixture of serious and comic which is inimitable. An
adult writer, indeed, would be foolish to try anything like this description of the first night at the holiday farm:

> 'Fun!' Bridget stood on the bed in her excitement. 'We shall
> have that all right; but this isn't a place for fun only. It's a place
> for travel, discovery, adventure. How do we know that there are
> not hundreds of hidden valleys, dozens of unscaleable peaks, heaps
> of unrideable rides; all waiting to be found, climbed, and accom-
> plished by us? Oh, we shall have fun here all right—but more as
> well, much more.'
> After which spirited speech she added a hasty good night and,
> seizing her sponge-bag, barged back into her room.
> Katharine Hull and Pamela Whitlock. THE FAR-DISTANT
> OXUS (Collins, 1960. First published, 1937) p. 17.

This kind of style, supported by goodwill and talent in equal
proportions, is irresistible, but it is also apt to be long-winded, and I
think any children must find these stories long and at times difficult
to follow. The hunt for Maurice, for instance, in OXUS IN SUMMER,
must be read in one enthusiastic sitting if it is not to be muddling.

All this serves to emphasize the sad but salutary fact that, on the whole, it is better for adults to write children's books—not so much because of superior powers of expression as because of a more experienced and objective sense of form.

CROWNS, a story outside the Oxus sequence, and written later, has a far more mature construction, but has retained the intensely romantic, personal feeling of the earlier adventures. This is the tale of a dream world, imagined by four children who are rapt away in spirit as they crouch hidden in an attic during a London party. In the kingdom they rule together, each finds the deepest desire fulfilled. Charlotte, who is a masterful child, explores over the frontier and narrowly escapes death; indeed, one of her servants is killed, and there is no boggling at the horror of the moment. Andrew, whose temperament is solitary, goes into the marshlands to live with shepherds; Eliza enjoys peacocks and silken cushions at the palace; and Rob, the real ruler among them, indulges a love of power and exposes the Chancellor's plots against them.

The source of this vividly imagined world lies, presumably, in some unusually stimulating history lesson or a vivid textbook. There is throughout the book an intense fusing of intellectual and emotional life, sometimes offered almost as the raw material of a story, as in this description of the dwarfs' tapestry:

> Eliza gazed at the yards already worked, hanging along the walls. Here was the beginning of time, the age of ice, the plains and hills in long cream-white stretches of snow, the frozen glacier in grey-white, mauve-white silk. Here were flames of scarlet and yellow fire spiking across the ice. Here were the plains and hills, and the river, melted into life; a team of oxen were at plough, shepherds were driving a flock across the hills, sailors lugging up nets of fish. Here were miniatures of the town and the market-place. Here the ragged range of mountains which could be seen from the palace when the weather was especially clear, and here last of all was the building of the new palace, boulders being rolled up the cliff by gangs of workmen as ants roll barley seeds.
>
> Katharine Hull and Pamela Whitlock. CROWNS (Cape, 1947) p. 118.

The whole of this fascinating tale reads as though one of the children in THE AMULET had taken the pen from Edith Nesbit's hand; the authors have looked back unerringly from their older stance and have seen the wonderful kingdom, still, as girls would see it.

The most difficult task for a young person writing *con amore* is to find universal utterance for private thoughts; and if this is what she wants to do, she is allying herself to all those adult writers, from Ransome downwards, who have enclosed children firmly in their own world. A different kind of selectiveness is needed in those family stories which present children as they fit into a larger world. One of the most striking stories published in 1960 was THE GREAT GALE by Hester Burton, a story based on the East Anglian floods of 1953. A boy and a girl, children of the local doctor, are the central figures, but they are there definitely as members of a community, not as the little hero and heroine. They belong to Reedsmere. They know and love the old couple, Jim and Hepzie, whose cottage is so dangerously near the sea; they are used to the trenchant remarks of Canon Crowfoot; they understand the village hierarchy and its routine. All this stands them in good stead when they find themselves alone in their house when the floods begin. Their actions thereafter are brave and resourceful; they are also well-organized. We have an eye on the children right through the story. We sympathize with Mary when her best friend from the post-office is in danger. We watch Mark sizing up the situation at the Hall, where the villagers have collected. But the children never take our attention away from the whole picture, the picture of a village in difficulties. There is nothing portentous about this book but, indirectly, it shows individuals living in a community and depending on one another, and it is a welcome change from the innumerable stories in which children seem to drift on the fringe of real life.

Another story with a sober realism of its own is Elizabeth Grove's WINTERCUT, about a canal family held up for repairs at a lock-side. Sal and Joe, the younger children, make friends with Don Landreth and stay at his home, the lock-house, and from here the children set out into the winter hills to prospect an old canal route. The Landreth parents enter into the spirit of the expedition, but in a sensible, partial way, and the feeling of home comforts side by side with enterprise is most attractive. If the sincere picture of the Landreth home gives depth to the story, so does the description of the narrow boat, and the summing-up of the canal dweller's outlook by Sal, as she prepares to set off once more:

Drawing by William Stobbs for Elizabeth Grove's WINTERCUT (Cape)

The water in the dipper was icy on her skin. When she had washed, she went to the closed cupboard ... and brought out a long bundle which she laid out on the side-bed. Pushing the little folding table back again against its shelves, she started to take off her shabby dungarees. 'Uhuh,' she said to the woollen frock and the stockings which Mrs Landreth had lent her and which were hanging over the stove ... 'Ta very much, but not my rig.'
Elizabeth Grove. WINTERCUT (Cape, 1957) p. 187.

Two worlds have met, their inhabitants have made some impression on each other, and they have parted. The simplicity of the theme, echoed by the fine, strong style and the equally strong drawings, make this a book in a thousand.

Unique among writers for children is William Mayne, who gives to his wildest treasure-hunts a background of balanced and complete

Drawing by Christopher Brooker for William Mayne's
THE ROLLING SEASON (O.U.P).

family life. THE THUMBSTICK, with its hunt over the Yorkshire dales for an old religious emblem, always comes circling back to the farm, to the rapid, idiosyncratic, absolutely authentic talk of a family—of Mrs Bargate, humorous and sensible, of John, with his flurries of enthusiasm and his moods of despair, of that splendid, trenchant centenarian, Great Aunt Airey. THE ROLLING SEASON roams up and down dried-up Wiltshire hills and in and out of two houses, and the finding of water to save the hamlet, the gang of toughs poling down the muddy canals, the brassy sky and the dry grass, the casual chatter, all make up a wonderfully real whole. I know no recent children's stories more *actual* than William Mayne's, whether he is writing about a school or a village or a small town; and perhaps he is a little difficult for children to appreciate just for this reason, because he utterly ignores any compromise, any of the formulas which endear more popular writers to children. But the child who plunges into his stories, forgetting fashion, listening to the dry, crisp dialogue, and seeing in his mind's eye the scenes so minutely and economically visualized, has found a companion for life, no less.

Now Ransome does not give us a *round* study of family life, as Mayne does, for he is committed to the children's point of view; but they have among themselves very clear and changeable relationships, though their relations with grown-ups are static. If you want to read a shrewd account of child behaviour, look at WINTER HOLIDAY, where the Blacketts and Walkers cautiously approach Dorothea and Dick, newcomers to the district. See how the two strangers stand aloof, envying the solidarity of the little group, and see how each individual learns to get used to a change of friends. It is a wonderful piece of social management. And what child with imagination does not warm to Titty Walker, with her shrinking from noise and heartiness, her burning courage in a crisis? In PIGEON POST Titty finds she is a natural dowser. Terrified at first, she faces her responsibility (for their holiday plans depend on finding water in the hills). She goes away alone, screwing herself up to test her gift; and when she has found water, her first impulse is to boast about it. Every stage of her feelings is beautifully described, but within the action of the story, and at the same time we see how this incident affects the other children. To Nancy Blackett the new-found spring is a challenge: 'Barbecued billygoats!' she exclaims, 'If it's there, we'll get it out all right if we have to dig through to Australia', and you can hear the ring in her voice. But to Dorothea, a budding author, there is more to it than this:

> 'I'm going to put it in a story . . . Different, of course. I'm making you a boy, and you do that business with the stick all by yourself and you've got a spade with you and you start digging. It's at night, and the moon rises through the clouds, and all of a sudden you've dug deep enough and the water comes spouting up into the moonlight . . .'
> 'Go on,' said Titty. 'What happened next?'
> 'I'm not quite sure yet,' said Dorothea.
> Arthur Ransome. PIGEON POST (Cape, 1936) p. 162.

There are children who find Ransome's books tedious because they are not interested in sailing, camping or skating, but there are few who will not change their minds if they have the patience to look beyond the technical details to the characters. They will find, in the end, that Ransome's stories last them longer than the similar tales of Kitty Barne or Lois Lamplugh or Tyler Whittle. I enjoy stories by these writers enormously. I like the free air the children breathe, their rousing conversations, their ingenuity; but I can never remember which is which—not even if I look at the illustrations; and in fact the unmistakable, squarish faces of William Stobbs's children (appearing in stories by the three writers I have just mentioned) give me an odd feeling that I am meeting the same boys and girls over and over again. Stobbs is a magnificent illustrator, and few people can create atmosphere as he can in an historical story, but his portraits interrupt the imagination as it rolls together known faces, impressions and dreams, so that eventually a character in a book takes on the semblance of a real person—but a different person to each reader. Harold Jones, who has illustrated several of M. E. Atkinson's family stories, has clearly a good idea what her characters are like, but he subordinates this knowledge to his ideas of design, and the result is a collaboration of artist and writer from which each gains.

An author must find time to establish his characters, no matter how much else he has to do. His details may date his story, but this will hardly matter if his characters are interesting. Who can now read E. V. Lucas's pioneer tale, THE SLOWCOACH? It has dated badly, not because the Avories go off in a horse-drawn van, leaving behind them a house run by four servants, but because the characters are not interesting enough to keep your attention from these period details. Nor are they any better in Lucy Bellhouse's story of twenty-five years later, THE CARAVAN CHILDREN, which is dedicated 'To all Nurses, Maid-servants, and Governesses who with such care and devotion look after and love other people's children'. And Barbara Willard's boys and girls who take the road with an unorthodox grown-up in SNAIL AND THE PENNITHORNES are going to suffer the same fate, long before it is old-fashioned to tow caravans behind cars.

But now look at a twenty-year-old camping story by a writer who is, above all, a creator of character. The plot of E. H. Young's CARAVAN ISLAND is far from original. Cicely and Stephen, who go to Skye with their young Aunt Judy, are furious because at the last minute two younger cousins, Laura and Hugh, are added to the party. Nothing out of the way happens in this camp, but everything that does happen seems memorable, because the children and their aunt are established as individuals right from the start. When Laura is lost in the hills, it is not only the hunt for her that makes you want to read on, it is also the fact that Aunt Judy, who believes that children should be resourceful, now wonders guiltily whether she has left them alone too much. When the bull gets out, it is not only the dramatic incident that matters, but Stephen's view of it, his plan to get a good audience for his untruthful version:

> . . . he was wondering what would be the best time to tell the story of the bull. Tonight, perhaps, when they were sitting round the fire in the twilight; it would seem more terrifying then, when every shadow could be mistaken for the animal and every sound might herald his approach.
> E. H. Young. CARAVAN ISLAND (Black, 1940) pp. 196–7.

The small adventures of the children are no more exciting than the ebb and flow of their feelings, their cross-alliances, the wearing away of hostility between the two families, the drawing-out of Cicely and the suppressing of Stephen, and a hundred and one little points subtly conveyed.

When we are reading stories about families, we must have some idea how the children regard each other. Personality will not do unless it is live, changeable personality. I would almost suggest that a family story without a quarrel was not worth reading—not because of the dramatic value of a quarrel, but because it is natural for children to be constantly rubbing corners off each other. E. Nesbit's Bastables live in the memory, never out of date, because they are children as we all know them, quarrelling, disagreeing, arguing, taking sides; they know each other in the way members of a family do, and at the same time they are always discovering new things about each other. Elizabeth Enright's New York Melendys, Gillian Avery's Victorian Smiths and Squerryes, and the riotous Cares children drawn by E. C. Spykman—all these have the hall-mark of the real *family*. This is the kind of thing which really happens in families:

> Theodore, who was thirteen and had red hair, green eyes and freckles, would do anything when he was in a temper, especially if someone had managed to hit him squarely in the neck with a mud-pie. Jane had decided to run and her neat new sneakers had carried her like wings. She had escaped into the house and upstairs where she had packed a few clothes, and by jumping into the soft loam of the geranium bed while Ted was banging at her locked door, had got off across the fields. Her intention had been to climb up to the middle of the old maple at the lower end of the barn field, unpack, and set up housekeeping in a place of peace and quiet, where in the cool shelter she could concentrate on hating Theodore. It had seemed a good idea . . . But now she was on her way home, because it had not worked. Living in a tree was quite impractical. Nothing would stay where you put it.
>
> E. C. Spykman. A LEMON AND A STAR (Macmillan, 1956) p. 2.

M. E. Atkinson's CRUSOE ISLAND stands out among many similar tales because of its family relationships. The opening chapter, with five children cooped up by rain and snarling at each other, is gloriously real, and so is the aunt who admits to herself that, fond as she is of her young relations, she would far rather be by herself. And (not to insist too much on the sharpness of quarrels) how valuable is the constant shift of loyalties in PATTERSON'S TRACK, an excellent story by Eleanor Spence about three Sydney children, on a back-country visit, trekking through the bush with local friends. The story is memorable for its plot, which rests on the unravelling of a piece of local history, but still more on the behaviour of the children during their exacting journey. At the end of it, town-bred Barry has thought twice about the yokels and his sister has questioned his authority for the first time; none of the children is quite the same as before. These are cheerful, extroverted children; there is no dreary musing over emotions. All the same, you can watch the family pattern of town and country children changing and re-forming. This is a splendid study of character in action.

For girls, character-drawing is always an essential part of fiction. Schoolboys demand more fact and less feeling, and, for them, stories based on a sport offer a specially suitable version of the family story, where they can see how people behave almost without noticing it. The method is not essentially different from the method that produced LITTLE WOMEN or the stories of the Melendys, but the emphasis is different. For instance, in Hugh de Selincourt's agreeable tale of village cricket, THE SATURDAY MATCH, the real point of the story is the delicate development of the relationship between father and son, between brother and sister, but every conversation, every nuance of expression relates to the match. In the same way, Clare Huchet Bishop's unusually good story, THE BIG LOOP, depends both on her vivid account of the Tour de France and on her portrait of young André and his efforts to triumph over poverty and inexperience and make himself worthy of his famous cyclist father. Robert Bateman, in YOUNG CRICKETER, YOUNG CLIMBER and YOUNG FOOTBALLER, combines technical detail (used dramatically) and a view of how character is tested in very ordinary situations.

Stories like this have, among other things, helped to widen the social background of children's stories. The dominant adults in Bateman's stories do not belong to the professional classes. They are a police inspector, a small farmer, a clerk and so on. Up to twenty years ago, children's books were keyed to the middle-classes, where most of their readers were to be found, and the rare stories about working-class or lower middle-class families suffered from an inevitable self-consciousness.

If you go back to the children's books of the last century, of course, you will find class-distinctions taken for granted. In Mrs Molesworth's story, THE RECTORY CHILDREN, Mrs Vane, the vicar's wife, is at first doubtful whether she should allow her young daughter to make friends with Celestina, whose father keeps a stationer's shop. But Celestina is well-behaved and intelligent,

Bridget needs a companion in her lessons, and the problem is solved frankly and with no loss of dignity on either side.

It is when writers begin to feel guilty about class that trouble sets in. You get the curious sentimentality for instance, of Alice Hegan Rice, whose stories of fifty years ago, MRS WIGGS OF THE CABBAGE PATCH and LOVEY MARY, turn humble characters into something foolishly music-hall in behaviour. This was still a danger at a much later date. Eve Garnett's stories about the Ruggles family are warm-hearted and sincere, but until she has really written herself in and is completely at ease with them, there is a facetious note, a note of apology and condescension; the Dustman and the Cleaner are put into inverted commas as well as into capital letters. There is some fine writing in THE FAMILY FROM ONE END STREET but there is also this note:

> In spite of a wife and seven children (not to speak of Ideas) Mr. Ruggles was a very contented sort of man. When the wind was in the East and blew bits of dirt from his dustbins and cart into his eyes and mouth he spat and swore a bit, but it was soon over. So long as he had his job and his family were well and happy, and he could smoke his pipe and work in his garden, see his mates at the Working Men's Club once or twice a week, dream about his Pig, and have a good Blow Out on Bank Holidays, he wanted nothing more.
>
> Eve Garnett. THE FAMILY FROM ONE END STREET (Penguin 1942. First published, 1937) p. 120.

It is a relief to turn to FURTHER ADVENTURES OF THE FAMILY FROM ONE END STREET, which perhaps owes its more relaxed tone to the climate of the 'forties and 'fifties. Here the author is thinking about children first and foremost, and in this enchanting picture of town children coming to terms with the country there is not a breath of condescension. Without Eve Garnett, probably, we should not have had MAGNOLIA BUILDINGS, a recent story by Elizabeth Stucley with the same loosely constructed plot, the same setting in a London working-class flat. The Berners family recalls the Ruggles at every turn. Mum is a cleaner; Gloria at fourteen thinks in terms of nail varnish and glamour, as Eve Garnett's Lily did; like Kate, Doreen hankers after education. But in style and presentation there is all the difference. Elizabeth Stucley may have had to learn about the kind of life the Berners lived, but she writes about them as people she knows, not as members of one class.

If they are left to themselves, children probably will not notice the point of class in a story, unless someone suggests that they should. It is a mistake to assume, as some critics do, that Secondary Modern children in the country, for instance, want to read about Secondary Modern children in the country. A book like GRIFF AND TOMMY by John Griffiths, with its entertaining picture of a family in a mining village, or Christine Price's DAVID AND THE MOUNTAIN, with its picture of a Welsh shepherd boy, do not address themselves to any particular set of children; they stand on their own merits as honest pictures of a particular environment. A BOX FOR BENNY, Leila Berg's touching story of a boy in the Jewish quarter of Manchester, is already established as a minor classic because it describes with grace and humour and precision a particular small boy belonging to a particular class and race—describes him as an individual, with his own problem. This is a book for children of all ages and all backgrounds.

The sensible author lets his young heroes and heroines take the problems of class, such as they are, in their stride. Mrs Molesworth knew what she was doing when she made Biddy disregard the difference between her own home and Celestina's (though she was aware of it), and, allowing for the social changes of the last half-century, that is just what James Reeves is doing, for instance, in MULBRIDGE MANOR, when he describes a group of children playing on the common. They know quite well that Anne is poor, that her background is not the same as theirs, but the only difference it makes to them, and to old Miss Matilda at the Manor, is that Anne can't get away often to help to find the missing will because her mother needs her at home.

In MINNOW ON THE SAY, by Philippa Pearce, one of the best children's books of recent years, young David, whose father is a bus driver, realizes his home life is different from Adam's. He sees the difference in practical terms. Adam lives in a large old house on the river, not in a council house, he has his meals at different times, and he does not always have enough to eat. It is for David's mother to work out how she can offer Miss Codling a cake without hurting her pride, for Mrs Moss realizes the intangible differences which David and Adam can happily ignore. This exquisite story has innumerable threads in its rich canvas—the pervasive presence of the river, every ripple exactly described; the treasure hunt, with its intricate and unexpected ending; the sure handling of a child's joy in living, which Ardizzone echoes in his drawings. But one of the most interesting threads is the sensible, subtle treatment of class difference; the contrasting, by implication, of the Moss household, with its safe, small prosperity, and the old house where Miss Codling fights to preserve her standards.

It might surprise those who think Britain is clinging to her class distinctions in defiance of the rest of Europe, to find in a Swedish story an extremely interesting use of this very subject to produce a dramatic plot. Harry Kullman, in THE SECRET JOURNEY, makes it the cornerstone of his tale of young David, who lives in a well-to-do part of Stockholm. David's father warns him against the other end of the town, where, he says, the children are nothing but savages. David, left alone for the day and feeling bored, decides to prove this to himself. He takes a bus ride to a factory district, gets involved in a gang fight, and after some uneasy moments, becomes the friend and ally of Dumpy and Skinny and their uninhibited lieutenant Rose-Marie. David is intrigued by the contrast between their life and his:

> He noticed to his surprise that their life seemed much more lively, and much less patterned than his own. They had no piano lessons, no dancing classes, and their father never took them for an evening stroll. Nor could he really understand whether they were rich or poor. One moment he thought they must be tremendously rich (Dad bought an accordion last year—although an uncle has it now), and in the next moment Skinny explained, giggling:
> 'We'll have to make the best of living here while we can, ha-ha, because we haven't paid the rent this month.'
> Harry Kullman. THE SECRET JOURNEY. Translated by Evelyn Ramsden (University of London Press, 1959) p. 121.

The urchins, in turn, regard with misgiving David's collar and tie, his accent and his apparent timidity. But prejudice dies a natural death. The children retire to a room where there is a gramophone. They put on a record and David teaches the little girl to dance, while the boys look on admiringly. That moment, when they agree to differ, is memorable for its honesty. Geoffrey Trease makes the same point in THE MAYTHORN STORY, where a boy from a back street in a Midland town goes out for a day on the hills and meets Sandra, who is influenced by a snobbish grandmother. There is perception in the story of Mike's friendship with Sandra, his visit to her home (where her grandmother deliberately tries to upset the girl by showing up his manners), and his unfortunate entanglement with the affairs of Shirley next door.

There have been a good many stories in the last few years about children of different backgrounds learning to get on together. For a time the theme may well become hackneyed, but gradually it will be treated with less conscious purpose. Already the tone seems to be easier; for example, in Ann Thwaite's story of London grammar-school girls, THE HOUSE IN TURNER SQUARE, which combines antiquarian research and personalities most skilfully. Books like this are still, not surprisingly, written from a middle-class point of view, but here is an author who is not disconcerted by this. Joanna Shepherd, the librarian's daughter, and Audrey Pitt, who lives in a council flat, are slow to make friends. Audrey is afraid of her friend's posh house and Joanna of Audrey's bluff manner. Their approach to each other is helped by their mutual interest in the Georgian houses and their history, and by the matter-of-fact attitude of their parents. Common sense and a warm interest in people have given this book a quality lacking in many others of its kind.

What writers like this have done is to bring their stories nearer to the world of grown-ups, not by giving grown-ups a more prominent part in the story, but by giving a child's view of adult problems. They have contributed to that reality which can exist in a family story even when it has an improbable plot; whereas a story where every scratch on the door, every honeycomb on the bedspread is exactly described, lacking the active participation of the author and his characters, may have nothing to offer to the lively-minded young reader. A family story must be about people. Without people—alive, variable, interesting—no matter what superlatives may be quoted on the back flap of the book, the dust-jacket is likely to remain unblemished and untorn by the fingers of enthusiastic readers.

Reading List

Family stories (See also p. 331.)

*Atkinson, M. E. AUGUST ADVENTURE. *Bodley Head* 1936. Illustrated by Harold Jones.

*Atkinson, M. E. CRUSOE ISLAND. *Bodley Head* 1941. Illustrated by Harold Jones.

*Avery, Gillian. THE WARDEN'S NIECE 1957, TRESPASSERS AT CHARLECOTE 1958, illustrated by Dick Hart. JAMES WITHOUT THOMAS 1959, THE ELEPHANT WAR 1960, illustrated by John Verney. *Collins.*

*Badcock, J. C. THE TRUANTS. *Hutchinson* 1953. Illustrated by Margaret Wetherbee.

Baker, Margaret J. ACORNS AND AERIALS 1956, THE BRIGHT HIGH FLYER 1957. *Brockhampton.* Illustrated by Terence Freeman. Domestic adventures for eight and upwards, with good use of village background and sharp observation of character in action.

Ballantyne, Joan. HOLIDAY TRENCH. *Nelson* 1959. Illustrated by Edward Ardizzone. Children on holiday trying to keep cars from spoiling their beach: full of authentic talk and behaviour of children.

Barne, Kitty. DUSTY'S WINDMILL. *Dent* 1949. Illustrated by Marcia Lane-Foster. Charming story of troubles and adventures in a Sussex family business: exceptionally well-described background.

*Barrett, Anne. THE JOURNEY OF JOHNNY REW. *Collins* 1954.

*Bateman, Robert. YOUNG FOOTBALLER 1958, YOUNG RUNNER 1958, YOUNG CRICKETER 1959, YOUNG CLIMBER 1959, YOUNG JOCKEY 1960. *Constable.* (See also p. 331.)

Beddington, Roy. THE PIGEON AND THE BOY. *Bles* 1957. North Country industrial town; a boy learns how to rear and train racing pigeons.

*Bellhouse, Lucy. THE CARAVAN CHILDREN. *Harrap* 1935. Illustrated by Barbara Moray Williams.

*Berg. Leila. A BOX FOR BENNY. *Brockhampton* 1958. Illustrated by Jillian Willett.

*Bishop, Clare Huchet. THE BIG LOOP (1955 U.S.A.). *Dent* 1958. Illustrated by Carl Fontseré.

Boden, Hilda. MARLOWS AT NEWGALE 1956, MARLOWS DIG FOR TREASURE 1958, MARLOWS IN DANGER 1959, MARLOWS AT CASTLE CLIFF 1960. *Brockhampton.* Illustrated by Lilian Buchanan. Unexacting domestic adventures intended for children of eight and upwards: good, easy characterization and dialogue: setting mainly Pembrokeshire.

Boucher, Alan. THE RUNAWAYS. *Nelson* 1959. Illustrated by Margery Gill. Practical and exciting tale of three children hiding from unwelcome aunt in New Forest.

*Burton, Hester. THE GREAT GALE. *O.U.P.* 1960. Illustrated by Joan Kiddell-Monroe.

*Chauncy, Nan. THEY FOUND A CAVE. *O.U.P.* (1949) 1958. Illustrated by Margaret Horder.

Chauncy, Nan. TIGER IN THE BUSH 1957, illustrated by Margaret Horder. DEVIL'S HILL 1958, illustrated by Geraldine Spence. *O.U.P.* Tales of the Lorennys in their remote Tasmanian home: wild life and daily adventures, from the angle of a small boy. (See also p. 343.)

*Coatsworth, Elizabeth. ALICE-ALL-BY-HERSELF (1938 U.S.A.). *Harrap* 1959. Illustrated by Marguerite De Angeli.

*Cox, Patricia Ann. SANDAL ASH. Harrap 1950.

Eager, Edward. HALF MAGIC 1954, MAGIC OR NOT? 1959. *Macmillan.* Illustrated by N. M. Bodecker. American family tales with freakish humour and some sharp drawing of personality. (See also p. 377.)

*Enright, Elizabeth. THIMBLE SUMMER (1938 U.S.A.). *Penguin* (Puffin Story Books) 1955. THE SEA IS ALL AROUND (1940 U.S.A.). *Heinemann* 1959. Illustrated by the author.

*Enright, Elizabeth. THE SATURDAYS (1941 U.S.A.) 1955, THE FOUR-STOREY MISTAKE (1942 U.S.A.) 1955, THEN THERE WERE FIVE (1944 U.S.A.) 1956, SPIDERWEB FOR TWO (1951 U.S.A.) 1956, *Heinemann.* Illustrated by the author.

*Enright, Elizabeth. GONE-AWAY LAKE (1957 U.S.A.). *Heinemann* 1959. Illustrated by Beth and Joe Krush. (See also p. 333.)

Estes, Eleanor. THE MOFFATTS (U.S.A. 1941) 1959, THE MIDDLE MOFFATT (1942 U.S.A.) 1960, RUFUS M. (1943 U.S.A.) 1960. *Bodley Head.* Illustrated by Louis Slobodkin. Lively tales of American small town of Cranbury between the wars, and the everyday exploits of average but highly amusing children.

Estes, Eleanor. GINGER PYE. *Harcourt*, New York 1951. PINKY PYE (1958 U.S.A.). *Constable* 1959. Illustrated by Edward Ardizzone. A family and their cat and dog: whimsical literary flavour and an endearing humour, setting Cranbury and New York Bay.

Fennimore, Stephen. BUSH HOLIDAY. *Heinemann* 1948. *Penguin* (Puffin Story Books) 1958. Illustrated by Sheila Hawkins. English boy getting used to Australian backblocks; very natural.

*Fischer, Marjorie. STREET FAIR (1935 U.S.A.). *Routledge* 1936.

*Garnett, Eve. THE FAMILY FROM ONE END STREET. *Muller* 1937. *Penguin* (Puffin Story Books) 1942. Illustrated by the author.

*Garnett, Eve. FURTHER ADVENTURES OF THE FAMILY FROM ONE END STREET. *Heinemann* 1956. Illustrated by the author. (See also p. 333.)

*Graham, Eleanor. THE CHILDREN WHO LIVED IN A BARN. *Routledge* 1938. *Penguin* (Puffin Story Books) 1955 (revised edition).

*Griffiths, John. GRIFF AND TOMMY. *Dent* 1956. Illustrated by Antony Lake.

*Grove, Elizabeth. WINTERCUT. *Cape* 1957. Illustrated by William Stobbs.

*Hull, Katharine and Whitlock, Pamela. THE FAR-DISTANT OXUS. *Cape* 1937. *Collins* 1960 (slightly abridged). ESCAPE TO PERSIA 1938, OXUS IN SUMMER 1939, CROWNS 1947. *Cape*. Illustrated by Pamela Whitlock.

Kaeser, H. J. MIMFF (1937 Sweden) 1939, translated by Kathleen Williamson. MIMFF IN CHARGE 1949, MIMFF TAKES OVER 1954, translated by David Ascoli. MIMFF-ROBINSON 1958, translated by Ruth Michaelis-Jena and Arthur Ratcliff. *O.U.P.* Illustrated by Edward Ardizzone. Enchanting stories about a small boy and his adventures, at home in Denmark, at school or camping on a Swedish island.

Kästner, Erich. LOTTIE AND LISA (1949 Germany). *Cape* 1950. Translated by Cyrus Brooks. Illustrated by Walter Trier. Two girls at holiday school discover they are identical twins, and succeed in reconciling their divorced parents. Light-hearted but with sound sense and principles.

'Kim'. THE BOYS OF PUHAWAI. *U.L.P.* 1960. Illustrated by Dennis Turner. Two Maoris and an Irish boy, their everyday adventures in and around a New Zealand dairy farm: told from boys' point of view.

*Kullman, Harry. THE SECRET JOURNEY (1953 Sweden). *U.L.P.* 1959. Translated by Evelyn Ramsden. Illustrated by Claes Bäckström.

*Lamplugh, Lois. NINE BRIGHT SHINERS 1955, THE PIGEONGRAM PUZZLE 1955, VAGABOND'S CASTLE 1957, ROCKETS IN THE DUNES 1958. *Cape*. Illustrated by William Stobbs.

Lavrin, Nora and Thorp, Molly. THE HOP DOG. *O.U.P.* 1952. Illustrated by Nora Lavrin. East-enders hop-picking in Kent. Level-headed study of a variety of men, women and children.

Lloyd, Marjorie. FELL FARM HOLIDAY 1951, FELL FARM FOR CHRISTMAS 1954, FELL FARM CAMPERS 1960. *Penguin* (Puffin Story Books). Illustrated by the author. The five Brownes and their domestic and holiday adventures in the Lake District: gay and readable.

Lockhart, David. THE HOUSE THAT MAC BUILT. *Dent* 1960. Illustrated by Geraldine Spence. Easy, convincing tale of children building a look-out house.

Love, Margaret. AN EXPLORER FOR AN AUNT. *Blackie* 1960. Illustrated by Susan Einzig. Gang of cousins in Cornish house instructed in enjoying adventure by unorthodox aunt: good fun, excellent studies of children sorting out their differences.

*Lucas, E. V. THE SLOWCOACH (1910). *Edward Arnold* 1955. Illustrated by M. V. Whielhouse.

Masefield, Judith. LARKING AT CHRISTMAS 1953, APRIL FOOLS 1954. *Collins.* Illustrated by Shirley Hughes. Boy and girl in manor house, acting plays, arranging circus in the village: distinguished by gusto, inventiveness, and natural dialogue.

*Mayne, William. THE THUMBSTICK 1959, illustrated by Tessa Theobald. THE ROLLING SEASON 1960, illustrated by Christopher Brooker. *O.U.P.*

Michael, Manfred. TIMPETILL (1937 Switzerland). *O.U.P.* 1951. Translated by R. P. Aston. Illustrated by Richard Kennedy. Children of a German-Swiss village run it for a week in parents' absence: neat and interesting story, with plenty of good characterization.

*Molesworth, Mrs M. L. THE RECTORY CHILDREN. *Macmillan* 1889.

*Parker, Richard. MORE SNAKES THAN LADDERS. *Brockhampton* 1960. Illustrated by Jillian Willett.

*Pearce, A. Philippa. MINNOW ON THE SAY. *O.U.P.* 1955. Illustrated by Edward Ardizzone.

Pertwee, Roland. THE ISLANDERS 1950, ROUGH WATER 1951. *O.U.P.* Illustrated by Ernest Shepard. Three boys on river island in Devon, fending for themselves and dealing with a crook and an unpleasant relation.

*Price, Christine. DAVID AND THE MOUNTAIN. *Bodley Head* 1959. Illustrated by the author.

Pullein-Thompson, Diana. THE SECRET DOG. *Collins* 1959. Illustrated by Geraldine Spence. Cockney and Jamaican boy fight for the right to keep a mongrel they rescue from river: good London working-class background.

Pullein-Thompson, Diana. THE BOY AND THE DONKEY. *Collins* 1958. Illustrated by Shirley Hughes. London working-class streets and a boy training a ragman's donkey for the Donkey Derby.

Pye, Virginia. RED-LETTER HOLIDAY. *Faber* 1940. Illustrated by Gwen Raverat. One of the earliest holiday adventure tales, about Kensington middle-class children fending for themselves in a Cornish cottage.

*Ransome, Arthur. SWALLOWS AND AMAZONS, 1930. SWALLOWDALE 1931. *Cape.* Both republished with Ransome's illustrations 1938.

*Ransome, Arthur. PETER DUCK 1932, WINTER HOLIDAY 1933, COOT CLUB 1934, PIGEON POST 1936, WE DIDN'T MEAN TO GO TO SEA 1937, SECRET

WATER 1939, THE BIG SIX 1940, MISSEE LEE 1941, THE PICTS AND THE
MARTYRS 1943, GREAT NORTHERN? 1947. *Cape.* Illustrated by the author.

Redlich, Monica. JAM TOMORROW. *Nelson* 1937. Children of absent-minded
Rector housekeeping when help walks out: good impression of ordinary
family on its mettle.

*Reeves, James. MULBRIDGE MANOR. *Heinemann* 1958. Illustrated by Geraldine
Spence.

*Rice, Alice Hegan. MRS WIGGS OF THE CABBAGE PATCH (1901 U.S.A.) 1902,
LOVEY MARY (1903 U.S.A.) 1903. *Hodder & Stoughton.*

*Selincourt, Hugh de. THE SATURDAY MATCH. *Dent* 1937.

Seredy, Kate. THE OPEN GATE (1943 U.S.A.). *Harrap* 1947. Illustrated by the
author. American family moving from New York and settling on a farm:
homely encounters with neighbours, the seasons and a new way of life.

Sheppard-Jones, Elizabeth. THE SEARCH FOR MARY. *Nelson* 1960. Illustrated by
Jane Paton. Adopted child runs away, two children follow clues across England
to Wales: natural and convincing.

Sindall, Marjorie A. MATEY. *Macmillan* 1960. Illustrated by Sheila Rose. Girl
and her father moving from Battersea slum to caravan in the country.

Sindall, Marjorie A. THE BUDDS OF PARAGON ROW. *Heinemann* 1954. Illustrated
by Vera Jarman. Working-class widow with a clever daughter and a son led into
bad ways: sincere and touching, with plenty of humour.

*Spence, Eleanor. PATTERSON'S TRACK. *Angus & Robertson* 1959. Illustrated
by Alison Forbes.

Spence, Eleanor. THE SUMMER IN BETWEEN. *O.U.P.* 1959. Illustrated by Marcia
Lane-Foster. Girls in Australian township during long holiday: friendships,
projects and adventures.

Spence, Eleanor. LILLIPILLY HILL. *O.U.P.* 1960. Illustrated by Susan Einzig.
Australia in the 1890's: English family settling in township and learning new
social pattern.

*Spykman, E. C. A LEMON AND A STAR (1955 U.S.A.) 1956, illustrated by
Prudence Seward. THE WILD ANGEL (1956 U.S.A.) 1957. *Macmillan.* (See
also p. 337.)

Street, Dorothea. THE DOG-LEG GARDEN. *O.U.P.* 1951. Illustrated by Evelyn
Cooke. Doctor's family playing in rented garden, learning about gardening and
people.

*Stucley, Elizabeth. MAGNOLIA BUILDINGS. *Bodley Head* 1960. Illustrated by
Dick Hart.

Theobald, Tessa. A SHADOW ON THE SEA. *O.U.P.* 1957. Illustrated by the
author. Straightforward tale of four children looking after themselves.

*Thwaite, Ann. THE HOUSE IN TURNER SQUARE. *Constable* 1960. Illustrated by Robin Jacques.

*Trease, Geoffrey. THE MAYTHORN STORY. *Heinemann* 1960. Illustrated by Robert Hodgson. (See also p. 338.)

Urmston, Mary. THE FIVE BRIGHT KEYS. *Doubleday,* New York 1946. American family settling in the country track down their keys and so meet neighbours who become friends.

Wayne, Jennifer. CLEMENCE AND GINGER. *Heinemann* 1960. Illustrated by Patricia Humphreys. Friendship between middle-class girl and a rackety boy of poor family who helps her in money-making plans.

Weaver, Stella. SISTERS AND BROTHERS. *Collins* 1960. Family relationships tackled with honesty: a family makes adjustments when a foreign orphan is brought to live with them.

Weir, Rosemary. THE SECRET JOURNEY. *Parrish* 1957. Children making their way from Cornwall to Windsor in a tilt-cart: good details of housekeeping, routes, etc.

Weir, Rosemary. THE HUNT FOR HARRY. *Parrish* 1960. Intellectual family moves to poor London district, becomes involved in muddled affairs of a coloured man and his child. Cross-country travelling, clues and chance-met people all brilliantly described.

*Whittle, Tyler. SPADES AND FEATHERS 1955, illustrated by Raymond Sheppard. THE RUNNERS OF ORFORD 1956, CASTLE LIZARD 1957, illustrated by William Stobbs. *Cape.*

Whittle, Tyler. THE BULLHEAD. *Dent* 1958. Illustrated by Geraldine Spence. Lively story of family navigating sea-going barge to East Coast.

*Willard, Barbara. SNAIL AND THE PENNITHORNES 1957, SNAIL AND THE PENNITHORNES NEXT TIME 1958, SNAIL AND THE PENNITHORNES AND THE PRINCESS 1960. *Epworth.* Illustrated by Geoffrey Fletcher.

Willard, Barbara. THE HOUSE WITH ROOTS. *Constable* 1959. Illustrated by Robert Hodgson. Family threatened with eviction because of new road: lively story about real personalities.

Willard, Barbara. EIGHT FOR A SECRET. *Constable* 1960. Illustrated by Lewis Hart. Village, newly enlarged by factories and housing-estate: good study of clash of children from different backgrounds, with adventure on a lake and an island.

Woodberry, Joan. RAFFERTY TAKES TO FISHING 1959, FLOODTIDE FOR RAFFERTY 1960. *Parrish.* Illustrated by the author. Domestic adventures of a small boy in an Australian coastal town. The atmosphere is cheerful and authentic. (See also p. 339.)

Wright, Alison. THE BLAKES. *Dent* 1952. Illustrated by Sheila Macgregor.
  Factory-worker looking for a job buys a bus and takes his family across
  country: real and lively, but with an unconvincing happy end.
*Young, E. H. CARAVAN ISLAND. *Black* 1940. Illustrated by H. J. Haley.

Drawing by Edward Ardizzone for Philippa Pearce's MINNOW ON THE SAY
(O.U.P.)

Chapter 15 | *Growing Up*

It is, after all, a fair test of a book, whether it still has its dust-jacket on or not—unless it is a second or third copy bought for a family of obsessive readers. A reviewer wrote recently:

> In the bad old Victorian days children's books made (we are told now) not nearly enough concessions to their diminutive readers. Their authors crammed them with instruction and moral uplift. They used an uncompromising, polysyllabic, adult vocabulary. They bombarded the youthful mind with raw, if not unadulterated, heroic legend. They were not what is today known as 'entertainment', or anywhere near; and the denizens of the nursery undistracted by TV or the Pleasure Principle, read and re-read them till they fell to bits.
> Ulysses in Modern Dress. *The Times Literary Supplement*, 20 May, 1960.

Why do children still read LITTLE WOMEN? What does Louisa Alcott give them still which they do not always find in contemporary stories? Could it be that her gently humorous tales are nearer to reality than the more up-to-date versions children take, mint-new, from the library shelf?

From their first junior books onwards, children should be able to find something of what people and places are really like. The writer who studies his public too closely may well leave out, on some misguided principle, a good deal of adult comment that children really need. It is only too easy to underestimate the understanding of the young. What we give them must be strong and honest. Victorian story-books are criticized for their repressions and omissions. We would do well to ask whether writers of today give children any more of the truth, or indeed as much.

How many family stories there are in which the plot centres round poverty: how few in which you can really *smell* that poverty. LITTLE WOMEN has a permanent place on the bookshelves of the young because of its sterling honesty. The author herself described the book as 'Not a bit sensational, but simple and true, for we really lived most of it, and if it succeeds, that will be the reason for it.' Whoever doubted, when reading about the scorched breadth in Jo March's evening dress, that these girls were poor? And it is the same with every issue that touches the Marches. Love, social adventure, jobs, friction among themselves, illness and death—the author looks at everything squarely. Brought up in a liberal family, where children were treated as sensible individuals, it never occurred to her that her young readers would expect anything else.

Ethel Turner, whose children's stories (especially SEVEN LITTLE AUSTRALIANS and THE FAMILY AT MISRULE) have been in print continuously for nearly seventy years, has the same forthright attitude to her material. These two splendid writers did not put death-bed scenes into their stories out of custom or morbid interest, but because death was part of the life they were writing about. It happened. Beth got ill, Judy Woolcot was hurt, and for once there was no happy ending. Their brothers and sisters faced the loss, some with complaint, some quietly, some only partly realizing it, but they all faced the fact of death, and there is no reason why young readers today should not do the same when a story demands it.

This is not to suggest that every story for older boys and girls should include a death-bed scene. Any scene that arises will be the better for being played straight. In LION AT LARGE, Richard Parker describes a dangerous situation and makes sure that it does impress the readers as being really dangerous. In the middle of the night a primary schoolboy wakes and sees from his window a lion standing by the gate. It is hardly surprising that he is not believed when he tells this story next morning, for he hardly believes it himself. All the same, he and his ally Ingrid, a farmer's daughter, do find the lion, hiding in a hollow tree. Together they plot and plan, buy food, think up excuses for being absent from school. At first the lion, hungry and wounded, seems friendly enough; but this is a wild beast, even if it does come from a circus. Barry has wonderful dreams of walking back to the village with a docile lion at his heels, but things do not happen like this. The children are in real, frighten-

Drawing by Paul Hogarth for Richard Parker's LION AT LARGE
(Brockhampton). Emphasizes the author's description of real danger

ing peril before rescue comes, and the author hides none of it from
his readers (who will be, incidentally, between eight and ten).

The problem of realism is more complicated, naturally, when we
come to books for older children, between thirteen and fifteen.
What is the writer to give them? How is he to make sure that they
still want to read what he writes? How is he to satisfy their craving
for experience without hustling them away from the last tentative
years of childhood? They must, now, have books that will tax and
stimulate them. If they can still cheerfully read adventure stories,
and most of them can, they will get more out of these if they show
some grasp of moral as well as physical danger and development.
In THE MAN FROM DEVIL'S ISLAND, Arthur Calder Marshall
has used a theme which could have been treated in a romantic,
unreal fashion. The setting is the island of Trinidad. A prisoner has
escaped from a French penal settlement. Three children in their
early teens find him on the beach, in a distressed condition, and deter-
mine to help him. What begins as an exciting adventure ends by being
a serious, even a bitter experience. Gradually the children realize
how many issues depend on their action. They see dimly the neces-
sities of the law. Through the reaction of their parents, they begin
to understand how little in real life is clear-cut. Their gay deter-

Drawing by Keith Vaughan for P. H. Newby's THE SPIRIT OF JEM (John Lehmann)

mination to do good flags and diminishes under pressure from the external world which they have blithely ignored. This is certainly not a moral story. No lesson is preached to interrupt the action. Excellent as this adventure story is, however, no child can finish it without having second thoughts about his own niche in the adult world.

A later story, THE FAIR TO MIDDLING, is still more exacting. Here the children of an orphanage are taken to a fair through the kindness of Lady Charity Armstrong, their gracious patron. Behind the familiar coconut-shies and merry-go-rounds are booths with less obvious attractions. Devils and angels, in human guise, wrestle, as it were, for the souls of the orphans and their preceptors; their wares are at once actual and symbolic. A boy who is going blind, and an ugly, unwanted schoolmistress who loves him, wander together through the blare of catchpenny tunes and hear together the glorious music of the soul which the boy now knows he can create.

Two nasty children suffer a prolonged sojourn in a very modern hell. Lady Charity herself wanders hysterically through a maze with the Superintendent, both seeking lost youth and innocence.

There is a story here, as well as a hidden meaning, and a compelling story it is. The simple force of allegory can be found too in a Kafkaesque tale by P. H. Newby, THE SPIRIT OF JEM, limpid in style and alarming in its implications. It is a mature story, with bold, uncompromising illustrations. The devil walks here, as he walks through Mr Calder Marshall's fair. He walks now in the shape of Jem, a boy who can make people forget their identity. Ostensibly, he is saving them from a mysterious enemy whom only he knows: really, he is destroying their individuality. The boy who tells the tale is at first deceived by Jem. When he realizes that this is, in fact, the enemy of freedom, he tries desperately to get support from his fellow-men, and to save Mr Bowler, who, playing the pipe which stands for grace and hope, has been imprisoned by Jem. Anti-war, anti-fascist, anti-totalitarian, a sermon for the freedom of man's mind—all these things, and, besides, a story which moves forward quickly, smoothly and with a grand simplicity.

Books like this are not for every child. But if some find allegory puzzling and even tedious, they still appreciate the truth about human nature, in the most straightforward family tale. There is no reason why such stories should not be outspoken about what people are like. Writers need not pretend that parents are always kind and tolerant, always interested in what their children are doing: their readers know otherwise. We can only hope that those writers who prefer to forget the acuteness of children about grown-ups will put up their pens for lack of readers; and, with family stories for older children growing tougher, more aware of life, more adult all the time, I believe this is what will happen, if parents will help by accumulating or suggesting books like this, contemporary or classic. Harvey Darton was justified, perhaps, in calling THE WIDE, WIDE WORLD 'that astonishingly lachrymose work,' but, putting up their umbrellas against Ellen's tears, children of today still learn from her relations with bitter Miss Fortune, as they learn from THE SECRET GARDEN, with its hints of deep unhappiness. These are not depressing stories, they are expandable. They open a window on the world, through which children will see more and more each time they read; and they do still read these books.

Let us hold fast by the writer of today who gives our children expandable stories, stories which draw them forward into knowledge of people. By Ruth Adam, for instance, because, in A STEPMOTHER FOR SUSAN OF ST BRIDE'S, she puts into a rather sensational story about a hospital sister some uncompromising, shrewd scenes where a prospective stepmother and a girl come to grips with each other. By William Mayne, who in UNDERGROUND ALLEY describes another kind of stepmother whose insensitive behaviour does more harm than direct cruelty. The truth of the following passage is sifted through the personality of a schoolgirl:

> The affair of the exchanged socks was the first thing to meet her at home. Gwen had looked for them to sew tapes on when Patty was out, and there was a battle of words and opinions about it. It stopped when Daddy came up from the cellar for his tea, but the matter was not settled at all, and Gwen said she would take the grey socks back and change them again. After tea Patty disposed of the argument by sewing tapes on both pairs and putting one pair on. Gwen found out too soon, and was very angry. Patty went down into the cellar, taking the alarm clock to remind her of the time, and fastened herself away.
>
> She calmed her rage by stirring paint and listening to Daddy sawing and chiselling next door at his secret construction.
>
> 'I've got my secret, Daddy's got his, and Gwen's got the baby,' she thought. 'Why can't she manage that and leave me as we were?'
>
> William Mayne. UNDERGROUND ALLEY (Oxford University Press, 1958) p. 78–9.

Adult relationships must make their appearance in books for young people in the right way, to the extent that they would notice them in their own lives. It is no use thrusting a complex story of human relations on a schoolgirl, disguised as an adventure story. In THE SPARROW CHILD, by Meriol Trevor, the quest for a lost chalice is mingled with a complicated love-affair, past and renewed, between young Philip's relations. A girl of twelve might become interested in the adventure but would probably be confused by the hints at an ancient issue between Barny and Carey; an older girl would find the love-story precious, and irritating in its vagueness. A better proportion is achieved in TAWNY BRUSH, a story by Peggy

Cannam about a Gloucestershire farm where Mrs Blake, whose husband had left her ten years before, is battling, with the help of her four sons, to keep the place and the family going. There is much to attract a girl in this book—the glowing picture of the country, the precise account of how Lexy tames a fox-cub, the candid comment and affection between the girl and her mother and brothers, and, above all, the picture of Mrs Blake, lonely, often bad-tempered, facing the difficult task of adjustment when her husband comes back.

Books like this are a necessary corrective to the sickly, unreal view of life and love thrust at schoolgirls in the pages of magazines designed for them, and the 'junior novels' which form a growing side of children's publishing are, too often, gentle, rosy and unreal also. If these so-called novels are intended for twelve-year olds, the writers would do better to confine themselves to adventure and slip romance in as the sideline it normally is at this age; as Elisabeth Kyle does in CAROLINE HOUSE, or Kathrene Pinkerton in her stories about the Bairds and Randolphs in Alaska, or as Geoffrey Trease does in his undergraduate story, THE GATES OF BANNER-DALE. Trease, indeed, was among the first writers of family stories to allow a place for the moments when boy and girl comradeship becomes something deeper. His earlier stories about Bannerdale show Bill and Penny talking with a rough jocularity that hides a delicate awareness of each other. Relationships of this kind will appear more and more now that such stories cast about more widely for their subjects and settings, and we must watch for those writers who can treat boy and girl love sensibly as well as sensitively; for we do not want to jump from the determinedly sexless note of the past to an unattractive sensationalism. A recent story by Catherine Storr, MARIANNE AND MARK, brings out interesting points about this change. The author contrasts Alice and Josie, two fifteen-year-old girls in Brighton, with their jobs and their boy friends, and Marianne, who has grown to an unaware fourteen in an intellectual home and feels she is missing something. The comfortable friendship she establishes with Mark, after a disastrous mistake over Alan and his motor-bike, rounds off a story that is very shrewd about young people and has an agreeable distinction in style and treatment.

If a young love affair is the subject of a story, it must be treated with this kind of shrewdness and without evasion. A younger sister could learn much and achieve a better understanding of her elders if she reads Maureen Daly's SEVENTEENTH SUMMER, with its delicate but frank picture of an American small town and a girl working through her first love affair. Angeline Morrow belongs to a comfortable middle-class home and is disconcerted as well as flattered when Jack Duluth, who works in her father's bakery, begins to take her out. There is an anthropological exactness in the descriptions of drug-store and dance-hall, and of the stylized behaviour of young people who like to think themselves grown-up. Above all, Angeline's feelings, her fear and excitement and the inconvenient warnings of her fastidious mind, are convincingly described. When Jack first visits her house she is strung up; his spoon clicking on his teeth, as he eats ice-cream, becomes a symbol of all the mannerisms she has been trying not to mind:

> I saw my mother raise her eyebrow just a little. Just a little, as if a quick thought had passed through her mind, and my heart shrank up into a tight ball of loathing till I felt that my whole inside would rattle around like a hard, brown peanut in a shell. In my mouth was a bitter taste as if I had been sucking a penny and I couldn't even raise my eyes to look at anyone.
> Maureen Daly. SEVENTEENTH SUMMER (Hollis & Carter, 1947) pp. 158-9.

We could do with more novels of this kind in England, and though we would not now echo exactly the definition of girls' literature offered by a critic in 1888*—'while it advances beyond the nursery, it stops short of the full blaze of the drawing-room'—there is a lot of sense in the view. Mrs Molesworth's novels, which date from that period, give many shrewd comments on the behaviour of young people which are still interesting today, and there are later romances, like Gene Stratton Porter's A GIRL OF THE LIMBERLOST, which fill the gap between school and adult reading. Lush and exaggerated as this story seems now, it is no superficial romance, but a candid, at times a cruel study of a repressed woman taking out her loneliness and disappointment on her daughter, and of that

---

*Edward Salmon. JUVENILE LITERATURE AS IT IS. H. J. Drake, 1888, pp. 221-2.

daughter meeting romance eagerly because of what she has learned
from her mother's failure.

Elnora is not a schoolgirl, of course. She is working her way
through college, earning her right to independence. Stories for
children commonly ignore or minimize the importance of jobs.
Does it really matter, in most family stories, what father does for a
living? We are told this merely as a way of defining the status of the
family. 'Daddy is a doctor', you read, or 'Father is in the Treasury',
or 'Dad is a clerk at the Town Hall'; even, occasionally, 'Dad is on
night-shift at the factory.' But though the head of the family may
sometimes be described as coming home tired, his children show
little interest in his work. More often than not the writer seems to
have chosen it to keep him occupied while his children proceed with
their adventures.

As for these children, they need not always be on holiday from
school; and indeed, with the widening of the social content of children's stories, more and more of them have young heroes and
heroines who are working, and who find adventure in and through
their jobs, rather than outside them.

One of the most readable books of this kind is Lois Lamplugh's
THE SIXPENNY RUNNER, a good-luck tale and none the worse
for it. Leaving her middle-class children whose adventures in NINE
BRIGHT SHINERS and ROCKETS ON THE DUNES were so vigor-
ously told, Miss Lamplugh has turned her attention to their friends
the Allens, who live in a converted railway-carriage on the dunes.
Ned, the oldest boy, has maturity thrust upon him when his father
has an accident and has to give up his groundsman's job. The boy
leaves school at fifteen, goes to work with a greyhound-breeder,
and studies for G.C.E. in his spare time. An attractive setting and a
bit of fairy-tale (Ned is given a runt pup to bring up and she turns
out to be a brilliant racer) make this an engaging tale for a twelve-
year-old, but there is plenty to interest an older child. Ned works
hard and the author takes care that we appreciate this, that we know
how often he doubts whether this exhausting night-work is worth
the trouble. The problems of a working-class schoolboy have been
tackled honestly within the framework of a first-class story.

This is the real strength of Richard Armstrong's splendid yarns,
the tales of Merchant Navy apprentices and also SABOTAGE AT
THE FORGE and THE WHINSTONE DRIFT, where boys working in a

foundry and an iron-working come upon adventures which rise out of their jobs and which their training helps them to tackle. The author has explained the serious purpose of his stories:

> I wanted as far as possible to forearm the boy at the beginning of adolescence—not ramming a weapon into his hand willy-nilly, but showing him the size and shape of it and where it lies in such a way that he would take it up without realizing he was doing so and find himself using it when he needed to.
>
> So in the book (he is writing of SEA CHANGE here), I try to give him a factual picture of life as it comes at a boy in the Merchant Service, to make him familiar with the tools and instruments used there and show him how they fit into the general scheme of things. I bring him into contact with the kind of people he would meet and outline some of the problems and emotional conflicts he would have to face, the difficulties and the possibilities such a life would hold for him. And finally, I try, whether this is ultimately the line of activity he chooses to follow or not, to make him aware through it of his own power, his value as a human being; to give him confidence in himself, in the richness of life in the real world and his capacity for living it.
>
> Richard Armstrong, in CHOSEN FOR CHILDREN. Edited by Marcus Crouch. (Library Association, 1957) pp. 52–3.

This is a fine aim, and Richard Armstrong has fulfilled this while giving his readers thrilling yarns and a sympathetic gallery of heroes in the process of growing-up but still retaining the angular contours of boyhood. There is no reason why stories should not be purposive in this way so long as they still keep the hall-mark of the author's personality in style and narrative.

The 'career-novel' which has become so popular in recent years does not stand up well in comparison, but it is only fair to judge this type of book by its own standards. It is necessarily a compromise between the junior novel and the handbook. So that the information about careers may be as complete as possible, the hero or heroine is pushed up the ladder or through the mill with unnatural speed. It is usually, in fact, up the ladder, for no author can get far if his hero stays in the outer office; but sometimes the load of experience is shared between two friends or two rivals. In JANET CARR,

JOURNALIST, Josephine Kamm takes the reader into the office of a woman's magazine, where two girls fresh from secretarial school are drafted, one into the fashion department and one into features. Within the limited pattern of the career novel, the temperaments of these two are effectively contrasted, and their rivalry animates a very thorough account of the routine of a magazine.

Although the formula for this kind of book leaves little room for restablishing characte, it is character, all the same, that really counts. More than one writer has drawn an efficient picture of life at a riding-school. In RENNIE GOES RIDING, Monica Edwards goes further. She presents as her heroine a girl suffering from the effects of wartime bombing, a girl who seems unsuitable for a job that is tough physically and perhaps tedious to the intelligence. Rennie's career is far from easy, and her disappointments and moments of despair are very real to the reader because she is so real a person; horse-obsessives, reading the book for its subject, will find they have got an unexpected pleasure from the interplay of character.

I particularly enjoyed Duncan Taylor's BOB IN LOCAL GOVERN-MENT for the same reason. An unpromising title, and Bob is a very ordinary boy, but the author finds adventure in the tastelessly-decorated local office, where an unpleasant senior clerk torments tenants and underlings with his ruthless interpretation of the official code. Information in plenty can be dug out of this story, but it is a fine study of character, too, of the perils of work in close association with an uncongenial personality.

No career novel, of course, gives a full picture of real life. Sex is presented as romance, and only incidentally. Virtue inevitably triumphs. It must be stressed that these are properly books for school-children, not for anyone much over the age of fourteen. They serve as an introduction to adult life, not as a complete version of it.

Not that any work of fiction attempts to provide this, but in so far as it must be attempted, many stories for school-children make a more honest attempt than a great many adult novels. All the same, young people must plunge into adult fiction, from twelve or so on-wards, and must do this unafraid and unchecked. We can advise and suggest, but we should not select or censor. The glitter of the forbidden is potent for young people. We must trust them, rather, to choose, as they should have been choosing all along, the books which are most valuable to them. They will form their taste after trial and error and in no other way.

The most valuable quality a child can have, in his reading life, is curiosity. Easily squashed, it is as easily encouraged by the provision of books varied in style and content. If our children can advance into the world of adult fiction with an intense curiosity about human relations, about the position of man in the world, about the technique of writing, they will not go far wrong. If they have grown up with good will towards reading as a necessity of life and one of its major pleasures, they will confirm what they have long unconsciously known, that 'all books are children's books.'

Reading List

*Adam, Ruth. A STEPMOTHER FOR SUSAN OF ST BRIDE'S. *Hulton* (Girl Novel) 1958.

*Alcott, Louisa. LITTLE WOMEN (1868). *Dent* (Children's Illustrated Classics) 1948. Illustrated by S. Van Abbé. *Penguin* (Puffin Story Books) 1953.

Alcott, Louisa. LITTLE WOMEN GOOD WIVES (1871). *Collins* 1954.

Alcott, Louisa. JO'S BOYS (1886). *Blackie* (1939) 1949.

Alcott, Louisa. LITTLE MEN (1871). *Blackie* (1937) 1949.

*Armstrong, Richard. SABOTAGE AT THE FORGE 1946, illustrated by L. P. Lufton. THE WHINSTONE DRIFT 1951, illustrated by M. A. Charlton. *Dent.*

*Burnett, Mrs Hodgson. THE SECRET GARDEN (1911). *Heinemann* (New Windmill Series) 1950. *Penguin* (Puffin Story Books) 1951.

Byers, Irene. TIM OF TAMBERLEY FOREST. *Max Parrish,* 1954. Agreeably written story of a boy learning forestry.

*Cannam, Peggy. TAWNY BRUSH. *Lutterworth* 1957. Illustrated by Sheila Rose.

*Daly, Maureen. SEVENTEENTH SUMMER (1942 U.S.A.). *Hollis & Carter* 1947.

Furlong, Agnes. ELIZABETH LEAVES SCHOOL. *Harrap* 1956. North Country town; secondary school girl goes to work in big store and makes a success of it. Very natural story.

Hogarth, Grace Allen. AS A MAY MORNING. *Hamish Hamilton* 1958. Girl and her first adult emotions: sincere and attractive.

Knight, Captain F. FAMILY ON THE TIDE. *Macmillan* 1956. Illustrated by Geoffrey Whittam. Girl growing up and realizing complexity of other people.

*Kyle, Elisabeth. CAROLINE HOUSE. (see Chap.13).

*Lamplugh, Lois. THE SIXPENNY RUNNER. *Cape* 1960. Illustrated by William Stobbs.

*Marshall, Arthur Calder. THE MAN FROM DEVIL'S ISLAND 1958, THE FAIR TO MIDDLING 1959. *Hart-Davis.*

*Mayne, William. UNDERGROUND ALLEY. *O.U.P.* 1958. Illustrated by Marcia Lane-Foster.

Meader, Stephen. BLUEBERRY MOUNTAIN. *Bell* 1960. Illustrated by Edward Shenton. Two boys selling berries by roadside, starting their own plantation. Technical details and characters equally good.

*Newby, P. H. THE SPIRIT OF JEM. *John Lehmann* 1947. Illustrated by Keith Vaughan.

Norris, Phyllis. MEET THE KILBURYS. *Nelson* 1947. Girls helping their mother to start a hostel for a day school: domestic tale full of good sense and shrewdness

*Parker, Richard. LION AT LARGE. *Brockhampton* 1959. Illustrated by Paul Hogarth.

*Pinkerton, Kathrene. HIDDEN HARBOUR (1951 U.S.A.) 1954, SECOND MEETING (1956 U.S.A.) 1956, THE SECRET RIVER (1958 U.S.A.) 1958. *Bodley Head.*

*Porter, Gene Stratton. A GIRL OF THE LIMBERLOST (1909 U.S.A.). *Hodder & Stoughton* 1912. Abridged edition, *Brockhampton* 1959. Intelligently edited.

Raymond, Margaret. A BEND IN THE ROAD. *Longmans* 1934. Welsh steel-worker in American town, troubles of his daughter in her search for independence.

*Storr, Catherine. MARIANNE AND MARK. *Faber* 1960.

*Trease, Geoffrey. NO BOATS ON BANNERMERE 1949, UNDER BLACK BANNER 1951, BLACK BANNER PLAYERS 1952, BLACK BANNER ABROAD 1954, THE GATES OF BANNERDALE 1956. *Heinemann.* Illustrated by Richard Kennedy.

*Trevor, Meriol. THE SPARROW CHILD. *Collins* 1958. Illustrated by Martin Thomas.

*Turner, Ethel. SEVEN LITTLE AUSTRALIANS (1894) 1949, THE FAMILY AT MISRULE 1895. *Blackie.*

*Wetherell, Elizabeth. THE WIDE, WIDE WORLD (1851 U.S.A.) 1852. *U.L.P.* 1950. Edited and illustrated by Joyce Lankester Brisley.

Career novels

Allan, Mabel Esther. HERE WE GO ROUND. *Heinemann* 1954. Girl helping in nursery school while waiting for training college: characters exceptionally interesting, a touching story.

Denniston, Robin. THE YOUNG MUSICIANS. *Chatto & Windus* 1955. Lively
  story of College of Music, with good characters and plenty of variety.
*Edwards, Monica. RENNIE GOES RIDING. *Bodley Head* 1956.
Edwards, Monica. JOAN GOES FARMING. *Bodley Head* 1954.
  Excellent characters and an interesting outline of practical training.
*Kamm, Josephine. JANET CARR, JOURNALIST. *Bodley Head* 1953.
Mack, Angela. CONTINUITY GIRL. *Chatto & Windus* 1958. Lively tale with
  plenty of hard fact.
Meynell, Laurence. POLICEMAN IN THE FAMILY. *O.U.P.* 1953. Illustrated by
  Neville Dear. Takes a recruit through training school and practical training
  up to his first beat: interesting and extremely readable.
Meynell, Laurence. THE YOUNG ARCHITECT. *O.U.P.* 1958. Illustrated by David
  Knight. A particularly good combination of fact and convincing fiction:
  Colin Winter goes from small Bucks town to a London college.
Summers, D. O. KEN JONES, ELECTRICAL ENGINEER. *Chatto & Windus* 1959.
  Straight-forward story of two boys climbing the ladder, one by university
  training, the other through apprenticeship. Extremely interesting.
*Taylor, Duncan. BOB IN LOCAL GOVERNMENT. *Chatto & Windus* 1958.
Wilson, Granville. JONATHAN ENTERS JOURNALISM. *Chatto & Windus* 1956.
  Boy on provincial newspaper: good picture of small town and its doings.

Chapter 16 | *Realism and Reality*

Not long ago a reviewer wrote scathingly about THE TIDY HEN, an attractively illustrated story by Antony Groves-Raines in the Potter tradition:

> The kind of book that should have died out by now—and most certainly not sold at this price. Crudely illustrated little story about a hen who tidies up a small girl's bedroom after she is scolded by (wait for it) *Cook*.
> Anne Barber in BOOKS AND BOOKMEN, December 1963, pp. 37–38.

It is perhaps unfair to take too seriously an ephemeral review which may be deliberately exaggerated, but it is symptomatic of the difference between what a writer wants to write and what critics think he should write. It provokes the question, deeper than an opinion about one book, whether a writer for children has the same kind of rights as any other, and whether a writer of any kind can please himself and not be ruled by public taste and public beliefs. As I write, the question is being argued fiercely in regard to so-called obscene books, and it is argued as fiercely, though less publicly, whenever a group of adults meet who are concerned with children's reading. In the case of THE TIDY HEN, the question is a social one. An author has chosen to write what is really a period piece. Should this be reviewed for what it is, or should we expect him to conform to public taste?

There can be no doubt that tastes change, though it is impossible to say how far it is the taste of *children* and how far the taste of those who choose or recommend books for them. The early 1960's brought a hardening in the drive towards realism, in family stories in particular, which began far earlier. This was in part an answer from writers (and publishers) to the popularity of non-fiction for children. This has improved strikingly, under the encouragement of being wanted, and has the obvious advantage of ready-made markets and ready-assembled readers. More important, children's fiction today may reflect the desire of young people to get out and about and see life as it is—no new wish but, with every year, more readily expressed and gratified. The family story is too young for many (I would almost say most) children after thirteen or so: the move to adult fiction comes earlier all the time. But even in the years below this, children seem to look more and more for stories with a background like their own or at least one which is topical in some way or another. This tendency could help to bring such stories nearer to their Victorian counterparts—and what a good thing that would be. It could also discourage good writers who for one reason or another wanted to use apparently old-fashioned themes and settings. For them, there is the risk that criticism will be tinged with social prejudice. If SWALLOWS AND AMAZONS were to appear now as an unknown book, I wonder how it would fare.

The sanctions working against the upper-middle-class family story are especially hard on the orthodox pony-book. When the Great House has become a home for backward children, it is not easy to write of it unselfconsciously, as if at the present time, with Cook in residence, and yet it is too soon for this kind of story to become a period piece. The arbitrary addition of topical detail hardly helps. The most skilful exponents of the pony story, the Pullein-Thompson sisters, are certainly trying to move with the times. In THE OPEN GATE Christine Pullein-Thompson uses a group of Teddy boys and girls from the village to shape the plot; they are presented in a bunch, crudely contrasted with the children who go to the riding-school, and never seem to belong in the story. In THE LOST PONY and its sequel, FOR WANT OF A SADDLE, the change is more successful because it is integral to the story. The Smallbone brother and sister, whose father works in a factory, are sent to foster-parents in the country because their town flat is overcrowded. They are engaging and probable children, and their relations with parents and foster-parents are made to seem natural; so is their friendship with Paula, who teaches them to ride on the old pony from the market garden, but not before they have had to overcome a lot of nervousness about her accent and her old but elegant jodhpurs.

Other writers meet the supposed wishes of today's readers in other ways. Gillian Baxter has always concentrated on the hard knocks and rewards of working with horses, and although her recent stories, THE STABLES AT HAMPTON, THE DIFFICULT SUMMER and THE PERFECT HORSE, are in every way traditional, they are not dated. It is pleasant, too, to come upon a new young writer who blithely ignores any hostility to middle-class riders. Bernagh Brims was fifteen when she wrote RUNAWAY RIDERS and she is solely interested in enjoying the exuberance of the boys and girls who camp their way down to Dublin, swigging lemonade and exchanging prep-school jokes on the way. The orthodox pony story persists, but it is the oddities we remember—like Cledwyn Hughes's benevolent piece of nonsense, PONIES FOR CHILDREN. This starts in time-honoured fashion, or apparently so, with two children sitting in a tree-house in a large garden, talking about ponies—but there *are* no ponies. Mr Bynner is writing a book about them, and then he may earn enough money for Nandi and Mathew to have their own. Meanwhile, they listen to extracts from their father's book and learn the mysteries of tack and the aids, while around these readings unfolds a wildly improbable spy story. In this ingenious and elegant tale, the pony story is very much alive, even if it is upside-down.

The criterion must always be a literary one. Is the author using a formula or genuinely re-creating an old form? Mary Treadgold's story, THE HERON RIDE, presents horse-mad children resident at a riding-school. But are they wholly horse-mad? And is this the usual riding-school? There is Ethne Blake, a juvenile television star whose producer has decreed that she must learn to look natural on a horse. There is Sylvia, dumped there by globe-trotting parents, who bursts out, 'I hate my beastly horse.' There is Julian, immersed in intellectual pursuits, and Harry, whose love of horses comes from a country-bred grandfather, but whose working-class father puts into his head the idea of a Teenage Strike against their cantankerous and neglectful teacher, Major Mogg. To Sandra and her brother Adam, town children staying in the village, the string of horses they see on the skyline is entirely romantic, but they soon find out how different the truth is. Nor is Sandra's luck like the luck we come to expect for the heroine of a run-of-the-mill pony story. Her longing to ride has to be satisfied by Toby, who in his old age pulls the Vicar's lawn-mower. Toby is given a new pride in himself, just as Sandra is brought to a more sensible outlook on life, by a Hungarian refugee who was once a groom in the Vienna School. This interesting and plausible conglomeration of individuals is beautifully managed by the author, and her story is shot through with a humour that is neither adult nor juvenile but just a nice personal appreciation of the incongruous and the absurd. Mary Treadgold has a talent for working out a mystery. The children in THE HERON RIDE rightly suspect that the Major is up to something, and their detective work provides a strong plot. In the sequel, RETURN TO THE HERON, the story depends still more on clues and investigation. The Heron now becomes the scene of a hunt for the lost Stubbs which could help the Denes family to return to their ancestral home. But this is just the outward shape of the story. The person who really matters is Kathryn Denes, a child of nine who, because of an unstable family background, has come to resent the idea that family history has any claim on her. The discovery of the picture, which is described in most varied and likely detail, is less important than Kathryn's discovery that she has inherited from the Denes's ancestors a talent that can help her to be happier.

In short, the village as the venue for a story promises to be rather more interesting than it has sometimes been in the past. I wonder if it has ever, in fact, been treated realistically? You can hardly call *Mary's Meadow* or *Daddy Darwin's Dovecot* realistic, though to the reader the settings are triumphantly real. The writers of the last century have their share of the idealization of the country and country life that belongs to any branch of literature in an urban society. The nostalgia for a countryside that is visibly vanishing can be seen today in the stories of Barbara Willard and Jenifer Wayne and Rosemary Weir. Their imagined village, with its rustic cottages, its duckpond and all-purpose shop, has one foot in the past. In those agreeably humorous tales of Jenifer Wayne, THE DAY THE CEILING FELL DOWN and THE NIGHT THE RAIN CAME IN, incomes have been levelled, everyone uses the same soap-powder and eats the same kind of food (whether they call it supper, tea or high tea), but although the scene is noticeably more democratic, the general effect is not realistic; it is an ideal village indeed that houses such a collection of curious types.

Drawing by Juliette Palmer for Barbara Willard's THE PENNY PONY
(Hamish Hamilton)

Social realism hardly belongs to comedies like this, any more
than it belongs to stories for younger children, where the country is
a background for exploration and play. What is needed here is an
impression—of space and sky, roofs and walls, and people only as
part of the landscape. In short books for children between six and
eight, the illustrator can help the author to suggest a country scene
economically but clearly. A fruitful partnership like this lies behind
the charm of Eilís Dillon's A PONY AND TRAP, with Monica Brasier-
Creagh's drawings, or of Barbara Willard's exquisite miniature, THE
PENNY PONY, which Juliette Palmer has interpreted in line, or of
Mary Cockett's THE COTTAGE BY THE LOCK, in which author and
illustrator, Shirley Hughes, concentrate on just those visual details
of canal life that would entrance a child.

All these writers have brought their stories into line with the present
day, with housing estates and frozen foods and the 11-plus, but they
are still, basically, writing in the pastoral tradition. Rosemary Weir,
to take another example, chooses to pose problems very much of our
times in stories which take a light-hearted and amusing view of

village life. In WHAT A LARK, for instance, the Tooleys, when their
East-End house is condemned, turn their back on the London
housing estate and escape to a double-decker bus in Sussex. The
note is gay, even facetious. The Tooleys are never more than mildly
disconcerted by their homelessness, and when orders come that they
must move their bus, fate intervenes through Mr Abbot of Matcham
Court, who has a solution and a home ready. The author has chosen
the problem as a device for getting together a number of people
from differing backgrounds, to make a pleasantly entertaining, and
topical, story. The village has been modernized, as it were, but tactfully. Her intention can also be seen very clearly in the opening
paragraphs of SOAP-BOX DERBY:

> Andy Harper lived on the Harepath Housing Estate, on the out-
> skirts of Axford in Devon. Axford is a market-town, and every
> Wednesday huge cattle trucks arrive from all over the country and
> disgorge their loads of cows and sheep and pigs into the neat
> concrete pens of the cattle market. The town fills up with red-faced
> farmers in shiny leggings and stout farmers' wives with shopping
> baskets. Stallholders set up their stalls in the square outside the
> old grey church and sell interesting things like brandy-snaps and
> Real Cream Toffee, and buckets and cow chains and plants and
> lengths of brightly-coloured cotton.
> ... By four o'clock everyone has gone home, in time for the
> milking, and Axford is quiet again until half-past five when the
> factory workers come out.
>   There are three factories in Axford. One of them makes gloves,
> and one makes wooden huts, and one, the biggest of the three,
> makes tooth-paste. The tooth-paste is called Kleeny and is quite
> nice, green, and tasting of peppermint. A great many women and
> girls are employed at the Kleeny factory and among them, when
> this story begins, was Andy's mother.
> Rosemary Weir. SOAP-BOX DERBY (Brockhampton Press, 1962)
> p. 7.

The Harper family is skilfully drawn, but the author is neither old-
fashioned nor grimly sociological in her treatment of them. This is
essentially a story about two children—Andy, who sets out to earn
money to buy old Mr Billings's donkey Kitty, and Andy's friend

Mary-Alice, whose mother's cottage, dark and inconvenient but smelling of home-made buns, draws him with a warmth he cannot find in his own polished and electrified villa. The young reader may or may not notice the moral of the story, but he will follow with pleasure the description of how Andy finds and then loses a pram chassis, comes to grips with the village bully, wins the soap-box race at the local carnival, and at long last gets his donkey. Biro's lively illustrations emphasize that this is a tale of busy small boys with a setting part-old and part-new.

Among the many writers who prefer a village to a town scene, Barbara Willard stands out for the quality of her work. THE SUM-MER WITH SPIKE is similar to WHAT A LARK in its plot. A field of caravan squatters is suddenly threatened, and saved by a blatant story-telling device; the local boy who has made good returns from Canada, and we know at once that he will start up the disused brick-works and frustrate the plans of nasty Nog Merrow. Certainly the author has used more convincing plots than this. But, again, the story depends not on its plot but on its theme—the friendship of two boys with differing backgrounds. Spike lives with his grandfather in a caravan while his father is at sea: Perry Trevelyan, whose school-master father has been sent to the country to recover from an illness, has a totally different home and home life. The author is interested to work out just what the two boys have in common and how they find this common ground. Everything else is subordinated to the theme which is so firmly concluded in the final paragraph:

> Summer will come again . . . They always said that, Perry thought, as though every summer was the same . . . It was hard for him to believe that any season of any year could be as good as the one that had ended. It had been the best he could remember. It had been the summer with Spike.
> Barbara Willard. THE SUMMER WITH SPIKE (Constable, 1961) p. 191.

Hinds Cross, glimpsed through the activities of children, seems real to the reader, and that is what matters; it is not a photographically exact picture, but a selectively drawn background, with elements of the old and the new shaking down together.

And so to the most real village of all. In one sense, *realism* implies

a conscious effort to find details that will *seem* real, and this effort
often keeps a book from being a spontaneous and unhampered
work of art. William Mayne's books are distinguished not by laborious realism but by an innate reality. A PARCEL OF TREES is perhaps

Drawing by Margery Gill for William Mayne's A PARCEL OF TREES (Penguin)

his best book to date. The village of Burwen, where Susan Brown's
father keeps the bakehouse, is located somewhere on the Cheltenham-
Hereford line. This is important not as a piece of realistic detail, but
because the story turns on the small triangle of land, lying below the
railway embankment and within the company's fence, which had
once belonged to Susan's family, and which she wants for her own
territory. From the literary point of view, this book is as nearly per-

fect as a book could be. Each character, each detail, is meant, selected, properly placed. Susan's much younger sister Rosemary, whose tape boundary in their shared bedroom drives Susan to look for privacy elsewhere; the lads, Denis and Neddy, in their first jobs, and respectfully admired by Susan; stammering Tom Royal, presented straight away as a gambler (when he comes to the shop to buy rolls for his lunch, he explains that betting isn't allowed at the fishing contest, and so, easily, the author introduces a fact essential to the story); the solicitor, Mr Ferriman, who brews his own wine and finds legal loopholes for Susan; even the secretary of E. D. Kessel and Son, in the near-by market town, where the tombstones were made for Mr Monsy's dogs—each and every character has his place in the story, and also his accredited place in the village. This is not a story about the clash of social interests; it is a story about individuals in a community. It is important, as well, that each of the characters is seen through a child's eyes, though in no archly juvenile way. The book is about fourteen-year-old Susan, her difficulties, her determination, her victory over circumstance. Everything is referred back to her. Here she is talking to Mr Ferriman:

'I could just pay forty shillings,' said Susan.
'I didn't mean the fine,' said Mr. Ferriman. 'I meant lawyer's fees. They don't always work for nothing—it's just that the fancy takes me to work on an arid little problem like this. Besides, you see, I'm interested in railways. I'll show you my trains one day.'
'Thank you,' said Susan, not at all interested in trains. 'And can I go in the orchard now?'
'You could,' said Mr. Ferriman. 'Say you are taking measurements for me, or something. You could, anyway, make a plan. But don't cross the line any more, or it *will* be forty shillings.'
William Mayne. A PARCEL OF TREES (Penguin, 1963) p. 46.

Mr Ferriman is the only person who can safely know about the forgotten lodge and orchard. 'She would have liked to tell Mum, if it would have been mere information, but what Mum knew became before morning what Daddy knew as well; and if Daddy knew he had an orchard, then it would not be private any more.'
This is a shrewd study of a girl's character. It is also a shrewd cross-section of a village—like all villages, at once unique and familiar.

Seen from Susan's point of view, the essential elements of village
life are all here—the community feeling (indicated by the casual
evening gathering on the green), the importance of weather and time
of day, the dovetailed routine of the inhabitants, the impression of
space and leisure. It is Mayne's feeling for locality that gives substance to this book, and stories of treasure-hunts (for this, in the
long run, is what A PARCEL OF TREES is) also owe their attraction
to their local history. Sheena Porter, for instance, a new writer
whose books are reminiscent of Mayne's, uses exact details of place
to substantiate her stories; up till now, at least, she seems to rely
more on this than on characterization. The woods in THE BRONZE
CHRYSANTHEMUM and the neglected fields of HILLS AND HOL-
LOWS seem more real than the characters in them. THE BRONZE
CHRYSANTHEMUM, particularly, has a note of strain as soon as the
author has left the middle-class people she understands for the
villagers and gipsies who are drawn from outside:

> Constable Pilgrim went into the house looking for his helmet
> to make him more official, and then walked quickly up the hill
> to the Leylands'. As he turned the corner by the back door,
> he trod heaviiy on Angus's tail as he lay stretched out in a
> patch of thin sunlight, and stooped hurriedly to make apology
> for it.
>   ... Roger opened the door as they got to it, and found Con-
> stable Pilgrim knocking on the air.
>   'I'm sorry,' he said, and closed it again.
>   This time Constable Pilgrim knocked on it with both fists,
> beating a small tattoo, and saying, 'Let me in. Open in the name
> of the law.'
>   Roger opened it again. 'I ain't done nothin',' he said. 'And if
> I had you couldn't prove it.'
>   'Ha,' said Timothy. 'You underestimate me, Master Roger.
> My record is a brilliant one, and by rights I should be a sergeant,
> or even an inspector.'
> Sheena Porter. THE BRONZE CHRYSANTHEMUM (Oxford
> University Press, 1961) p. 51.

In a later book, JACOB'S LADDER, though the setting is just as carefully visualized, the theme depends on character, and the change in

the relationship of two schoolgirls is as important, and as interesting, as the discovery of an ancient chalice in a long forgotten chapel. In Eric Houghton's SUMMER SILVER, the finding of a hoard of seventeenth-century silver depends on exact topography, and when Colin Trant works out the alignment between the church spire and the river-front of the paper-works, he is energetically learning local history. These authors are not slavishly following fashion, but they are in the fashion none the less. In recent years, local history has been growing more and more popular as a subject for amateur work, for the young as well as for adults. A nice compromise between instruction and entertainment can be found in E. W. Hildick's MAPPER MUNDY'S TREASURE HUNT, in which the young reader can follow a simple children-v.-crooks story, and can also, if he likes, put in some practice with an ordnance survey map.

This book is suitably illustrated with diagrams and map-sections: illustrators have to decide how far accuracy is important in stories with a strong local flavour. In her drawings for A PARCEL OF TREES, Margery Gill has followed out exactly Mayne's careful indications of place. It is noticeable that she does not depict the village so much as the people who live there, but the railway embankment and orchard, whose ownership is in dispute, are shown just as the author describes them. A precise idea of the place, as well as the impression of its sunken, remote character, is essential. In THE LAST BUS, one of Mayne's stories for younger children, Margery Gill has taken similar pains. The second part of this superbly imagined short tale describes two small boys running across country to intercept David's last bus home. The reader must be made to feel their breathlessness and the way the route seems to lengthen before them, and the drawings help him to do this just as much as the author's words do.

Of course illustration can easily hinder imagination. Many stories call for an impression of reality rather than a transcription of it. There are moments in Paul Berna's FLOOD WARNING where the scene is very important. This story, set in the Anjou district of France, shows brilliantly the effect of a sudden and disastrous flood on a group of masters and boys in a small boarding-school. To appreciate the story we need to have certain points clear in our minds—that the school is built round three sides of a square, with a walled garden and playing-fields on the fourth side leading to the river, and

Drawing by Charles Keeping for Paul Berna's FLOOD WARNING
(Bodley Head)

that the whole block is dominated by a massive medieval mill-tower.
All this Berna makes clear in the story, not by set descriptions, but
bit by bit, often through dialogue, and the reader must use his
imagination to put the scene together. It is unobtrusively done and
you hardly realize how skilfully he has given you the means of imag-
ining the crisis of the story, when the waters of the Alouette finally
break through the sandbags on the garden wall. The picture of the
widening cracks, the towering wall of water, and the watchers sprint-
ing to safety, is painfully vivid from the text, and drawings of action
would be superfluous. Instead, Charles Keeping provides one that
enhances the atmosphere, using a swirling, broken line that partly
obscures shape and *suggests* action. The effect of danger and tension,
of a boy battling with flood-water, is immensely fine, and really
complements the text. In the same way, Brian Wildsmith has illustrated Véronique Day's story, LANDSLIDE!, in a style that stimulates
and does not limit imagination. This is a sharp, startling tale about
five children who are trapped in a lonely cottage in France and are
not found for many days. Confronted by darkness, cold, hunger and
loneliness, each child reacts in a personal way, and the author is
helped by the artist's illusion of darkness, which he achieves even
when inevitably using some light in his pictures. Illustrations like
this are far more effective than, for instance, those by an anonymous
artist for Ivan Southall's HILLS END. This is a story of a group of

children isolated in an Australian township in a freak storm. The accidents and terrors of their days alone are most adequately described by the author, and the drawings, which try to represent various critical scenes of action, only have a weakening effect on the excitement of the story.

All these stories could be called realistic, in that they set out to show natural cataclysms as they might be in real life, but their first preoccupation is, after all, with character. Nearest of all to the documentary is Robert Bateman's TV REPORTER, which draws on the author's personal experience and presents it under the heading of *Real Life Adventure*. When the sea wall breaks and Nabsby Head floods, young Mick Johnson is the only person there; so far, a familiar device for attracting attention at the beginning of an adventure story. But there is much of the inconsequence and waste of real life in this story. Mick sees his scoop reduced to part of a single sentence in a television news report; he learns the difficulty, in practice, of questioning people in trouble; even the mystery that fills out the story (he gets on the track of a fraud in a professional football team) is exceptionally topical and treated in an authentic manner. A book like this holds out one hand to the reluctant reader of fourteen or so who thinks books should be like life as he knows it, and another to the child of ten to whom adventure can happen anywhere.

English fiction may have been given a push in the direction of realism by some of the stories that have come from the Continent in recent years, stories like AVALANCHE by Rutgers van der Loeff, with its glimpse of the Pestalozzi scheme in action, or Michel Bourguignon's LINE OF ATTACK. Here are the children of two Breton villages enthusiastically carrying on a feud started so long ago that nobody remembers more than that the villagers of generations back had failed to agree on the running of the branch railway. Headed by Junkshop, a confident amateur engineer, the Belmont gang have got the diesel engine back into working order and propose to use it to launch an attack on the enemy and recapture the Lone Tower, their forest stronghold. The book violates many of the taboos which have somehow established themselves in regard to English stories for children. The story runs like the report of a military campaign. The author accumulates details of fist-fighting and smoke-grenades with healthy relish. For all the confidence of the boys, a train is hardly a normal plaything, and sabotage on the track could be really dangerous; as Junkshop says:

> 'It was lucky I saw it in time, in spite of the curve, and that the brakes held. Otherwise we'd have gone straight down and ended up with this lot at the bottom of the ravine and the rest of us pushing up the daisies.'
>
> Michel Bourguignon. LINE OF ATTACK. Translated by John Buchanan-Brown. (Bodley Head, 1958) p. 125.

Moreover, the moral of the story, that peace is more comfortable and more constructive than war, is not enforced through an unconvincing change of heart. The truce is occasioned first by the dramatic collapse of one of the boys with threatened peritonitis; common sense comes first, tolerance and generosity afterwards. These are proper boys, just as the other characters, with their work and their adult preoccupations, are proper people; and, as in the classic English story of boyish enterprise, *The Otterbury Incident*, parents and the Law have the last word.

A century-old extension of the meaning of *realism* is, as the dictionary puts it, 'the implication that the details are of an unpleasant or sordid character.' The popular story about crooks and children often seems to set out to exploit this kind of material, but the effect is most often one of dilution; a thief or a spy or a smuggler is presented as a cardboard dummy and his actions as futile and insignificant. The outstanding stories with a crime plot, in recent years, have been not about adult criminals, who would inevitably have to be treated with a certain reticence, but about young people whose troubles can be honestly described and understood by readers not much younger. If children today are precocious in their knowledge of events, they are not necessarily any more mature than their parents or grandparents at the same age. Since they cannot read any family story, however hastily, without absorbing *some* impressions about human behaviour, the writer has it in his power to help or to confuse them with his handling of such material. THE RACK-ETTY STREET GANG, by the Australian novelist L. H. Evers, presents an adult crime as it is seen by boys in their early 'teens, with a measure of adult commentary implied for the reader who can find it. The story is made up of two interwoven strands. Anton Smertzer and his parents are trying to learn to be new Australians and to forget the past; in the same street, fat Tommi and his associates are planning to rob the bank on the corner. Attention is mainly focused on the gang who adopt Anton—the Prof., with his inventions and his grand speech; Bob, who is on probation and has a drunkard for a father; Stanley, who is jaunty and secretly unsure of himself. The activities of the crooks are seen through the inquisitive eyes of the boys, the need for the brotherhood of man is seen as it affects Anton. The author has something to say that is pertinent to the times, but he says it within the framework of a good adventure story. In the treatment of Anton's family, though, and in the character of Evans, boss of the crooks, this is near to the tone of an adult novel, and so is John Rowe Townsend's interesting GUMBLE'S YARD, in which a man drifts into petty crime as a last resort in his feckless life. Kevin and Sandra are not well served by their father or by Doris, his self-styled housekeeper. The author faces the implications of his plot. Though he introduces a parson and a welfare officer, these are no angels in disguise to make all bright and clear, for the children finally decide to stay in their home, with poor meals, sluttish mistress and all. There is nothing sordid about the story and nothing evasive either; it is, in detail and in outlook, a contemporary story.

Taboos have been broken in this story, again—among them, the idea implicit in much reviewing of children's books, that adults should never be shown as unsympathetic, weak or cruel. This is a point on which writer and consumer may never wholly agree, though many critics feel that children's understanding is too often underestimated. The point is relevant to a book like THE THURSDAY KIDNAPPING by Antonia Forest. Kathy Fisher is neither a delinquent nor a deprived child, but though her home is comfortable in a material sense, her parents are insensitive and lazy, and they nag at her for lying and showing off without realizing how far they are responsible for her behaviour. Bored and lonely, Kathy has come to resent the large, lively middle-class Ramsey family next door, and when the chance offers one day, she pushes off the pram with charming baby Bart in it. All she wants is to fuss over a baby and to feel that she has upset other people, and neither she nor the Ramsey children are capable of dealing with the complications that follow. It is the way they try, and especially the difference between the conscientious fears of Ellen and Neil and the gay abandon of the much younger boy and girl, that makes this such a fine story. It is an answer, really, to all the authors who confuse excitement with sensationalism and petty crime with human complexity.

There is enough drama and action in THE THURSDAY KIDNAP-PING to hold the attention of a child of ten, and plenty for an older child to ponder over. One of the difficulties facing the writer today is the question of reading ages. With some children exhausting the scope of children's books by the time they are twelve and others only getting up a reading momentum at that age, it becomes harder as time goes on to choose situations and styles to suit the apparent sophistication of the young and still to satisfy the writer's own impulses. This is particularly obvious in that abominably tricky, dangerously limited sphere, the young romance. It may be taken for granted that, with the present popularity of realistic family stories, the capricious, experimental boy-and-girl relationship will crop up everywhere. How this is to be dealt with in a story that will be read by numerous ten-year-olds is another matter. Few authors seem to feel easy about it. In NO GOING BACK, Monica Edwards introduced, tactfully and sympathetically, the dawn of affection between the Westling comrades, Tamsin Grey and Meryon Fairbrass. Now she is stuck with the situation. In three subsequent stories—THE OUTSIDER, THE HOODWINKERS and DOLPHIN SUMMER—she seems to be finding it a nuisance, to judge by the perfunctory and rather mawkish snatches of dialogue she gives to these two characters at regular intervals. This is a problem that will obviously beset any writer who starts a series and finds her characters growing up and bursting out of the confines of the family story. There can be no simple solution. Gently readable novels about girls in their late 'teens finding work and happiness under sunny skies—these are still produced in quanti-ties, and promise adult subjects only to disappoint older girls by their unfailingly juvenile approach. Better an honest adult novel than an evasive fairy-tale that purports to be about life as it really is. No doubt writers for children have always been bedevilled by the compulsion to understand their readers and the trends of the day, but I can think of no period when this was so evident as our own. A story written with the dogged intention of showing 'what modern youth is like' is not always going to be a good piece of literature.

To give an example, John Berrington, author of TO CLEAR THE RIVER, writes out of experience as a teacher. In the space of a shortish book he introduces a large cast of characters to illustrate such talking points as sex in youth, the atom bomb and industrialized society. His hero, young Tony Finley, son of a bus driver, is at a technical school. His heroine, Christine, is working for G.C.E. at a comprehensive. The young people explore their feelings for each other, argue in cafés and private houses, do their homework, help to deal with a gang of Teds, join in a C.N.D. march. This is a good-hearted attempt to reproduce the climate of our times, but as a story it never gets off the ground. Most young readers will suspect that it has been written in a spirit of moral suasion and not from the compulsion to tell a story. All the same, the author is right to direct the attention of his readers to what they *can* understand in the more difficult aspects of social life—the domestic background to any personal relationship; and there are writers who have done this with more success. Josephine Kamm, in OUT OF STEP, looks at the problem of colour in suburban society, through the story of Betty Fielding, sixteen years old, training in a London store, who falls in love with a young coloured man from British Guiana. Like any other girl of her age, Betty has no idea how closely her life is interwoven with family, friends and neighbours. This is the author's theme. Kitchen, club room, street and café, the settings are ordinary and familiar; the dialogue is natural without being over-larded with slang; the characters are well-drawn and right for their setting. This is not meant to be a treatise nor a profound character-study; it is an open-minded, honest story which satisfactorily fits a crucial problem into the technical form of a story acceptable to the young.

Children ask nowadays, it seems (and they have a right to ask), that the people in the family stories they read shall be reasonably like the people they meet in their own lives, the scenes and events not too far from those of everyday. They are asking not for realism in a superficial sense, but for reality in a form they can recognize. From Lettice Cooper's delightfully sardonic BOB-A-JOB, which will do for children as young as seven, to Hugo Charteris's CLUNIE, a girls' story most maturely conceived, the past few years have seen a great range of family stories that should satisfy these wishes, because they use, in a contemporary setting, problems and situations that are universal. All children have had the experience of learning to live in a new environment. It may be a new country. If so, they will appreciate the experience of the Dutch girl in Australia, in Richard Parker's story, THE HOUSE THAT GUILDA DREW. It may be a new school. They can read Mary Harris's subtle story, PENNY'S WAY, which takes a lively girl from primary to grammar-school. Every child has her way of retreating from difficulties. With Penny, it is painting. The associations of poetry and stories support the hero of an exceptionally interesting story by Ruth Tomalin, THE SEA MICE. Paddy Weir is sent to boarding-school when his mother has to be away from home, and a favourite book, *Tom Brown's Schooldays*, makes him eager to see what this new world has to offer. Unfortunately it offers, among other things, two old enemies from his home life, Hooky and his ferocious dog Sicker. Hooky has become the school's odd-job man, and Sicker seems to threaten not only Paddy's ankles but also his pet mouse Jan, which he keeps in the school yard. There is only one thing to do. He runs away to London, where he wanders and hides for three days in the huge news-agency building, not knowing that his journalist father is on an assignment overseas. Paddy faces a situation beyond his years with his own resources. He is haunted by his father's story of the sea-mice, the Dutch lads carried on fishing boats, and the agency building takes on the semblance of a vast ship. Then, too, he has the flexibility of a boy and his power to change mood with circumstance. He has learned from an overseas broadcast that his father may be in danger:

The sad voice was still speaking. Paddy put out his hand to get rid of it. He turned the switch again, and heard another voice—quite different: a man's voice, not sad at all, but crotchety: an actor's voice from a play. It said, '*Why* shouldn't we sit down and make ourselves comfortable?' He clicked the switch round again, and the clipped voice said, '—precisely.'

It was like a real answer; a piece of good advice. And suddenly he found that he was ravenous. He finished the ship's biscuit and cheese, gave himself a ration of chocolate, and thirstily sucked at a lemon through a hole in the rind. He remembered one of Asher's ditties:

'Julius Caesar,
Silly old geezer,
Caught his nose
In a lemon squeezer . . .'

He laughed; and in the middle of laughing he was tired, tired.

He turned off the light, lay down under his coat, and was asleep
before the clipped voice could have added more than thirty seconds
to her courteous, amiable, endless pacing in step with time.
Ruth Tomalin. THE SEA MICE (Faber, 1962) pp. 91–2.

Here is no unlikely shouldering of an adult problem; this is a true
picture of a boy. The Australian writer, Joan Phipson, has the same
probability in her stories. THE FAMILY CONSPIRACY turns on a
hackneyed situation—children (on a New South Wales sheep station)
trying to help out in a financial crisis. Because the children have the
solid reality of Nesbit or Alcott children, the situation comes to the
reader fresh, newly explored. Lorna stays in Sydney at the end of the
school term to earn money as a baby-sitter; the whole project is a
secret, so she has to put up with being misunderstood by her parents,
who think she is bored with her home. Robbie, selling rabbit-skins,
begins to look like a miser; Belinda gets eye-strain making baby-
clothes for sale and is depressed to find her standard is not high
enough. Each child finds his own level, in this book and in a sequel,
THREAT TO THE BARKERS, where they are united again in a campaign against sheep-stealers. Within an exciting and entertaining
story, the author makes shrewd comments on character in a situation
that is entirely probable, and she does this most of all in THE
BOUNDARY RIDERS, which I think is her best book so far. This is
the story of three children lost in the ranges beyond the Thompson's
boundary fence. It is also the story of fourteen-year-old Vincent
and how he loses his authority to Bobby, who is only ten. Beautifully
told, with the assurance of someone who knows the scene well and
can describe it for those who do not, this book has, finally, the
reality that comes from a straight, honest look at people.

Stories of this calibre can be set against the great children's
stories of the last century—like *The Secret Garden* or *Jan of the
Windmill* or *The Little Duke*—stories which are not for children
of X years or Y aptitude, but expandable stories for everyone.
Philippa Pearce's story, A DOG SO SMALL, is recommended, in its
paper-back edition, for children between eight and eleven, but it does
not stop here. The theme, the conquering of disappointment, can be
equated by any reader of any age with his own experience. In this
case, it is the disappointment of a boy of about ten, Ben Blewitt,
whose father works on the London Underground. Ben is a pleasant,

everyday kind of boy, who wants one thing and one thing only—a dog. He daydreams about a chihuahua who seems to follow him and know him as its master; his dream brings trouble, and brings, too, a dog of a very different kind, which he must learn to accept. This is an absolutely real family, with its affection, its squabbles, its councils and makeshifts, a family named and described and placed in a certain setting, but like every other family in the world too. Through this book, with its blithe humour and its sure handling of concrete detail, its vitality and strength, a young reader can reach out to a world bigger, richer, more interesting than his own, and yet related to it.

Many who read A DOG SO SMALL know the Thames at Westminster Bridge, but now they will see it as Ben did:

The expanse of the River reminded him conveniently of the enormous expanses of Russia, the home of the borzoi . . . The land was a level and endless white, with here and there a dark forest where wolves crouched in the daytime, to come out at night, howling and ravening. For Ben, it was daytime in Russia. Sleighs had been driven out into the snow, and left. Each sleigh was covered with a white woollen blanket to match the snow . . . Wolves came out. They were rushing past the sleighs. Men concealed in the sleighs threw back the blankets and, at the same time, unleashed their coupled borzoi dogs. Magnificent, magnificent beasts! They leapt forward after the wolves. The wolves were fast, but the borzois had greyhound bodies, their whole bodies were thin, delicately made, streamlined for speed. . . . They caught up with the wolves: one borzoi on each side of a wolf caught it and held it until the huntsman came up with his dagger—

At this point Ben always stopped, because, although you couldn't have wolves, he wasn't so keen on killing them either. Anyway, from the far side of the bridge the moon-face of Big Ben suddenly spoke to him and said half-past seven. The wolf-hunt with borzois had taken a long time. Ben Blewitt turned back from the River to go home to breakfast.

Philippa Pearce. A DOG SO SMALL (Constable, 1962) pp. 11–12.

Just so, at the end of the story. Hampstead Heath takes on another aspect as Ben calls across its darkening stretches to the gangling mongrel he has tried to lose. To each scene the author has given her own reality, and this means the reality of Ben, an ordinary boy to whom books are a passport to vividly imagined scenes of adventure that transcend real life. This story belongs very much to our own times, but its realistic details, which will date as time goes on, serve only to throw into the foreground the boy who will always seem familiar to any child who reads about him.

Drawing by Brian Wildsmith
for Véronique Day's
LANDSLIDE!
(Bodley Head)

Reading List

1.*Family stories, Family Adventure, School, Sport and Career stories*

Adema, Wim Hora. ODD GIRL OUT (1953 Holland). *Methuen* 1962.
Translated by Arnold J. Pomerans. Illustrated by Elisabeth Grant. A Dutch girl at school and a new, more prosperous friend from France; a natural and perceptive story.

Armstrong, Richard. OUT OF THE SHALLOWS 1961, TRIAL TRIP 1962. *Dent.*
Illustrated by D. G. Valentine. Two stories of young Merchant Navy apprentices learning the hard way on their first ships. Fast-moving, shrewd and realistic. (See also p. 222.)

Bateman, Robert. YOUNG SKATER 1961, YOUNG BOXER 1962, YOUNG CYCLIST 1962. *Constable.* Technical detail combined with a well-told story of contemporary life. (See also p. 290.)

*Bateman, Robert. TV REPORTER. *Brockhampton* 1963. Illustrated by James Russell.

Baudouy, Michel-Aimé. MICK AND THE P.105 (1959 France). *Bodley Head* 1961. Translated by Marie Ponsot. Illustrated by Robert Micklewright. Problems of class and of mechanics (including the restoration of a 20-year-old motorbike) combine in an exciting story.

*Berna, Paul. FLOOD WARNING (1960 France). *Bodley Head* 1962. Translated by John Buchanan-Brown. Illustrated by Charles Keeping.

*Berrington, John. TO CLEAR THE RIVER. *Heinemann* 1964.

*Bourguignon, Michel. LINE OF ATTACK (1958 France). *Bodley Head* 1959. Translated by John Buchanan-Brown. Illustrated by Geraldine Spence.

Buckingham, M. E. ODD BOY OUT. *Faber* 1963. Illustrated by Mary Watt. Chronicle centring round George Clyde, his dog Shuffleboots, his friend Mad Malcolm the naturalist and his Scottish home. Spontaneous, amusing and perceptive.

Canfield, Dorothy. BETSY (1916 U.S.A. as UNDERSTOOD BETSY). *Bodley Head* 1962. Illustrated by Heather Copley. One of the best family stories ever written. A cosseted little girl learns to enjoy life on a farm in Vermont more than half a century ago.

*Charteris, Hugo. CLUNIE. *Heinemann* 1963. Illustrated by Victor Ambrus.

Clarke, Pauline. KEEP THE POT BOILING. *Faber* 1961. Illustrated by Cecil Leslie. The Carlisle children have to make money quickly: a lively episodic tale of a middle-class family who supply their own amusements in life.

Cleary, Beverly. FIFTEEN (1956 U.S.A.). *Penguin* (Peacock Books) 1962. A fifteen-year-old girl in an American town and her first romance. Touching and true to life, the portrait of an individual.

Corbin, William, HIGH ROAD HOME (1954 U.S.A.). *Methuen* 1962. Illustrated by Reg Gray. A French boy wanders across the Middle West to avoid an adoption which turns out well in the end. A vivid procession of places and people.

Ćurčija-Prodanović, Nada. BALLERINA. *O.U.P.* 1961. Illustrated by Dušan Ristić. Beautifully written story, authentic in detail, about a girl from the provinces making a difficult start at the State Ballet School in Belgrade.

*Day, Véronique. LANDSLIDE! (1958 France). *Bodley Head* 1961. Translated by Margaret Morgan. Illustrated by Brian Wildsmith.

Duncan, Jane. CAMERONS IN THE HILLS. *Macmillan* 1963. Illustrated by Victor Ambrus. Relaxed, vivid story of children visiting an aunt in the Highlands; adventures with a crashed aeroplane, a lost baby and a severe snowstorm. (See also p. 343.)

*Edwards, Monica. NO GOING BACK 1960, THE OUTSIDER 1961, THE HOODWINKERS 1962, DOLPHIN SUMMER 1963. *Collins.* Illustrated by Geoffrey Whittam. (See also p. 194.)

Enright, Elizabeth. RETURN TO GONE-AWAY (1961 U.S.A.). *Heinemann* 1962. Illustrated by Beth and Joe Krush. American children return to that best of playgrounds, a deserted house. (See also p. 291.)

Finlay, Winifred. ALISON IN PROVENCE. *Harrap* 1963. Illustrated by J. S. Goodall. Au-pair girl, confronted with the social complexities of another country, finds romance after misunderstanding. Warm-hearted, mature.

Forest, Antonia. PETER'S ROOM. *Faber* 1961. The younger Marlows, imitating the Brontës, begin a romantic saga in collaboration and find themselves carried away by it. An unusual study of character. (See also pp. 192, 267.)

*Forest, Antonia. THE THURSDAY KIDNAPPING. *Faber* 1963.

Freeman, Barbara. A BOOK BY GEORGINA. *Faber* 1962. Illustrated by the author. Attractive story of two sisters finding out the history of an old house in their home town.

Friermood, Elisabeth Hamilton. THE LUCK OF DAPHNE TOLLIVER (1961 U.S.A.). *Constable* 1963. Family chronicle starting before World War 1, and giving an equally good picture of young people and the Indiana background of their joys and difficulties.

Garnett, Eve. HOLIDAY AT THE DEWDROP INN. *Heinemann* 1962. Illustrated by the author. Kate Ruggles recovers from measles in a village where a flower-show, a concert, a naughty small boy and a smug small girl keep her busy. Gently humorous. (See also p. 292.)

Garnett, Richard. THE SILVER KINGDOM 1956, illustrated by Jane Dickins. THE WHITE DRAGON 1963, illustrated by Graham Oakley. *Hart-Davis.* Mark Rutter helps to make archaeological discoveries off the Cornish coast and in the Fen country. Exceptionally vivid, varied and exciting.

Gibson, Michael. LE MANS 24 HOURS. *Brockhampton* 1962. Illustrated by John Ross. A lad unexpectedly gets the chance to drive for a British team in the celebrated race. Sensible, factual and extremely exciting.

Godden, Rumer. MISS HAPPINESS AND MISS FLOWER 1961, LITTLE PLUM 1963. *Macmillan.* Illustrated by Jean Primrose. Japanese dolls are the means by which two cousins, Nona and Belinda, learn to understand a little about people and their ways. Stories full of wit, artistry and tenderness.

Guillot, René. THREE GIRLS AND A SECRET (1960 France). *Harrap* 1963. Translated by Joan Selby-Lowndes. Illustrated by Jane Paton. Three friends in Paris keep house and mind a lost baby in a building due for demolition. Sharp domestic detail and a warmly sympathetic tone.

*Harris, Mary K. PENNY'S WAY. *Faber,* 1963. Illustrated by Sheila Rose.

Hewett, Anita. THE ELWORTHY CHILDREN. *Bodley Head* 1963. Illustrated by Margery Gill. A family in the 1920's, with a new car and a plan for a picnic that is frustrated by all sorts of domestic crises. Charming, quiet style and illustrations.

Hildick, E. W. BIRDY JONES. *Faber* 1963. Something new in reading for the backward boy of fourteen or so; a swashbuckling farce about two boys from a secondary modern school who go to London to seek their fortune, as a pop-whistler and his manager.

Hildick, E. W. JIM STARLING TAKES OVER. *Blond Educational* 1963. Illustrated by Roger Payne. The gang in a competition to turn an initial 2/6 into the largest possible sum. Simple reading and simple arithmetic, but the author's craftsmanship means no feeling of impoverishment in style or characterization. (See also p. 192.)

Hope-Simpson, Jacynth. YOUNG NETBALL PLAYER. *Constable* 1961. The author shows that an orthodox girls' school story can be interesting in action and characterization.

*Houghton, Eric. SUMMER SILVER. *Oliver and Boyd* 1963. Illustrated by Shirley Hughes.

Huddy, Delia. JANE PLAYS HOCKEY. *Constable* 1963. Behind accurate details of sport lies a sympathetic study of a girl from a poor home learning to get on with girls of very different backgrounds. Especially good dialogue.

Inyart, Gene. TENT UNDER THE SPIDER TREE (1959 U.S.A.). *World's Work* 1961. Illustrated by Carol Beech. Camping in Illinois. Nothing much happens, but the story has the sophisticated wit that can be so attractive in American stories of young people and their enterprises.

Jenkins, Alan. PAULO AND THE WOLF. *Oliver and Boyd* 1963. Illustrated by Margery Gill. A family of charcoal-burners in southern France, a marauding wolf, a boy taking on adult responsibilities. Exceptionally attractive setting and style.

Kalnay, Francis. THE RICHEST BOY IN THE WORLD (1959 U.S.A.). *Methuen* 1962. Illustrated by W. T. Mars. An institute for underprivileged boys, in Hungary, and a boy who learns that to be rich (if only in a currency of marbles) is not necessarily to be happy. Unforgettably vivid and true to life.

*Kamm, Josephine. OUT OF STEP. *Brockhampton* 1962. Illustrated by Jillian Willett.

Konttinen, Aili. KIRSTI COMES HOME (1959 Finland). *Methuen* 1961. Translated by Oliver Coburn and Ursula Lehrburger. Illustrated by Faith

Jaques. Subtle, gently humorous story about a child evacuated from a small farm in Finland to a rich Swedish house, and finding it hard to adjust herself to her family again.

Ladébat, Monique P. de. THE VILLAGE THAT SLEPT (1961 France). *Bodley Head* 1963. Translated by Thelma Niklaus. Illustrated by Margery Gill. A boy, a girl and a baby, sole survivors of an air crash, make a world for themselves in a deserted mountain village. Forceful in domestic detail and insight into character.

Lavolle, L. N. NUNO (1959 France). *U.L.P.* 1962. Translated by James Kirkup. Illustrated by Hans Schwarz. Boy in a fishing village in Portugal, bent on taking the place of his dead fisherman father but forced to take a job in a draper's shop. A melodramatic ending does not spoil the steady veracity of the book.

*Loeff, Rutgers van der. AVALANCHE (See p. 269.)

Lynch, Patricia. RYAN'S FORT. *Dent* 1961. Illustrated by Elisabeth Grant. A travelling family makes a home in a deserted stone hut; domestic effort and happiness described with the immediacy of a true story-teller.

MacGibbon, Jean. PAM PLAYS DOUBLES. *Constable* 1962. A level-headed story of sport, romance and clash of character, in a suburban setting.

MacGibbon, Jean. THE RED SLEDGE 1962, THE VIEW-FINDER 1963. *Hamish Hamilton*. Illustrated by Janet Duchesne. Brother and sister in convincing situations, helping old people in a snow-bound Yorkshire and contending with an unpleasant gang of boys on Hampstead Heath. Good style and perceptive view of children.

Mayne, William. THE CHANGELING. *O.U.P.* 1961. Illustrated by Victor Ambrus. Miss Durnthwaite's past is linked with a deserted garden-house and when three children find and re-furbish it, the years her memory has lost come rolling back. One of Mayne's strangest plots, with finely visualized village background and characters to make it plausible.

*Mayne, William. A PARCEL OF TREES. *Penguin* (Puffin Original) 1963. Illustrated by Margery Gill.

Mayne, William. SUMMER VISITORS. *O.U.P.* 1961. Illustrated by William Stobbs. Boy from an industrial town joins the school's summer camp in Yorkshire and sees something of country ways and people. Impeccable style, subtle images of farm, field and fell.

Mayne, William. THE TWELVE DANCERS. *Hamish Hamilton* 1962. Illustrated by Lynton Lamb. An old cup and an old custom in a remote part of the Severn Valley; a girl and her mother help to work out a fascinating puzzle.

Mayne, William. WORDS AND MUSIC. *Hamish Hamilton* 1963. Illustrated by
Lynton Lamb. Another story of the choir school, in which Owen and his
friends help homesick boy to settle down and track down a centuries-old
ghost. (See also p. 193.)

Morris, Ruth. THE RUNAWAY. *Michael Joseph* 1961. A twelve-year-old girl
wanders through Australian back-country with an old hack, and finds
many good friends. Supremely authentic in atmosphere and characters.

Morrow, Charlotte. THE WATCHERS. *Hutchinson* 1963. Illustrated by Brian
Wildsmith. Children roaming Suffolk marshes on foot and by bicycle,
involved with a derelict engine on a branch line and a mysterious man with
field-glasses. Vividly and unusually well-written.

Nordstrom, Ursula. THE SECRET LANGUAGE (1960 U.S.A.). *Methuen* 1961.
Illustrated by Mary Chalmers. Little girls at a boarding-school, their games,
alliances and troubles. Charming and delicately written.

Nortje, P. H. THE GREEN ALLY (1960 South Africa). *O.U.P.* 1963. Translated
by Jean Beynon. Illustrated by William Papas. A group of children earn
money so that a needy comrade can go to grammar-school. Afrikaans and
English children in a Cape setting brilliantly visualized.

O'Farrell, Kathleen. NUMBER ONE VICTORIA TERRACE. *Blackie* 1962.
Illustrated by Shirley Hughes. Cherry from a London back street goes to
visit grand relations in the country. Sound comments on children and their
unsuspected fund of common sense and good-will: an entertaining story.

Park, Ruth. THE HOLE IN THE HILL. *Constable* 1962. Illustrated by Jennifer
Murray. Two children in the North Island of New Zealand learn to get on
with the Maoris of their neighbourhood and find a unique relic of their
ancestors. Good use of setting.

*Parker, Richard. THE HOUSE THAT GUILDA DREW. *Brockhampton* (Brock
Books) 1963. Illustrated by Prudence Seward.

Parker, Richard. A VALLEY FULL OF PIPERS. *Gollancz* 1962. Illustrated by
Richard Kennedy. Forthright story of a family in Tasmania with a long-
standing feud involving young and old.

*Pearce, Philippa. A DOG SO SMALL. *Constable* 1962. Illustrated by Antony
Maitland

*Phipson, Joan. THE BOUNDARY RIDERS 1962, THE FAMILY CONSPIRACY
1962, THREAT TO THE BARKERS 1963. *Constable* and *Angus and
Robertson*. Illustrated by Margaret Horder.

*Porter, Sheena. THE BRONZE CHRYSANTHEMUM 1961, illustrated by Shirley
Hughes. HILLS AND HOLLOWS 1962, JACOB'S LADDER 1963, illustrated
by Victor Ambrus. *O.U.P.*

Reid, Meta Mayne. SANDY AND THE HOLLOW BOOK. *Faber* 1961. Illustrated by Richard Kennedy. Archaeologist's daughter involved in mystery of a stone figurine that seems to have a strange power. (See also p. 372.)

Reid, Meta Mayne. THE TOBERMILLIN ORACLE. *Faber* 1962. Illustrated by Richard Kennedy. Tiffany the cat brings magic to help the unknown girl who has lost her memory. A distinguished time-fantasy. (See also p. 151.)

Richardson, Henry Handel. THE GETTING OF WISDOM. *Heinemann* (1911) 1961. Illustrated by Kay Dattner. Classic story of country girl sent to boarding-school in Melbourne; an unforgettable picture of growing up.

Roberts, Daniel. MARMOT VALLEY. *O.U.P.* 1962. Illustrated by M. A. Charlton. Group of children, French, Swiss and visiting English, work to save a Swiss valley from developers.

Selby-Lowndes, Joan. FAMILY STAR. *Collins* 1961. Illustrated by Dick Hart. Working class family at home, and one member of it (and an old horse) rehearsing for a pantomime. Good details of back-stage; warm-hearted tone.

Smith, Emma. OUT OF HAND. *Macmillan* 1963. Illustrated by Antony Maitland. Guerilla warfare between independent children and repressive grown-ups. Set in Wales; an unusual and absorbing story.

Smith, Eunice Young. THE JENNIFER WISH (1949 U.S.A.) 1959, THE JENNIFER GIFT (1949 U.S.A.) 1960, THE JENNIFER PRIZE (1951 U.S.A.) 1960, JENNIFER IS ELEVEN (1952 U.S.A.) 1961, JENNIFER DANCES (1954 U.S.A.) 1963. *Edmund Ward.* A little girl before World War I, in Chicago and on a farm; pleasant domestic tales, simply written.

*Southall, Ivan. HILLS END. *Angus and Robertson* 1962. Illustrated.

Spykman, E. C. TERRIBLE, HORRIBLE EDIE (1960 U.S.A.). *Macmillan* 1961. The Cares family again; eccentric view of a pack of wildly individual American children. (See also p. 294.)

Streatfeild, Noel. APPLE BOUGH. *Collins* 1962. Illustrated by Margery Gill. An unconventional family, steeped in the love and practice of music, and especially Myra, who longs for domestic security and peace.

Streatfeild, Noel. NEW TOWN. *Collins* 1960. Illustrated by Shirley Hughes. The Bell family leave St Mark's Vicarage for what seems a far less congenial place, and come to like it.

Stucley, Elizabeth. SPRINGFIELD HOME. *Bodley Head* 1961. Illustrated by Charles Mozley. A girl and a boy, brought up in a children's home, find a new life and new friends; a warm study of a variety of people.

Taylor, Sydney. ALL-OF-A-KIND FAMILY (1951 U.S.A.). *Blackie* 1961. Illustrated by Helen John. A richly-varied chronicle of a Jewish family in East Side New York.

*Tomalin, Ruth. THE SEA MICE. *Faber* 1962. Illustrated by Sheila Rose.

Treadgold, Mary. THE WINTER PRINCESS. *Brockhampton* 1962. Illustrated by Pearl Falconer. Attractive story, with an element of mystery. Three girls and a boy visit an old lady at Hampton Court and hear about her life.

Trease, Geoffrey. CHANGE AT MAYTHORN. *Heinemann* 1962. Illustrated by Robert Hodgson. This lively book continues the adventures of Mike and his friend Sandra in a west country town; vividly topical in scenes of home and school. (See also p. 295.)

Unnerstad, Edith. THE SPETTECAKE HOLIDAY (1956 Sweden). *Michael Joseph* 1959. Translated by Lilian Seaton. Illustrated by Iben Claute. A boy of six stays with his grandmother in South Sweden; a happy mixture of fireside tales, friendly animals and country air.

Unnerstad, Edith. GRANDMOTHER'S JOURNEY (1959 Sweden). *Michael Joseph* 1960. Translated by Lilian Seaton. Illustrated by Claes Bäckström. The craft of hair-weaving illustrated in a story of an old woman's journey to find work: an enchantingly human tale.

Unnerstad, Edith. A JOURNEY IN ENGLAND (1960 Sweden). *Michael Joseph* 1962. Translated by Lilian Seaton. Illustrated by Ulla Sundin-Wickman. A tale of eighty years ago, when a boy and a girl from southern Sweden wander through the Cotswolds looking for their mother, who has been working in England. A touching story with a surprising end.

Unnerstad, Edith. THE SAUCEPAN JOURNEY (1949 Sweden). *Michael Joseph* 1962. Translated by Lilian Seaton. Illustrated by Iben Claute. Riotous adventures of the large Larsson family journeying from Stockholm to Norrköping in beer-wagons turned into caravans, and selling, by the way, an experimental whistling saucepan.

Ware, Jean. ROWDY HOUSE. *Faber* 1961. A girl of thirteen growing up in the happy but frustrating atmosphere of an energetic, noisy family.

*Wayne, Jenifer. THE DAY THE CEILING FELL DOWN 1961, THE NIGHT THE RAIN CAME IN 1963. *Heinemann*. Illustrated by Dodie Masterman.

Wayne, Jenifer. KITCHEN PEOPLE. *Heinemann* 1963. Illustrated by Margaret Palmer. A lost Strad, a large old house, a visiting family almost too much for an elderly bachelor uncle. Entertaining and well-turned.

*Weir, Rosemary. WHAT A LARK 1961, SOAP-BOX DERBY 1962. *Brockhampton*. Illustrated by B. S. Biro.

West, Joyce. CAPE LOST 1963, THE YEAR OF THE SHINING CUCKOO 1963. *Dent*. Illustrated by the author. New Zealand sheep country forms a well-described background for family stories in which adult and youthful problems intertwine very naturally.

*Willard, Barbara. THE SUMMER WITH SPIKE. *Constable* 1961. Illustrated
by Anne Linton.

Willard, Barbara. HETTY. *Constable* 1962. Illustrated by Pamela Mara.
Tells about a little girl whose father keeps a draper's shop seventy years
ago, and her part in the family vicissitudes.

Willard, Barbara. THE BATTLE OF WEDNESDAY WEEK. *Constable* 1963.
Illustrated by Douglas Hall. An English widow with two children marries
an American widower with four; an interesting situation which the author
explores with humour and understanding.

Willson, Robina Beckles. LEOPARDS ON THE LOIRE. *Gollancz* 1961. Illustrated
by Gwyneth Cole. A SERAPH IN A BOX. *Hart-Davis* 1963. Illustrated by
Victor Ambrus. Interlinked stories about a boy and his adopted sister and
their life with amateur music: humour and mystery and technical detail.

Wilson, Barbara Ker. LAST YEAR'S BROKEN TOYS. *Constable* 1962. Four
girls in a provincial town whose lives are given a new course by World
War II. Well documented, and mature enough to satisfy older girls.

Woodberry, Joan. RAFFERTY RIDES A WINNER 1961, RAFFERTY MAKES A
LANDFALL 1962. *Parrish*. Illustrated by the author. More cheerful adventures
of the Australian boy. (See also p. 295.)

Wrightson, Patricia. THE ROCKS OF HONEY. *Angus and Robertson* 1961.
Illustrated by Margaret Horder. Richly-imagined story of a boy on an
Australian farm, how he comes to understand the aborigine way of life
through his new friend Eustace and through the search for an ancient stone
axe. Wonderful background.

Wrightson, Patricia. THE FEATHER STAR. *Hutchinson* 1962. Illustrated by
Noella Young. A girl, on holiday at the sea in New South Wales, growing
into an awareness of other people's lives; an appealing and wise story.

2.*Junior Family Stories* (*well suited to children between six and nine*)

Almedingen, E. M. ONE LITTLE TREE. *Parrish* 1963. Illustrated by the author.
The Russian Revolution and a family on the Finnish border whose
Christmas was threatened.

Briggs, Raymond. SLEDGES TO THE RESCUE. *Hamish Hamilton* (Antelope
Books) 1963. Illustrated by the author. Tim and Mary help the milkman
on a snowy Christmas morning; lively text and pictures.

Carlson, Natalie Savage. THE HAPPY ORPHELINE 1960, A BROTHER FOR
THE ORPHELINES 1961, A PET FOR THE ORPHELINES 1963. *Blackie*.
Illustrated by Pearl Falconer. Happy, idiosyncratic tales of an orphanage
in Paris, with sharply-defined characters and delicate drawings.

Clarke, Pauline. JAMES THE POLICEMAN 1957, JAMES AND THE ROBBERS 1959, JAMES AND THE SMUGGLERS 1961, JAMES AND THE BLACK VAN 1963. *Hamish Hamilton* (Antelope Books). Illustrated by Cecil Leslie. Compact, active stories for all children who like to play a grown-up role.

*Cockett, Mary. COTTAGE BY THE LOCK. *Methuen* 1962. Illustrated by Shirley Hughes. (See also p. 48.)

Cooper, Lettice. BLACKBERRY'S KITTEN. *Brockhampton* 1961. Illustrated by Mary Shillabeer. Crisply and sympathetically written, the story of a domestic problem happily solved.

*Cooper, Lettice. BOB-A-JOB. *Brockhampton* 1963. Illustrated by Mary Dinsdale.

Cresswell, Helen. JUMBO SPENCER. *Brockhampton* (Brock Books) 1963. Illustrated by Clixby Watson. Vigorous, amusing tale of a young Napoleon who sets out to put his village on the map.

Dehn, Olive. THE CARETAKERS 1960, THE CARETAKERS AND THE POACHER 1961, THE CARETAKERS AND THE GIPSY 1962. *Burke* (Wren Books). Illustrated by Dorothy Clark. Adventures of the Meredith children whose mother looks after the Big House in a village where plenty happens; good family atmosphere, especially in dialogue.

*Dillon, Eilís. A PONY AND TRAP. *Hamish Hamilton* (Antelope Books) 1962. Illustrated by Monica Brasier-Creagh.

Gebhardt, Hertha von. THE RIVER POST (1956 Germany). *Burke* (Wren Books) 1961. Translated and adapted by Oliver Coburn and Ursula Lehrburger. Illustrated by Irene Schreiber. How three boys send messages in bottles from an island in the river and how they are answered. Delightfully vivid description of a village and of inventive children.

*Groves-Raines, Antony. THE TIDY HEN (1953 U.S.A.). *World's Work* 1961. Illustrated by the author.

Hawthorne, Jennie. DAVID AND THE PENNY RED. *Harrap* (Flying Foal Books) 1962. Illustrated by Geoffrey Fletcher. Excitements that result from a stamp collection and a boy's first auction sale. Good domestic detail.

Hope-Simpson, Jacynth. DANGER ON THE LINE. *Hamish Hamilton* (Antelope Books) 1962. Illustrated by Janet Duchesne. A crowd of prep-school boys use Hobbies Thursday for their narrow-gauge railway; lively and amusing.

*Mayne, William. THE LAST BUS. *Hamish Hamilton* (Antelope Books) 1962. Illustrated by Margery Gill.

Mayne, William. ON THE STEPPING STONES. *Hamish Hamilton* (Antelope Books) 1963. Illustrated by Prudence Seward. A vivid glimpse of three little girls watching a river flood and how Grandpa manages his horse and cart.

Mayne, William. PLOT NIGHT. *Hamish Hamilton* (Reindeer Books) 1963. Illustrated by Janet Duchesne. A gang of children collecting material for Guy Fawkes Night and looking for somewhere to have their bonfire; good study of individual children.

Mayne, William. THE MAN FROM THE NORTH POLE. *Hamish Hamilton* (Antelope Books) 1963. Illustrated by Prudence Seward. Yorkshire under snow, and three little boys who help a stranger (with a red costume and beard) to find his way.

Morgan, Helen. MEET MARY KATE. *Faber* 1963. Illustrated by Shirley Hughes. Charming vignettes of a little girl of four with her cat and dog, her toys and parents.

Oterdahl, Jeanna. APRIL ADVENTURE (1958 Sweden). *Macmillan* 1963. Translated by Annabelle MacMillan. Illustrated by Birgitta Nordenskjöld. A little girl visits a great-aunt who understands the delights of cooking, turning out drawers and listening to stories.

Peterson, Hans. MAGNUS AND THE SQUIRREL (1956 Sweden) 1960, translated by Madeleine Hamilton. MAGNUS AND THE VAN HORSE (1957 Sweden) 1961, MAGNUS IN THE HARBOUR (1958 Sweden) 1962, translated by Marianne Turner. *Burke* (Wren Books). Illustrated by Ilon Wikland. Brisk, amusing tales of a small boy who lives in an apartment-house in Gothenburg and has many friends and adventures.

Pudney, John. THE HARTWARP LIGHT RAILWAY 1962, THE HARTWARP DUMP 1962, THE HARTWARP CIRCUS 1963, THE HARTWARP BALLOON 1963. *Hamish Hamilton* (Reindeer Books). Illustrated by Eccles Williams. A village where some peculiar people live, including Olly Took and his brother the Gaffer, who run a narrow-gauge railway and transform the life of lonely young Charley.

Pullein-Thompson, Diana. THE HIDDEN RIVER. *Hamish Hamilton* (Reindeer Books) 1960. Illustrated by Sheila Rose. A small boy on a visit in Kentish Town determines to find the old River Fleet; the author makes good use of a London setting.

Rongen, Bjørn. OLAF AND THE ECHOING CAVE (1956 Norway). *Methuen* 1962. Translated by Evelyn Ramsden. Illustrated by Ilon Wikland. Grandmother tells a family anecdote about a small goatherd trapped in a cave by a landslide during a thunderstorm; a gentle, repetitive style gives a homely fireside appeal.

Storr, Catherine. LUCY 1961, LUCY RUNS AWAY 1962. *Bodley Head* (Acorn Library). Illustrated by Dick Hart. Stories of a tomboy and her exploits; subtle and well written.

Treece, Henry. THE JET BEADS. *Brockhampton* (Brock Books) 1961.
Illustrated by W. A. Sillince. A boy concerned with the 11-plus is involved
unexpectedly with other people's problems; an experiment in plain, realistic
writing that really comes off, because of the author's humour and keenness
of observation.

*Willard, Barbara. THE PENNY PONY. *Hamish Hamilton* (Antelope Books)
1961. Illustrated by Juliette Palmer.

Williams, Ursula Moray. BEWARE OF THIS ANIMAL. *Hamish Hamilton*
(Reindeer Books) 1963. Illustrated by Jane Paton. A billy-goat terrorizes
the village and gets young George into trouble: a lively story full of realistic
touches.

Wölfel, Ursula. TIM FIRESHOE (1961 Germany). *O.U.P.* 1963. Translated by
E. M. Prince. Illustrated by Annette Macarthur-Onslow. A fat boy, much
teased at school, goes on a walking holiday with his father and learns to
take things as they come. A charming tale with considerable point.

3.*Children and Crooks*

Andrew, Prudence. GINGER OVER THE WALL 1962, GINGER AND BATTY
BILLY 1963. *Lutterworth*. Illustrated by Charles Mozley. An alert cockney
boy involved with small-time crooks, in London and in Wales. Fascinating
characters and settings, excellent prose.

Berna, Paul. THE MYSTERY OF SAINT-SALGUE (1962 France). *Bodley Head*
1963. Translated by John Buchanan-Brown. Illustrated by Robert Broomfield. The Louvigny gang, much older now, are travelling to southern
France in search of a lost village, but meet with some opposition. (See also
p. 266.)

Bonzon, Paul-Jacques. THE GOLD CROSS OF SANTA ANNA (1960 France).
U.L.P. 1962. Translated by Thelma Niklaus. Illustrated by Margery Gill.
A miscarriage of justice is put right with the help of a brave boy. Fine
setting on the mountain border of France and Italy.

Bonzon, Paul-Jacques. THE FRIENDS OF CROIX-ROUSSE (1961 France).
U.L.P. 1963. Translated by Godfrey Burston. Illustrated by Geraldine
Spence. A boy, come from Provence to Lyons, loses his dog and finds both
crooks and good friends. Domestic affection and street adventure nicely
blended.

Brunner, Fritz. TROUBLE IN BRUSADA (1960 Switzerland). *U.L.P.* 1962.
Translated by James Kirkup. Illustrated by Klaus Brunner. An unusual
plot involving local history, afforestation and nature reserves, with good
characterization and an interesting setting in southern Switzerland.

Chauncy, Nan. THE ROARING 40. *O.U.P.* 1963. Illustrated by Annette Macarthur-Onslow. Badge Larenny, travelling to Tasmania's West Coast with his father, finds a new friend and sees an old wrong righted. A story that goes deep. (See also p. 291.)

Dawson, Mitchell. THE QUEEN OF TRENT. *Abelard-Schuman* 1961. Illustrated by Charles Keeping. Two children, who stow away on a narrow-boat, journey on the canal and are involved in the theft of a secret invention. Superb characterization and setting and very natural dialogue.

Duncan, Jane. CAMERONS ON THE TRAIN. *Macmillan* 1963. Illustrated by Victor Ambrus. Witty, racy story of children doing some amateur detection in the Highlands when saboteurs have designs on an experimental aerodrome. (See also p. 332.)

Edwin, Maribel. THE HIDDEN HOUSE. *Nelson* 1963. Illustrated by Prue Theobalds. A Scottish estate threatened by drifting sand and a pressing landlord, and children who set out to find the luck of Broom. Fine use of setting.

*Evers, L. H. THE RACKETTY STREET GANG. *Hodder and Stoughton* 1961.

Fuller, Roy. WITH MY LITTLE EYE (1948). *Penguin* (Peacock Books) 1963. Son of County Court judge does some sleuthing after a murder; a subtle and most intriguing story.

Grice, Frederick. THE MOVING FINGER. *O.U.P.* 1962. Illustrated by Joan Kiddell-Monroe. Men and boys hunting for rock-paintings on an archaeological expedition in the Sahara and foiling plot to take these from their proper place.

Hildick, E. W. JIM STARLING AND THE SPOTTED DOG. *Blond Educational* 1963. Illustrated by Roger Payne. The gang hunting for a Dalmatian and the villain who stole it from its old master. Primarily for backward readers in their early 'teens, but a story brisk enough for bright younger boys too. (See also pp. 192, 334.)

Hildick, E. W. MEET LEMON KELLY. *Cape* 1963. Illustrated by Margery Gill. A gang of youngsters, under a lively leader, come to grips with much older boys who are doing damage in a new town. Authentic in dialogue and event; good, well-constructed story.

*Hildick, E. W. MAPPER MUNDY'S TREASURE HUNT. *Blond Educational* 1963. Illustrated by John Cooper.

Hope-Simpson, Jacynth. THE MAN WHO CAME BACK. *Hamish Hamilton* 1962. Compelling tale of a feud from World War II, with an adult attitude to danger, and an interesting setting in a prep-school with children at a loose end in holiday time.

Lavolle, L. N. THE LOST LAKE (1959 France). *Abelard-Schuman* 1961.
Translated by Hugh Shelley. Illustrated by J. Daymé. In the Landes marshes,
two cousins set out to solve a family problem of land ownership, against
some opposition. Surroundings superbly described.

Mantle, Winifred. THE HIDING-PLACE. *Gollancz* 1962. Unpleasant fraud
involves a group of children who chase the crooks to the Lake District
and escape from danger with difficulty. Good characterization.

Meynell, Laurence. THE DANCERS IN THE REEDS. *Hamish Hamilton* 1963.
Thriller in Buchan idiom concerning art treasures stolen in the War. Most
exciting, subtly contrived; for older children.

Morrison, Strang. THE MONACH LIGHT. *Macmillan* 1961. Illustrated by
Drake Brookshaw. Radar station secretly installed by foreign power near a
British rocket range in the Hebrides; a group of young people on a cruise
who stumble on plot. Distinguished by seascapes and sailing technique.

Park, Ruth. THE ROAD UNDER THE SEA. *Macmillan* 1963. Illustrated by
Jennifer Murray. Adults and children join to investigate the loss of a
schooner, and expose crooks trying to steal treasures from ancient drowned
city. Exciting though improbable.

Sargent, Shirley. STOP THE TYPEWRITERS! (1963 U.S.A.). *Abelard-Schuman*
1963. Illustrated by Prue Theobalds. In an American small town, children
edit a news-sheet and frustrate land-grabbers. Unusually good dialogue and
highly individual characters.

Styles, Showell. THE LOST POTHOLE. *Brockhampton* 1961. Illustrated by
C. W. Bacon. A 'Real Life Adventure' involving a rescue and a treasure
hunt. Good background detail and characterization.

Taylor, Reginald. THE BOY FROM HACKSTON N.E. *Hamish Hamilton* 1962.
Frank study of a boy whose father is going against the law and who is
under persuasion. London setting and characters excellent.

*Townsend, John Rowe. GUMBLE'S YARD. *Hutchinson* 1961. Illustrated by
Dick Hart.

Townsend, John Rowe. HELL'S EDGE. *Hutchinson* 1963. Boy in a West Riding
town, his well-brought-up London cousin, and a lonely spinster who has
some land badly needed by the town. People and environments most
intelligently contrasted.

Verney, John. FEBRUARY'S ROAD. *Collins* 1961. Illustrated by the author.
Another adventure for the Callendars, involving spies, foreign powers and
other excitements. (See also p. 268.)

4.*Pony stories, stories of horses*

*Baxter, Gillian. JUMP TO THE STARS 1957, THE DIFFICULT SUMMER 1959,
   illustrated by Anne Gordon. THE PERFECT HORSE 1963, illustrated by
   Ivan Lapper. *Evans.*

Baxter, Gillian. THE STABLES AT HAMPTON. *Evans* 1961. Illustrated by
   Anne Gordon. A dashing cavalryman from Vienna turns an English stable
   into a school for dressage. Romantic tale with accurate technical details.

*Brims, Bernagh. RUNAWAY RIDERS. *World's Work* 1963. Illustrated by
   Juliette Palmer.

Bruns, Ursula. THE SNOW PONIES (1959 Germany). *U.L.P.* 1960. Translated
   by Katya Sheppard. Illustrated by Princess Marie Luise of Salm. Town
   boy is put through it by tough country cousins on a stud farm for Iceland
   and Shetland ponies; a fascinating story.

Griffiths, Helen. THE WILD HEART. *Hutchinson* 1963. Properly, an animal
   biography of distinction, about an ugly, fast mare whom many men on the
   South American pampa try to tame. Superb background and knowledge of
   horses. (See also p. 65.)

*Hughes, Cledwyn. PONIES FOR CHILDREN. *Routledge* 1962.

Kalashnikoff, Nicholas. JUMPER (1944 U.S.A.). *O.U.P.* 1963. Illustrated by
   Victor Ambrus. Fine picture of old Russia and its changing pattern, and a
   horse before and during World War I.

Leitch, Patricia. JANET YOUNG RIDER. *Constable* 1963. A girl working in a
   riding-stable, and a difficult horse. Exceptional character interest as well as
   good technical details.

Patchett, Mary Elwyn. THE BRUMBY 1958, illustrated by Juliet McLeod.
   COME HOME BRUMBY 1961, CIRCUS BRUMBY 1962, illustrated by Stuart
   Tresilian. *Lutterworth.* Interlinked stories, set in Australia, about a boy and
   his father and their horses of Lipizzaner stock.

Peel, Hazel M. PILOT THE HUNTER 1962, PILOT THE CHASER 1964. *Harrap.*
   Stories of Ann Barton and her gelding, whose training culminates in the
   National. Interesting in detail and sensibly presented.

*Pullein-Thompson, Christine. THE LOST PONY 1959, illustrated by Sheila
   Rose. THE EMPTY FIELD 1961, illustrated by Anne Bullen. THE OPEN
   GATE 1962, illustrated by Barbara Crocker. FOR WANT OF A SADDLE 1963
   illustrated by Anne Bullen. *Burke.*

*Treadgold, Mary. THE HERON RIDE 1962, RETURN TO THE HERON 1963.
   Cape. Illustrated by Victor Ambrus.

Chapter 17 | *Standards and Achievements*
1961–1964

Facts worked upon by imagination are at the back of any story, and it is well for the state of children's literature that the distinction between fiction and non-fiction is not really clear-cut. The many children who want to find out about the last war, for instance, may be as well satisfied by a story as by something more directly informative, when the story is as good as László Hámori's DANGEROUS JOURNEY, or Karl Bruckner's uncompromising picture of a family in Hiroshima, THE DAY OF THE BOMB. Each of these authors has documentary evidence behind the incidents he uses—and in the case of Hámori, personal experience of escape from Hungary. Each is dominated by a sense of compassion, but never mastered by it; these are not sentimental tracts disguised as fiction, but stories well written, properly constructed and presenting believable characters. During the last few years it seems that the classic adventure story, with its mature themes and mature heroes, has given ground to the war story. It is true that classic adventure belongs properly to adult fiction (and nearly always did until the 1930's). Boys and girls in their 'teens can look to adult authors like H. E. Bates and Nevil Shute and Hammond Innes to take them into worlds of adventure. Jack Schaefer's SHANE AND OTHER STORIES is an adult volume, and a fine one; it has recently been published, unaltered, in a series for children. Eilís Dillon's tales for children, which transport young readers so thoroughly to the Atlantic coast of Ireland, could well be adult novels, if it were not for a certain simplification of motive.

For those awkward years between twelve and fifteen, all the same, stories about the war have a special appeal, as recent history that involved the generation before, and the theme of a young person proving his worth through adversity is readily transplanted from the exotic regions of Africa or the South Pacific to the battlegrounds of

Europe or Asia. Richard Armstrong has never used this theme better than in ISLAND ODYSSEY, where he tells how Stan Bryant, a Merchant Navy apprentice, is caught up in the British retreat across Crete and put to the test in desperate days of escape. And if children need to be reminded of the life of civilians in time of war, there is THE WINGED WATCHMAN by Hilda van Stockum, a touching story of a boy growing up in the country during the German occupation of Holland.

The young readers of the last century expected their story books to contain a lesson, whether it was about nature or the behaviour of man, and no writer of today need be ashamed of an educational purpose so long as literary standards are not forgotten. The blurring of the distinction between fiction and exposition is noticeable in many new stories about the children of other lands. Now that educationists and parents are increasingly anxious that children should think internationally, it is not surprising that there should be an increase in stories like Andrée Clair's BEMBA, which shows a West African village in transition between superstition and science, or Shirley Arora's WHAT THEN, RAMAN?, which describes how an Indian lad learns to use his schooling to help his friends, or the appealing stories by Aimée Sommerfelt, THE ROAD TO AGRA and THE WHITE BUNGALOW, which bring everyday life in India nearer to our own. The description of a foreign country and proper human problems are combined in a natural way, in these books, within a well-told story. The increasingly high standard of books like these may force improvement on that awkward travel-cum-story formula that has too often imposed mediocre reading on children in the name of education. Certainly there are signs that writers are trying to make the fictional side of such books more convincing; Betty Cavanna's PEPE OF ARGENTINA and PAULO OF BRAZIL, and the charming commentary in Peter Buckley's DIMITRIOS, BOY OF GREECE are notable in this respect.

The past three years have seen also a striking rise in the general standard of historical stories, where writers face this same problem of enlivening fact with imagination. I do not believe that children are as much obsessed by fact as we are sometimes asked to believe. I talked recently with two average schoolboys who had enjoyed their first sample of historical fiction because, they said, they liked the way the hero had to decide between one kind of life and another. The

Drawing by Victor Ambrus for Rosemary Manning's ARRIPAY (Constable)

book was Rosemary Manning's ARRIPAY. The period of this book is the early fifteenth century, the place Poole Harbour in Dorset, and the character who provides the title is Harry Paye, appointed Vice-Admiral of the Cinque Ports by Henry IV and carrying out his duties mainly by piratically attacking French and Spanish ships. The dilemma of Adam Morden, round which the book turns, is one that could belong to any period. Adam might well sail with Harry Paye, as his father and brothers have done, but his mother has destined him for the church. Adam frets against the discipline of learning, but when he finally joins the pirate, he is sickened by the realities of fighting. Throughout a rousing story, the author keeps the emphasis on Adam's perplexities, and so far prepares the ground that we can accept his final decision to be a swanherd at Abbotsbury. A fine prose style and a mature outlook distinguish this book from many others with a similar theme. The message is clear enough for the young reader of today, but the author has felt herself (as well as researched herself) into the past, and with well-placed period details she takes us there with her. Family loyalties are involved also in Hester

Burton's TIME OF TRIAL, a story, again, conceived in a mature spirit. Here is Margaret Pargeter living in London, near St Paul's, at the opening of the last century. Like any other girl in her 'teens, she would like to spend her life in harmony with her neighbours and be free to muse about the man she loves—Robert Kerridge, a medical student who had once lived with the family. But Margaret's father is a reformer. He expresses his concern for the ragged poor of his district in a pamphlet denouncing rent-racking landlords. He is imprisoned for sedition, and Margaret's courage is taxed by the months that follow, when she has to live frugally in a Suffolk village and stand against the hostility of Robert's intolerant parents. This could be any girl embarrassed to the point of danger by a parent's actions, but respecting him for them: as the author presents her, she is also very much a girl of Regency London. Anyone who reads this story can feel a bond with the heroine and yet, through her, can be taken into the past.

Here, as always, the author has had to take the risk that a modern point of view may not suit the setting, but the historical novel is valuable because it can suggest, in a way relevant to our own times, the movement of ideas or causes in a nation as they affect the lives of individuals. This is not necessarily done in a solemn or didactic way, and may even have a deceptive light-heartedness to decorate it. Gillian Avery's pictures of the late Victorian world reflect shrewdly the social and educational views of the time, but in a most hilarious fashion. Her three stories THE GREATEST GRESHAM, TO TAME A SISTER and THE PEACOCK HOUSE, which overlap in characters and plots, are full of absurd situations—as when Julia Gresham, so properly brought up, rides through the suburban streets on a milk-cart, in her nightgown. Like the most delightful charades, these books revive the past with few but well-used stage-properties. In THE PEACOCK HOUSE, for example, these include a baby-carriage, an autocratic stationmaster and the weather (so important to children in badly-heated country houses). Out of a terrifyingly authentic atmosphere of frustration and chilled hands, there resound, in appropriate idiom, the voices of energetic and mischievous children of all time. In their way these stories are as clearly portraits of an age as, let us say, the far more serious LOOKING FOR ORLANDO, Frances Browin's penetrating story about escaping slaves in the American Civil War, or Rosemary Sutcliff's haunting book, DAWN

WIND, which shows Britain defeated by Saxon invaders but with new hope of national unity. Each of these books has its own particular value in carrying a picture of the past and a moral for the present.

The pressure of fact on the historian becomes yearly more heavy, but also more stimulating. The science of carbon-dating, modern anthropological studies and archaeological discoveries have brought new facts for the novelist's imagination to work on. In recent years there has been an increased interest in ancient worlds and in the psychology of alien and ancient peoples. In ANTELOPE SINGER, for instance, Ruth Underhill has used her specialist knowledge to describe in lucid detail the life of the primitive Paiute Indians in the desert country of Utah. This is no dry study of racial habits. To make a story, the author has contrasted the white pioneers, travelling towards unknown California, and the Indians, accustomed to use natural resources in their marginal existence. There is a clash of temperaments as well as of customs, made sharper by the assured scholarship behind the story. Again, Roderick Haig-Brown, in THE WHALE PEOPLE, writes of the Hobsath Indians on the North West Pacific coast of Canada. Stories of taboos and initiations and tribal contests can easily seem naïve, and (which is worse) can pass on to children the idea that primitive *means* naïve. There is nothing of that attitude here. The author has even contrived a rhetorical style for dialogue which quite naturally suggests the solemnity of the ancient community. In RANGATIRA, two Australian anthropologists have put together up-to-date knowledge to make a fine and exciting story of the first coming of the Polynesians to New Zealand. Most remarkably of all, another anthropologist has collaborated with a writer of fiction, in THROW STONE OF THE ARCTIC, to build up a credible picture of man in one of his earliest known homes, 25,000 years ago, during the last Ice Age.

This is to use science to create literature. But the past can also be a mystery, in the old sense. Bible stories and early religious practices have inspired some writers in recent years to write novels which are akin to poetry. Among these, J. E. Hood, in GUARDIANS OF THE FOREST, tells a strange tale of a princeling rounding up his father's horses after rumours of coming invasion, and here the power of the Druids, which is felt throughout the book, is contrasted with the efficiency of the Roman legionaries. To me, Donald Suddaby's

TOWER OF BABEL is the most fascinating among stories of this kind. The characters are human types that can be readily understood. Nimrod is so mad for power that he will even challenge Jehovah; Zillah, Queen of Nineveh, is the eternally curious female, as Asshur the Master-Builder is the very model of the upright craftsman. But none of the characters is quite as simple as he seems. Nimrod is power-mad, but is he not also a visionary, as he pushes the tower of stone and lapis lazuli higher and higher towards the heavens? As for the negro Gomer, the agitator, he remains an enigma to the end. This is immensely exciting as an adventure story, but entirely satisfying in historical detail—detail that depends essentially on objects and everyday actions. Suddaby can set a scene marvellously. Here is the city after a day of ceremonial propitiation:

> Some, under a reckless mixture of wines, fell to thinking that all would be climbing above the sky in a few days and they started to pack their belongings. Absurd articles were thrown into the streets for assembly in baskets—kneading tubs, hoes, children's garments, wine bottles, rushlight holders, torn bits of dusty material, all the necessities of daily life which look so shoddy in the open air. Petty thefts created roars of rage. Every street had its own quarrel, and at the lighting of lamps Babel looked and sounded like a vast madhouse.
>
> Donald Suddaby. TOWER OF BABEL (Collins, 1962) p. 125.

Accumulation of detail helps the reader to make mental pictures of the various scenes and it helps, too, to carry an air of mystery and strangeness that provokes thought as well.

A story like this is in a way very close to fantasy, especially in its feeling for *place*. The fantasies of Tolkien and Alan Garner and Margaret J. Miller belong with our native landscape poetry, and many of the characters in them are emanations from nature. This is easy to see in Margaret J. Miller's two stories, THE QUEEN'S MUSIC and THE POWERS OF THE SAPPHIRE, which are set in the Highlands of Scotland. The stories follow a familiar pattern. A queen dies, her son and heir vanishes, her kingdom is left in a state of confusion. Two children and their mother are chosen to find her treasure and her heir and to oppose Them, dwarfish, twisted beings with magic powers that can offset the strength of humans three times their size.

This is the old quest story, set in a period of time, marked by faintly archaic dialogue, that belongs to tapestry rather than to history. The stories are notable for the way the author uses a familiar and well-loved landscape. The flat-topped Torridonian hills, the secret lochs, the mists and the soft skies of the Highlands are all here. The powers of good (magic music and magic jewel) derive from a love of wind and air, as the crises of the story are drawn out of natural features—dangerous shaly heights, claustrophobic piles of rock, choking fog. Margaret Miller offers her readers, as well, the delight of humour. Her human characters are generalized, as befits fairy-tale, and have caught even a little priggishness from their function, but the two good members of the dwarfish race, Boomer the stout gastronome and his nephew Lukey, are as entertaining as lively children taken unawares; and Robbie, the cowherd, in the second book, is a touching character who belongs in part to the everyday world, but seems also to be a personification of the lonely hills. These stories are delusively simple in style, but there is a quiet poetry in them that comes directly from their landscapes.

Two more new writers must be mentioned here. Joyce Gard builds her stories from a Tolkienesque mixture of landscape and knightly legend. WOORROO and THE DRAGON OF THE HILL are concerned with a schoolboy and the odd associate from whom he learns so much—Woorroo, an aboriginal being with the power of flight; but even more than this, they are concerned with the Lakeland Fells, and the force of imagination is felt through natural scenes. In the following passage, evil is suggested through the description of a deserted corner:

There stood the grey buildings against the darker grey of Hag Wood. It was a barren wood of thin ash-trees, straggling up the hillside behind the forge; no proper flowers grew there since the rain washed away the soil; there were only a few docks and wild arums—lords and ladies—with their brilliant green spearheads and strange pallid sheaths which would be unrolling now to reveal the tall black lord or the tall pale lady within. Unless they were blighted . . . The forge had been secured with a chain and a pad-lock, but now the chain had rusted away and the heavy door sagged on one hinge. Gowan peeped inside. Thin grass was grow-ing on the floor, among heaps of old litter and rusty horseshoes.

Trails of ivy which had forced their way through the broken roof hung festooned in the shadows. A frog jumped out through the doorway and startled Gowan.

Joyce Gard. THE DRAGON OF THE HILL (Gollancz, 1963) pp. 43–4.

And in the happy end to this conflict of good and evil there is the poetry of space and light and the spring:

Behind her the lake was silver grey after the sunset; they could hear the waves lapping on the beach, and in a sycamore beside them a blackbird was singing at the top of its voice. The small ferns in the wall were unrolling their new fronds, covered in russet down, and a primrose root by Jenny's feet was full of flowers shining out pale from the shadow.

Ibid., p. 173.

In this second book, especially, the writer has kept up the illusion of danger and strangeness without exaggerating the natural features of the district. The smell of scorched earth after the dragon has flown wrathfully by, the underground caves where Gawain and many others lie in enchanted sleep, the sound of wind and water—the fantasy comes from elements such as these.

Joyce Gard's stories depend in a general way on legends of dragon hoards and on evidence of Romano-British settlements in the Lake District. Alan Garner, in THE WEIRDSTONE OF BRISINGAMEN and THE MOON OF GOMRATH, uses more local lore. His stories are set fair and square on Alderley Edge and the action follows the map; there are references, too, for anyone who wants to follow up the local beliefs he uses. But he never allows scholarship to interfere in the free flow of his imagination. That sinister and extraordinary witch-woman, the Morrigan, the horsemen who are conjured up to oppose new evil with Old Magic, the bonfire rites and incantations, the pathway revealed by moonlight at certain times—as far as the reader is concerned, these appear spontaneously in the narrative. And a spanking, electrifying narrative it is, with a blend of energy and mystery that deserves comparison with Tolkien's *Lord of the Rings*, and with that essential gift for turning the other side, as it were, of ordinary scenes and objects. To a literal-minded child, the following paragraph could suggest simply the chance of a few scratches for a girl who walks through a wood full of half-wild cats:

> . . . the concentration in the air throbbed like plucked strings. Susan stared so hard all around her that the blackness seemed to be spotted with light—pale flecks of green; and then she noticed that, instead of swimming in rainbow patterns, as such lights do when the eyes strain against darkness, these lights did not change colour, but were grouped close to the ground, motionless, *in pairs*. They were eyes. She was surrounded by a field of green, unwinking, hard eyes—every one fixed on her.
>
> Alan Garner. THE MOON OF GOMRATH (Collins, 1963) p. 97.

Submit to the author, and how much more it is!

Colin and Susan range far into a magic world and meet very real danger, but behind them is the sturdy, stone-built Cheshire farm-house where they are staying and where their host talks in a reassur-ingly homely dialect. This helps to make children feel at ease in stories that are, in many ways, not children's books but ageless fairy-tales. The type of domestic fantasy which is more specifically planned to suit children has also produced examples, in the last few years, which I am sure will have a long life. I can perhaps best illustrate the difference, as I see it, between the two kinds of fantasy, if I mention Clive King's STIG OF THE DUMP. Here, again, there is a strong sense of place; the action takes place in or around a chalk-pit in Kent, and to some extent depends upon it, but the magic is not in the place, vividly though this is described. It is in the person of Stig, a survivor from the Stone Age who is discovered by young Barney in his present-day rummagings. Any chalk-pit offers delights to a small boy, but for this one there is the joy of a secret hiding-place where he and Stig, communicating without difficulty across the centuries, can contrive plumbing from a vacuum-cleaner tube, a stovepipe from tins and a window from jam-jars, can eat odd con-coctions and escape from soap and routine. This is an enjoyable frolic and on the whole the time-fantasy is lightly handled, though at one point a deeper note sounds, when Barney and his sister, out of doors on Midsummer Eve, suddenly find themselves in a Stone Age settlement. Easily and humorously, too, Eleanor Estes touches on ancient superstitions in THE WITCH FAMILY. This American story must conquer many readers with its gaiety and charm. Two little girls are responsible for the fantasy, and it is easy to believe that when Amy and Clarissa draw Old Witch, they bestow real life on her, whether they like it or not. The idea is wittily developed. Old Witch must have a nasty place to live in—so she is banished to a bare cottage at the top of a glass mountain; but she is not so wicked that she does not deserve a little company, and Little Witch Girl is created to keep her company. And so the story gathers pace, always psychologically shrewd and sound, real in domestic detail, natural in dialogue, a fantasy of playful childhood.

The sinister has little place in this story, though there are moments (for instance, when Old Witch goes for the rabbits in the Painting Field) when terror casts a momentary shadow. Terror belongs to fantasy as much as beauty does, and even the most domestic tale may have a liberating effect just because it brings into the open some deep-seated childhood fear. Barbara Freeman's TWO-THUMB THOMAS is a vigorous and amusing adventure story about a boy brought up by cats. Everything in the setting is ordinary—Thomas's diet of milk and sardines, the class-room cupboard where he hides for his stolen lessons, the exercise-books in which Lynette helps him to do his homework. When the rats arrive and lay claim to Thomas's house, when they bare their teeth and prepare for war, a new note enters the story. What lies beyond or behind the familiar domestic scene may be sinister or benign. A fantasy may reflect the destructive side of a child's nature, as in Honor Prime's sharp little tales, MOONFACE and MOONFACE AND MATTHEW, where an old vest becomes possessed with life. It may give a twist of humour to every-day things, as Alf Prøysen's stories of Mrs Pepperpot do, or it may light them up as in Dana Faralla's enchanting tale, THE SINGING CUPBOARD. In his drawings for this book, Ardizzone creates just the right mood of delicate fancy, the mood in which Hans Mus, familiar spirit of the cupboard, describes a larder as a treasure-hoard, the mood in which a nursery song is enacted in the dreams of Nils and Ulla:

Then Hans Mus did an amazing thing. He climbed up on the throne and then up the ladder of braided flax. And perched among the branches he began playing the little harp. It was a song that put dancing into everyone's feet, and so the garland of little people

began dancing on the golden carpet. Colours were scattered everywhere like bright flowers moving in the wind. Hans Mus played
and played, one happy song, one jolly tune after another. Even the
grey pussywillows began dancing on the branches, and one of them
tumbled to the ground and hid under the throne—a small grey
kitten, very shy and timid. There was no end to the music, no end
to the dancing, or so it seemed. But at last it was morning, and
none too soon or again every boot and shoe and slipper would
have been danced to shreds.

Dana Faralla. THE SINGING CUPBOARD (Blackie, 1962) p. 87.

In fantasy like this a child sees his dreams come true—of flying,
going small, becoming invisible. In 1962 the Carnegie Medal was
deservedly won by THE TWELVE AND THE GENII, an outstanding
example. This book recalls stories like *The Brownies* or Mrs
Molesworth's *The Caged Lions*, for it is essentially a family story,
with a moral and a point, and with magic rising out of character.
Here we have an ordinary family newly come to live in a farm-house
near Haworth. Because Max is eight, it is he who finds the wooden

Drawing by Edward Ardizzone for Dana Faralla's
THE SINGING CUPBOARD (Blackie)

soldiers which were given to Branwell Brontë at the same age, and which, in the imagination of the Brontë children, became the Young Men. It is Max who first realizes the soldiers are alive, but they evoke some reaction from each member of the family. With the determined common sense of fourteen, Philip would like to make money out of them; Jane secretly thinks of them as dolls; only Max comes to know them as individuals who should decide their own future. This is a very fine piece of writing. The author uses the youthful writings of the Brontës most tactfully. She enjoys, and makes her readers enjoy, the minutiae of the fantasy—exactly how the soldiers use a piece of string round the banister rail when they first go downstairs, exactly how they make a roller-skate into a carriage and a marble-bag into a forage-sack in the cornfield. Her sense of scale is impeccable:

> Philip and Max decided at once that they must march, and march quickly, in case the patriarch should be recognized for what he was, an antique soldier, and in case the fame of the Brontë soldiers should cause the farmer to search in his straw and round his land for the rest. Meanwhile the thoughtful Jane fed them. She had brought crumbs and sugar and wild strawberries and milk, and the starving Twelves fell upon these like locusts. (For they had only essayed a few hasty rushes for chicken seed, and that when the greedy chickens had had most of it.) Bravey even began to sing 'Cannikin clink' as he seized the acorn cup she had brought and took his turn at the milk. But finding it a feeding rather than an intoxicating fluid, he made a face and swigged it down for duty. Their spirits rose after their meal and when they set out several of the Twelves sported small, curled, white chicken feathers in their hats, like tiny ostrich plumes.
>
> Pauline Clarke. THE TWELVE AND THE GENII (Faber, 1962) pp. 157–8.

Above all, the book has depth because the fantasy is related to character all the way through. Many writers in the past few years have attempted this attractive version of family story, among them William Herschel, Mary Schroeder and Josephine Lee, but THE TWELVE AND THE GENII stands alone for its richness and its truth.

Recently the fantasy seems to have attracted to itself other forms of writing. There seem to be fewer Mrs Bunny stories now than there used to be. Nobody has ever matched Beatrix Potter and perhaps it is time the stream of imitations dried up. It would be rash to suggest, on the basis of three years' output, a radical change in the humanized animal story, but I have found lately that young children are reading and enjoying stories nearer to nonsense than to nature—like Josef Čapek's HARUM-SCARUM, in which a dog and a cat invent their own ways of housekeeping, or Claude Aveline's daintily odd tales of fleas, plush lions and flying fish, or George Selden's A CRICKET IN TIMES SQUARE, a very sophisticated piece of satirical fantasy.

Historical stories have embraced new material as it came along, and animal stories could take the same course, but at present this does not seem to be happening. The findings of animal behaviour studies could well be used in animal biography, for instance, even though the animal in question is humanized. In this connexion Arthur Clarke's piece of science fiction, DOLPHIN ISLAND, is interesting, for it imagines a twenty-first century when man is talking freely with dolphins and whales. This possibility is taken more seriously by Andre Norton, in a remarkable space story, CATSEYE, where she considers the implications of a common language. Other writers pursue their usual paths. B.B. has always written with a naturalist's accuracy, and his animal biography, LEPUS THE BROWN HARE, is as good as ever. The choice among the works of René Guillot has fallen lately on romantic rather than naturalistic stories. THE KING OF THE CATS and REX AND MISTIGRI, tales of circus life, have a measure of fantasy in them. Meindert de Jong still explores with minute care, and with increasing sentimentality, the relations between people and domestic animals. His stories reflect the public conscience about the welfare of animals which belongs especially (though not exclusively) to the past ten years or so. Ideas about conservation, for instance, are beginning to creep into stories for children. In Barbara Willard's DUCK ON A POND, a boy and a girl, to help an injured bird, make a dogged, difficult journey from London to the Wildfowl Trust in Gloucestershire. By far the most striking story in this mood is, in the long run, unclassifiable—A STRANGER AT GREEN KNOWE by L. M. Boston. In all the stories she has woven round Green Knowe, there has been an unspoken plea that innocence might be kept from harm; here it is the dominant theme. This latest story concerns the refugee boy Ping and a gorilla escaped from the London Zoo. It opens with a description of the

Drawing by D. J. Watkins-Pitchford for B. B.'s
LEPUS THE BROWN HARE (Benn)

young Hanno with his family in the wild, which is a wonderful blend
of accurate fact and intuition:

> He ate, as a matter of course, the canes he lived among, like
> Hansel and Gretel eating their toffee-and-barley-sugar house. His
> toys were fern leaves or feathers which he put on his head, imitating
> father who often covered his head when he snoozed; or sticks to
> bang with, or swings of tough creeper stems; or he pelted his
> brothers with anything that came to hand, or played with them the
> really important game of Disappear, at which his giant father was
> an expert, vanishing without a sound. This was an art that every
> gorilla must learn young. It was their best defence. Instinctively
> perhaps a baby guessed that to be alive is to be in danger, though
> it was difficult to imagine any in their private paradise. But the
> Old Man knew, and his authority impressed them.
> L. M. Boston. A STRANGER AT GREEN KNOWE (Faber, 1961)
> pp. 14–15.

The story carries the same depth and subtlety throughout its intricate
way. This is a generous, humane, living work of art, which asks the
reader to respond to charity and tragedy, to the spirit of a place, a boy
and a gorilla. Very much in tune with our time, it is in the end time-
less.

The only books that can be mentioned in the same breath, different
though they are in character, are two adventure stories first published
half a century ago. A. J. Dawson, the author of FINN THE WOLF-
HOUND and JAN, SON OF FINN, was experienced in dog-breeding
and showing, and his portraits of the wolfhound and bloodhound
breeds are both faithful and sympathetic. Each story has a plot

exciting by adventure story standards but carefully devised to show Finn's loyalty and courage, Jan's endurance and tracking skill. The scenes in Australia and the Yukon have an open-air vigour and a kind of rough candour of atmosphere which is refreshing in these days when adventure is cut to fit children; they also give opportunities for comparison between the two canine heroes and other dogs—a swagger's terrier bitch, a dingo, the savage husky and the malingering sledge-dog. These books were not written for children, but no child should miss the chance to read them.

There is room for more experiment and more originality in animal stories and latterly these qualities seem to exist mainly in picture-story books for the very young. If I think of the most striking picture books of recent years, they seem often to have animal characters—Gerald Rose's horse in CHARLIE ON THE RUN; the mouse in Brian Wildsmith's superb A.B.C., or the animals he painted so exquisitely for the fable THE LION AND THE RAT; the hero of the Standons' book THE SINGING RHINOCEROS; John Burningham's goose BORKA; Stobbs's multifarious cats in the stories of Joan Cass; horses again beautifully depicted by Alie Evers in an Australian gem of a book, BARNABY AND THE HORSES. Because of the type of book they are illustrating, most of the artists here are indulging in a degree of humour, but most of all their books show a departure from naturalism, a concentration on the demands of colour, line and design. Yet the dignity of the animal is never lost. Edward Standon, interpreting his wife's tall story of a rhinoceros who trained as an opera singer, uses a technique reminiscent of John Skeaping's, preserving the natural shape of the animal and letting the humour make itself felt in the situations (the earnest pupil spreading over a chair in the music-room) or in details (the shower of grace-notes in the air as the rhinoceros sings wistfully in the garden). Stobbs's cats have a chunky, ceramic quality, and the near-human expressions of china models, but they are always feline, just as his beautiful designs for Anita Hewett's THE LITTLE WHITE HEN never spoil the farmyard spirit. Looking at books like these, I seem to be back thirty years, to the time when the work of Ardizzone and Lewitt-Him startled picture-books into new life.

The books I have mentioned are distinguished by rich, bold colour and, for the most part, by broad effects. In other books, the drama small children love in stories is seen in the kind of detail, elegant and witty, which Jean de Brunhoff and Kathleen Hale, in their stories of Babar and Orlando, established so long ago for the delight of the young. In this tradition, Gaby Baldner has explored, in THE PEN-GUINS OF PENGUIN TOWN, the possibilities of humour as well as design in the slab of a fish-shop, and V. H. Drummond, in her stories of Little Laura and in an early work revived, THE FLYING POSTMAN, gives a vivid and peculiar life to ordinary things like flower-pots, bicycles and parcels. In Peter Spier's illustrations for THE FOX WENT OUT ON A CHILLY NIGHT there is wit and subtlety in some of the details (like the Confederate statue in the village square or the pictures of ancestors on the wall of the Slipper-Slopper bedroom) as well as a beautifully flowing line in the landscapes. A young artist who made his début a short time ago, Antony Maitland, showed a striking talent for line in MRS COCKLE'S CAT and a sure sense of colour, in his pictures of London roof-tops and Channel beaches. This is an artist who has not always come up to expectation, but at his best his drawings have a special domestic charm, and a kindly eye for the homely elements of life. His illustrations for A PROPER PLACE FOR CHIP and THE TEN TALES OF SHELLOVER, in particular, are outstandingly good.

One last point must be made about these new and exciting picture-stories—they have good texts. By good, I mean rhythmical, selected but not restricted in vocabulary, evocative as well as economical. The authors have not worried about keeping to 108 simple words or finding a psychologically reputable theme, great though the pressure is on them to do so. They have written in the style that seemed best for the story, and what a medley of attractive and personal styles it is. Here is Joan Cass using dialogue cleverly to distinguish her cats one from another:

Early next morning, when almost everyone was still in bed, the cats met by arrangement in Mr Humber's garage. They were all very concerned about Blossom.

'I should not be a bit surprised if Circus Annie went and pushed that kitten of hers into the river, or left her behind somewhere,' said Esmeralda anxiously.

Sarah and Arabella raised their paws in dismay.

'She's a disgrace to the cat world,' said Sarah indignantly.

'Let's go and see what's happening,' said Bill Briggs's five little tabbies, who were always ready for an adventure. They soon got bored with conversation.

Joan Cass. BLOSSOM FINDS A HOME (Abelard-Schuman, 1963) pp. 22–3.

Here is Elizabeth Rose simulating the movement of a river, in words:

Otters dived and gambolled in the still pools beyond the falls, twisting their gleaming bodies in the sunlight as they chased the water-beetles. The stream eddied round them, slowed down and rested. She explored the overhanging banks, spread out, and basked in the sun-warmed shallows.

But a day came when she was scarcely moving and she wished she had not lingered so long among the warm, smooth stones. She felt herself getting weaker. She thought of the ocean ahead and wondered if she would ever reach it.

'I shall never be a big river now,' she whispered sadly to the sheep which came to nibble the tender, sweet grass which grew by the water. She trickled slowly between the rocks.

Elizabeth Rose. THE BIG RIVER (Faber, 1962) pp. 8–10.

Here is Lydia Pender using prose-poetry to suggest the majesty of the draught-horses and the wonder of their obedience to a small child who has rounded them up:

Once there was Barnaby, a boy on a farm by the river; and close to his home, in a wide, green, grassy, warm-in-the-sunshiny paddock, lived the horses of Barnaby's farm.

Oh, the horses!

Such fine, fierce, friendly, munching, crunching creatures, with their huge, fur-fringed hooves, and their wild, fly-swishing tails.

Barnaby loved the horses.

Lydia Pender. BARNABY AND THE HORSES (Abelard-Schuman, 1961) pp. 1–4.

And here, most accomplished of all, is Philippa Pearce, opening and closing a story for small children with as much artistry as she uses for her long novels:

Old Mrs Cockle lived at the top of a very tall house in London. Most of the people who knew her were sorry for her, because she had to climb eighty-four stairs before she reached her own front-door; but she did not mind. It is true that all that climbing made the backs of her knees ache, but then there were advantages. Mrs Cockle lived so high that, from her window, she had a view of the sky over the top of the tall house opposite—which was more than most people had. In the mornings she could look out and think, The sky is blue all over—I'll wear my straw bonnet today; or, The sky is white with snow coming—I'll wear my woollen shawl today; or, The sky has clouded right over—I'll take my biggest umbrella. Mrs Cockle had three umbrellas for different weathers, and the biggest of the three was larger than umbrellas are ever made nowadays . . .

Mrs Cockle never told that Peter had once lived with her in London and then left her: she would not have had people think that Peter was light in his affections. She knew in her heart that, after fresh fish for his tea, Peter Cockle valued her company more than anything else in the world.

Philippa Pearce. MRS COCKLE'S CAT (Constable, 1961) first and last paras.

No writer can write too carefully for children, and especially for the youngest, but the choice of words is his and his alone. So long as he is offering his work to the public, he has to reconcile a personal vision with certain known demands and capacities—but the vision comes first. I have been haunted for many years by a remark Ben Jonson made about himself: 'He hath consumed a whole night in lying looking to his great toe, about which he hath seen Tartars and Turks, Romans and Carthaginians, fight in his imagination.' This definition of a creative artist should as well restrain the hasty critic as encourage the writer of fiction. In the years to come, the middle-men (teachers, critics, librarians and the rest) will be more and more prominent in regard to children's books as the study of childhood develops and deepens. Let us be sure that we, the critics, remember that we *do* stand in the middle, between writer and young reader. *Their* relationship is a very simple one. Unless they are pressed to put their opinions in a literary form, children will express them in honest exclamations of approval or condemnation. We can give useful service to both sides as tasters, sorters, cheer-leaders, even advisers, but we have somehow to avoid the 'plagues of judging and pronouncing', which Jonson listed as 'envy, bitterness, precipitation, impudence, and scurrile scoffing.' Then we can enjoy our share of the pleasures of the imagination.

Drawing by Antony Maitland for Ruth Ainsworth's
THE TEN TALES OF SHELLOVER (Deutsch)

Reading List

1.*Classic adventure*

Dillon, Eilís. THE FORT OF GOLD 1961, THE CORIANDER 1963. *Faber.*
Illustrated by Richard Kennedy. Adventure, mystery and treasure, with the
setting of islands off the Galway coast, brilliantly described, together with
their inhabitants, who have the sea and superstition in their blood.

Guillot, René. MOUNTAIN WITH A SECRET (1958 France). *Collins* 1963.
Translated by John Marshall. Illustrated by B. L. Driscoll. Adventures of a
Dutch boy in New Guinea bent on solving the mystery of an outlaw and a
hidden valley: compelling atmosphere, vivid sense of place.

Hamre, Leif. BLUE TWO . . . BALE OUT (1958 Norway) 1960, OTTER TWO
THREE CALLING (1958 Norway) 1960, READY FOR TAKE-OFF (1959
Norway) 1962. *U.L.P.* Translated by Evelyn Ramsden. Illustrated by Arne
Johnson. Robust, practical stories of an air station and the men of the
Norwegian Air Force who train and experiment there. Exciting and shrewd.

Patchett, M. E. WARRIMOO 1961, DANGEROUS ASSIGNMENT 1962, THE
VENUS PROJECT 1963. *Brockhampton.* Illustrated by Roger Payne. Exploits
of Jeff James, special agent, and his friend Tex, among Australian
aborigines, in North West Africa and, again, in Australia, where they are
tracking down visitors from outer space. Fast-moving and well-sustained.

*Schaefer, Jack. SHANE AND OTHER STORIES (1954 U.S.A.). *Deutsch* 1963.
Illustrated by Robert Micklewright. (See also p. 223.)

Syme, Ronald. THE MOUNTAINY MEN. *Hodder and Stoughton* 1961. Illustrated
by Roger Payne. By far the best of his later work. Set on a Pacific island
and opposing hill aborigines and lowland cultivators, with white settlers
intervening to settle the conflict.

2.*World War II and its aftermath*

Ambrose, Kenneth. THE STORY OF PETER CRONHEIM. *Constable* 1962.
Illustrated by Elisabeth Grant. Documentary tale of a Jewish boy growing
up in a north German town from 1932 and escaping finally to a new life in
England. Truthful and unsentimental.

*Armstrong, Richard. ISLAND ODYSSEY. *Dent* 1963. Illustrated by Andrew
Dodds.

Bateman, Robert. JIM'S FIRST CONVOY. *Brockhampton* 1962. Illustrated by James Holland. A junior radio officer on a merchant ship and how he behaves in a crisis.

Benary, Margot. A TIME TO LOVE (1962 U.S.A.). *Macmillan* 1963. Translated by Joyce Emerson and the author. A German girl grows up through the war: a quietly written chronicle of a family.

*Bruckner, Karl. THE DAY OF THE BOMB (1961 Austria). *Burke* 1962. Translated by Frances Lobb.

Daniell, David Scott. SANDRO'S BATTLE. *Cape* 1963. Illustrated by Colin Spencer. Italian boy keeps an eye on his composer father and his donkey while Germans and British battle round the house. Half humorous, wholly exciting.

Gray, Elizabeth Janet. THE CHEERFUL HEART (1959 U.S.A.). *Macmillan* 1961. Illustrated by Kazue Mizumura. A mother and her children returning to Tokyo, and a new home, during the war; told with charm and feeling.

*Hámori, László. DANGEROUS JOURNEY (1962 U.S.A.). *Constable* 1962. Illustrated by W. T. Mars.

Held, Kurt. GIUSEPPE (1955 Switzerland). *Constable* 1963. Translated by Kay Ockenden. Illustrated by Audrey Smith. Adventures of a homeless Italian boy seeking relatives in Naples during the war. A notable picture of the city and daily contrivances of its poorer inhabitants.

*Stockum, Hilda van. THE WINGED WATCHMAN (1962 U.S.A.). *Constable* 1964. Illustrated by the author.

3.*Children of other lands*

Ainsworth, Ruth. FAR-AWAY CHILDREN. *Heinemann* 1963. Illustrated by Felice Trentin. Small domestic episodes for young children, each set in a different country.

*Arora, Shirley L. WHAT THEN, RAMAN? (1960 U.S.A.). *Blackie* 1963. Illustrated by Margery Gill.

*Buckley, Peter. DIMITRIOS, BOY OF GREECE. *Methuen* 1962. Photographs by the author.

*Cavanna, Betty. PAULO OF BRAZIL (1962 U.S.A.) 1963, PEPE OF ARGENTINA (1962 U.S.A.) 1963. *Chatto & Windus*. Photographs by George Russell Harrison.

*Clair, Andrée. BEMBA (1957 France). *Hart-Davis* 1963. Translated by Marie Ponsot. Illustrated by Harper Johnson.

Ik, Kim Yong. THE DAYS OF HAPPINESS. *Hutchinson* 1962. Illustrated by Artur Mirikvia. A small Korean village builds its own school; a gay, tender story, with a well-drawn background.

Kaye, Geraldine. KOFI AND THE EAGLE. *Methuen* 1963. Illustrated by Sheila Hawkins. A small boy in West Africa finds he is not the best guardian for a wild fledgeling; an exquisite little tale for younger children.

Lewis, Janet. KEIKO'S BUBBLE (1961 U.S.A.). *World's Work* 1963. Illustrated by Kazue Mizumura. A little girl in a Japanese fishing-village finds luck for her needy family. Simple and fine in words and pictures.

Lunn, Peter. THE HOLIDAY MOON. *Abelard-Schuman* 1963. Illustrated by Peter Thompson. A great day in China—the New Year Kite Festival.

Mackay, Margaret. DOLPHIN BOY. *Harrap* 1963. Illustrated by Peggy Fortnum. A group of Hawaiian children and how one of them makes friends with a dolphin. Exceptionally attractive in text and pictures.

Piggott, Juliet. THE BIGGER FISH. *Abelard-Schuman* 1962. Illustrated by Peter Thompson. A great day in Japan—the Boy's Festival in Tokyo, and a boy on his birthday waiting for his wind-fish to be flown.

Richardson, Tracy. NICHO OF THE RIVER (1958 U.S.A.). *Methuen* 1962. Illustrated by Herbert Rogers. A family of Indians in Nicaragua, especially a boy of thirteen proving his worth by taking charge of the annual expedition down river for stores. Wise and well-told.

*Sommerfelt, Aimée. THE ROAD TO AGRA (1959 Norway) 1961, THE WHITE BUNGALOW (1962 Norway) 1963. *U.L.P.* Translated by Evelyn Ramsden. Illustrated by Ulf Aas.

Thampi, Paravathi. GEETA AND THE VILLAGE SCHOOL. *Gollancz* 1963. Illustrated by Ronni Solbert. A girl in a remote village learns that school is not as frightening as she had imagined. Quiet, thoughtful writing.

4.Stories for the youngest

Ainsworth, Ruth. RUFTY TUFTY AND HATTIE. *Heinemann* 1962. Illustrated by D. G. Valentine. The little golliwog has a baby sister. (See also p. 46.)

Ainsworth, Ruth. THE TEN TALES OF SHELLOVER. *Deutsch* 1963. Illustrated by Antony Maitland. A tortoise, newly come to Mrs Candy's cottage, tells her pets stories of animals, children and magic beings.

Bisset, Donald. NEXT TIME STORIES 1959, ANOTHER TIME STORIES 1963. *Methuen.* Illustrated by the author. Odd nonsense stories about anything under the sun. (See also p. 168.)

Bruna, Dick. TILLY AND TESSA (1961 Holland) 1962, THE LITTLE BIRD (1961 Holland) 1962, CIRCUS (1962 Holland) 1963, THE FISH (1962 Holland) 1963. *Methuen.* Brightly-coloured pictures, tiny text, for the very youngest.

Chapman, Elizabeth. MARMADUKE GOES TO FRANCE 1962, MARMADUKE
    GOES TO HOLLAND 1963. *Brockhampton*. Illustrated by Eccles Williams.
    Adventures abroad for Joe and his red lorry. (See also p. 47.)
Colwell, Eileen. TELL ME A STORY. *Penguin* (Young Puffin Books) 1962.
    Illustrated by Judith Bledsoe. A collection, for under-fives, of stories to be
    told or read aloud. Every kind of fantasy and domestic incident, all
    distinguished by rhythmic prose, gay simplicity.
Colwell, Eileen. A STORYTELLER'S CHOICE. *Bodley Head* 1963. Illustrated by
    Carol Barker. Fairy tale and fantasy, domestic and animal tales; the
    leading exponent of the art of story-telling has selected stories and extracts
    that are particularly suitable, and adds suggestions for their telling.
Duchesne, Janet. THE GOOD DOGS 1963, THE PICNIC 1963, THE FAST CART
    1963, THE CAR AND THE TRICYCLE 1963. *Hamish Hamilton*. Illustrated
    by the author. Domestic incidents, briefly described in captions under good,
    simple drawings.
Guthrie, Kathleen. MAGIC BUTTON TO THE MOON. *Brockhampton* 1962.
    Illustrated by the author. Kitty Flewett leaves her caterpillar in a cocoon
    and takes her mouse travelling. (See also p. 151.)
Hough, Charlotte. THREE LITTLE FUNNY ONES. *Hamish Hamilton* (Antelope
    Books) 1962. Illustrated by the author. Adventures of three small boys,
    tenderly and humorously told, attractively illustrated.
Hourihane, Ursula. TRAVELLER'S JOY. *Methuen* 1962. Illustrated by Betty
    Middleton Sandford. Small fantastic tales starting in an ordinary domestic
    scene; great variety of incidents and simple rhythmical prose.
Mosheim, Lily. WHERE IS JOHN? *Constable* 1963. Illustrated by Sally Ford.
    A little boy who doesn't like his bath runs away and gets lost; very short,
    natural and entertaining. In three versions: English, English/French and
    English/German.
Sedgwick, Modwena. THE ADVENTURES OF GALLDORA 1960, NEW
    ADVENTURES OF GALLDORA 1962. *Harrap*. Illustrated by the author.
    Charming little tales of a rag-doll who believes 'experience is the best
    education'.
Stockum, Hilda van. LITTLE OLD BEAR (1962 U.S.A.) 1963, JEREMY BEAR
    1963. *Constable*. Illustrated by the author. Simple, charming tales of a boy
    and a teddy-bear.
Thwaite, Ann. TOBY STAYS WITH JANE 1962, JANE AND TOBY AT THE
    SEASIDE 1962. *Constable*. Illustrated by Janet Martin. A clear, sympathetic
    look at the amusements of two small children.

5.*Historical stories*

*Avery, Gillian. TO TAME A SISTER 1961, THE GREATEST GRESHAM 1962, THE PEACOCK HOUSE 1963. *Collins*. Illustrated by John Verney.

Bartos-Höppner, B. THE COSSACKS (1959 Germany) 1962, TO SAVE THE KHAN (1961 Germany) 1963. *O.U.P.* Translated by Stella Humphries. Illustrated by Victor Ambrus. The Russian move into Siberia in the 16th century, seen from the point of view first of the invading Cossacks, then of the defending Tartars. Powerful stories, superbly told.

Baumann, Hans. I MARCHED WITH HANNIBAL (1960 Germany). *O.U.P.* 1961. Translated by Katharine Potts. Illustrated by Ulrik Schramm. A boy attaches himself to an elephant-driver and sees the general in victory and defeat. A profound book, deep in detail and mood.

Bothwell, Jean. OMEN FOR A PRINCESS (1963 U.S.A.). *Abelard-Schuman* 1963. The story of 17th century Jahanara, whose father built the Taj Mahal; a picturesque tale of romance and war in ancient India.

Boucher, Alan. THE PATH OF THE RAVEN 1960, THE GREENLAND FARERS 1961, THE WINELAND VENTURE 1963. *Constable*. Illustrated by Toni Patten. Interlinked stories starting in 12th-century Iceland; a young man is sent into exile ventures to new colonies in Greenland and goes to find the unknown land now called America. Scholarly and exciting.

*Browin, Frances Williams. LOOKING FOR ORLANDO (1961 U.S.A.). *O.U.P.* 1961. Illustrated by Victor Ambrus.

Burton, Hester. CASTORS AWAY! *O.U.P.* 1962. Illustrated by Victor Ambrus. A Suffolk family affected by domestic and national events at the time of Trafalgar. Most vivid and well written.

*Burton, Hester. TIME OF TRIAL. *O.U.P.* 1963. Illustrated by Victor Ambrus.

Capon, Paul. WARRIOR'S MOON 1960, THE KINGDOM OF THE BULLS 1961, LORD OF THE CHARIOTS 1962. *Hodder and Stoughton*. Encounters of a British prince, a thousand years before Christ, with Myceneans, Cretans and other seafaring people. Enormously dramatic and full of colour.

Carter, Bruce. PERIL ON THE IRON ROAD (1953). *Hamish Hamilton* 1963. Illustrated by Charlotte Hough. The building of the railway between Euston and Watford Tunnel: a melodramatic plot but not far different from possible events in those wild times over a century ago.

Daniell, David Scott. POLLY AND OLIVER BESIEGED. *Cape* 1963. Illustrated by William Stobbs. Another adventure of a resourceful pair of children in the Peninsular War; slight but entertaining. (See also p. 245.)

Dawlish, Peter. THE BOY JACKO. *O.U.P.* 1962. Illustrated by William Stobbs. A boy travels from Exeter to Virginia, in the late 17th century, to claim an inheritance, and is pursued by enemies he can't identify. Action by land and sea vividly described.

Drewery, Mary. REBELLION IN THE WEST. *Oliver and Boyd* 1962. Illustrated by William Stobbs. The rebellion of Hotspur, Mortimer and Glendower against Henry IV; set mainly in Wales, with a young page as central character, trying to be loyal to a time-serving master.

Drewery, Mary. DEVIL IN PRINT. *Oliver and Boyd* 1963. Illustrated by William Stobbs. How Tyndale's Bible was printed in Holland and smuggled into England. Good material well used.

*Haig-Brown, Roderick. THE WHALE PEOPLE. *Collins* 1962. Illustrated by Mary Weiler.

*Hood, J. E. GUARDIANS OF THE FOREST. *Hutchinson* 1961.

Houghton, Eric. THE WHITE WALL. *Brockhampton* 1961. Illustrated by Robin Jacques. A boy joins Hannibal's army in the crossing of the Alps. For younger children; good action and an interesting personal problem that the boy has to work out.

Houghton, Eric. THEY MARCHED WITH SPARTACUS. *Brockhampton* 1963. Illustrated by Robin Jacques. The rebellion of 73 BC seen through the eyes of a young slave. Interesting use of detail to create mood.

Household, Geoffrey. XENOPHON'S ADVENTURE. *Bodley Head* 1961. Illustrated by Bernard Blatch. A free re-telling, in modern style, of this historian's account of the war between Persia and Greece in 401 BC. A clear picture, among other things, of a mercenary army living off the country.

Hunter, Mollie. HI JOHNNY. *Evans* 1963. Illustrated by Drake Brookshaw. A sidelight on James V and his Scottish kingdom in 1540; a pedlar, a marauding lord, a beautiful lady, a gipsy king—put together in a relaxed and interesting way to make a good story.

Jamison, *Mrs* C. V. LADY JANE (1891). *Hart-Davis* 1963. Illustrated by Robin Jacques. A story of New Orleans seventy years ago, and of the violent changes in the life of a gentle little orphan. A story full of compassion and strong drama; superbly drawn characters and setting; fine illustrations.

Johnson, Annabel *and* Edgar. THE BLACK SYMBOL (1959 U.S.A.). *Brockhampton* 1960. Illustrated by Brian Sanders. A boy, seeking his father in the mining camps of the 1850's, is helped, and exploited, by a travelling quack doctor. An exceptionally vivid tale.

Johnson, Annabel *and* Edgar. TORRIE (1960 U.S.A.). *Brockhampton* 1961. Illustrated by Pearl Falconer. A girl, journeying with her family from St Louis to California in the 1840's, learns through hardship to value different things in life. Fine atmosphere of covered-wagon days.

Kamm, Josephine. RETURN TO FREEDOM. *Abelard-Schuman* 1962. Illustrated
by William Stobbs. Jewish families in London under Cromwell's Protectorate;
a well-constructed story of individuals in a time of stress.

Kaufmann, Herbert. THE KING'S CROCODILE (1959 Germany). *Methuen*
1962. Translated by Stella Humphries. Illustrated by Anne Linton. Slave-
trading and intrigue in the Niger Delta towards the end of the 19th century;
distinguished by the author's sharp eye for character and his marked power
for describing action and place.

Knight, *Capt.* Frank. CLEMENCY DRAPER. *Macmillan* 1963. Illustrated by
William Stobbs. Sussex in the 1790's—coach roads, inns and travellers, and
daily news of the French Revolution. An exciting and romantic story.

Knight, Peter. THE BOREAS ADVENTURE. *Nelson* 1963. Illustrated by Nigel
Lambourne. A young British lieutenant is sent to France during the
Napoleonic Wars to find out about a reported new weapon. Fast-moving
adventures in the Paris slums.

Knudsen, Poul E. THE CHALLENGE (1960 Denmark). *Methuen* 1962.
Translated by L. W. Kingsland. A forceful picaresque novel, set in the first
century AD, about a Danish horseman who seeks his fortune abroad, is
enslaved in Gaul and rises to fame as a charioteer. A succession of
extremely vivid scenes of action.

Lee, M. *and* C. ROSAMOND FANE (1870). *O.U.P.* 1963. Illustrated by Heather
Standring. A quietly written story of the Civil War, in which a girl is
involved in a conflict of loyalties when she becomes playmate to the
children of Charles I. Beautiful style, moving scenes.

Leeuw, Cateau De. GIVE ME YOUR HAND (1960 U.S.A.). *Deutsch* 1963. A
girl taking charge of the household after her mother's death; a quietly
truthful picture of Ohio nearly a century ago.

Lewis, Mildred. THE HONOURABLE SWORD. *Deutsch* 1962. Illustrated by
Panos Ghikas. Written in elegantly formal style, the story of a nobleman's
son in 17th-century Japan, and his good fortune after bad times.

McGiffin, Lee. ON THE TRAIL TO SACRAMENTO (1962 U.S.A.). *Deutsch*
1963. Illustrated by Ann Swyer. The California Gold Rush, and a boy
overlanding a flock of sheep from Iowa to sell at the diggings. The journey
and the people on it are finely described.

McLean, Allan Campbell. RIBBON OF FIRE. *Collins* 1962. The end of the 19th
century, in Skye, with crofters seeking redress against the oppression of the
laird and his factor; a stirring tale with a fine background.

*Manning, Rosemary. ARRIPAY. *Constable* 1963. Illustrated by Victor
Ambrus.

Mitchison, Naomi. KARENSGAARD. *Collins* 1961. Illustrated with photographs. A Danish boy explores the history of his own farmstead and then of his country; an effective mixture of fact and fiction.

Oliver, Jane. FARAWAY PRINCESS. *Macmillan* 1962. Illustrated by Jane Paton. A troubled England at the time of Edward the Confessor's death, seen from the point of view of a princess newly come from exile in Hungary; an unusual combination of intrigue and personal feeling.

Peyton, K. M. WINDFALL. *O.U.P.* 1962. Illustrated by Victor Ambrus. The fortunes of a fishing family on the Essex coast 70 years ago; a fine blend of action and the clash of character.

Picard, Barbara Leonie. LOST JOHN. *O.U.P.* 1962. Illustrated by Charles Keeping. Moral dilemma of Norman boy looking for his father's murderer and taking refuge with an outlawed knight. Scholarly and picturesque.

Plaidy, Jean. MEG ROPER. *Constable* 1961. Domestic in tone, the life and times of Sir Thomas More from the point of view of his favourite daughter.

Polland, Madeleine. THE TOWN ACROSS THE WATER. *Constable* 1961. Illustrated by Brian Wildsmith. An Irish fishing community in the 16th century, under an English government and friendly with seafaring Spain. The adventures of two children are described vividly in a story of quality.

Polland, Madeleine. BEORN THE PROUD. *Constable* 1961. Illustrated by William Stobbs. A Viking boy and a captured Irish girl; a story of human relationships, and action on land and sea, ranging from Ireland to Scandinavia in the time of Leif the Lucky.

Polland, Madeleine. THE WHITE TWILIGHT. *Constable* 1962. Illustrated by William Stobbs. A Dutch girl goes with her architect father to Elsinore, in the 16th century; a story that takes the reader easily into the past by its selection of detail and event.

Polland, Madeleine. THE QUEEN'S BLESSING. *Constable* 1963. Illustrated by William Stobbs. Set in the 11th century: the Saxon queen of Malcolm of Scotland befriends two orphans from a Northumbrian fishing town. A warm and decorative story.

Reid, Meta Mayne. WITH ANGUS IN THE FOREST. *Faber* 1963. Illustrated by Zelma Blakely. A time-fantasy which gives a girl from the present day a vision of England in the 9th century, through an illuminated manuscript. (See also p. 337.)

Ritchie, Rita. THE YEAR OF THE HORSE 1961, THE SECRET BEYOND THE MOUNTAINS 1962. *Hutchinson*. Illustrated by Lorence F. Bjorklund. Haunting tales of Asia in the times of Genghis Khan; exotic backgrounds, mysterious events. Exceptionally good story-telling.

Rush, Philip. THE CASTLE AND THE HARP. *Collins* 1963. Illustrated by
Charles Keeping. Henry II's reign; a good account of the siege of Bedford
Castle by a rebellious baron, and a romantic picture of Hugh de Breauté
taking the road with a wandering minstrel.

*Sayles, Edward *and* Stevens, Mary. THROW STONE OF THE ARCTIC. *Deutsch*
1962. Illustrated by Barton Wright.

Softly, Barbara. PLAIN JANE 1961, PLACE MILL 1962. *Macmillan.* Illustrated
by Shirley Hughes. Excellent tales of the Civil War from the Royalist point
of view; especially good use of locality (Devon and Cornwall in the first
book, Hampshire in the second).

Speare, Elizabeth George. THE BRONZE BOW (1961 U.S.A.). *Gollancz* 1962.
A moving story of a Galilean boy at the time of Christ, learning to exchange
general hostility to Rome for a better understanding of individuals.

Steele, W. O. THE LONE HUNT (1957 U.S.A.) 1957, THE FAR FRONTIER
(1959 U.S.A.) 1960, THE PERILOUS ROAD (1958 U.S.A.) 1960, WINTER
DANGER (1954 U.S.A.) 1963. *Macmillan.* Illustrated by Paul Galdone.
Straightforward tales of Tennessee in the late 18th century and through the
19th; in each one, a boy is up against nature and man and proves his
worth. Exceptionally good in settings and dialogue.

Suddaby, Donald. CROWNED WITH WILD OLIVE. *Collins* 1961. Illustrated by
William Stobbs. Not long after the Trojan War, a lad of noble birth and
one plebeian-born adventure through Greece; an exciting blend of myth
and historical detail.

*Suddaby, Donald. TOWER OF BABEL. *Collins* 1962.

Sutcliff, Rosemary. KNIGHT'S FEE. *O.U.P.* 1960. Illustrated by Charles
Keeping. A dog-boy, part-Norman and part-Saxon, pushing sturdily from
the Welsh Marches into a larger world. A wonderfully vivid picture of the
times of William Rufus.

*Sutcliff, Rosemary. DAWN WIND. *O.U.P.* 1961. Illustrated by Charles
Keeping.

*Tindale, Norman B. *and* Lindsay, Harold A. RANGATIRA. *Harrap* 1959 (in
association with *Reed*, N.Z.). Illustrated by Douglas F. Maxted.

Trease, Geoffrey. FOLLOW MY BLACK PLUME. *Macmillan,* 1963. Illustrated
by Brian Wildsmith. An English boy and his tutor are involved in a critical
stage of Garibaldi's rising; action and personality expertly mixed. First-
rate marshalling of historical fact to make a clear-cut, exciting story.

Treece, Henry. THE GOLDEN ONE. *Bodley Head* 1961. Illustrated by William
Stobbs. 1204 in Constantinople: a gallery of portraits—Franks, Venetians,
Knights Templars, Greeks, Tartars—and a most exciting story.

Treece, Henry. WAR DOG. *Brockhampton* 1962. Illustrated by Roger Payne. A short, crisp story, well suited to arouse a child's interest in the Roman invasion of Britain.

Treece, Henry. HORNED HELMET. *Brockhampton* 1963. Illustrated by Charles Keeping. A tough, thrilling tale of Jomsvikings and of an Iceland boy who joins them, told in a style derived from the sagas.

*Underhill, Ruth M. ANTELOPE SINGER (1961 U.S.A.). *Penguin* (Puffin Story Books) 1963. Illustrated by Peter Barrett.

Welch, Ronald. CAPTAIN OF DRAGOONS 1956, MOHAWK VALLEY 1958, ESCAPE FROM FRANCE 1960, FOR THE KING 1961, NICHOLAS CAREY 1963. *O.U.P.* Illustrated by William Stobbs. A series of stories about members of the Carey family at various periods of history, from the Civil War onwards. Variable in standard but uniformly interesting in material.

6.*Animal stories*

*Aveline, Claude. THE BIRD THAT FLEW INTO THE SEA (1946 France). *Harrap* 1961. Translated by Margaret Ledésert. Illustrated by Françoise Estachy.

*'B.B.' LEPUS THE BROWN HARE. *Benn* 1963. Illustrated by D. Watkins-Pitchford.

Baudouy, Michel-Aimé. BRUNO, KING OF THE WILD (1953 France). *Bodley Head* 1962. Translated by Marie Ponsot. Illustrated by Johannes Troyer. A bear in the French Pyrenees and his relationship with a youth and a girl who feel responsible for him in the wild and when he is captured by local smugglers. A fine story with a fine setting.

Bingley, Barbara. THE STORY OF TIT'BÉ AND HIS FRIEND MOUFFETTE. *Abelard-Schuman* 1962. Illustrated by Margery Gill. A French-Canadian boy and his real friendship with a skunk. A story with charm and point.

Bond, Michael. A BEAR CALLED PADDINGTON 1958, PADDINGTON HELPS OUT 1960, PADDINGTON ABROAD 1961, PADDINGTON AT LARGE 1962. *Collins.* Illustrated by Peggy Fortnum. A bear from South America adopts an English household and leads an adventurous life that often embarrasses his hosts. Delightful domestic fantasy.

*Boston, L. M. A STRANGER AT GREEN KNOWE. *Faber* 1961. Illustrated by Peter Boston. (See also p. 129.)

*Čapek, Josef. HARUM-SCARUM (1954 Czechoslovakia). *Methuen* 1963. Translated by Stephen Jolly. Illustrated by the author

Clarke, Arthur. DOLPHIN ISLAND. *Gollancz* 1963.

Cunningham, Julia. MACAROON (1962 U.S.A.). *Harrap* 1963. Illustrated by
Eveline Ness. A witty and exquisitely illustrated tale of an arrogant raccoon
meeting a child who is a match for him.

*Dawson, A. J. FINN THE WOLFHOUND (1908) 1962, JAN, SON OF FINN
(1917) 1963. *Brockhampton.* Illustrated by Richard Kennedy.

Dillon, Eilís. THE CATS' OPERA. *Faber* 1962. Illustrated by Kveta Vaneček. A
whimsical tale of a small boy permitted to see a performance by talented
and idiosyncratic cats.

*Guillot, René. THE KING OF CATS (1959 France). *Collins* 1962. Translated
by John Marshall. Illustrated by B. L. Driscoll.

*Guillot, René. REX AND MISTIGRI. *Bodley Head* (Acorn Library) 1963.
Translated by Gwen Marsh. Illustrated by William Stobbs.

Johnston, Roy. THE SCRUFF RAFFERTY DOG STORIES. *Faber* 1962. Illustrated by Alistair Grant. Tales told by an Irish terrier about his companions;
rollicking, rhythmical stories with an acute observation of dog behaviour.

*Jong, Meindert de. THE LITTLE COW AND THE TURTLE (1955 U.S.A.) 1961,
HURRY HOME, CANDY (1953 U.S.A.) 1962, THE SINGING HILL (1962
U.S.A.) 1963. *Lutterworth.* Illustrated by Maurice Sendak.

*Jong, Meindert de. SMOKE ABOVE THE LANE. *Harper*, N.Y. 1951. Illustrated
by Girard Goodenow.

Kalashnikoff, Nicholas. THE DEFENDER (1951 U.S.A.). *O.U.P.* 1962.
Illustrated by Feodor Rojankovsky. A widower in northern Siberia consti-
tutes himself a protector of a herd of wild sheep; a richly written, thoughtful
story.

Lampman, Evelyn Sibley. THE CITY UNDER THE BACK STEPS (1960 U.S.A.).
Faber 1962. Two children translated to ant size and put in servitude in an
ant citadel. Exciting mixture of fact and fantasy.

*Norton, Andre. CATSEYE (1961 U.S.A.). *Gollancz* 1962.

Patchett, Mary Elwyn. IN A WILDERNESS. *Hodder and Stoughton* 1962. A
small boy on an Australian cattle-station trying to tame a dingo pup and
protect it when it returns to wild life and marauding habits. A touching
story with a fine setting.

Prescott, John B. MOUNTAIN-LION (1961 U.S.A.). *Deutsch* 1962. Arizona, and
a forester's son who adopts a puma and has to give him back to the wild.

*Selden, George. A CRICKET IN TIMES SQUARE (1960 U.S.A.). *Dent* 1961.
Illustrated by Garth Williams.

Sharp, Margery. MISS BIANCA. *Collins* 1962. Illustrated by Garth Williams.
More adventures of the Ladies' Guild of the Mouse's Prisoners' Aid
Society. (See also p. 66.)

Stephen, David. RORY THE ROEBUCK. *Bodley Head* (Acorn Library) 1961.
  Illustrated by Don Higgins. Simple, tender, accurate account of how a
  keeper's small daughter rears an orphaned deer in Scotland and releases
  him to a natural life.
Svinsaas, Ingvald. TOM IN THE MOUNTAINS (1955 Norway). *O.U.P.* 1961.
  Translated by Marianne Turner. Illustrated by Gunvor Edwards. A
  domestic cat, left behind after a summer holiday, has to learn to live in a
  cold and dangerous world. Beautifully told from an animal's point of view.
Weir, Rosemary. THE SMALLEST DOG ON EARTH. *Abelard-Schuman* 1963.
  Illustrated by Charles Pickard. Part-fantastic, part-realistic; the adventures
  of a chihuahua who has to change her home every six months, and who
  goes from riches to rags and back to riches again.
Whitney, Leon. PIGEON CITY (1931 U.S.A.). *Ward* 1963. Illustrated by
  Ernest Hart. A sturdy, fascinating tale about boys in Brooklyn buying,
  breeding and flying pigeons. Good character studies, fine descriptions of
  tests and long-distance races.
*Willard, Barbara. DUCK ON A POND. *Constable* 1962. Illustrated by Mary
  Rose Hardy.
Windsor-Richards, A. THERE CAME THE LITTLE FOXES. *Hutchinson* 1961.
  Illustrated by Edward Osmond. A simply-written account of the life of Ren
  and his vixen and family, which sets out to give children an accurate and
  unsentimental idea of wild life.
Young, Noella. FLIP THE FLYING POSSUM. *Methuen* 1963. Illustrated by the
  author. An Australian feathertail 'possum looking for a new home; a
  tender story for younger children with delicate and accurate pictures.

7.Fantasy

Baker, Margaret J. AWAY WENT GALLOPER. *Methuen* 1962. Illustrated by
  Norman Thelwell. A rocking-horse takes two bored children to unexpected
  places and involves them in odd situations.
Baker, Margaret J. THE CATS OF HONEY TOWN. *Harrap* (Flying Foal Books)
  1962. Illustrated by Keith Money. A strange adventure in a deserted village.
Baker, Margaret J. HOMER IN ORBIT. *Brockhampton* 1961. Illustrated by
  Terence Freeman. The intelligent tortoise again. (See also p. 150.)
Blum, Lisa-Marie. THE MYSTERIOUS MERRY-GO-ROUND (1959 Germany).
  Abelard-Schuman 1962. Translated by Geoffrey Strachan. Illustrated by the
  author. Wooden animals escape from a new, unsympathetic owner to
  pleasant homes of their own with the children who believe in them. A
  gentle story with good descriptive touches.

Clare, Helen. FIVE DOLLS AND THE DUKE. *Bodley Head* 1963. Illustrated by
Cecil Leslie. The dolls' house entertaining Vanessa's grand relative.
(See also p. 47.)

*Clarke, Pauline. THE TWELVE AND THE GENII. *Faber* 1962. Illustrated by
Cecil Leslie.

Eager, Edward. THE WELL-WISHERS (1960 U.S.A.) 1961, SEVEN DAY MAGIC
(1962 U.S.A.) 1962. *Macmillan.* Illustrated by N. M. Bodecker. Stories of
magic adventure in the Nesbit tradition, with lively American children as
actors. (See also p. 291.)

*Estes, Eleanor. THE WITCH FAMILY (1960 U.S.A.). *Constable* 1962. Illustrated
by Edward Ardizzone.

*Faralla, Dana. THE SINGING CUPBOARD. *Blackie* 1962. Illustrated by
Edward Ardizzone.

Farjeon, Eleanor. KALEIDOSCOPE. *O.U.P.* 1963. Illustrated by Edward
Ardizzone. An allegory of a child growing up in close contact with nature;
a sequence of dreams and reminiscences, with magic showing through the
everyday world.

Farmer, Penelope. THE SUMMER BIRDS (1962 U.S.A.). *Chatto & Windus*
1962. Illustrated by James J. Spanfeller. Children find adventure through the
strange boy who comes to the village school; a moving fantasy of flight
with a strong moral.

Fletcher, David. THE CHILDREN WHO CHANGED. *Michael Joseph* 1961.
Illustrated by Belinda Hodson. Two dolls get their own back on their
owners; a tart and vivid little story.

*Freeman, Barbara. TWO-THUMB THOMAS. *Faber* 1961. Illustrated by the
author.

Freeman, Barbara. BROOM-ADELAIDE. *Faber* 1963. Illustrated by the author.
A Ruritanian fancy in which a little grand-duchess outwits a witch; charming
and unusual.

*Gard, Joyce. WOORROO 1961, illustrated by Ronald Benham. THE DRAGON
OF THE HILL 1963. *Gollancz.*

*Garner, Alan. THE WEIRDSTONE OF BRISINGAMEN (see p. 94), THE MOON
OF GOMRATH 1963. *Collins.*

Gray, Nicholas Stuart. DOWN IN THE CELLAR. *Dobson* 1961. Illustrated by
Edward Ardizzone. An extraordinary mixture of crook-adventure and black
and white magic; most exciting.

Gray, Nicholas Stuart. GRIMBOLD'S OTHER WORLD. *Faber* 1963. Illustrated
by Charles W. Stewart. A farm cat at night rules a world of magic and
watches over two boys who only partly inhabit it. Strange, haunting tales.

Herschel, William. KING LIZARD. *Nelson* 1962. Illustrated by Geraldine
Spence. Children on a visit to a strict aunt in Hampstead find an exiled
lizard king on the Heath and help him to defeat his mysterious enemies.

Juster, Norton. THE PHANTOM TOLBOOTH (1961 U.S.A.). *Collins* 1962.
Illustrated by Jules Feiffer. A fascinating book but an acquired taste. Milo
in his little car journeys to the land of Ignorance to rescue the princesses
Rhyme and Reason. Linguistic jokes, plenty of incident, freakish illustrations.

*King, Clive. STIG OF THE DUMP. *Penguin* (Puffin Original) 1963. Illustrated
by Edward Ardizzone.

Lee, Josephine. JOY IS NOT HERSELF. *Cape* 1962. Illustrated by Pat Marriott.
An ordinary horse-mad family, but one member of it keeps breaking out
into strange behaviour.

L'Engle, Madeleine. A WRINKLE IN TIME (1962 U.S.A.). *Constable* 1963.
A compelling space and time fantasy, mature in style and in the way it
relates the fantasy directly to the characters who dare such strange adventures.

Manning, Rosemary. GREEN SMOKE 1957, DRAGON IN DANGER 1959,
THE DRAGON'S QUEST 1961. *Constable*. Illustrated by Constance Marshall.
A dragon, surviving from antiquity in Cornwall, takes young Susan for
some dashing expeditions into the past.

*Miller, Margaret J. THE QUEEN'S MUSIC 1961, THE POWERS OF THE
SAPPHIRE 1962. *Brockhampton*. Illustrated by Robin Jacques.

Muir, Lynette. THE UNICORN WINDOW. *Abelard-Schuman* 1961. Illustrated
by Pauline Baynes. Heraldry and the orders of chivalry contribute to a
story in which two children visit the land of Armorie.

Norton, Mary. THE BORROWERS ALOFT. *Dent* 1961. Illustrated by Diana
Stanley. The closing book of the series, telling how the Borrowers find a
home at last. (See also p. 115.)

Poole, Josephine. A DREAM IN THE HOUSE. *Hutchinson* 1961. Illustrated by
Peggy Fortnum. An allegory of a girl who seeks a lost sister.

Preussler, Ottfried. THE LITTLE WATER-SPRITE (1957 Germany) 1960, THE
LITTLE WITCH (1958 Germany) 1961, THOMAS SCARECROW (1959
Germany) 1963. *Abelard-Schuman*. Translated by Anthea Bell. Illustrated
by Winnie Gayler. Fascinating stories, with unforced, subtle humour.

*Prime, Honor. MOONFACE 1961, MOONFACE AND MATTHEW 1963.
Faber. Illustrated by Geraldine Spence.

*Prøysen, Alf. MRS PEPPERPOT TO THE RESCUE (1960 Sweden). *Hutchinson*
1963. Translated by Marianne Helweg. Illustrated by Björn Berg. (See also
p. 151.)

Rhys, Julia. THE TINSEL NOVEMBER. *Hart-Davis* 1963. Illustrated by Carol

Barker. A boy and a girl in London trying to collect together a scattered band of Harlequinade puppets who have a secret life of their own.

Ross, Diana. THE MERRY-GO-ROUND. *Lutterworth* 1963. Illustrated by Shirley Hughes. More stories of Miss Pussy and Jackanapes, with magic and domesticity delicately blended. (See also p. 96.)

Sauer, Julia. FOG MAGIC (1943 U.S.A.). *Woodfield & Stanley* 1960. An incomparable American time-fantasy of a girl in Novia Scotia who visits a village long deserted and gets to know its history.

Schmidt, Annie M. G. WIPLALA (1957 Holland). *Abelard-Schuman* 1962. Translated by Henrietta Anthony. Illustrated by Jenny Dalenoord. A tiny man turns the Blom family into confusion when he gets his magic mixed; beautifully neat and comical domestic fantasy.

Schroeder, Mary. MY HORSE SAYS. *Chatto & Windus* 1963. Illustrated by Phillida Stone. A family looking for a house, and how Elizabeth's imaginary animal seems to help; pleasant middle-class country story.

Symonds, John. DAPPLE GRAY. *Harrap* 1962. Illustrated by James Boswell. A rocking-horse trying to find his way home; gay and full of inventive fantasy.

Todd, H. E. BOBBY BREWSTER 1954, BOBBY BREWSTER—BUS CONDUCTOR 1955, BOBBY BREWSTER'S SHADOW 1956, BOBBY BREWSTER'S CAMERA 1959, BOBBY BREWSTER'S WALLPAPER 1961, BOBBY BREWSTER'S CONKER 1963, BOBBY BREWSTER—DETECTIVE 1964. *Brockhampton*. Illustrated by Lilian Buchanan. Short, plainly told stories of a small boy whose domestic adventures take a fantastic turn; gay, everyday humour.

Yeoman, John. THE BOY WHO SPROUTED ANTLERS. *Faber* 1961. Illustrated by Quentin Blake. Wildly improbable and cleverly sustained.

8.*Myths, Legends, Folk and Fairy-Tales, and some modern analogues*

Almedingen, E. M. THE KNIGHTS OF THE GOLDEN TABLE. *Bodley Head* 1963. Illustrated by Charles Keeping. Tales of Vladimir of Kiev and his comrades in arms, deriving from about AD 1000, brilliantly re-told.

Asbjørnsen, Peter Christian *and* Moe, Jørgen. NORWEGIAN FAIRY TALES. *Allen & Unwin* 1963. Translated by Pat Shaw and Carl Norman. Illustrated by Eric Aarenshold and Theodor Kittelsen. A scholarly and fascinating collection made 150 years ago by two folk-lorists.

Bishop, Sheila. GEORDIE'S MERMAID. *Methuen* 1961. Illustrated by Zelma Blakely. Set in Tyneside, humorous tales of magic with a piquant flavour.

Courlander, Harold. THE KING'S DRUM (1962 U.S.A.). *Hart-Davis* 1963. Illustrated by Enrico Arno. African stories, classified by regions; an extremely varied and interesting collection.

Gág, Wanda. THREE GAY TALES FROM GRIMM 1962, MORE TALES FROM
GRIMM 1962. *Faber*. Illustrated by the author. A story-teller's rhythms and
an assured touch with folk-tales.

Graves, Robert. THE SIEGE AND FALL OF TROY. *Cassell* 1962. Illustrated by
C. Walter Hodges. A very personal, robust version for children of the Iliad
and Odyssey.

Gray, Nicholas Stuart. THE SEVENTH SWAN 1962, illustrated by Joan Jefferson
Farjeon. THE STONE CAGE 1963, illustrated by the author. *Dobson*.
Sophisticated modern tales based on *The Wild Swans* and *Rapunzel*,
published at the same time in play form.

Green, Roger Lancelyn. THE LUCK OF TROY. *Bodley Head* 1961. Illustrated
by Margery Gill. An episode of the siege of Troy, told as an adventure.

Green, Roger Lancelyn. MYTHS OF THE NORSEMEN. *Bodley Head* 1962.
Illustrated by Brian Wildsmith. A compact and interesting arrangement of
the Norse legends. A new edition of THE SAGA OF ASGARD (*Penguin* 1960).

Hawthorne, Nathaniel. THE COMPLETE GREEK STORIES OF NATHANIEL
HAWTHORNE. *Gollancz* 1963. Foreword by Kathleen Lines. Postscript by
Roger Lancelyn Green. Illustrated by Harold Jones. Beautifully produced
edition of A WONDER BOOK and TANGLEWOOD TALES, slightly edited and
with the preambles omitted.

Hunter, Mollie. PATRICK KENTIGERN KEENAN. *Blackie* 1963. Illustrated by
Charles Keeping. An Irishman brags that he can outwit the little people
and is put to the test; a fascinating series of tales written in a persuasive
style and superbly illustrated.

Irving, Washington. STORIES OF THE ALHAMBRA. *Heinemann* 1962. Adapted
by Iva Howard. Illustrated by Richard Kennedy. Tales of the Moors in
Spain, richly romantic and exciting.

Korel, Edward. LISTEN AND I'LL TELL YOU. *Blackie* 1963. Illustrated by
Quentin Blake. A Chinese-box arrangement of witty animal fables.

Lang, Andrew. TALES OF TROY AND GREECE (1907). *Faber* 1962. Illustrated
by Edward Bawden. A classic re-telling in rich, rhythmical prose.

Manning-Saunders, Ruth. A BOOK OF GIANTS 1962, A BOOK OF DWARFS
1963. Illustrated by Robin Jacques. *Methuen*. Varied and fascinating
collections.

Mitchison, Naomi. THE FAIRY WHO COULDN'T TELL A LIE. *Collins* 1963.
Illustrated by Jane Paton. A tale of malice and affection, set in the Highlands
and involving fairies and children, and Brec, who is in between.

Montgomerie, Norah. TWENTY-FIVE FABLES. *Abelard-Schuman* 1961.
Illustrated by the author. Traditional tales neatly told.

Montgomerie, Norah. TO READ AND TO TELL. *Bodley Head* 1962. Illustrated by Margery Gill. A varied collection of stories, classified by subjects and ages.

Morgan, Mary de. THE NECKLACE OF PRINCESS FIORIMONDE (1880). *Gollancz* 1963. Original illustrations by William de Morgan, Walter Crane and Olive Cockerell. Introduction by Roger Lancelyn Green. Told for a group of children in Victorian times, fairy-tales full of colour and fancy.

Perrault, Charles. PERRAULT'S COMPLETE FAIRY TALES. *Constable* (1921) 1961. Translated by A. E. Johnson and others. Illustrated by W. Heath Robinson.

Picard, Barbara Leonie. THE STORY OF RĀMA AND SĪTĀ. *Harrap* 1960. Illustrated by Charles W. Stewart. An Indian legend re-told in decorative prose.

Piggott, Juliet. JAPANESE FAIRY TALES. *Muller* 1962. Illustrated by Harry Toothill. Distinguished style; stories macabre, delicate or comic.

Preussler, Ottfried. THE WISE MEN OF SCHILDA (1958 Germany). *Abelard-Schuman* 1962. Translated by Anthea Bell. Illustrated by F. J. Tripp. Folk tales in comical version of a town that took itself very seriously.

Ransome, Arthur. THE SOLDIER AND DEATH. *Ward* 1962. Illustrated by Charles W. Stewart. A Russian legend told in rich prose and decorated with exciting drawings.

Rickard, J. A. THE OLD AZTEC STORY TELLER. *Barnes* 1962. Illustrated by Will Brady. Little known, interesting stories.

Serraillier, Ian. THE GORGON'S HEAD 1961, THE WAY OF DANGER 1962, THE CLASHING ROCKS 1963. *O.U.P.* Illustrated by William Stobbs. Fine, vigorous re-tellings of the legends of Perseus, Theseus and Jason.

Sheppard-Jones, Elizabeth. WELSH LEGENDARY TALES 1959, SCOTTISH LEGENDARY TALES 1962. *Nelson.* Illustrated by Paul Hogarth. Varied and beautifully written, with haunting coloured illustrations.

Sutcliff, Rosemary. BEOWULF. *Bodley Head* 1961. Illustrated by Charles Keeping. Stirring language brings this version near the spirit of the original.

Sutcliff, Rosemary. THE HOUND OF ULSTER. *Bodley Head* 1963. Illustrated by Victor Ambrus. A rich, exciting version of the story of Cuchulain of Ulster, his exploits, wars and death.

Thurber, James. THE 13 CLOCKS (1950 U.S.A.) *and* THE WONDERFUL O (1957 U.S.A.). *Penguin* (Puffin Story Books) 1962. Illustrated by Ronald Searle. A convenient edition of two odd, entrancing tales. (See also p. 96.)

Uttley, Alison. THE LITTLE KNIFE THAT DID ALL THE WORK. *Faber* 1962. Illustrated by Pauline Baynes. As always, endless inventiveness, a delicate touch with detail, a sure use of words.

Williams-Ellis, Amabel. ROUND THE WORLD FAIRY TALES. *Blackie* 1963.
Illustrated by William Stobbs. A collection beginning and ending in Korea,
and covering the globe; an excellent collection from an experienced and
scholarly teller of folk-tales and fairy-tales.

9.Picture-story books

Abrahams, Anthony. POLONIUS PENGUIN COMES TO TOWN. *Dobson* 1963.
Illustrated by Hilary Abrahams. A gay book in every way.

Adamson, Gareth. OLD MAN UP A TREE. *Abelard-Schuman* 1963. A cumulative
story full of zest and humour.

Ardizzone, Edward. TIM'S FRIEND TOWSER 1962, PETER THE WANDERER
1963. *O.U.P.* Matchless, as always. (See also p. 32.)

Ayer, Jacqueline. A WISH FOR LITTLE SISTER (1960 U.S.A.) 1961, THE
PAPER-FLOWER TREE (1962 U.S.A.) 1963. *Collins*. Stories set in Japan and
Thailand respectively, beautifully illustrated in fine line and colour wash.

Baker, Laura Nelson. TORKEL'S WINTER FRIEND (1961 U.S.A.). *Abelard-
Schuman* 1962. Illustrated by Juliette Palmer. A little American boy in a
snowy landscape, beautifully visualized.

*Baldner, Gaby, THE PENGUINS OF PENGUIN TOWN (1962 Germany).
Heinemann 1962. Illustrated by Gerhard Oberlander.

Baldner, Gaby. JOBA AND THE WILD BOAR. *Constable* 1961. Illustrated by
Gerhard Oberlander. Exceptionally rich colour. English/German text.

Bates, H. E. ACHILLES THE DONKEY 1962, ACHILLES AND DIANA 1963.
Dobson. Illustrated by Carol Barker. A donkey in Greece and his various
homes and friends. Text slightly marred by whimsy, but illustrations superb.

Baumann, Hans. TINA AND NINA (1963 Germany). *O.U.P.* 1963. Translated
by Edward Blishen. Illustrated by Wanda Zacharias. A lost doll finds her
way home; charming story, entrancing filigree pictures.

Bemelmans, Ludwig. MADELINE AND THE GYPSIES (1959 U.S.A.) 1961,
MADELINE IN LONDON (1961 U.S.A.) 1962. *Deutsch*. Lively tales in verse
of a children's home in Paris, the humour partly carried on unusual words
skilfully and wittily used. (See also p. 32.)

Briggs, Raymond. THE WHITE LAND. *Hamish Hamilton* 1963. Tiny traditional
rhymes, illustrated imaginatively and with a fascinating range of colour.

Broomfield, Robert. DAME WIGGINS OF LEE AND HER WONDERFUL CATS.
Bodley Head 1963. A new look, and a charming one, for an old favourite.

Brunhoff, Laurent de. BABAR'S CASTLE (1961 France). *Methuen* 1962. (See
also p. 33.)

*Burningham, John. BORKA: the adventures of a goose with no feathers. *Cape* 1963.

Cass, Joan. THE CAT THIEF 1961, THE CAT SHOW 1962, BLOSSOM FINDS A HOME 1963. *Abelard-Schuman*. Illustrated by William Stobbs. A community of cats in a fishing town; a sharply imagined bunch of animals.

Charters, Janet *and* Foreman, Michael. THE GENERAL. *Routledge* 1962. A fable for our times, in light-hearted prose with exciting pictures in colour.

Clark, Dorothy. JULIA AND THE SPARROWS. *Methuen* 1961. A little girl whose hair is always untidy gets into a quandary. Humorous text and casual, lively pictures.

Cooney, Barbara. CHANTICLEER AND THE FOX (1958 U.S.A.). *Constable* 1960. Adaptation by R. M. Lumiansky (1948 U.S.A.). Derived from medieval illuminations. Beautiful line and colour work.

Cooney, Barbara. THE LITTLE JUGGLER (1961 U.S.A.). *Constable* 1961. An adaptation of an old French legend, beautifully illustrated.

Drummond, V. H. THE FLYING POSTMAN (1948). *Constable* 1964. Enchanting domestic comedy, re-drawn and re-written.

Drummond, V. H. LITTLE LAURA AND THE LONELY OSTRICH 1963, LITTLE LAURA AND THE THIEF 1963, LITTLE LAURA AND HER BEST FRIEND 1963. *Nelson*. A lively child and some fantastic adventures.

Duvoisin, Roger. THE HAPPY HUNTER (1961 U.S.A.). *Oliver and Boyd* 1962. How a hunter kept his animal friends in spite of his gun.

Fatio, Louise. RED BANTAM (1963 U.S.A.). *Bodley Head* 1963. Illustrated by Roger Duvoisin. Unusual shades of colour illustrate a pointed tale of barnyard fowls.

Fisher, David. TILLY BALLOONING. *Abelard-Schuman* 1961. An enterprising little girl goes off on her own; entrancing, spiky illustrations.

Hall, Donald. ANDREW THE LION FARMER. *Methuen* 1962. Illustrated by Ann Reason. A gloriously logical fantasy with striking, simple pictures in orange and black.

*Hewett, Anita. THE LITTLE WHITE HEN. *Bodley Head* 1962. Illustrated by William Stobbs.

Hewett, Anita. THE TALE OF THE TURNIP. *Bodley Head* 1961. Illustrated by Margery Gill. A spirited version of a favourite folk-tale.

Ireson, Barbara. THE GINGERBREAD MAN. *Faber* 1963. Illustrated by Gerald Rose. Wonderful sense of movement in text and coloured illustrations.

Lindgren, Astrid. THE TOMTEN (1962 Sweden). *Constable* 1962. Illustrated by Harold Wiberg. Adapted from a poem by Viktor Rydberg, this old legend communicates country warmth and simplicity.

Lionni, Leo. LITTLE BLUE AND LITTLE YELLOW (1959 U.S.A.). *Brockhampton* 1962. A tour de force, in which blobs of colour behave like people; vital and imaginative.

Lobe, Mira. JOHNNY AND THE BOOPLE (1961 Germany). *Harrap* 1963. Translated by Gwen Marsh. Illustrated by Susi Weigel. A child's imagination has an outlet in paper-tearing and in dreams; enchanting colour.

Maitland, Antony. THE SECRET OF THE SHED. *Constable* 1962. Congenial subject of two children and a newly invented vehicle that takes them by land, sea and air.

Michels, Tilde. KARLINE'S DUCK (1960 Germany). *O.U.P.* 1961. Illustrated by Lilo Fromm. An old woman cherishes a chance-come duck; entrancingly illustrated in black and white, with fascinating and minute detail.

Molloy, Anne. A PROPER PLACE FOR CHIP. *Constable* 1963. Illustrated by Antony Maitland. A little boy wants to release the sparrow he has rescued; charming text, excellent canal scenes.

Moss, Elaine. TWIRLY. *Constable* 1963. Illustrated by Haro. A piece of string takes on a personality; a tiny, attractive book.

Opie, Iona *and* Peter. THE PUFFIN BOOK OF NURSERY RHYMES. *Penguin* 1963. Illustrated by Pauline Baynes. A wise and scholarly collection, convenient in size and illustrated with wit and charm.

*Pearce, Philippa. MRS COCKLE'S CAT. *Constable* 1961. Illustrated by Antony Maitland.

*Pender, Lydia. BARNABY AND THE HORSES. *Abelard-Schuman* 1961. Illustrated by Alie Evers.

Pender, Lydia. DAN MCDOUGALL AND THE BULLDOZER. *Abelard-Schuman* 1963. Illustrated by Gerald Rose. A visitor from the outback causes picturesque confusion in an Australian city.

Petrides, Heidrun. HANS AND PETER (1962 Switzerland). *O.U.P.* 1962. Two German boys take over a builder's hut and make a house. The author, in her 'teens, conveys youth and high spirits in the story, and her pictures are exciting in design and colour.

Postgate, Oliver. IVOR THE ENGINE. *Abelard-Schuman* 1962. Illustrated by Peter Firmin. A Welsh engine joins the choir; riotously witty and wholly delightful.

Regniers, Beatrice Schenk. THE SNOW PARTY (1959 U.S.A.). *Faber* 1961. Illustrated by Reiner Zimnik. An American social comedy, with crisp, eccentric drawings.

Rey, Margret. ZOZO FLIES A KITE (1958 U.S.A.). *Chatto & Windus* 1963. Illustrated by H. A. Rey. A story for beginner-reading. (See also p. 48.)

*Rose, Elizabeth. CHARLIE ON THE RUN. *Faber* 1961. Illustrated by Gerald Rose.

Rose, Elizabeth. WUFFLES GOES TO TOWN 1959, OLD WINKLE AND THE SEAGULLS 1960, THE BIG RIVER 1962, PUNCH AND JUDY CARRY ON 1962, ST GEORGE AND THE FIERY DRAGON 1963. *Faber*. Distinguished combinations of lively text and thrillingly-coloured pictures.

*Spier, Peter. THE FOX WENT OUT ON A CHILLY NIGHT (1961 U.S.A.). *World's Work* 1962.

*Standon, Anna. THE SINGING RHINOCEROS. *Constable* 1963. Illustrated by Edward C. Standon.

Titus, Eve. ANATOLE AND THE ROBOT (1960 U.S.A.) 1961, ANATOLE OVER PARIS (1961 U.S.A.) 1962. *Bodley Head*. Illustrated by Paul Galdone. More adventures of the super-intelligent French mouse. (See also p. 66.)

Ungerer, Tomi. THE MELLOPS GO FLYING (1957 U.S.A.). *Methuen* 1962. A family of pigs and a do-it-yourself aeroplane; whimsical and ingenious humour.

Wildsmith, Brian. A.B.C. *O.U.P.* 1962. A work of art; single objects supremely and subtly portrayed on pages of rich colour.

*Wildsmith, Brian. THE LION AND THE RAT. *O.U.P.* 1963.

TITLES
Authors
Illustrators